Elementary School Curriculum

Elementary
School
Curriculum

Celia Stendler Lavatelli
University of Illinois at Champaign-Urbana

Walter J. Moore
University of Illinois at Champaign-Urbana

Theodore Kaltsounis
University of Washington

Holt, Rinehart and Winston, Inc.
New York   Chicago   San Francisco   Atlanta
Dallas   Montreal   Toronto   London   Sydney

Preface

For some time now, investigators in the field of child development have been pointing out how prone that field is to fads in child rearing. Since the 1900s, fashions in how to raise children and particularly how to discipline children have changed roughly every ten years. Reports have documented the shift from Victorianism to Freudianism, from a strict approach to a permissive one, with the pendulum swinging back and forth and sometimes resting in between.

To educators it may seem that changes in curriculum occur in the same faddish cycle. I began my career in the 1930s when the theory and practice of Progressive Education were being enthusiastically endorsed. The war and its aftermath limited fresh activity in the 1940s. There were attempts in the early 1950s to adjust the curriculum to the needs of the poor and the disadvantaged; reformers at the University of Illinois advocated the inclusion in basic subjects of topics geared to problems of living. In mathematics, for example, they argued for the study of such problems as the hidden costs of borrowing money, of financing a car, and of evaluating insurance policies. But there were other critics of the curriculum, the Bestors and the Rickovers, who argued that such topics were soft and foolish, and that instead *all* students should be required to take as many years of mathematics, science, and foreign languages as European and Soviet schools required. Better education was simplistically defined as more of the same curricula in the traditional disciplines.

At the same time, however, a group of reformers was at work to plan new curricula in mathematics and science. Their aim was to move the teaching of these subjects into the twentieth century. Men like Beberman in mathematics education at Illinois and Zacharius in physics at M.I.T. felt that the traditional curricula in these subjects (on both sides of the Atlantic) needed basic reform in both content and teaching methods. "New math" and new physics were born, to be followed by a new chemical-bonds approach to the chemistry curriculum, the oral–aural approach to foreign-language teaching, and a multidisciplinary approach to teaching biology. Subject-matter reform was concentrated at first at the secondary level but spread rapidly to the elementary. Curricular reform was dominated by a concept approach, with concepts for teaching selected by professional educators and by teams of scholars in the discipline. There was a great deal of emphasis upon identifying the gifted and providing advanced instruction for them.

Then in the 1960s we discovered the poor. We discovered them first at the preschool level but then discovered, too, the price the poor pay in school failure for the deprivation they suffer as a result of poverty. The poor began to be heard and to insist that school failure was due not to genetic deficiencies, but to deficiencies in the school itself. The blacks, in particular, were active in articulating the schools' deficiencies and in crying for reform. "Compensatory" education began at the preschool level and gradually spread into the primary.

In the late 1960s, another group of reformers had mustered enough strength to constitute a real force in changing the curriculum. These were the writers, "romanticists" to some, like Holt and Kozol, who decried both the content and the process of education. They railed against what the schools were doing to the human spirit; they saw the schools stifling creativity, individuality, and freedom in children, with large city schools being the worst offenders.

Simultaneously a movement began toward informal education, toward making the classrooms less rigid and teacher-dominated. Educators began to visit the informal classrooms of Britain and were impressed by what they saw. The psychological theory of Piaget began to have an impact; reformers asked and are still asking that the child be considered as the agent of his own learning, and that the school environment be structured so as to make accessible to the learner the acquisition of that knowledge identified as significant by scholars and educators.

I know I speak for my coauthors when I say that we have tried to support exactly that point of view in this book. We see a marriage of the new curricula of the 1960s and the informal, individualized approach to teaching, with special attention to the needs of children of the poor. Children may pace their own learning, but the teacher's planning makes possible the acquisition of important concepts in mathematics, sciences, and the social studies. Unless both partners in the marriage are recognized, we will see history repeating itself in foolish activities in "informal" classrooms (like the sixth-grade girls who voted to study "cosmetology" and invited the local owner of a beauty-supply house to speak), to be followed by the Bestors, who will cry out for the "fundamentals," to be followed in turn by other reformers whose kind we will have seen before. We hope that this book will help future teachers develop the common sense that comes with a sense of history and a solid foundation in values, values that will insist upon equal educational opportunity for *all* America's children.

My coauthors are responsible for five of the chapters: Professor Moore for the chapters on selection of content, reading, and evaluation; Professor Kaltsounis for the chapters on grouping and the social studies. Chapter 4 has been prepared by Professor Herbert Kliebard of the University of Wisconsin. Most of Chapter 14 has been written by Professor Marjorie Souder of the University of Illinois. We are indebted to Professor John Easley, Jr., for his help with the chapter on mathematics.

Celia Stendler Lavatelli
University of Illinois
January 1972

Contents

CHAPTER 1

Contemporary Demands upon Curriculum

Introduction

This book is written for all those concerned with elementary education in the 1970s. Judging from the way in which the decade began, it will be an exciting although troubled one for education. Some of the troubles will be resolved only as the social ills of the nation are resolved. But some depend for their resolution on the reshaping of schools in fundamental ways to meet clearly defined purposes. We, the authors of this book, see a dual purpose: the task of helping children acquire knowledge of man's cultural heritage and the task of preparing children to live creative, humane, and sensitive lives. This dual purpose is not new. What is new is the vigor of the demand that the schools be reshaped to meet that purpose.

Other decades have also been concerned with reshaping the schools. In the 1920s and 1930s, the ferment was over progressive education. In the 1950s and 1960s, reform centered on certain elements of the curriculum—particularly mathematics and the sciences, on ways of grouping children for instruction—particularly the nongraded school, and on establishing new programs for children of the poor. The demand now is for teachers to recognize that the child is the principal agent of his own learning, and for educators to reform conventional schooling in recognition of that fact. We propose in this book to examine that demand as well as others, and to consider both what presently goes on in the classroom and what should go on. We will concentrate on *curriculum*, which we will first define.

Curriculum: A Definition

The subject matter of this book is the curriculum for the elementary school. By *curriculum* is meant the set of learnings and experiences for children planned by the school to attain the aims of education. The term includes

1. *concepts* drawn from man's vast reservoir of knowledge and traditionally organized into subject-matter areas such as the social and natural sciences and mathematics;
2. *skills* essential for acquiring and coping with concepts—language skills, for the most part, such as reading, writing, and speaking since man's cultural heritage is encoded largely in words, but also skills for communicating graphically and with nonverbal symbols;
3. *processes for valuing and decision making,* particularly about one's role as a human being in contemporary society;
4. *mental processes* or problem-solving abilities that enable the child to iron out inconsistencies, make comparisons, and arrive at logical deductions from a set of facts;
5. *esthetic experiences* in art, music, and the dance, which form an important part of man's cultural heritage and enhance daily living.

In contrast to some other countries, such as France and the Soviet Union, the United States has no national curriculum. Our schools are largely under state and local control, and decisions as to what children are to learn are made at the state and local level. (*How* they are to learn, which is the concern of the new reformer, is typically not specified.) How, then, can one discuss curriculum in any kind of general way that will be meaningful across the nation? The reason it is possible to do so is because there is not the great diversity one would expect under state and local control; in fact, one finds far more similarity than difference in various courses of study in subjects such as mathematics, science, and social studies. The set of learnings set forth in a course of study in mathematics prepared for Florida schools, for example, differs little from that prepared for Illinois schools. Some states and local communities are more advanced than others, but there is a broad area of agreement with respect to what children should learn that makes possible an examination of curriculum practices and issues at a national level. The uniformity is due to a considerable extent to the uniformity in textbooks. There are probably only a dozen or so major textbook series in the various subject areas—social studies, reading, arithmetic, science. These dozen series are used by the majority of schools in the country; they differ from one another in the extent to which they have incorporated curricular reform and attention to learning processes into the texts, but there is considerable similarity in the topics covered. (One can safely predict that American colonial history will be covered in the fifth and sixth grades and that ecology will be represented at several grade levels.) Some writers argue that the growth in the 1960s of the educational-industrial complex, or education as big business, will exercise a nationalizing influence upon the curriculum, they believe that the proliferation of audiovisual and other teaching aids, and the adoption of performance contracting (whereby a private business contracts to raise performance levels of students in basic skills, or lose money) may produce greater uniformity of curriculum throughout the country. Actually, we know little about whether these developments will change the curriculum, and we can only speculate about whether a definite trend toward a national curriculum would be a good thing or not. There are obvious pros and cons on both sides.

To say that there is a broad area of agreement regarding the curriculum of the elementary school does not imply that the curriculum is static. Schools are slow to change, but change they do; they change in response to social and political demands, and the curriculum changes also. A hundred years ago, America faced the problem of absorbing millions of immigrants into the nation, and building national unity out of a diverse mixture of ethnic and social-class groups. The school was the agency assigned the task, and its responsibilities were to build a literate nation inculcated with the virtues of democracy, nationalism, and equalitarianism. The curriculum of the early 1900s reflected these responsibilities. Today the school faces these demands and more; as one writer (Schrag, 1965) has put it, ". . . the schools are being asked to win the Cold War, stop tooth decay, restore the national fiber, prevent Communist brainwashing, warn about the evils of alcohol and tobacco, close the missile gap, entertain the community, open the college gates, teach 'spiritual values,' save the cities and promulgate cleanliness." In addition, we are faced with a knowledge explosion, one in which man's knowledge appears to be expanding at an exponential rate, making the choice of what is important to teach even more difficult.

Schrag, in writing about demands upon the schools, stated the case facetiously in the above quotation, but the point is true: that the "basic dedication of the school has been shifting more and more toward the meeting of broad *national* needs and the facilitation of *national* policies. The teacher is currently called upon to exert efforts in the development of a citizenry not simply *literate* but literate *in relation to* pressing political and social realities" (Lee, 1966). In this chapter we analyze pressures upon the curriculum stemming from broad national needs and consider how these pressures are reflected in the schools.

Political Demands upon Schools

The pressures upon the schools to meet national needs and facilitate national policies come mainly from federal legislation. In the 1950s and until the mid-60s, national needs were defined in terms of meeting the Soviet challenge. The Soviets had sent up Sputnik in 1957; they were ahead of us, so the argument went, and national pride as well as national security were considered to be at stake. To close the gap and catch up with the USSR, scientists, educators, and other scholars argued for a strengthening of the teaching of mathematics, science, and foreign languages. But the teaching of these key subjects could be strengthened only by the infusion of large sums of money into school systems, sums available only at the national level. There followed a rash of federal legislation to make available financial support for the remediation of subject-matter deficiencies in both students and teachers. The National Defense Education Act was the legislation that made federal support possible. The U.S. Office of Education and the National Science Foundation were the chief instruments for carrying out federal policy; large private foundations like the Ford and the Carnegie foundations also generously supported curriculum change. Curriculum revision projects in mathematics, science, foreign-language teaching and learning processes —for the most part the joint efforts of subject-matter specialists and professional educators—sprang up in various university centers and resulted in some of the curricula in the schools today. (These curricula in different subjects will be reviewed later in appropriate chapters.) Summer and year-long institutes were set up for teachers to update their background in the critical subject-matter fields, with teachers' expenses being financed by federal or foundation money, a revolutionary new development.

The federal government, by financing specific curriculum developments, became a powerful force in education. This is not to say that Washington exerts control over the schools. Grants from Washington do not specify in detail what kind of program grantees must develop; usually they specify only that the program show some reasonable relationship to the purpose for which money is being allocated. Control of the curriculum still rests with state and local school systems. The federal government provides the carrot in the way of funds for programs, which are initiated at the local level but for purposes designed *to further the national interest* as defined at the time of the enabling legislation.

Politics and Education

Who defines national interest and determines how education can best serve it? Such decisions are made politically as the result of pressures from the electorate, more often organized than not, upon members of Congress. We are in a new era in which politics and education have entered into a union with schools to carry out programs designated and funded by Congress as being in the national interest.

We have been inclined to look upon *politics* as a nasty word, and the notion of a relationship between politics and education is at first shocking. Furthermore, we have been jealous of our prerogative to control schools locally, and have been slow to realize the decisive impact of federal legislation upon the schools. As one writer puts it (Bundy, 1968),

> There was a time not so very long ago when it would have been offensive to connect the word "politics" and the word "education" in any affirmative sense. . . . We would have supposed that a well-run school system was a system insulated from politics. . . . We would have supposed in fact that the merit and quality of the school system could be measured almost by the degree to which it could be given protection against politics—politics construed in this fairly crude, fairly limited, fairly dated way.
>
> What I think is most important about the problem of education today is that too many of the professionals working in the field of education . . . still think in terms in which this separation is the defining proposition. And they hold fast to this proposition in a time in which, for all kinds of reasons, the separation is neither possible nor right, a time when the name of the game is to find the right and constructive connection between education and politics. Perhaps the easiest demonstration of this necessary connection is—and there is something of a paradox in this—the record of the last four years in Washington. What has happened there is that by a revolution as permanent as it is quiet, Federal government has become to the world of education the supplier of last resort. The world of education knows it, and the Federal government knows it, and Congress has approved it, and the country accepts it, and it is a fact.
>
> It is a fact of such depth and meaning—so quietly achieved, still so imperfectly understood—that it is, I think, correctly described as a silent revolution. And quite remarkably, the fact has been achieved without any of the ordinary difficulties—the kinds of difficulties that those who opposed this or that part of the program initially predicted. I do not here seek to explain all this; I merely observe it and say that it means that politics and education have had themselves a marriage. The fact that it was not celebrated, not reported on the society page in large columns, that there were not many ushers and still fewer bridesmaids, and that the dowry is still inadequate—none of these facts separates the partners. The marriage is made.

The "marriage" today, however, is more controversial than it was during the early '60s. When political pressures upon Congress initiated mainly with scientists and educators and was in the direction of remedying subject-matter deficiencies, there were few voices raised in protest. (See the *Appendix* for an outline history of federal educational activities.)

Today, however, pressures that involve schools in basic social change are coming from the civil rights movement, and counterpressures from those who oppose change. Involved is a basic way of life separating black and white children, an unconstitutional way of life, as the Supreme Court has ruled. The first challenge to that way of life came with the Supreme Court decision of 1954.

The Impact of the Supreme Court Decisions of 1954, 1964, and 1971

The unanimous verdict of the Supreme Court in the *Brown et al.* v. *Board of Education of Topeka et al.* proved to be one of the most violently attacked of all decisions in the history of the Court. What the decision did was to reverse previous verdicts of the Court that had enunciated a "separate but equal doctrine," by which school systems could maintain segregated schools, provided physical facilities and other tangibles were equal for both Negro and white. The question in the *Brown* case was whether segregation solely on the basis of race, even though other factors were equal, deprived children of the minority group of equal educational opportunities. The answer was short, "We believe that it does." In other words, the Court held that segregation is inherently unequal; it is an arbitrary deprivation of liberty, and hence is contrary to a Constitution that guarantees every citizen equal treatment under the law.

Some of the readers of this text may recall the uproar that ensued as a result of the Court's order to the defendants in the *Brown* case to proceed "with all deliberate speed" to admit children to schools regardless of race. In Little Rock, Arkansas, in 1957, federal troops were rushed in to control mobs trying to prevent nine black children from enrolling in an all-white school. The scene was to be duplicated in various cities of the South in the next few years, as black parents sought to register their children in white schools. Yet the pace was so slow that by 1964, ten years later, only 30,798 Negro students in the South, a scant 1 percent, were attending schools with whites. Similarly in the North, because of the existence of *de facto* segregation, the 1954 decision had little impact. Segregation was not written into the law in northern states, but since housing restrictions kept blacks in the ghetto, and since the principle of the neighborhood school (that is, children must attend the school within their school district) kept blacks in ghetto schools, blacks continued to attend segregated schools. In fact, as white urban dwellers moved in increasing numbers to the suburbs, school populations in many city schools become *more* black rather than less.

In 1964, Congress passed a Civil Rights Act, which, among other things, empowered the Attorney General to bring suits on behalf of individuals to speed school desegregation, and forbade payment of federal funds to school districts still practicing segregation. The Supreme Court promptly upheld the constitutionality of the law, and during the next year, probably more blacks entered white schools in the South than in the preceding eleven-year period since the *Brown* decision.

A third momentous decision of the Supreme Court, the *Swann* v. *Charlotte Mecklenburg* decision of 1971, declared that the Constitution required desegregation and that there must be busing to achieve an equal racial balance in every school within a school district. The court-ordered busing was implemented by plans mapped out by the Department of Health, Education, and Welfare, and in September of 1971 over a quarter of a million children, some of whom lived a stone's throw from a school, were bused to a different school to achieve racial integration. Both blacks and whites were bused, blacks into white schools and whites into black schools. As might be predicted, children took the busing in their stride, many adults were up in arms, and schools opened with what, for many teachers and children, was a radical departure from the past—classrooms with more than a "token" black or white pupil. The burden fell hardest on cultural groups like the Chinese, who feared that integration would dilute their cultural heritage and weaken their children's sense of identity.

No one likes busing. But once the decision was made to make the schools, rather than housing, the instrument for desegregating society, busing was inevitable. President Nixon's open disavowal, as schools were about to open in 1971, of a busing plan for Austin, Texas, and his warning that busing operations should be pressed only to the "minimum required by law," added to an already trying and confusing issue.

We can expect that desegregation suits against local boards of education will continue to be filed. The pace is a creeping one, but we can safely predict that the 1970s will see blacks and whites in North and South attending school together in greater numbers than ever before.

The Impact of School Desegregation

We are concerned here with the impact of school desegregation upon the curriculum. How does the busing of children to achieve integration affect the school program? What changes in curriculum does the admission of black children to all-white schools (and vice versa) bring? One effect has been to expose the fact that black children educated in segregated schools, in both North and South, score below grade norms on achievement tests.

The explanation is a multiple one. In some cases extreme poverty has resulted in undernourished children whose health handicaps are serious

Education and the environment. Sixth graders observe changes in a micro-ecosystem in SCIS (Science Curriculum Improvement Study) unit, Ecosystems. *Ecological relationships become more meaningful after such first-hand experiences. Courtesy of SCIS.*

to the point where learning ability is impaired. In all too many cases, schools have treated minority children as if they were *unable* to learn, and, indeed, have demanded little of them. "Adjustment" of curriculum usually means teaching children skills and concepts a grade or two below the standard, and assuming that the children can do no better. Sometimes such an adjustment is accomplished by putting black children in a separate class in an otherwise white school; sometimes a track system is used, with the slowest track composed almost entirely of children of minority groups. Critics point out that procedures such as these groom children to accept their own inferiority, and their motivation and level of aspiration are affected accordingly. Teachers who expect pupils to be slow learners rarely have their expectations challenged, and do not like it when they are. In a study of teacher expectation and pupil achievement,

Pygmalion in the Classroom (Rosenthal & Jacobson, 1968), the experimenters found that when teachers were told a group was superior (which it was not), the teachers demanded *and got more* from the group as measured by standardized test scores than from a control group. While replication studies failed to reveal as dramatic shifts as Rosenthal and Jacobson found, nevertheless the existence of a self-fulfilling prophecy is not to be denied.

The Impact of the War on Poverty

We have witnessed the fact that many black children, bused out of the ghetto to white schools, are a grade or more lower in school achievement than their white middle-class counterparts. The Coleman Report (1966) confirmed this fact. However, we have also witnessed the fact that children of the poor, regardless of color, are below middle-class children in school achievement, a fact attributed largely to differences in environmental stimulation. The term *disadvantaged* has been coined for those who come to school with no exposure to the "curriculum" that exists in middle-class homes in the way of books, educational toys and games, conversation conducive to language development, trips, and motivation to do well in school—a "hidden" curriculum that ensures readiness for school learning in middle-class children.

One argument for the low intelligence and achievement test scores of children from the poorest socioeconomic level is that these children have inherited a lower intelligence potential. However, the notion of a fixed I.Q. is rejected by research evidence (Hunt, 1961); the poor scores of lower-class children are generally attributed not so much to low inherited intelligence as to the poverty of experience that poorly prepares them for middle-class schools. As a result, pressures have increased over the past decade for a program of compensatory education, preschool through high school, that would make up for the educational deficiencies that exist in poverty-stricken homes. Such a program would be costly, far too costly a burden for local communities to assume; only the federal government, the largest collector of taxes, could make funds available on a scale demanded by the enormity of the problem. Head Start, the well-known preschool program, was one imaginative effort devised at the federal level to help young children of the poor overcome deficiencies—in some cases for only a summer, in some cases for a school year. Although inadequately funded, hampered by bureaucracy, and probably unfairly evaluated (see Chapter 14), it sparked the imagination and aspirations of many of the poor. The Elementary and Secondary Education Act of 1965 provided funds for various kinds of help for school-age children.

The Elementary and Secondary Education Act of 1965 (ESEA)

This revolutionary piece of legislation was designed to strengthen and improve educational quality and educational opportunities in elementary and secondary schools. Because of its tremendous importance, we review its provisions here.

Title I. Under this title financial assistance was to be provided to local educational agencies for special educational programs in areas having high concentrations of children of low-income families. The money could be used to hire additional staff, construct facilities, acquire equipment, and so on. The amount assigned to each local school district would depend on two factors: (1) the average annual current expenditure per school child in the entire state; (2) the number of school-age children in the district from families with annual incomes of less than $2,000 and those in families receiving more than $2,000 annually from the program of Aid to Families with Dependent Children. Over one billion dollars was appropriated in fiscal year 1971 to meet the educational needs of deprived children.

Title II. This title was designed to provide school library resources, textbooks, and other instructional materials. Educational specialists have long emphasized the importance of well-stocked libraries, audiovisual materials, and up-to-date textbooks and materials in an effective program of instruction. Where there are central libraries in elementary schools, research has found that children not only read more but show significant educational gains between the fourth and sixth grades. Despite this and other evidence of the value of elementary school libraries, nearly 47 percent of public and more than 50 percent of nonpublic elementary school students in 1965 had no library. This title authorized the allotment of money to states for school library resources, textbooks, and other instructional materials. Materials could include books, periodicals, documents, magnetic tapes, phonograph records, and other printed and published materials. Allotments would be made on the basis of the number of children enrolled in public and nonpublic elementary and secondary schools within each state.

Title III. Supplementary educational centers and services were to be provided under Title III. Among the variety of supplementary services that make the difference between a poor school and a good school are special instruction in science, mathematics, languages, music, and the arts; counseling and guidance; health and social work; access to such resources as technical institutes, museums, art galleries, and theaters; and the availability of innovative programs to serve as stimuli to local planning and operation. Provision might be made under this Title for such supplementary educational services and activities as guidance and counseling, remedial instruction, school health services, vocational guidance, adult education, dual enrollment programs, and, especially in the area of early childhood education, innovative programs to overcome deficiencies in language and cognitive development. Materials centers and learning centers could be established to furnish modern instructional equipment to area schools.

Other titles under the Elementary and Secondary Education Act were designed to strengthen education research and training, the operations of state departments of education, and, more recently, the education of bilingual children. Although education is big business (over 30 billion dollars a year), very little money has been available in the past for research on the educational process—much less than a large corporation typically spends on research and development. Under appropriate titles this act made funds available through both the U.S. Office of Education and the state departments of education for experimental work on innovations in educational methods, preschool through high school.

There is considerable flexibility in the titles, and the U.S. Office of Education has great power in deciding which aspect of a title will be funded. A school in Maine found that its proposal to improve health services received ecstatic reviews, but was turned down because the children, while indeed at the poverty level, were French-Canadian Americans, and that year the Office was funding projects for Indian children. Or, the word may come that Washington is funding innovations, but giving priority to those involving the open classroom or curricula based upon behavioral objectives. In fact, school people frequently complain about federal whims and that too-frequent changes in funding often result in the abandonment of promising programs. Amount of funding is also a problem, for funding depends upon annual congressional appropriations, which can be delayed to such a point that schools do not know, until too late to make effective plans, whether they will be operational or not.

American Education, a publication of the U.S. Department of Health, Education, and Welfare, in its December 1970 issue, listed seventy-nine different programs under which federal money for education is distributed to the schools for programs, instruction, and administration. Authorization for these programs came from a number of different acts of Congress (School Aid to Federally Impacted and Major Disaster Areas, P.L. 874; Office of Education Appropriation Act of 1971 for desegregation assistance; National Defense Education Act; and Vocational Education Act are examples), but by far the largest appropriations were made under the Elementary and Secondary Education Act. Public schools in all sections of the country are feeling the impact of this Act, particularly Titles I, II, and III. Some idea of the scope of the impact can be attained by reading summaries of research in progress (over 200 innovative projects were listed by Fallon in 1967). In some cases, money has been used to hire reading and other remedial teachers, to establish a transition grade between kindergarten and grade one, to set up programmed instruction, to provide additional teaching personnel, to purchase audiovisual and other instructional aids, to add new courses of instruction to the curriculum. So far, there has been no systematic study of the impact of these titles upon educational reform; as might be expected, there have been cases of foolish and tragic uses of the money for purposes unrelated to quality of education. However, the visitor to many school systems already feels a heightened awareness of the needs of the disadvantaged and of attempts to meet those needs. Many of the innovative programs will be described in this text. Although the surface has been scratched, we are still a long way from achieving equality of educational opportunity for large numbers of the American population. A far greater expenditure of federal monies is necessary to help school systems pull themselves up by their bootstraps, but drastic remedial measures other than financial are also needed to improve public education. In fact, many educators are calling the notion of measuring equality of educational opportunity solely by counting educational dollars a simplistic one. The Coleman Report, to which we turn next, is in part responsible for this attitude.

The Coleman Report on Equality of Educational Opportunity

Under the mandate of the Civil Rights Act of 1964, the Office of Education carried out a study directed by James Coleman of Johns Hopkins University, designed to assess the lack of equality of educational opportunity. The survey was to include the *effects* of schooling; equal educational opportunity was defined in terms of equality of results, given the same individual input. What Coleman and his staff expected to find, and what most people thought that they would find, is that for children of minority groups, school facilities are sharply unequal, and that the inequality is related to student achievement. The data (Coleman et al., 1966) did not support this expectation. The survey staff did not find direct evidence of great inequalities in educational facilities attended by children from different majority and minority groups. The staff *did* find that for scores on achievement tests, all white averages were higher than Negro; all Northern averages were higher than those of Southerners; all urban averages were higher than rural. In other words, there are large group differences in scores on measures of school achievement, but there is no evidence that these differences in the performance of different groups are due to inequalities of educational treatment, to inferior schools, to poor and underpaid teachers, or to inferior physical facilities.

This major finding may come as a shock to the reader who has a stereotyped image of the poor child of a minority group attending a dilapidated school taught by an underpaid teacher—as, indeed, it did to many readers when the report was first released. Yet the reader can probably call to mind an example of a particular ghetto school with fine teachers and excellent facilities—better teachers and facilities, in fact, than in some of the middle-class schools in the same community. The reader can also call to mind an example of very bad teaching under very bad physical facilities in middle-class white neighborhoods. And for the tumble-down shack that serves as school for poor blacks in Mississippi, one can find its poor white counterpart in the hills of West Virginia. The Coleman Report did not deny inequalities; there are wealthy suburban communities in many states, as we have pointed out, that spend three times as much on education per child as do some poor communities. There *are* gross inequalities in educational facilities that should be corrected, but the Coleman Report would indicate that removing such inequalities will not by itself solve the educational problem for disadvantaged children. School achievement does not depend upon "trained" teachers ("trained" in the conventional sense of a college degree that includes certain professional courses), better school buildings, smaller class size, or large budgets, and the data show that equalizing educational opportunity as measured by such tangibles will not produce equality of results.

But what of the intangibles? The Coleman Report stated that the factor of pupil attitude appears to have a stronger relationship to school success "than do all the school factors together." Under pupil attitude are subsumed such factors as self-concept, motivation, industry, and the like, factors strongly influenced by teacher-pupil relationship, as we shall see. And the investigators reported that black students who were enrolled in well-integrated white schools did significantly better than those in segregated schools. Some writers have explained the superior performance of black children in "well-integrated white schools" as due to the fact that these blacks are middle-class, with a middle-class value system, and are expected by home and school to perform according to middle-class standards. What poor blacks might do, given classrooms more suited to their needs, we are beginning to realize from the scattering of positive results presently available from experimental programs.

The Coleman Report has been subjected to massive criticism since its publication. It is, of course, a limited study; it does not follow children over a period of years, so it tells nothing about past educational experience. Nor does it control factors like social class considered to be a very important correlate of school achievement. It *does* help to set priorities: that the "tangibles" of educational quality, like buildings and teacher-pupil ratio, are not as important as the "intangibles" of social attitudes. Thus the report is used to support arguments for those curriculum programs which stress the social context of learning. The British Infant and Junior Schools, comparable in grade range to our kindergarten and elementary grades, are an example. Their emphasis is upon vertical or family grouping, with groups made up of a range of ages, and upon open education where children are the discoverers of knowledge. Such instructional programs are discussed in detail later in the text.

Pressures from Educational Technologists

Also to be included in our discussion of pressures is that of pressure upon the curriculum from educational technologists. Late in the 1960s, government planning agencies (notably the Office of Education) began a drive to popularize, through funding educational research, a curriculum based upon behaviorally stated objectives, that is, upon pupil performance specifically stated. The thinking behind the drive went something like this, as analyzed by Atkin (1968): "To utilize the techniques for long-term planning and rational decision making that have been developed with such apparent success in the Department of Defense, and that are now being applied to a range of domestic and civilian problems, it is essential that hard data be secured. . . . Fuzzy and tentative statements of possible achievement and questions of conflict with respect to underlying values are not compatible with the new instructional systems management approaches. . . . In fact, delineating instructional objectives in terms of identifiable pupil behaviors or performances seems essential . . . for assessing the output of the educational system." Atkin's critical analysis of a behavioral objective approach to curriculum follows along much the same lines as that developed in Chapter 4; as he points out, stating objectives very specifically may sound admirable, but is not the way knowledge is acquired by children, as we shall see in Chapter 2. In passing, however, we cannot refrain from observing how ironic it is that education—which has a long history of turmoil and progressive ideals—should borrow a model from the Department of Defense, whose objectives are hardly idealistic and whose cost accounting has been glaringly inefficient.

An additional pressure upon curriculum, also stemming from the federal government through educational technologists, is the pressure for accountability of quality of the schools. Many different groups—including teacher organizations, professional educators, parents and community leaders—have spoken in favor of the principle that school systems must be held responsible for the academic progress of their students, and in many fine school systems that principle has been put into action. In others, substandard performance of pupils is taken for granted, and teachers are not held responsible for low scores. In 1970 the government announced its program to ensure accountability through private contracting. Under this technique, private industry assumed part of the teaching load in twenty-one school districts with large numbers of disadvantaged youths, to be paid in accordance with how well students' performance improved. The contractors use a variety of educational devices including teaching machines, programmed learning, reorganized classroom materials, and incentive payments to teachers.

Since the federal government announced its plan, a number of school systems on their own have entered into contracts with business firms to bring students up to grade. The approach of one firm is described as follows:

> The approach consists of establishing a High Intensity Learning Center in a school for each subject area involved. Twenty-five to thirty students will be scheduled into the center on a daily basis for a period of one hour for each academic subject in which they are enrolled. At the outset of the project each student will be diagnosed to determine his particular needs and behavioral competencies. Appropriate instruments have been developed for this purpose. Subsequently, each student has learning activities and materials prescribed for his involvement. These have been selected from those of over 15 different publishers to provide maximum responsiveness to the student's need in terms of skill, content, level and rate of learning. The materials are for the most part self directing and self correcting. Most are carefully sequenced so that students can move on independently, once diagnosis and prescription have been completed, with a minimum of teacher direction. The teacher subsequently focuses on continuing diagnosis and prescription and assists students who are experiencing difficulty in progressing.
>
> Motivation for continuing attendance in the center and involvement in the learning activities is enhanced by providing immediate and direct feedback to the student on his responses so that he experiences reinforcement or "pay off." The reinforcement system is translated into charts, graphs or the opportunity to spend more time in the center. Additionally, the centers are designed to be different in appearance and function from the usual classroom. Centers will be carpeted, and air conditioned, and have comfortable living room type furniture. One of the unique features will be bins containing books suitable for a wide range of interests and reading levels. (Learning Research Associates, 1971)

Such plans have been widely criticized, first, on the grounds that favorable results could be obtained by teaching students answers to the evaluative tests, and second, that performance contracting is "an abdication of responsibility for educational leadership." Many opponents also argue that the child's learning environment outside of school must first be improved for real school progress. However, the very real attempts made by some companies to change self-image, individualize instruction, and create environments for learning are to be commended.

Clark (in Engel, 1970) refuses to acknowledge that the urban slum must be improved to provide a better learning environment before schools can be improved. His position is that black children *can* succeed in an urban school system, if that system is reformed. Not an inferiority of environment, but poor teaching and low expectations are the stumbling blocks. Children can be urged toward success by group competition; there should be no grouping of children into slow and fast tracks. He has proposed an alternative to performance contracting that will still hold schools accountable for pupil achievement. Through the Metropolitan Research Center of New York, a program for schools in Washington, D.C., where the schools are 90 percent black, was devised and put into operation in 1970. The elements of the program are

1. *Curriculum.* For one entire "reading mobilization year," the whole curriculum was geared to competence in reading and reading comprehension. All activities, including dramatics, chorus, special clubs, and even athletics stressed the basic component of reading and precise writing and speech.

   The program ruled out the theory that ghetto children should be allowed to perpetuate their street dialect and grammar. The school's first obligation is "to see that the English language is taught effectively, and respected and learned by all children," a controversial position, as we shall see later.

2. *Teachers.* Dr. Clark believes that the old "sentimentalist appeals" for dedication, self-sacrifice and social dedication, self-sacrifice and social sensitivity, must be replaced by greater competence and professional dignity. Teachers are considered qualified, not by virtue of a degree, but only after being supervised in on-the-job training, similar to medical internship and residency.

   Under this plan, the following categories of teachers were introduced: staff teachers, who study and teach at the same time; senior teachers, who are comparable to associate professors and paid on an equal level with assistant principals; master teachers, the equivalent of full professors, at a principal's salary, whose rank signifies proven ability to stimulate pupils; distinguished teachers, a rank reserved for a few classroom teachers who have contributed to the improvement of education beyond the local schools.

Rank is linked to proven capacity and classroom performance. It makes the reward for such performance equal to that for administrators, and thus would incidentally give equal career opportunities to women in a field where supervisory posts are still largely a male monopoly.

3. *Administration.* A special group of experts deals with service functions and record keeping while the academic leadership devotes its energies to education.

It is too early to evaluate the programs for accountability, but there is the danger that the goal of education will become the passing of tests that to date do assess only part of educational quality. In fact, in Texarkana, glowing reports of gains in test scores in an accountability experiment were followed by reports that the children had been drilled on test questions! Real achievement *is* important, even of paramount importance; furthermore, the student who succeeds in school subjects after several years of being a school failure has a different opinion of himself. It has been nothing short of a national disgrace that thousands of children have failed to learn to read in our schools, and that the failure has been taken for granted. But literacy in reading and arithmetic is only one step toward quality education; the curriculum of the elementary school includes other facets as listed in the beginning of this chapter.

Pressures from Progressive Idealists

For some years now, a number of writers variously labeled as "Romantics" or "Progressive Idealists" have been criticizing the schools for systematically oppressing, stifling, and boring children while at the same time failing to educate them. Some of these writers have centered their criticism on urban schools, some on education of blacks, but all agree on the need for reform in the educational system for preschool through college. Their angry voices, including those of A. S. Neill, John Holt, Paul Goodman, George Dennison, Edgar Friedenberg, and, more recently, Ivan Illich and Charles Silberman, not only have called for reform but also have been singularly in agreement over the direction that reform should take. That agreement centers on certain aspects of education: that learning should be a matter of discovery rather than indoctrination; that the teacher's job is to guide learning rather than only to impose rules and regulations; that the child has the capacity to organize his own learning, given freedom and some help to do so. In the early

1970s their voices were taken seriously, first by the foundations and then by the U.S. Office of Education, and a full-fledged movement to change education was under way.

Pressures from Foundations

American foundations, both public and private, with vast sums of money that can be used to influence the direction of public education, have interested themselves in educational reform for the last quarter of a century. The first reforms were for excellence, for improvement of intellectual content of the curriculum. The Carnegie Foundation, for example, supported early efforts in the 1950s to develop the "new math." The National Science Foundation likewise supported innovative programs in both science and mathematics. More recently, however, the push from foundations has taken a different turn. The emphasis has shifted to the learner, and to development of programs that will free the learner from the joyless, conformity-inducing programs that, critics claim, exist in most schools today. It is not that excellence has been abandoned as a goal, but that a more open approach to it is seen as desirable and necessary.

The British Infant School

A movement that is attracting considerable attention on this side of the Atlantic at the present time, largely as the result of support from the Ford Foundation, is that of the British Infant School. Infant schools are government-supported (public) schools enrolling children from five to seven or eight years of age. In these schools fundamental changes have taken place as the result of the Plowden Report, an official report that called attention to deficiencies and outlined tentative foundations for what schools for young children should be like. The British classes, of forty children each, are characterized by informal methods: the children work in small groups—fives, sixes, and sevens in the same room, with older ones teaching younger ones. Learning is individual; classrooms abound with all kinds of materials, and as children work with the materials, they grow in basic knowledge. For example, in the area of mathematics, it is expected that by seven years of age, children will be able, among other things, to classify things into sets, to know the number line and understand place value, to invent their own units of measure or use standard ones, to understand the meaning of addition, subtraction, multiplication, and division, to work problems of shape and size including some simple proportions.

There are no formal lessons in reading and writing skills, but children make amazing progress, according to observers, in the two or three years they spend in the infant school. There are books in profusion, and children spend considerable time in the library corner before they begin to read. They seem to "pick up" reading as they hang around the library, looking at pictures in books, trying to find words they know, listening as the teacher hears other children read, asking classmates for words they want to know. As the teacher works with an individual or small group, she uses a variety of methods: sight reading, phonics, or whatever seems to work with a particular child.

Reading and writing are learned simultaneously. When he starts school, the child is given a large, unlined notebook in which he may put what he pleases. He may draw a picture, and as he tells the teacher about it, she may write down a word or phrase of what he says. He then makes a copy of the caption just underneath the teacher's. In this way, he comes to know the look and sound of his dictated words and phrases, and begins to enter the words in his own private dictionary as he learns them. Accuracy and neatness, as well as spelling, punctuation, and grammar are introduced gradually as ways to say more efficiently what one wants to say.

The British infant schools differ from our kindergartens and first grades in their informality. Children are not assigned to a particular seat in the classroom. Rather, centers are set up for mathematics, science, reading and writing, dramatics, and other types of activities. After a brief planning session, where the teacher lists the different activities available, small groups go to the various centers and, thereafter, move about on their own, talking quite freely as they do so. A teacher may use assignment cards. A card might ask, "How many acorns balance the pebble?" or "How many bolts balance nine bears?" Some assignment cards are to be worked individually, while others require the cooperation of a group of children to complete. The day is literally free for children to use as they wish, with the teacher circulating among them, encouraging, motivating, discussing, helping, prodding. Not all schools have a completely free day; some teachers, especially as they make the change from a formal, rigid program, begin with a free period, gradually extending it as they gain confidence that children can and do learn with the new methods.

In general, there is more emphasis upon cognitive learning, and more materials are provided that will encourage cognitive learnings, than is true in schools in our country. The theoretical basis is derived largely from Piaget although the impact of Dewey and Montessori is also evident. There is a strong belief that telling is not teaching, and that, as children use good, open-ended materials, their intelligence grows, and basic concepts develop.

The question continually raised about open education is, "Does it work?" Do the children really learn? Do the children in London slums, with the same problems of dialect and deprived environment as our children of the poor, achieve a satisfactory level of competence in reading, arithmetic, and language skills? The question is hard to answer, for the British are not as test-happy as Americans and do not use standardized tests extensively. The British seem satisfied. In this country, open classrooms are still too new to pass any judgment on and, furthermore, there is a strong feeling on the part of specialists in evaluation that new instruments must be designed, just as was true for schools in the era of Progressive Education, to assess fairly the accomplishments of open education.

Educators are in agreement that the British model cannot be imported "as is" into this country. There is danger, however, that with the American tendency toward faddism we may see classrooms with quantities of "junk" material out of which children are to fashion their own curriculum. Hapgood (1971), after describing the high quality of the environment in British classrooms, goes on to say:

> Small wonder that American educators have tried to follow suit. Yet what has resulted is a poor copy. In it, the class is "activity-centered" but the activity is often aimless and noisy and sometimes destructive. Books are used very little, and children are allowed to disturb other children with dramatic play, or carpentry, or blocks, or musical instruments. The teacher is so busy trying to maintain some semblance of order that she has no time to help children individually, or to record growth. Her classroom is chronically disorganized: the flexible order she has admired in the British model has become chaos. Some children may well be asking to withdraw to a "quiet" room. Some parents may well be asking for a return to the 3 R's.

Hapgood goes on to analyze what has gone wrong. She notes two factors in particular: one, the goal of American educators to accomplish instant reform, to change overnight and in one step what England has done in many small steps and over a period of a dozen or more years; and the other, the lack of recognition of very real differences between English institutions and our own. For example, the British teacher conceives of her role in a very special way—as a gentle but firm guide in helping children to direct their own learning, as some typical quotes from teachers illustrate:

> Off you go now, and come back and show me when you've finished those three.
> Jolly good, now you bring your book about the Normans and let me have a look at that, would you?
> I should do some printing with other colors if I were you.
> Well, that's very good, because every time you've added twelve more. That's really your twelve times table, isn't it?

The basic notion that children can direct their own learning is a sound one, but this does not mean that children should follow their own instincts and interests exclusively. This was the error made by some progressive educators in the 1930s, and we should not allow history to repeat itself. It is possible, as we shall see in Chapter 2, to incorporate newer ideas about how children acquire knowledge into school programs, but the curriculum must have structure, the shape of which we will develop in subsequent chapters.

The Silberman Report

This report (1970), *Crisis in the Classroom*, supports the thesis that, despite curriculum reforms, schools have changed but little in postwar years. Silberman argues that American schools are, by and large, joyless places preoccupied with order and control. He bases his conclusions upon a three-year study commissioned by the Carnegie Foundation during which time he surveyed the literature on education and visited classrooms in all parts of the country. He talks about the "tyranny of the lesson plan" and of rigid time schedules that "often start before children are interested—if, indeed, they get interested at all—and end before interest is exhausted or understanding achieved."

Following are excerpts from the Silberman Report:

> It is not possible to spend any prolonged period visiting public school classrooms without being appalled by the mutilation visible everywhere— mutilation of spontaneity, of joy in learning, of pleasure in creating, of sense of self. The public schools—those "killers of the dream," to appropriate a phrase of Lillian Smith's—are the kind of institutions one cannot really dislike until one gets to know them well. Because adults take the schools so much for granted, they fail to appreciate what grim, joyless places most American schools are, how oppressive and petty are the rules by which they are governed, how intellectually sterile and esthetically barren the atmosphere, what an appalling lack of civility obtains on the part of teachers and principals, what contempt they unconsciously display for children as children.
>
> Schools can be humane and still educate well. They can be genuinely concerned with gaiety and joy and individual growth and fulfillment without sacrificing concern for intellectual discipline and development. They can be simultaneously child-centered and subject- or knowledge-centered. They can stress esthetic and moral education without weakening the three R's. They can do all these things if—but only if—their structure, content, and objectives are transformed.

While Silberman writes in the tradition of those writers on education who have been labeled "Progressive Idealists" or "Romantics," he rejects the romantic's view that the child must live fully *as a child* to become a happy, useful adult. He would like some of the reform movement in curriculum that is reflected in new math and science programs to continue, but would like more attention on *how children learn.* He argues for more open, informal classrooms that encourage freedom, informality, and individuality, but that are also concerned with subject matter and intellectual discipline.

Educators may justly be cynical about these latest foundation efforts to influence the direction of American education. In their day foundations have promoted the efforts of those who criticized Progressive Education with its emphasis upon interests of the learner; yet today the precepts of the Progressives about child learning are receiving emphasis as if they were brand new. Foundations have supported the Bestorites and the Tellers who in an earlier day criticized efforts of the "life-adjustment" movement to make education relevant to the needs of the poor, and then the same foundations "discovered" compensatory education in the 1960s. However, there *is* need for reform, and in the direction of concern for individual growth and fulfillment. Let us hope that the concern for cognitive growth and intellectual discipline that developed in the '60s will not be thrown out in this latest wave of criticism and reform.

Other Sources of Pressure upon the Curriculum

The curriculum reforms we have reviewed so far grow out of cold-war politics, the civil-rights movement, and the war on poverty. Other aspects of the social revolution in which we find ourselves also demand curriculum reforms. We consider first the urban crisis. The plight of the cities in terms of slum housing, inadequate public health services and sanitation, bad air, poor transportation, high crime rate, a staggering welfare load, large numbers of unemployed, has been a primary concern of the nation for the past decade, although the concern has resulted in little, if any, improvement.

Population shifts account in part for the problems. The trend away from impoverished rural areas of the South accelerated during World War II and continues today. Conversely, there is also a population trend out of our very large cities (over 1,000,000 population) into the suburbs. Middle-class families have made up the bulk of those moving out of the city, leaving an inner core of the poor behind. These population shifts, accompanied by rising protests of minority groups, have created a crisis in urban education. Large-city school systems are in trouble, indeed in very great trouble.

The Crisis in Urban Education

The case against metropolitan schools has been dramatized in recent years by articles and by books such as Kozol's *Death at an Early Age* (1967). Kozol described his own experiences as an elementary school teacher in a Boston public school attended mainly by black children. Not only was the school, built at the turn of the century, in very bad repair, but instructional materials were inadequate, and, worst of all, some of the white teachers treated the students as if they were indeed second-class citizens.

Kozol's voice was not the only one being raised in protest against the inferior education blacks were receiving in large-city schools. In 1968 New York City was beset with teacher strikes brought about by the conflicting interests of black parents and the teachers' union. Parents were demanding more say in their children's education, even to a voice in the hiring and firing of teachers. They were aware that their children were a year or more behind national norms in achievement, aware of the high dropout rate, of the poor preparation for life attained even by those who finished high school.

A number of proposals for the reform of large-city educational bureaucracies have been advanced. One proposal seems at first glance to be revolutionary. It would give each parent a voucher for a sum of money equivalent to what the city is spending to educate a pupil. Parents could then find whatever means they wanted to educate their children, redeeming the voucher in any legitimate institution they might choose. One argument is that the plan would bring competition back to a field now dominated by one all-encompassing institution, which can now allow itself to grow lax through want of any substantial challenge save a handful of private schools. As might be expected, the voucher system has been denounced by many school leaders, not only because it poses a threat to the very existence of public schools as we know them, but also out of a genuine concern that children might be exposed to bizarre forms of education in some of the new schools that would be established. Not all critics of public education have a good alternative to suggest.

Decentralization has also been advocated as a means of reforming urban schools. One proposal for the decentralization of the New York City school system implies, at least in theory, a strategy similar to the voucher system. "While blank checks would not be handed out to individual parents, they would, in a genuinely decentralized system, be given to individual school districts to spend as the parents, represented by their community boards, saw fit. To many of the paternalistic proprietors of the present system, such an expedient must seem not only a threat to their personal security, but evidence of insanity, for the unspoken assumption of the liberal majority which has traditionally dominated public education in New York is that the poor, particularly the blacks, are not only rather hard to educate but they are constitutionally incapable of running their own institutions" (ICRD Bulletin, 1969).

Less revolutionary in its objectives of decentralizing large-city systems is the plan simply to break up the large system into a number of smaller, autonomous districts. "Smaller" is decidedly relative, however; districts in New York would include a school population considerably larger than most school districts have today. Nevertheless, such a unit size might offer the possibility of bringing control of the schools closer to the parents who are served, and control is what the parents in inner-city schools are seeking. They are militantly concerned over their children's learning problems and find the school at fault. This is the reverse of the attitude, prevalent until recently, that substandard scores on reading and other achievement tests were due to poor home environment and the consequent uneducability of the children, and not to differences in schools or teaching. Low scores were expected and accepted as normal; there was no great pressure to bring the children up to grade, for no one believed that it could be done. Now parents are demanding that schools be held accountable for failures, and they see decentralization as a possible way of achieving a voice in decisions affecting their children.

New York City has led other large cities in decentralization. In September 1970, the city system was divided into thirty-one school districts with newly elected community school boards and locally appointed superintendents. The local school districts have substantial operating control over elementary and junior high schools, while a chancellor has city-wide powers in curriculum, budget, and personnel.

Gordon (1968 and 1969), an educator who has been close to the New York City struggles, has this to say about possible advantages from decentralization:

> Decentralization of the schools is one means of achieving educational relevance in these three areas (accountability of schools to the community; responsibility for learning placed principally on the teacher and school; relevancy of education to needs of the child), since it provides a structure through which communities can decide on the specific capabilities and needs of their children. In a large educational system, one means of creating flexibility, and thus enabling the system to become more responsible to a wide variety of populations within it, is through the dispersal of responsibility and authority for educational planning and control to points nearer the beneficiaries. It should be easier for persons who share the culture and values of the families served to evolve educational goals, policies and programs which reflect these ideational commitments. Indeed, it is the eternal

hope of school people that the families and communities they serve will show their commitment to the values the school advances. If the values of the community become those of the school, an ideal marriage may be said to have occurred. (p. 3)

Decentralization is difficult to achieve in large school systems. Pressures from supervisors and from teachers' unions (which fear a loss of power if their ranks are splintered), pressure from boards of education, and pressure from the middle class and from some public officials, all operate to maintain the status quo. Probably there will eventually be some degree of decentralization that will make it possible for minority groups to have a voice in decision making. However, decentralization is no panacea. There are hundreds of small school systems in the country that are doing no better in educational reform than the metropolitan systems. The curriculum must be reformed and so must teaching methods.

One can find reform in isolated instances in individual schools under an inspired principal, or in classrooms taught by inspired teachers. I. F. Stone, the journalist, visited two schools in the Ocean Hill-Brownsville district of New York City, a district set up as part of the city's controversial decentralization plan. At the time of his visit, the district, almost 100 percent black, was under black control, and educational reform was already under way. He describes his visit:

> I watched a Mrs. Naomi Levinson teach an English class full of eager black children. I read some of the touching poems and essays they had produced. "It's the first time in my eight years as a teacher," she told us proudly, "that I have been allowed to use unconventional teaching methods." I talked with another teacher, Leon Goodman, whose face lit up with pleasure when he explained the new methods of teaching science he was allowed to apply. "We get them to think rather than simply to copy down abstractions from the blackboard."
>
> I sat in on a teacher-team conference of five English teachers, three black, two white, one of the whites a delicate-featured blond WASP, the other an intense and dark-eyed Jew. The two whites were volunteers. One of them had brought a bongo drum into the classroom to use with the reading of Vachel Lindsay's incomparably rhythmic "Congo" as a way to awaken the children to the wonders of poetry. The atmosphere of this mixed group was wholly devoid of any racial self-consciousness or tension. One felt their pleasure in working together. In the corner of one classroom we watched a young black teacher with a group of children who took turns at reading *The Prince and the Pauper*. On the blackboard was the assignment, "Write a story about something that went wrong in a person's life" and next to it in a row there were the helpful hints, "No money. Sickness. No food. No light. No home. No friends. No job." The words telescoped the familiar annals of the ghetto. (1968)

The Ocean Hill-Brownsville approach to reform is different from others that emphasize making the child a good learner without any radical change in the school's middle-class traditions. Here the approach takes into consideration what the child brings with him to school. It attempts to build upon his strengths, rather than, willynilly, to program him into the traditional curriculum, using traditional teaching methods. Many blacks, angry at schools for their disregard of the child's cultural background, applaud such an approach.

Additional Social Problems and Their Impact

We are in the midst of a social revolution, with man-made problems demanding solutions. Should the study of such problems be included in the curriculum?

Such a problem is that of an overcrowded and misused planet. We are rapidly reaching a point where population pressure may be intolerable. Increasingly we are seeing that the earth is a spaceship of limited resources whose continued satisfactory operation is threatened by overcrowding and what overcrowding engenders in terms of environmental deterioration—excessive waste, overconsumption of material goods, pollution of land, air, and water. There are many who believe that control of population growth, so that man can work out a satisfactory relationship to his environment, is essential for human survival. Should the science and social science curricula include attention to the effect of the population explosion upon the quality of life and to the ecological crisis we face?

Urban blight, with decayed housing, crime, unemployment, and overpopulation, make living conditions intolerable for millions. Should study of such problems and proposed solutions be part of the elementary school curriculum? Conflicts between private enterprise and conservation of natural resources are omnipresent and rise to public consciousness when, for example, oil from a drilling operation befouls miles of public beach. DDT and mercury residues from agricultural sprays and factory wastes threaten animal and human existence. Should such problems be included for study in the curriculum?

There is still another area of concern, perhaps the most serious of all, and that is the matter of war and peace. The world has become an armed camp, with at least two nations capable of destroying the earth and everyone on it several times over. America now finds itself with a multibillion dollar budget for national defense, by far the largest expenditure in the national budget, while problems of people are neglected for lack of resources. Young people protest against the growing power of our military-industrial complex; some take to the streets, while others retreat into rural communities to work out personal salvation in a society they have given up trying to reform. There are analysts who relate the increased use of drugs to the problems engendered by the Indochina war. Can and should the school curriculum reflect the existence of such problems?

And, last, there are the demands growing out of our increasingly complex, technological, impersonal society. Are these demands such that everyone who is educable be educated beyond the high school? If so, what demands does this place upon the elementary curriculum? The position taken in this text is that the curriculum, if it is to serve broad national needs, must take into account newly identified needs; it must adapt to social change although at the same time *it must avoid being faddish.*

The foregoing statements and questions are not intended to intimidate the prospective teacher or the teacher-in-service. If anything, the socio-political setting of education today makes teaching more exciting, more challenging, more promising than ever before. Witness the thousands of young men who are teaching, from kindergarten through high school in ghetto schools in Chicago and New York, young men who graduated from liberal arts colleges and who chose to teach during the Vietnam war rather than to be drafted. Many of these young men have been "hooked" on teaching, have found a deep satisfaction in helping children experience the joys of discovering knowledge and of developing an image of self as a worthwhile person. Ferment has brought a dissatisfaction with the status quo and with attempts to improve education by superficial tinkering. The times are ripe for basic curriculum reconstruction.

Curriculum Trends

But is the curriculum meeting the challenge? School systems, like other social institutions, have been slow to respond to demands for change. The lag between what society needs in the way of an educated citizenry and what schools do to meet the demands has been great. Despite the near-revolutionary changes that have taken place in society, content, methods, and organization of the curriculum, as practiced in the average elementary school, have changed but little. Nevertheless, despite Silberman's gloomy report, there are positive trends, and one can find examples of the trends in schools throughout the country. The trends are

1. *Subject-matter content*: toward selection of concepts the importance and validity of which have been (a) "certified" by scholars in the

respective discipline (for example, economists identifying basic economic concepts to be taught in grades 1–6), and (b) inclusion of problems that are considered to be relevant to present-day society (for example, ecology, use of drugs).

2. *Role of the teacher*: toward the teacher as a specialist in the basic fields of learning and child development, who sets up the environment and provides the opportunity and guidance for children to discover knowledge.

3. *Function of the school*: toward the viewpoint that the school has the *unique* function of developing intellectual power, of helping children become logical thinkers, in a setting that respects the child's individuality and rights as a human being.

4. *Teaching methods*: toward inductive teaching fortified by the use of programmed learning, technological aids, and audiovisual materials, and, in primary grades in particular, a trend toward "open education" adapted from British Infant School methods, based, within limits, upon what interests the learner rather than "what interests the teachers."

5. *Organization of classroom*: toward a variety of grouping arrangements, including team teaching, departmentalization, and vertical grouping with several age groups represented in a classroom.

The first two trends can be traced to the political and social demands upon the schools that we have been analyzing. The "new math," revised science curricula, teaching of foreign languages in elementary schools, ecological concepts, "black" studies, compensatory programs—all stem from demands that the schools pay attention to the nation's needs. The last three trends are more directly related to changing concepts about how the child acquires knowledge, and how theories of learning can be applied to classroom problems. The two chapters to follow, "How the Child Acquires Knowledge" and "The Learner and the Teaching-Learning Process," are intended to serve as a foundation for further discussion of curriculum.

Summary

Historically, the task of the American school has been to meet certain national needs, defined differently at different periods in history. In response to recently defined needs, schools have upgraded math, science, and foreign language teaching, and embarked upon innovative programs chiefly for children of the poor. The federal government, together with foundations, has played a key role by providing funds to make specified changes possible.

Desegregation in response to Supreme Court decisions has brought to light long-buried problems of differences between black (or Chicano) and white, lower-class and middle-class students, in school achievement. While some argue that these differences are due to heredity, the body of opinion of educators, geneticists, and psychologists is to be found in early and continuing environmental deficit, and in failure of the schools to educate. Various measures are being tried to raise achievement levels of the poor, including accountability contracts between boards of education and private business and decentralization of large-city systems.

Other pressing problems of society make demands for curriculum consideration. Although schools have been slow to respond, certain positive trends have been noted and are listed in the chapter.

READING LIST 1

Central Advisory Council for Education (England). *Children and their primary schools*. London: Her Majesty's Stationery Office, 1967 (two volumes). This is the so-called Plowden Report, after the chairman of the Council, Lady Bridget Plowden. Volume 1 provides the philosophical foundation for a new approach to English primary education.

Children of Barbiana. *Letter to a teacher*. New York: Random House, 1970. Students in a school attended by poor children in the countryside near Florence, Italy, have written a criticism of the Italian school relevant on this side of the Atlantic as well, particularly as it points up how education is used to perpetuate class distinctions.

Coleman, I., et al. *Equality of educational opportunity*. Washington, D.C.: U.S. Government Printing Office, 1966. This controversial report presents results of standardized achievement tests to black and white, Puerto Rican, Indian, Mexican, and oriental Americans, and offers possible explanations for low minority-group scores.

Coons, J., Clune, W., III, & Sugarman, S. *Private wealth and public education*. Cambridge, Mass.: Harvard University Press, 1970. This is an impressive review of inequities in educational spending, the causes of the inequities, and a proposal to achieve economic equalization.

Holt, J. *How children fail*. New York: Pitman Publishing Corp., 1964. Holt's argument, like those of Jonathan Kozol, Herbert Kohl, and other critics of the schools, is that children who are failing in schools today *are* educable and that it is the fault of the schools that they are failing. At least one of the books of this genre should be read by every teacher and prospective teacher.

Illich, I. *Deschooling society*. New York: Harper & Row, 1971. More controversial than most, this book argues that education has become "schooled," that the school is a monopoly, and that society needs to be "deschooled." Schools confuse teaching with learning, grade advancement with educa-

tion, and a diploma with competence. Illich makes a provocative proposal
for a deschooled society and suggests how it might work.

National Society for the Study of Education (NSSE) Yearbook, *The changing American school*, Volume 65. Chicago: University of Chicago Press, 1966. The chapter by Lee, "The changing role of the teacher," presents a thoughtful analysis of demands upon the schools and how demands are reflected in curriculum change.

Silberman, C. *Crisis in the classroom*. New York: Random House, 1970. A survey of American education, based upon classroom visits, talks with educators, and a study of the literature. Silberman found a need for sweeping and thorough changes and suggests the direction for some of these.

Professional Journals To Become Acquainted With

Harvard Educational Review. Harvard Graduate School of Education, Appian Way, Cambridge, Mass. 02138.

Nation's Schools. McGraw-Hill, 330 W. 42nd Street, New York, New York 10036.

CHAPTER 2

How the Child
Acquires
Knowledge

Curriculum texts for teachers traditionally include a discussion of school learning in which the writers draw heavily upon certain areas of psychology (learning theory, motivation, problems of transfer) to find suggestions for the improvement of learning. Typically such discussions have addressed themselves only to the problem of how children can be helped to learn more efficiently what the school wants to teach. The emphasis has been upon the *products* of learning—upon mastery of a specified body of subject matter, and not upon *how* the child acquires knowledge. However, writings of cognitive psychologists in recent years suggest two things: (1) children's reasoning ability may not be sufficiently developed to learn what the school wants to teach; (2) reasoning ability can be sharpened as children acquire knowledge, provided the curriculum is organized and subject matter is presented in such a way as to further this goal. Therefore, in this chapter we put the emphasis upon the processes by which children acquire knowledge, and what schools can do to develop the logical reasoning powers of children to facilitate acquisition of knowledge. We use the terms *reasoning ability, thinking processes, logical reasoning, critical thinking, problem solving* interchangeably in the presentation that follows.

A great deal has been written in recent years about developing children's problem-solving abilities or critical thinking powers. It has been generally recognized that such abilities are tremendously important, perhaps even necessary for survival, in the kind of world in which we live today. We need to be able to recognize fuzzy-minded thinking, faulty analogies, and general illogic in politicians of both the Left and the Right, in new social movements that spring up in society, and in the commercial advertising with which our senses are bombarded. Problem-solving abilities, or ability to do critical thinking, stem from man's special capacity for logical thinking.

Yet despite our lip service to the aim of developing thinking abilities, far too little classroom time is spent in the process. Part of the difficulty lies in the fact that too often we are puzzled by errors in children's thinking and do not know what to do about them. Consider these examples:

A group of fifth-grade children were experimenting with cylinders of different weights and volumes, selecting two and immersing each in identical glasses of water. At first they had been sure that for the same volume a heavier cylinder would make the water level rise higher. They had tried out their prediction and found to their amazement that each cylinder of the same volume, regardless of weight, made the water rise to the same level in its respective glass. Once the initial shock of surprise was over, the children began to suggest and try out ways to make weight work, and also to try other variables. The interesting thing about their suggestions and their procedures was that not one of them had the notion of keeping all other factors constant while they varied only one. The children would say, "I'll try a heavy one in this glass and a light one in this glass," but it did not occur to them to keep the overall size of cylinders the same for each glass at the same time.

A first-grade teacher was teaching the new math. She drew a straight line on the board and a wavy line beneath. She put dots as in the drawing below and asked, "How many dots are above the straight line?" The children answered correctly. "How many dots are below the straight line?" The children answered, "Two." "Could it be five?" asked the teacher. The children, all of them, chorused "No." Despite the teacher's prompting, they did not accept the fact that an object can be below the wavy line and the straight line at the same time: that it is possible for something to belong to a class and a subclass simultaneously.

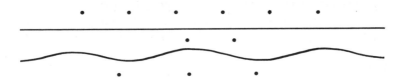

A college instructor was trying to explain to a psychology class the thinking processes involved in classifying. He asked, "How do we know whether a particular animal belongs to the class of birds? What are the characteristics or properties of a bird?" The class named some, to which the instructor added "warm-blooded." The students protested; birds could not be warm-blooded, because mammals were warm-blooded. Their difficulty lay in not thinking that several subclasses such as birds and mammals can *share* certain properties in addition to having others that are unique.

Instruction and Thinking

Teachers typically explain such responses as the three cited above as errors of fact. The learner does not know enough to give the correct response, the argument goes, but when his errors are corrected, he will revise his thinking—when he is told, for example, that *size* of cylinder is the critical factor, or that an object can belong to more than one class at the same time, or that a property such as warm-bloodedness can belong to members of different subclasses, he will give the correct answer.

A different explanation increasingly accepted by cognitive psychologists is that some erroneous answers that children give are due not so much to lack of knowledge of specific facts as to "poor thinking," that is, an inability to carry on certain mental operations. Even when a child is told the correct answer, he may refuse to accept mentally that dots can belong to a class of dots under the wavy line and a class under the straight line at the same time, because he lacks the mental structures for carrying on such operations. All teachers know the look of incredulity on the child's face when someone tries to convince him to give up a cherished belief. When the fault lies in thinking processes, the child is likely to say, "OK if you say so, but I don't really believe it."

Smith et al. (1962) reports from his analysis of tape-recorded classroom lessons that pupils are asked to perform mental operations throughout the day. Teachers call upon pupils to define, compare, contrast, find other examples of a phenomenon, hypothesize, deal with whole-part relationships, and perform other mental operations in the course of acquiring knowledge. But, in dealing with pupil answers, teachers have tended to concentrate on the products of the process; that is, they have been primarily concerned with the correctness of the answer the pupil gives to a question. If a pupil cannot answer a question as to whether Florida is a peninsula, the teacher goes on to ask another pupil. Rarely does he ask the pupil, "How can you decide? How do we know when something is a peninsula? What are the characteristics of a peninsula?" And then, once these have been named, to say, "Now let's check these out one by one against what we know about Florida." Even more rarely does he make clear to the pupil that *there is a mental process by which he can arrive at the correct answer*, and more rarely still does he say to the pupil, "When you have to decide whether something belongs in a particular class or can be called by a particular name, this is what you do," and then describe how a one-to-one correspondence can be made between properties attributed to the class, and properties of the thing being evaluated. Broudy and his coauthors (Broudy, Smith, & Burnett, 1964) describe the consequences of this neglect as follows:

Certain consequences flow from this fact. In the first place, instruction is far less challenging intellectually than it could be. Since the teacher seldom handles these processes with any marked degree of understanding, he is often unable to follow up points made by students in such a way as to challenge their thinking. If their explanations are inadequate, he does not know how to pry into what they have said so as to bring out the inadequacies. If their definitions are inappropriate or unacceptable, or if the class becomes engaged in a discussion of definition, the teacher ordinarily does not know how to handle such discussion, nor does he know how to point out the inadequacies of the students' defining procedures.

In the second place, one of the chief consequences of the failure to deal adequately with these operations is a rather low level of intellectual rigor. There is a sense in which we can say that intellectual rigor does not consist in the amount of information an individual retains and recalls, the number of problems he can work in a given domain, or his persistence in pursuing a task. Rather, intellectual rigor consists in the ability of the student to handle logical operations with marked precision in any domain of information with which he may be required to deal. The educational program only accidentally engenders the ability to think clearly and consistently. . . . (pp. 119–120)

Teachers and teachers-in-training are concerned with processes of instruction. They want pupils to be better learners. They take courses on the psychology of learning and find out about motivation and how lack of it can affect learning. They learn about reinforcement principles and the effectiveness of kind and scheduling of reinforcement. They read about intelligence and its assessment, and environmental influences upon I.Q. scores. All of these things are important for a teacher's understanding of children, but they have only a tangential effect upon instruction. The teacher still is at a loss as to how to help the learner who gives the wrong answer—except that he knows he must not shame him before the class, for that will result in an "emotional block"!

The moment of truth is essentially that moment in the teacher-pupil interaction when the teacher, having asked a leading question and received incorrect responses, attempts a cognitive restructuring. Such a cognitive restructuring enables the learner to arrive at "knowledge and understanding by perceiving the situation . . . before and then rearranging it, through central cognitive processes, in ways that yield meaning of a rational, logically consistent kind" (Gage, 1964, p. 278). And this the teacher can only do as he is aware of the mental processes involved in acquisition of knowledge. Stated colloquially, the teacher needs to know what is "bugging" the pupil.

To consider seriously how teachers can be better teachers, one *must* consider how children think about problems, and to consider how children think about problems one must consider what mental operations are involved in acquiring knowledge and how these operations develop. *Our aim in education should be to make children better thinkers* on the supposition that better thinkers make better learners. Any book dealing with instructional processes in elementary schools ought, then, to consider seriously the improvement of mental processes.

The school *does* have a stated concern with improvement of mental processes, and developing the intellect is high on any list of educational goals. The failure to deal adequately with mental processes has not stemmed from a lack of concern, but, rather, from a lack of precise definition of "good thinking," and identification of the operations of which it consists. Lacking a precise definition or even a concern for such a definition, educators have tried other approaches to the problem. We review some of these next.

Improvement of Thinking through Mental Discipline

Interest in the improvement of children's thinking goes back at least to the second half of the nineteenth century, when there were many scholars who advocated the study of classical subjects on the grounds that they strengthened certain mental faculties like reasoning, judgment, and memory. One could develop such faculties through exercise, the argument went, and the study of such subjects as Latin and mathematics would provide the "mental discipline" that would help one to become a logical thinker. Training the memory was also emphasized, a feat to be accomplished by having students memorize lengthy passages of literature. The concept of transfer was basic to the argument; the beneficial effects derived from studies that disciplined the mind would transfer to the general faculties of learning and memory.

The findings from both James's and Thorndike's classical research on mental discipline dealt the theory severe blows. The first was struck by James's finding that the capacity for memory is not improved by memorizing. James himself memorized part of a poem by Victor Hugo and then "trained" his memory for a month by memorizing lines from a poem by Milton. At the end of the training period he memorized another part of the Hugo poem, only to find that the task took longer than the initial effort. Follow-up research by many investigators convincingly demonstrated that memory is not an independent faculty that will improve the more one memorizes.

Thorndike dealt a similar blow to the notion that the study of certain subjects would improve one's mind. He found little or no connection between the study of a particular high school subject and improvement of general learning ability. Today one finds an occasional person questioning why the schools do not have pupils memorize more poetry to train the memory or insisting that the study of Latin will improve the mind, but faith in faculty psychology and mental discipline began to wane in the 1920s.

Improving Thinking by Teaching Children Scientific Methods

Beginning with John Dewey, attempts to improve reasoning ability took rather a special turn. While Dewey's philosophical and psychological interests embraced a wide spectrum of subjects; one of his concerns was with the process of reasoning itself and an analysis of the kinds of mental activities in which human beings engage as they solve problems. He identified five steps in the reasoning process: the learner becomes aware of some difficulty; he has a "felt need." The need serves as a stimulus to the intelligence to search for a suggested solution. An hypothesis is formulated, and the learner seeks evidence to confirm or refute his hypothesis. The evidence must be evaluated, and if the hypothesis is then rejected, the process begins again with more hypothesizing.

Dewey's work, *How We Think*, was published in 1933, but has a remarkably modern flavor and continues to influence curriculum. The reader may recognize his steps of thinking as very similar to those usually described in connection with the "scientific method." This method, the one that purportedly is used by scientists in solving problems, begins with careful observation out of which comes recognition and definition of a problem about which the scientist then hypothesizes, collects data, evaluates, and accepts or rejects the hypothesis.

There are those who reject such a pat formula for scientific methods, and who maintain that the scientist's method consists of "doing one's best, no holds barred." Nevertheless this step-by-step analysis has influenced teaching methods, and teaching the scientific method is advocated in some curriculum texts. While observing, hypothesizing, testing, and evaluating are certainly important in problem solving, it is questionable whether teaching pupils of their importance is the way to make children better observers, hypothesizers, and so on. The child in the primary grades *does* observe; the trouble is that he centers on only one property of an object or event as he observes. For example, if he pours juice from a tall narrow container into a lower broader one, he thinks that there is now not as much juice because, before, the juice went up to the top of the glass. Similarly, the pupil in intermediate grades *does* hypothesize, but if he picks out the wrong variable for testing, he does not know what to do next.

Recent Attempts To Improve Thinking Processes

There have been attempts in recent years to improve thinking processes and a whole new vocabulary developed in connection with these attempts. One reads of "strategies" for solving problems; of ways to make children "productive thinkers"; of "inquiry training." Such attempts are the result of an increased emphasis upon mediational processes. Learning theorists recognize that between the stimulus and the predicted response of the old S–R school, there are certain mental processes that intervene; previous learnings both cognitive and affective mediate to affect the response. Mediational processes may include "strategies" or preferred ways of tackling a problem, and, according to one school of thought, such strategies may be improved by teaching children to ask the "right" kind of questions. In "inquiry training," for example, the child is taught to ask questions that can be answered only by a "yes" or "no," as is true in such games as *Twenty Questions*, or the TV program *What's My Line?* However, there is no evidence to show that playing games like *Twenty Questions* or *What's My Line?* will make children better thinkers, nor do such training programs aid the teacher in figuring out what to do when a child gives the wrong answer. He may know that the child's strategy for solving problems is inadequate, but still be at a loss to know how to improve it.

Nor do such attempts to improve thinking as "inquiry training" help the teacher to be a better analyzer of learning problems. A fourth-grade class has experimented to find out what happens to a variety of materials when they are heated. The teacher asks under what headings the changes can be listed. The pupils list the headings for each class: melted, changed color, expanded, got hotter, temperature went up, and so on. They do not recognize, nor does the teacher help them to see, that their headings overlap, and that "got hotter" and "temperature went up" are repetitive. The problem is one of classification, and such fuzziness in classifying makes for fuzzy thinkers. The teacher needs to become aware of the mental operations involved in classifying before he can help children to think more clearly.

If the curriculum is to include experiences that will improve children's thinking processes, then we need to know more about how logical intelligence does develop in the child. We use the term *logical intelligence,* for development of the ability to deal with problems logically is our goal. We need, however, to define the term *logically,* for this term has been used ambiguously. Some use the term merely to say that the child's thinking is reasonable or sensible, while others use it to mean being systematic and "scientific" in problem-solving procedures. While such definitions are "commonsense" definitions of logical thinking, they do not reflect the logician's definition. When he says that a person is thinking logically, he means that that person is carrying on certain identifiable mental operations unique to human intelligence and used by all human beings regardless of culture. Reversibility is one such operation. Thought can reverse itself; we can go back in thought to the starting place. We do this sometimes in carrying on an argument. After the argument has gone on for some time, we may remind our opponent, "But you *said* in the beginning . . ." and then, by means of an identity operation, show him that all of his statements could not be true, and that his thinking is faulty, contradictory, inconsistent, or, in a word, illogical.

The examples of children's thinking given at the opening of this chapter can also be analyzed from the standpoint of logical operations. Or take the case of the pupils who do not know how to solve the problem of deciding what, instead of weight, might affect the time a pendulum takes to make a complete cycle (the period). The teacher demonstrates that different pendulums do indeed take different times to complete the full swing. What makes the difference? Children are asked to solve the problem and are given materials to do so. Involved here are a number of mental operations: identifying variables (length of string, weight, initial push, and so on) that *might* affect the outcome; keeping one of these the same for two pendulums while the others are varied, *one at a time*; being sure to test all possible combinations and keeping track mentally of the combinations as they are tested.

An observer in a classroom can find countless examples of both logical and illogical thinking that the teacher often does not recognize or does not know what to do about. Knowing what logical operations consist of and how they develop in children is a prerequisite to finding out how children acquire knowledge. For this knowledge, we turn to the developmental theory of Piaget and some of the implications of that theory.

The Developmental Theory of Piaget

Jean Piaget is a Swiss psychologist who, with his colleagues, has been studying the development of intelligence for over forty years. He has formulated a theory that has done for mental development what Freud did for the field of personality development. The starting point today for the serious student of the development of intelligence is the theory of Piaget, and his descriptions of stages in that development.

The Sensorimotor Stage

In contrast to the now discarded belief that intelligence is fixed at birth, Piaget, like most modern psychologists, believes that intelligence develops as the human organism carries on transactions upon objects or events in the environment. The human infant is born with a very large cortical area (the so-called gray matter of the brain where intelligent processes go on), but with few inborn responses. The infant comes into the world capable of reflex activity. Some of the reflexes, like that of the knee jerk, are not altered by experience. Others, however, like grasping, sucking, and reflexes involved in vision, are modified as the infant exercises them in response to stimulation. With the exercise, the infant assimilates information about objects and accommodates developing mental structures accordingly. That is, contact with an object modifies the activity of the reflex. The infant, for example, accommodates the grasping reflex to the shape of the object to be grasped, curving the fingers in one way for a long narrow object and differently to grasp a ring. The exercise of the reflexes serves as needed aliment for the reflex; as Piaget (1963) points out with respect to the eye, "Light is nourishment for the eye . . . the eye needs light images just as the whole body needs chemical nourishment" (pp. 42–43). And, as the reflexes are nourished by exercise, there is a tendency toward spontaneous repetition. Grasping leads to more grasping and looking to more looking. "The more a child has seen and heard, the more he wants to see and hear," is Piaget's way of summarizing the circular reaction of the first acquired adaptations. Through sensorimotor channels the infant is taking in information about the world, and the more he takes in, the more he wants.

The exercise of acquired adaptations leads to fresh discoveries, "every discovery historically entails a series of others." As the infant carries on activities with his environment, new behavior patterns are formed by differentiation and adaptation of preceding ones. Put an obstacle in the way of what a young infant is trying to grasp and he will abandon his attempt to find the object; out-of-sight is out-of-mind, for he lacks the concept of permanence of object. With experience, however, he comes to realize that objects *do* have permanence, and he will search for an object that an adult has shown him and then removed. Later, he may put to work here a response previously acquired in some other situation —that of pushing away or striking at the barrier in order to reach his goal. Parents and baby-sitters may recall the first time the baby discovered that striking at or pushing away an adult hand made it possible for him to reach the object which he now knows continues to exist.

During the first eighteen months, the infant carries on countless transactions involving space, time, matter, and causality. He assimilates information from these transactions, and because there are regularities and order in the physical world, mental structures become transformed as they accommodate themselves to new information. A baby tries to pull a ruler through the bars of the playpen. He discovers that held horizontally the ruler will not go through, but turned vertically it will. The discovery stimulates practice, and the infant may carry on a directed apprenticeship with variously shaped objects, and by twisting and turning them, assimilate information about how an object relates to space.

Piaget labels this early stage of intelligence, "sensorimotor intelligence." Sensorimotor intelligence is the intelligence of action; the infant "thinks" with action. If one moves a teddy bear from a chair to a bed while the infant looks on, and then says, "Where's teddy?", the baby will look first in the direction of the chair and then the bed. He does not have the capability for representational thought, for representing in his mind the displacement just carried out. He can carry on a series of displacements, of shifting data about, *but only in his actions* and not in his mind. He can move a toy physically, but he cannot visualize the move.

But according to the way in which Piaget traces the development of intelligent behavior in infancy, gradually the child comes to think about an action as he carries it out. Give an eighteen-month-old baby a closed box that he has never opened before and he does not grope for a solution. Rather, he puts to use the various schemata he has acquired for opening things, until he finds the correct one. This capacity to think out an action before representing it Piaget calls "mental invention." At this same stage the infant is capable of "representation"—that is, he has the capacity for imagining the environment other than as he directly perceives it. If the baby is asked, "Where's mommy?", after mommy has just left the room, he will point to the door she has passed through and say, "Dere mommy." He can conserve a part of the external world as a mental image, at least for a short time. And with the advent of language, events are increasingly represented linguistically, so that actions that previously had to be carried out in the sensorimotor system can now be carried out in thought.

The reader may wonder why we are concerned with the infancy period in a chapter on thinking processes of school-age children. The five-to-twelve-year-old is, after all, well beyond the stage of sensorimotor intelligence. For teachers, however, development in this first stage raises the interesting question of whether complex operations must first be enacted physically before they can be internalized. Bruner has written persuasively of such an enactive process in learning. He discusses the question of representation, or how a child gets to conserve past experience, in a model: "What is meant by representation? What does it mean to

translate experience into a model of the world? Let me suggest that there
are probably three ways in which human beings accomplish this feat:
The first is through action. We know many things for which we have no
imagery and no words, and they are very hard to teach to anybody by
the use of either words or diagrams and pictures. If you have tried to
coach somebody at tennis or skiing or to teach a child to ride a bike, you
will have been struck by the wordlessness and the diagrammatic impo-
tence of the teaching process. . . . There is a second system of represcnta-
tion that depends upon visual or other sensory organization and upon the
use of summarizing images. We may . . . grope our way through a maze
of toggle switches and then at a certain point in overlearning come to
recognize a visualizable path or pattern. We have come to talk about the
first form of representation as *enactive*, the second as *iconic*. . . . Finally,
there is representation in words or language. Its hallmark is that it is
symbolic in nature, with certain features of symbolic systems that are
only now coming to be understood" (Bruner, 1966, pp. 10–11).

There is the question of whether only motor skills, like playing tennis
or swimming, depend upon sensorimotor action, or whether certain cognitive skills do also. This is a question that must eventually be answered
by research. However, teachers would do well to keep the question in
mind and to experiment themselves to find which kinds of learnings
demand a sensorimotor underpinning. Learnings having to do with space
almost certainly do. The large floor maps that first-grade children draw,
and then walk their way from place to place on, very probably help them
to become oriented in space. Kindergarten children who set the table,
and in doing so must transform a place-setting 180°, keeping spoon,
napkin, and cup in the same position relative to the diner, are building
into their motor systems a concept of relativity. Perhaps the reason it is
difficult for adults to make certain transformations in thought is because
a sensorimotor underpinning for the operation is missing.

The Preoperational Stage

Piaget finds thinking processes changing with environmental transactions. The preoperational stage extends roughly from four to seven years
of age. (There are, of course, individual differences in the ages of children at a particular stage.) At this stage the child does not perform
operations of thought upon data when confronted with a problem. If
three dolls of various sizes were placed before the child, he could immediately pick out the largest. But if we say, "Amy is larger than Susie and
Susie is smaller than Mary; which one is largest," he cannot compare the
three because he cannot "serialize" (that is, he cannot place the three
dolls in his mind in order of size). If we show him a box of wooden

A preoperational view of space. In space relations, the concepts of vertical and horizontal become coordinated after seven years of age. This charming picture by five-year-old Susan is a preoperational version of how objects look upon a hillside. Courtesy of the Hapgoods, University of New Hampshire.

beads, eighteen of which are red and two of which are yellow, and ask him if there are more wooden beads or more red ones, he will say, "More red ones, because there are only two yellow ones." He cannot keep the whole in mind when one of the parts is so obviously larger than the other. If presented with a matrix puzzle where he must consider several properties of a figure (perhaps size and color), he will choose on the basis of one property alone, the one that stands out visually. Serializing, classifying by more than one attribute, dealing with whole-part relations, are logical operations the young child is not yet capable of mastering.

From research in Geneva and elsewhere, certain characteristics of mental processes at the preoperational stage have been identified (Stendler, 1966, pp. 8–11):

"1. *The child is perceptually oriented*; he makes judgments in terms of how things *look* to him. He may, for example, be confused in thinking about space by the objects placed in that space. When given a problem where two lines of ten sequential sticks are laid out in parallel rows, he will see that both are equal in length; that two dolls, walking along each path, would walk the same distance. But if one of the rows is rearranged in this fashion:

and the child is again asked if each doll takes as long a walk as the other, the child says, "No." Even when he counts the segments, he denies equality; the child does not see that there is a logical necessity by which ten must equal ten. Piaget has shown that this same type of perceptual judgment enters into the preoperational child's thinking about space, time, number, and causality. It is only as the child goes beyond his perceptions to perform displacements upon the data in his mind (for example, visualizing the second row of sticks straightened out again) that ability to conserve length even with a change in appearance appears.

"2. *The child centers on one variable only, usually the variable that stands out visually; he lacks the ability to coordinate variables.* For example, a kindergarten child is pouring juice into paper cups. The standard-size cups run out, and the teacher substitutes some that are much higher but are also smaller in diameter. As the children drink their juice, several comment on the fact that Jimmy, Eddie, and Danny have more juice. Why? Because those children have cups that are taller. The dimension of height, not width, stands out. The child's thinking is rigid; he does not perform operations on what he sees. Later he will reason that "higher than" is compensated for by "skinnier than," and that both kinds of cups may hold the same amount of juice. This ability to see reciprocal changes in two sets of data is an important logical tool available to older children but not to the preoperational child.

"3. *The child has difficulty in realizing that an object can possess more than one property, and that multiple classifications are possible.* It is hard for the child to see that one can live in Los Angeles and in California at the same time, that a bird is also an animal, and that, since there are animals other than birds, there are logically *more* animals in the world than there are birds. The operation of combining elements to form a whole and then seeing a part in relation to the whole has not as yet developed, and so hierarchical relationships cannot be mastered.

"So far, this consideration of preoperational thinking has been largely negative. We have seen that the child lacks the ability to combine parts into a whole, to put parts together in different ways, and to reverse processes. What, then, can the child do? The development of logical processes is not at a standstill during this period; there are some positive accomplishments. We see, for example, the rudiments of classification: the child can make collections of things on the basis of some criterion; he can also shift that criterion. Thus, if we present a kindergarten child with a collection of pink and blue squares and circles, some large and some small, and ask him to sort them into two piles with those in each pile being alike in some way, he can usually make two different collections on the bases of color and shape (a few children discover the third criterion of size). Such an ability, of course, is essential to the formulation of classes and eventually of a hierarchy of classes.

"The child is also beginning to arrange things in a series. He can compare two members of a set when they are in a consecutive order; he knows that Tuesday comes after Monday. But since Friday comes after Tuesday, which is after Monday, does Friday also come after Monday? This operation, involving seeing logical relations between things or events that are arranged in a series, is not yet possible to the preoperational child, but experiences with seriation are preparatory to the development of such operations. The "inching up" that an older pupil does in trying to establish equilibrium between two parts of a physical system (add a little to one side; then add a little to the other) is an example of a more sophisticated use of seriation.

The Concrete-Operational Stage

"Between seven and eleven years of age on the average, as the child assimilates information from his actions and accommodates mental structures to the new information, thinking processes change. The child abandons his perceptual judgments, and thought takes on certain logical properties. Piaget calls this stage the stage of *concrete operations,* because, while the child uses logical operations, the content of his thinking is concrete rather than abstract. One of the mental operations that develops is that of combining elements; the child begins to put two and two together figuratively as well as literally. He uses this combining operation to discover (though not until toward the end of this stage) that a substance like sugar added to water will make the water level rise, and that the water level will stay up even after the sugar dissolves. It dawns on the pupil that matter combined with matter produces more matter, that matter doesn't disappear into nothingness.

"Another property of logical thought is that elements of a whole can be associated in various ways without changing the total. Thus, in the problem of the ten sticks, the segments can be "associated" in a straight line or a zigzag line, but the total distance of the path to be covered remains the same, or is conserved. And in studying science, the pupil can use the associative operation to discover how to keep a system in equilibrium—how, for example, when a muscle is flexed, it becomes shorter but thicker; when relaxed, it is longer but thinner. In each case, the total amount of muscle remains the same; the amount of matter is conserved, though its shape is changed.

"A third property of logical thought is that of identity. The identity operation is basically a null operation; the child can mentally cancel out the effects of any operation by combining it with its opposite. He uses such an identity operation to reason that the effects of adding a force to one side of a balanced tug-of-war can be canceled out by adding a force to the other side (at the preoperational stage, he could solve the problem only by taking away the extra force that had been added). The pupil can also reason, as he thinks about a flexed muscle, that, since nothing has been added to the muscle and nothing has been taken away, then quantity of matter is identical before and after the flexing. An extension of the identity operation is the one-to-one correspondence a pupil carries on to establish identity between two sets. Is the spider an insect? The pupil must compare each characteristic in the set of insect characteristics with each in the spider set, on a one-to-one basis, to answer the question.

"Of all the properties of logical thinking, one of the most critical to develop is that of reversibility. Often when we are engaged in a discussion, it is necessary to go back in thought to the starting point and to compare what was said in the beginning with what is being said now. Children must be able to go back in thought, for example, when they are reading to find the answer to a question, so that they can compare what they are reading with what they started out to find."

The Stage of Formal Operations

Thinking processes change again at around eleven or twelve years of age, with the biggest change being the manner of attack on problems. Given a particular problem, a child at the level of concrete operations is likely to test out a possible solution, reject it if it does not fit, try another, and so forth. A student at the level of formal operations, however, "begins his consideration of the problem at hand by trying to envisage all the possible relations which could hold true in the data and then attempts, through a combination of experimentation and logical analysis, to find out which of these possible relations in fact do hold true. Reality is thus conceived of as a special subset within the totality of things which the data would admit as hypotheses" (Flavell, 1963, p. 204). He is capable of propositional thinking, of identifying the variables needed for testing, and putting them in a form for testing. This may be by *implication*: "If I try two mixtures in the hummingbird feeder, both of which are sweet and one of which is red while the other is colorless, and if the hummingbirds are attracted to the red, perhaps it is redness to which they respond." Or, it may be by *identity*: "I can test for redness by hanging up various red objects some of which are not food to see to which ones the hummingbirds will be attracted." Or the adolescent may use in his thinking processes *conjunction* (it's *either* this *or* that) or *disjunction* (it's this but *not* that) as he tests reality.

Piaget also points out that at the stage of formal operations the student can use a *combinatorial analysis* to make sure that all possible variables and combinations of variables have been tested. The student is not content with testing variable A, B, and C; he knows that he must also test for A and B together, or A and C, or any of the other combinations. We come back to specific examples of both combinatorial analysis and propositional thinking later in this chapter.

Implications of Piaget's Developmental Theory for Instruction

Disequilibrium as a Condition for Learning

It is clear from research findings that there are individual differences in children's ability to think logically, with some children being severely retarded in logical development. Can the schools intervene to foster maximum development? And, if so, what can teachers do?

Piaget makes it quite clear that maturation alone is not a guarantee of development; we cannot anticipate that children by virtue of having reached a certain age will have reached a certain state in logical development. Studies done in Martinique of culturally disadvantaged children showed a four-year delay in development over the Geneva norms. Nor is exposure to a particular experience enough. Deutsch found children of migratory workers, who had crossed the country many times as their parents followed the crops, whose knowledge of the geography of the region was minimal. Nor does instruction that depends upon verbal transmission apparently guarantee emergence of logical structures; readers of this text have probably had the experience themselves of listening to or reading about a clear account of the scientific discovery of a Nobel prize winner and feeling that they were understanding the explanation, only to find it totally impossible to explain the phenomenon to others.

How, then, *is* knowledge acquired and intellective development facilitated? For Piaget, twin processes of assimilation and accommodation are involved. As he acts upon his environment, the child assimilates certain elements into already existing mental structures. Equilibrium in mental organization is upset, the mental structures change to accommodate the new data, and equilibrium is restored. An analogy to homeostatic processes involved in temperature control may be helpful. As the body cools, temperature equilibrium is upset. Information on changes in the state of the system is assimilated in the hypothalamus, and the autonomic nervous system accommodates by setting in motion certain changes that enable the body to take care of the cooling. Blood vessels close to the skin contract so that less surface area is exposed to the cold; shivering increases production of heat in the body. In a somewhat comparable manner, one can postulate homeostasis in mental structures involving a sequence of assimilation—disequilibrium—accommodation—equilibrium. The obvious difference is that, whereas temperature adjustments are automatic and structures in the autonomic nervous system are not permanently altered as a result of the cycle, in the case of intelligence, there *are* changes in existing mental structures, and even new structures emerge at certain transition points in development.

Self-activity is crucial in the equilibration model described above. If equilibrium is to be achieved at a higher level, then the child must be mentally active; *he* must transform the data. The elements to be incorporated may be present in an experience, or the child may be told of the error in his thinking, but unless the mind is actively engaged in wrestling with data, no accommodation, or *false* accommodation, occurs. Children, like adults, are not convinced by being told they are wrong, nor by merely seeking evidence that contradicts their thinking. They have to act upon the data and transform them, and in so doing, make their own discoveries. As Piaget puts it, knowledge is not a copy of reality; to know something one must modify reality.

Does the foregoing presentation with its emphasis upon self-activity imply that such activity must be physical? Can the child carry on transactions in his mind, or must they always be upon actual objects? This question has already been raised in connection with sensorimotor intelligence, and again a reminder for the reader may be in order. Activity for Piaget is the activity of the mind. Physical activity may support, but mere physical involvement with material objects does not guarantee, mental activity any more than does verbal transmission. Mental activity is ensured when there is disequilibrium. When the learner is confronted with data that are fresh and challenging, or that contradict what he has always believed, he is more likely to carry on mental operations to resolve the dissonance and restore equilibrium. The data may be derived from experimenting with real objects, or they may come from other sources (books, maps, graphs, people), but disequilibrium is the necessary condition for acquisition of knowledge.

How, then, does the teacher create disequilibrium? How does he become a problem maker? He does so by changing the emphasis in his teaching from fact gathering to problem making. Bruner discusses a teaching technique used in the social studies that offers some clues. The topic was the geography of the North Central states and the children involved were fifth graders. Using a conventional approach a teacher might have listed such questions as

> What are the cities with a population over 250,000 in the North Central states and where are they located?
> What are the principal products of these states?
> What are the physical features?

Instead, the teacher in this instance did the following:

> We hit upon the happy idea of presenting this chunk of geography not as a set of knowns, but as a set of unknowns. One class was presented blank maps, containing only tracings of the rivers and lakes of the area as well as the natural resources. They were asked as a first exercise to indicate where the principal cities would be located, where the railroads, and where the main highways. Books and maps were not permitted and "looking up the facts" was cast in a sinful light. Upon completing this exercise, a class discussion was begun in which the children attempted to justify why the major city would be here, a large city there, a railroad on this line, and so on.
>
> The discussion was a hot one. After an hour, and much pleading, permission was given to consult the rolled-up wall map. I will never forget one young student, as he pointed his finger at the foot of Lake Michigan, shouting, "Yippee, *Chicago* is at the end of the pointing-down lake." And another replying, "Well, OK: but Chicago's no good for the rivers and it should be here where there is a big city (St. Louis)." These

children were thinking, and learning was an instrument for checking and improving the process. (Bruner, 1966, pp. 80–81)

When children are set to work to answer a question of fact, they must keep the question in mind and look for clues in the text to find the answer. Such mental operations are at a fairly low level. In contrast, in the example that Bruner cites, the mind must perform more complex operations, putting together, comparing and contrasting bits and pieces of information to form a hypothesis that might read, "Maybe cities get built up where two rivers come together." Does this hypothesis check with the facts? Perhaps not. The student may have chosen rivers that are not navigable or that do not lead to raw materials, and he may have to discard his hypothesis. Eventually, however, there *will* be learning, and he *will* acquire new knowledge. Disequilibrium of this kind begins with a problem that cannot be solved by recall of previously learned information.

A state of disequilibrium is motivating. The motivation may stem from what one psychologist calls competence motivation. White (1959) proposes the existence of an intrinsic need to deal competently with the unknown, a need that drives men to climb Mount Everest, monkeys to undo hasps that are fastened to a wooden slab and that open nothing, and children to solve problems and in so doing to acquire knowledge.

Implications of Theory for Planning Curriculum Sequence

Implicit in Piagetian theory is the notion of readiness. Intelligence consists of logical structures that permit the child to solve increasingly complex problems. The learner can have difficulty in mastering subject matter because he does not have ways of using the mind that certain concepts require for mastery. The boy or girl who cannot hold certain variables constant in his mind while another variable is experimentally manipulated is going to have difficulty in following a written description of the procedures of Pasteur. He will have even more difficulty in trying to set up an experiment where he must plan which variables will be held constant and which one will be manipulated. Similarly the child who is not nimble enough in combining classes and reversing an operation will find so-called two-step problems in arithmetic impossible to solve. We used to think that such pupils were stupid or stubborn, or both, or were poorly motivated, or had what we called, for lack of a better name, an "emotional block." One or more of these conditions may indeed be true, but there is gathering evidence that a cognitive deficit, an inability to manipulate data in particular ways, may be the basis of the learning problem.

One-to-one correspondence. The kindergarten child shown here is attempting to match pennies to horses on a one-to-one basis. If he succeeds, the teacher will then see if he can maintain the correspondence if she bunches the pennies together. The simple mental operation involved in solving this problem provides the foundation for the more complex matching that must be done to compare two sets of conditions, the type of problem posed on page 54 in connection with the kangaroo rat. From A Piaget Preschool Program in Action, "Number, Measurement and Space." *Copyright 1971 Center for Media Development, Inc. From Knowledge Tree Films, a division of Center for Media Development, Inc.*

A two-step problem:

How much change will Jimmy get from a one-dollar bill if he buys a pencil for 15¢ and a pen for 39¢?

Note that the student must first combine the prices of the two separate items, and then go back to the amount Jimmy started with, to solve the problem.

Research on classification structures in particular has yielded promising leads in planning sequence in curriculum. Classification structures are important, for being able to classify helps one to deal efficiently with a phenomenon. If one can identify a strange animal as a reptile and one has studied reptiles, one immediately has access to a whole body of knowledge about the new animal. If one recognizes a phenomenon as retrograde motion, and one has knowledge of this class concept, then one is more competent to deal with the new phenomenon. And if one can identify an arithmetic problem as belonging to a particular class of problems with which one is familiar, then the particular instance is easy to solve. The ability to classify is essential to the acquisition of subject matter.

Classification consists of a number of different operations involving a coordination of intension and extension. *Intension* (note the spelling) refers to the sum of the characteristics or attributes contained in a concept, while *extension* refers to the class of things to which the term is applicable. To be able to classify, a child must know what properties are common to a set of elements (the *intension* of the class). But his decision as to common properties can only be based upon comparison of "all" and "some" members of the class; he must ask, "Can I find this property in all members I know to belong to the class?" This is class *extension*, and the operations of intension and extension go on simultaneously. It is as if the child hypothesized, "I think that flying is one of the properties that is common to all birds; therefore, if an animal can fly, it is a bird and if it is a bird, it can fly." But when the child tries to extend that particular intension of the class, he finds that it does not work. There are animals besides birds that fly, and there are some birds that do not fly. So, in classifying, he must use operations of extension and intension at the same time, going backward and forward in thought, having both hindsight and foresight, remembering the properties with which he started and applying his criteria to all members of the class. When a teacher of biology says to students, "What are the characteristics of osmosis? Before we can label a process 'osmosis,' what things must be true?", he is asking students to define the intension of the class. And when the teacher asks, "Could such-and-such a process be called osmosis," he is calling upon students to extend the class.

Classification operations have been broken down and the following sequence at least tentatively identified:

1. Operations involving the matching of objects or collecting of objects into small groups that share common features. For example, a child's performance when asked to find blocks to match one that the teacher has, or to sort pictures of plants and animals into two groups following the teacher's lead, would be an indication of whether or not these operations had emerged. Approximately 90 percent of four-year-olds can solve such tasks, yet comparable tasks are assigned to six- and even seven-year-olds. In fact, most of the tasks of finding likenesses and differences in objects presently assigned to primary children are more

suitable to four-year-olds, and few, even disadvantaged primary children, are at this level. Knowledge of sequence can be helpful not only in identifying tasks too difficult for children but also, as in this case, those that are too easy.

2. Operations for dealing with multiple-class membership. Children in primary grades obviously need practice in seeing that an object can belong to more than one class at the same time, for successful solution to problems of multiple membership is not achieved until about seven years of age. They need training in seeing the redness and squareness of an object at the same time, in recognizing diameter as well as length, in conceptualizing a bean as a seed as well as something to be eaten. In many different contexts, conceptual as well as perceptual, they need to move away from centering on only one variable in a problem to recognition of multiplicative classification.

3. Operations for dealing with class inclusion. As we have already noted, in one of the Piaget tasks, the child is shown a box of twenty beads all of which are wood, eighteen of which are red, and two of which are yellow. He verifies that all are made of wood and that most are red in color while only two are yellow. Then he is asked whether there are more beads made of wood, or more red beads. The pre-operational child says there are more red "because there are only two yellow." Because he cannot yet perform transformations upon the data before him, he loses track of the property of woodenness; he is overwhelmed by the visual display and answers in terms of what he perceives. He cannot keep the whole and its parts in mind at the same time and successfully compare one part with the whole. The relations of "some" and "all" elude him. It is only when the child can mentally reverse an operation, when he can take the class of wooden beads apart and compare one subclass to the whole, that he can solve the problem.

Primary teachers will recognize similar problems in children's thinking. Boys and girls in the schoolroom make up the class of children. If the girls overwhelmingly outnumber the boys, the child will respond, when asked if there are more children or more girls, that there are more girls.

The alert teacher can be on the lookout for many situations that arise in the course of a teaching day to teach operations of class inclusion—that is, that a superordinate class is formed by putting subclasses together, and that when the superordinate class is taken apart, the whole is always greater than any of its parts. Wherever the opportunity exists, the teacher should ask the kind of questions that will force the child to compare a part with the whole, and to justify his responses. Then, if he gives the wrong answer, she can lead the pupil by her questioning to keep the whole in mind while he compares a part with it. Use of the chalkboard to provide a visual representation of the operation involved is helpful.

4. Hierarchical operations. These operations include combining subsets to form a hierarchy. Robins and bluejays and all birds not robins and bluejays combine to form the class of birds. Birds, reptiles, and mammals combine to form a class of animals with a backbone. Animals with a backbone combine with animals without a backbone to form a class of animals. Animals and plants together combine to form a class of living things.

Seventh- and eighth-grade teachers of civics can attest to the difficulty their students have with hierarchical classification. The hierarchical organization of city, township, county, state, and federal governments remains forever a mystery to some students simply because they lack the mental operations for dealing with hierarchies. Again the teacher would do well to search for opportunities to teach children how subclasses can be combined to make higher-order classes, and those classes in turn combined to make still higher orders, and so on. At the same time, she can, by adroit questioning, help pupils discover some of the logic inherent in hierarchical classification:

a. All elements must be classified. If there exists an element that is the only one of its kind, it must give rise to its own class.
b. Each class contains members having all of the elements characteristic of that class.
c. Every specific class characterized by its own property (a) implies its complement, characterized by *not* (a). The class of robins, for example, implies a complementary class of birds *not robins*.
d. A class is included in every higher ranking class that contains all its elements. Therefore, all robins are birds, and some birds are robins.

Facilitating Development of Logical Operations at the Concrete Level

There is some evidence to show that when pupils become aware of the actual logical operations underlying the solutions to problems, thinking processes improve. Wohlwill and Lowe (1962) found that some kindergarten children responded positively to training based upon addition and subtraction of elements to induce conservation of number. While the number of successes was not significant, results of the research were in the direction of support for Piaget's own contention that complex operations depend for their development upon simpler ones, and that teaching the simpler operations of addition and subtraction induced in some children the appearance of the more complex operations involved in conservation.

At the beginning of this chapter, we pointed out that when a pupil cannot give the proper response to the teacher's question, the teacher all too frequently moves on to ask another pupil. He assumes, we said, that the first pupil does not know enough to answer the question, although actually the case may be that the pupil lacks the logical operations for dealing with it. An alternative teaching procedure to that of calling upon another pupil would be to work out the logical processes involved in question answering with the pupil. For example, suppose the teacher has asked of a third-grade pupil in a class that has been studying adaptation of animal life to the desert, "Can you give me an example of an animal that lives in the desert and explain how the animal can live in such an environment?"

To answer the question, the pupil must first combine elements that make up a set of desert conditions: little water, extremes of temperature, scarcity of food, little ground cover. He remembers the kangaroo rat as living on the desert and combines elements that make up a set of rat characteristics: eats seeds and gets water from seeds, has sharp claws and can dig burrows, stays underground during heat of day and so needs less water, has eyes with many rods and so can hunt in the cool of the night. Then the pupil must set up a correspondence between elements in the desert-conditions set and elements in the rat set. If for the elements in the first set there are corresponding members in the second set, then the two sets fit, and one can say with certainty that the kangaroo rat is adapted to desert living. Identifying for children the logical processes for answering certain kinds of questions could conceivably aid the process of knowledge acquisition. To the pupil who is at a loss to answer a ques-

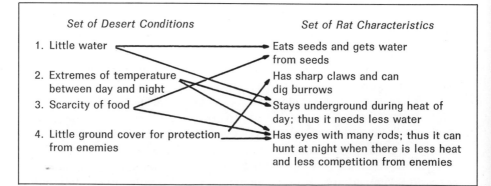

Kangaroo rat's adaptation to its environment. From C. Stendler, The Developmental Approach of Piaget and Its Implications for Science in the Elementary Schools, *booklet to accompany The Macmillan Science Series, p. 16. © Copyright The Macmillan Company, 1966.*

tion, the teacher might explain the procedure for composing two sets and comparing the two.

Building Readiness for Formal Operations

There are four stages in the development of logical thinking that Piaget has identified. Transition from one stage to another depends upon whether or not the simpler operations that form the basis for the more complex have developed. All children of normal intelligence, however, appear to achieve a level of concrete thinking. That is, they move from sensorimotor to preoperational to logical thinking at the concrete level, although, of course, some achieve a particular level at a much earlier age than others. Even the children in Prince Edward County, Virginia, deprived of schooling for a period of five years when the county closed school doors rather than integrate, displayed an ability to think logically about conservation tasks at a level not significantly worse than culturally disadvantaged children in a Detroit ghetto. True, the Detroit sample at nine years of age was several years below the norms reported by Piaget, but the children were capable of logical thinking about some types of problems (Sigel & Mermelstein, 1965).

The transition to the fourth stage, that of formal thinking, is a different matter. Supposedly the ability to reason at a formal level begins at about eleven or twelve years of age, yet it appears that many people, even the well-educated, do not become capable of the hypothetico-deductive reasoning that characterizes the formal stage. Hypothetico-deductive reasoning involves first of all the ability to identify variables in a problem. The adolescent can reason, "Well, it is clear from the data that A might be the necessary and sufficient condition for X, or that B might be, or that both together might be needed; my job is to test these possibilities in turn to see which one or ones really hold true in this problem" (Flavell, 1963, p. 205). He can then combine the variables systematically so as to make sure that all combinations are tested: (a) neither A nor B produces X alone or in combination; (b) A elicits X but B does not; (c) B elicits X but A does not; (d) both A and B can induce X, separately or jointly; and (e) A and B together produce X, but neither alone does; and so on.

Stendler (1967) reports a classroom example of the thinking of fifth-grade pupils that illustrates some of their difficulties with hypothetico-deductive reasoning. The unit under study was temperature, and the activity a ball-and-ring experiment. The experimental apparatus consists of a metal ball attached to a rod with a wooden handle, and a metal ring similarly mounted. The two pieces are so sized that the ball will just slip through the ring when both are at the same temperature. The children had already seen liquid expand and contract when warmed and cooled, and the ball-and-ring activity provided an exposure to expansion and contraction of a solid. To find out the level of the children's thinking with respect to hypothetico-deductive reasoning, the apparatus was explained to the children; they saw that the ball and the ring expanded when heated and contracted when cooled, and that evidence of the change came from the tightness or looseness of the fit. Then they were asked what experiments might be done to show what happens when metals are heated and cooled.

From the suggested experiments and the discussion that followed their listing, some interesting insights into the children's level of deductive thinking could be derived. Piaget has said that the concrete operational child is tied to reality, to concrete data before him, and can state in terms of action successive associations between one datum and another. Piaget's description did indeed fit the eleven-year-olds in question. They could make, without great difficulty, such associations as, "Heat the ball and not the ring"; "Heat the ring and not the ball," a simple reversibility; and when *asked* to predict what would happen in each case, could make the correct association. But the children *began* with action in each case and not with hypotheses. They did not begin, as one might at the formal stage, with a statement hypothesizing about the effect of heat and cold upon metals. Furthermore, because the children lacked a hypothetico-deductive scheme, because they did not start with hypotheses as generalized statements, they got bogged down in particulars, forgot what they started out to do, and lost track of transformations that they had made. In particular, they had difficulty in keeping successive transformations in mind. Many children, for example, suggested a procedure of heating the ball and then plunging it into ice; such a procedure, they predicted, would make the ball bigger. They could not keep in mind what was happening with each transformation.

Another interesting facet in the children's thinking was their inability to deal with inversions. Many children suggested heating both pieces of apparatus and then cooling them. They did not see that heating both pieces and then cooling both pieces changes nothing with respect to fit of ball and ring. Nor did they see that they neutralized the effect of a particular transformation on one piece of apparatus by carrying out an identical transformation upon the second piece. The question, "If we put both ball and ring in the ice at the same time, can we say from what happens anything about the effects of cooling upon metal? Can we stick both in ice at the same time and find out about cooling?" was a difficult one for most children. Their answer to the question was, "Yes, they will get smaller and the ball will go through"; they thought in terms of what was happening to one piece of equipment only.

One last sidelight on the children's thinking. It was obvious from their proposals that they lacked an appreciation of the need to keep all things the same in their experimenting except the one variable that was being tested. They thought that one could prove a causal relationship by varying two factors simultaneously. When asked to think of an experiment to test the statement, "Ice made the ring shrink and heat made the ball big," the children suggested, "Put the ring on ice and the ball on the flame, and the ball won't go through." They did not see that the reason for lack of fit might be both that the ball is bigger and the ring is smaller, and so one has not really "proved" the original statement.

From the analysis of children's thinking about the ball-and-ring problem, a teaching strategy for developing hypothetico-deductive reasoning skills can be devised. Such a strategy should be based upon the following needs of children:

1. Children need help in framing statements based upon hypothetico-deductive reasoning rather than upon action. Action statements such as "Heat the ball and not the ring" reflect fragmented thinking. If the student can be trained to state propositions—"Metal expands when heated"—for example, and then to state all the implications of that proposition—an example of one such statement would be, "If the ball is heated and not the ring, then the ball will expand and no longer go through the ring"—then experimentation will follow *after* deductions from preliminary hypotheses. Such training in stating deductions would seem to be a necessary condition for the emergence of formal thought.

2. Students need help in devising a system for keeping track of combinations of variables tested. Teaching the use of a simple gamelike device like a two-by-three matrix table (Ball-Ring; Heat, Cool, Do Nothing) would seem useful here.

3. Students need help in stating hypotheses and then following through successive transformations upon hypotheses. Here a model that has a visual component might be useful. A two-pan balance, for example, might be used where the child can actually see that doing the same thing to both sides of the balance changes nothing as far as equilibrium is concerned.

Thinking about how pupils are thinking and being concerned about what might stand in the way of logical thinking is an important step for teachers to take, if they are to help children acquire knowledge. Teachers can gain firsthand insight into how pupils are thinking if they themselves administer some of the Piaget tasks and listen to pupil explanations. Directions for administering some of the tasks are included in the Appendix in Lavatelli and Stendler, *Readings in Child Behavior and Development* (in press).

Bruner on Cognitive Growth

Piaget's theory of how the child acquires knowledge has attracted widespread attention on the part of educators, and there are serious attempts under way to identify implications of that theory for education. On this side of the Atlantic, the American whose ideas about cognitive growth have been most influential is Jerome Bruner, whose studies of how "human beings increase their mastery in achieving and using knowledge" have provoked considerable interest and some controversy. Much of the controversy stems from his statement that the child at any age can learn concepts considered to be respectable in the eyes of specialists in the field. There are those who interpret the statement to be in contradiction to Piaget, that Piaget believes a child cannot acquire concepts unless mental structures necessary to process the concept already exist. However, it should be noted that there is no real contradiction here; Bruner does not say that a child at any age can learn *anything*: in fact, nothing is said about the complexity of the concept, nor that simpler concepts, suited to the developmental level of the child, lack academic respectability.

Bruner's view of cognitive growth is organized around two central tenets concerning the nature of knowing. He maintains that since we can never "know" reality, we construct models of the real world which we test, when we can, against input from the real world. The models rest upon certain assumptions that we cannot test directly, notions of the conservation or invariance of time, space, matter, and number, and notions of cause and effect. The structure of these models is in part determined by the innate nature of or means of representing reality: in action, in imagery, in symbolism.

According to Bruner, the child represents the world first through motor activity. Suppose the learning involves how to operate a particular mechanism. We operate the mechanism over and over again, taking each step in turn, until we have built in a model of the mechanism at, one might say in slang terms, the "gut" level; one has the "feel" for it. Piaget's concept of sensorimotor intelligence is akin to this "action" representation, or enactive representation. In time, Bruner postulates, action becomes internalized: A schema becomes abstracted from a particular act and "becomes the basis for action-free imagery." At that point, the child's way of representing the world no longer depends upon an action image, although the child will continue to depend upon some forms of enactive representation when faced with new and difficult problems. Bruner cites the case where a child is given a rack containing forty-two pegs arranged in six columns and seven rows. The examiner has an identical rack; he places a ring on one of its pegs. The child is asked to put a ring on his rack in the same place as the examiner has put one. The examiner's rack may be side-by-side, at right angles, or back-to-back to the child's. The greater the angle of displacement, the greater the problem of carrying the action pattern in one's mind and solving the problem correctly.

A second stage in representation emerges about age two when a child can represent some aspect of the real world by an image. This is *iconic representation* and has definite limitations. Because iconic representation depends so much upon perception, it is field oriented; it is difficult for the child at this stage to see an object removed from the field and make judgments about it. Thus he cannot determine the position of a body in a tilted room or figure out where an object will be if a pictured landscape is rotated 180°. What Piaget describes as the characteristics of preoperational thinking, Bruner finds to be true of iconic representation.

The infant "knows" by doing (enactive); the young child "knows" by depicting in images. Both of these ways of knowing have their limitations. The third way of "knowing," of representing the world, is symbolically, through the use of language. To this stage Bruner gives the label *symbolic representation*. Bruner believes that, as the child acquires the language in an advanced society such as ours, he also acquires certain fundamental rules for dealing with objects and events—rules of category, hierarchy, function, and the like. Bruner finds symbolic activity and culture inextricably mixed; experience becomes organized to correspond in some measure to patterns in the culture that are represented in the structure of language.

Teachers find Bruner's stages of "knowing"—the enactive, iconic, and symbolic—useful in teaching certain concepts. Teachers of primary arithmetic, in using the number line, have children trace with a finger a jump from the "2" position to the "8" position, an enactive representation of 2 and 6. In teaching spatial transformation, a teacher may have a child choose from photos of a scene taken from different positions the one photo that matches what he sees from his position—iconic representation. And over and over again, teachers rely upon symbolic representation; they call upon the child to think about things that are not in the immediate present and that must be called to mind by the words the teacher uses. There appear to be social-class differences with respect to meeting this particular cognitive demand; teachers would do well to keep in mind that some children need special coaching in talking about objects or events removed in space or time from them. We return to this point in a later chapter, "The Language Arts Curriculum."

Summary

Children may have difficulty in acquiring knowledge because the mental processes necessary for acquisition of that knowledge have not yet developed. Teachers can foster the development of these mental processes, or logical way of thinking, as they become more aware of the processes themselves. Piaget's theory of the development of logical intelligence is helpful here. He postulates age-related changes in thinking processes. Teachers of young children (up to about seven years of age) can anticipate learning difficulties because the child's thinking tends to be egocentric and perceptually-oriented, and then modify their teaching accordingly. With the seven-to-eleven-year-old learner, teachers will find that taking into account Piaget's model of concrete-operational thought will facilitate learning processes. And at the fifth- and sixth-grade levels, teachers need to be alert to ways to assist development of hyptheticodeductive reasoning.

Bruner's model of how reality comes to be represented in thought is a three-stage model: enactive, iconic, and symbolic representation. The model complements the Piagetian one and provides the teacher with an additional tool for helping children acquire knowledge.

READING LIST 2

Bruner, J. *The relevance of education*. New York: W. W. Norton & Company, 1971. A series of essays written since 1965 and collected here for their special relevance to the problems of education in a deeply troubled society.

Bruner, J., Olver, B., Greenfield, P., et al. *Studies in cognitive growth*. New York: John Wiley & Sons, 1966. In addition to examining the growth of the three systems for representing reality reviewed in this chapter, Bruner and his coauthors present studies bearing on cognitive processes.

Jensen, A. How much can we boost IQ and scholastic achievement? *Harvard Education Review*, Winter 1969, 39:1–123. For readers who have not been exposed to the Jensen controversy in human development or educational psychology courses. Jensen revived the issue of heritability of intelligence in this article, along with the issue of racial differences in intelligence. The next issue of this same journal (Spring 1970) contains discussions of the Jensen paper by Bereiter, Cronbach, Crow, Elkind, and J. Mc V. Hunt, presenting evidence contrary to the Jensen position.

Lavatelli, C. *Piaget's theory applied to an early childhood curriculum*. Boston: American Science of Engineering, 1970. A text describing development of the mental structures: classification; number, measurement, and space; and seriation—up to about seven years of age, together with a curriculum designed to foster development of these structures.

Piaget, J. Development and learning. In C. Lavatelli and F. Stendler (Eds.),

Readings in child development. 3rd ed. New York: Harcourt Brace Jovanovich (in press). Piaget makes a distinction here between development and learning, and discusses the factors explaining the progression from one structure of operations to another.

Sigel, I., & Hooper, F., (Eds.) *Logical thinking in children.* New York: Holt, Rinehart and Winston, 1968. An anthology of research based on Piaget's theory. Papers by Wallach et al., Kohnstamm, and Dodwell are particularly recommended.

Professional Journals To Become Acquainted With

Child Development. Society for Research in Child Development, The University of Chicago Press, 5750 Ellis Ave., Chicago, Illinois 60637.

Merrill Palmer Quarterly. The Merrill-Palmer School, Detroit, Michigan.

CHAPTER 3

The Learner and the Teaching–Learning Process

In this chapter we will be concerned with learning and with how to make the learning process more effective. We will also be concerned with the learning of new behaviors, with strengthening motivation for school learning where it is weak, with weakening a too strong aggressive or other antisocial drive, and with helping pupils to learn to cope with their everyday problems. For help in the area of learning, we turn first to the work of behavioral psychologists, especially to those whose work has direct application to classroom learning.

Under the umbrella of Behaviorism, one can find many schools of thought, differing in certain respects but sharing a faith in the stimulus–response unit as the basic unit in behavior, and an abiding interest in the conditions under which a stimulus and a response become connected. The concept of reinforcement for most behaviorists is crucial; they believe that the learner must "get something" following the making of a response in order for that response to be learned. The "something" may be the satisfaction derived from drive reduction; that is, the learner may find satisfying the lessening of tension induced by the motivation that prompted the response in the first place. Or the satisfaction or "effect" may come from some positive or negative sign signalling success or lack of it. Repetition of responses with reinforcement strengthens that which is learned. In general, positive reinforcement through reward or success is considered to be more conducive to learning than negative reinforcement through punishment or failure.

Active in the field of child learning are those behaviorists using *operant conditioning* techniques to change the behavior of children. B. F. Skinner's name more than that of any other is associated with these techniques. In operant conditioning, the experimenter selects a particular response of the child and reinforces it, so that that response comes to be satisfying to the child and thus likely to be repeated. A key procedure is *shaping*. Granted that a desirable response should be reinforced, what if the response never appears? In shaping behavior, the experimenter searches in the child's repertoire of behaviors for those responses that resemble the desired behavior and reinforces them. A new set of responses will then be available, some of which will resemble the final response more closely than the first ones to be reinforced. The procedure is repeated, and each set of closer approximations is strengthened in turn until the desired behaviors appear and are available for reinforcing. Shaping can be of responses leading to word recognition in reading, or of responses leading to less aggressive behavior.

Ironically enough, developments in educational experimentation in recent years have drawn more and more heavily upon a Skinnerian view with heavy emphasis upon reinforcement. It is ironic because, after years of being told that one should *not* reward pupils for successful performance, that the reward should come from the learning itself, teachers are now discovering that the "in" thing to do is to pass out rewards. In fact, in early childhood education in particular, children are receiving material rewards (the worst kind according to the older view) in the way of raisins, M & M's, stickers, or handshakes. In fact, in some programs, children are saving up tokens and turning them in at the end of the week for more substantial rewards, and in so doing, learning to work, as we all must do, for delayed gratification rather than immediate. The term *behavioral modification* has come to be used as a label for an approach to changing child behavior through the use of reinforcement techniques. We return to behavior modification later in the chapter.

Four Components of Learning

Teachers have found useful a model of the learning act described by Neal Miller and John Dollard (1941). The Miller-Dollard Model includes four components: drive, cue, response, reinforcement. To paraphrase these terms, the authors say:

The learner must *want* something.
The learner must *notice* something.
The learner must *do* something.
The learner must *get* something.

The reader can discover these four components in his own mastery of the material presented here. If he is to understand the Miller-Dollard model, he must first be motivated to learn—a motivation that may spring from intellectual curiosity, or from a desire to do well in class recitation or the next hourly exam. Then he must focus his attention upon the important elements; perhaps such phrases as "wanting something," "noticing something," and the like will catch his eye. Next he must *do* something. If he is preparing for an exam, perhaps he will recite the four essentials of learning to himself or even write them down, and then compare his recall of the elements with those in the text. If he has been correct, there is a certain release from tension, a feeling, "Ah, I got *those* right," that reduces his initial drive and thus reinforces the correct response.

Drive

According to many psychologists, *drive* is the first essential of learning. If learning is to occur, the learner must want something so that he is impelled to act; he must be motivated. Some psychologists postulate the existence of internalized drive systems like independence and achievement which impel the child to work on his own and to do his "best" work in the classroom. Such drives are not present at birth; they are acquired through a conditioning process in which reinforcement plays a critical role.

The reader may recall the classical experiments of Pavlov. In his study of the digestion of dogs, Pavlov discovered that the mere appearance of food, and even the footsteps of the experimenter, elicited salivary secretions from the animals. After repeated associations of the sound of a buzzer with the presentation of food, the dogs came to salivate at the sound of the buzzer alone. Later investigators have shown that new drives, such as fear, can be learned by an animal, through association of a particular stimulus with the need to escape pain. If bell and shock are administered together often enough, a dog will learn to give the response to the bell alone. Through the same associative process, if the young child wants to please his mother, he will want to please some adults. He also discovers that doing well in school or doing things on his own pleases adults, and so he is motivated to achieve, to act independently. The psychological process involved is also conditioning; it differs from classical conditioning in that it is not based upon such innate needs as hunger or thirst, but upon learned needs.

Teachers emphasize the relationship between children's present drives and the learning task required by the school, often unconsciously. For example, a teacher says to first graders who are reading aloud:

> Good boy. Mother will be pleased. [You already want to please your mother; learning to read these words will please your mother.]
> That's fine, Harry, I like the way you did that. [You already want to please me; learning to read these words pleases me.]
> I like the way Susie is following along in her book. She'll learn some new words that way. [Susie wants to do well in reading; keeping place in the book will help her.]

Such reinforcement by the teacher teaches the child to know which behaviors will facilitate drive reduction. By singling out certain things that the child does for attention and praise, the teacher makes certain behaviors satisfying and thus increases the likelihood that those behaviors will be repeated. Furthermore, the drive itself will be strengthened; a child with a weak achievement drive who finds satisfaction in achieving may want more of the same satisfying state of affairs, and a generalized need to achieve will be more impelling than ever.

Motivation will also be strengthened when children have a chance to set goals. For example, a poor speller might work out a reasonable goal in terms of the number of words he will try to learn to spell in a week. A slow reader might set himself the task of reading a certain number of pages every day to build up speed. When children set goals for themselves they sometimes drive themselves much harder than the teacher would.

Additional general principles with respect to motivation can be found in the writings of Hunt (1963). He analyzes the work of Piaget, and particularly Piaget's observations of infant development, for the light these observations shed on motivation. Piaget had noted that "the more a child has seen and heard, the more he wants to see and hear." Hunt hypothesizes from this generalization that there may be an intrinsic motivation inherent in information processing and action. That is, "once children have been exposed to a given pattern of stimulation enough times to make it familiar, the emerging recognition of the pattern brings pleasure that motivates an effort to retain or re-elicit the pattern . . . after a pattern has continued to be familiar for a time, it is variation in that pattern that brings pleasure and the effort to find that variation in either the child's own activities or in external stimulation" (p. 273). The behavior of young children in Montessori schools is a case in point. Hunt notes that the young child will spend incredibly long periods of time with Montessori equipment, thoroughly immersed in teaching himself and with no prodding from the teacher. In British Infant and Primary Schools, also, observers note that children who have considerable freedom in planning their day within the limits set by the teacher work enthusiastically and diligently at learning tasks. It is intrinsic motivation of this kind that classroom teachers would like to see develop. Its secrets still evade us, but problem-solving activities that provide input for the child for the next phase of learning are a step in the right direction.

There are special problems of motivation with respect to children from low socioeconomic-status families. A number of investigators report that disadvantaged children are not motivated to achieve school success to the same degree as the middle-class child. The latter is *expected* to succeed in school, and motivation to do well is strengthened by parental interest and concern. The child receives positive reinforcement for the "good" papers and report cards he brings home, and for other evidences of satisfactory progress, all of which social reinforcement makes him want to continue to do well in school. Such social contingencies do not operate to the same degree in the disadvantaged home. As a result, grades and standardized achievement test scores show little improvement as the child goes through the elementary school, and the dropout rate remains high.

Zigler and Butterfield (1968) found that motivation also affects Binet scores. The design of their experiment was such that motivational factors could be separated from the cognitive in testing preschool children by setting up special conditions for testing designed to optimize I.Q. scores. Analysis of results indicated that the significant difference in improvement found between nursery and nonnursery groups was attributable solely to motivational factors; the nursery groups were better able to use their intelligence in a standard testing situation. The authors conclude:

> That the culturally deprived child has more intelligence than he is often credited with was indicated by the finding of a significantly greater increase from the standard to optimal testing (testing under conditions designed to optimize IQ scores) than from the standard to standard testing at the beginning of the year. The motivational position advanced in this paper would generate the expectation that such a great store of unused intelligence would not be found among middle-class children whose motivational systems are such as to produce a relatively optimal performance regardless of which testing procedure is used. (p. 10)

Wolf, Giles, and Hall (1968) report on a behavior modification program aimed at developing motivation through the use of reinforcement procedures. The students involved were sixth graders scoring at least two years below the norm in reading on the Stanford Achievement Test. In the experimental program, when a child completed an assignment correctly he received points, marked in his record book, much like a trading stamp book. When a page was completely filled, he could redeem it for a variety of reinforcers. Pages were of different colors; green pages were redeemable for a daily snack; blue pages for a weekly field trip; yellow pages for substantial long-range prizes; and pink pages for money. The authors report encouraging preliminary results. Children gained 1.5 years in achievement scores in one school year, as compared with 0.5 years in the two previous school years. The experimental classes were conducted after school, but school grades improved during the year from a D to C, reflecting improved skills and increased motivation to achieve school success. In this particular instance, reinforcement has served to teach responses through operant conditioning (which we will discuss at length at the end of this section). Some would argue that it also increases the strength of an underlying achievement drive.

Cue

The second essential of the learning process is cue; the child must *notice* something. He must be on the lookout for signs that tell him what to do. If he is not alert to the proper signs, he will make the correct response only accidentally, if at all, and the learning will be inefficient or negligible. Sometimes children look for the wrong signs and therefore make the wrong responses. It is not uncommon for elementary teachers to find pupils who can spell all the words in a spelling test correctly if the teacher dictates them in the sequence in which they appear in the spelling list, but who miss most of the words if they are dictated in random order. We do not know the reason for this interesting phenomenon, but it appears likely that the child in this case is paying attention to the wrong cues. Instead of looking at each word individually and selecting cues within the word, he notices how the words look in relationship to one another on the list. The learning feat that he accomplishes is a prodigious one, but it does not enable him to spell.

The child in our example has noticed the wrong *visual* cues. Pupils may also make the mistake of paying attention to the wrong sense receptors; they may listen to auditory cues instead of looking for visual signs. Many first graders can recite the contents of the preprimer from memory, without being able to read individual words. These children, too, have paid attention to the wrong cues; they have *listened* intently while the story was read to them instead of *looking* intently at the text for cues that would help them to distinguish one word from another.

Some recent research indicates that there may be social-class differences in the kind of cues to which children attend. Data from Orr and Graham (1967) indicate that low-income children score much closer to middle-income children in listening comprehension than in reading comprehension. Learning to read may thus be more difficult for poor children because of its great reliance upon visual context. Teachers of the disadvantaged might well consider placing more emphasis upon auditory stimuli rather than relying so exclusively upon the visual.

To make learning more efficient, the teacher needs to note student errors and analyze them from the standpoint of missed or incorrect cues. The student who continually spells "dinning" for "dining," or "hat" for "hate," is neither perverse nor stupid; he simply has not attended to the cues that would enable him to arrive at the correct spelling generalization. Asking the child to keep a record of his errors is helpful; the errors can then be analyzed to find a pattern, and then the proper cues pointed out to the child so that he is alerted to the pattern in the future.

Response

If learning is to occur, the pupil must not only need something and notice something; he must also *do* something. Learning to drive a car requires more than a theoretical knowledge of how to steer; the learner must actually practice driving, and many times. Learning to read involves more than the ability to recite the alphabet and to pronounce various letter combinations; the learner must apply these and other skills in actual attempts to read. The child does not develop the ability to think critically by memorizing a list of steps involved in critical thinking; he must repeatedly exercise certain intellectual skills.

If the child is to learn a certain response, he must first identify it correctly. In the early stages of learning, the pupil is often quite unsure of himself. When asked, "How much is 8 plus 8?" he may give the correct answer, but he usually does so tentatively, with a question in his voice. When he sits down at the piano, he has an idea of how the tune he wishes to play should sound, but he strikes some notes with an uncertain touch. The first responses of the learner are trial solutions, attempts to find a response that will relieve tension. At this stage of learning, the teacher must make sure that the pupils know when they have made the correct response so that incorrect responses do not become satisfying.

Then, in order to master the response, the pupil must practice. But he must practice the *correct* response. This means that the teacher must closely supervise the initial steps of learning. When first-grade pupils are learning to write, the teacher must make sure that they are making their strokes in the proper order. When pupils are forming a science concept, the teacher must make sure that they grasp the concept clearly and correctly before they apply it without supervision. Practice can "perfect" incorrect responses as well as correct ones. If pupils are not supervised closely, incorrect responses may become habitual and therefore difficult to change. Any teacher who has tried to change a left-handed writer's habit of writing with his wrist bent in an awkward position knows how difficult the task is. Painstaking attention to children in the initial steps of learning may save a great deal of time in the long run.

It would not be difficult to monitor a student's practice if a teacher were supervising only a handful of children. However, to monitor twenty-five or more pupils so closely that he can immediately call attention to an error is impossible. In recent years schools have taken giant strides toward solving the problem of providing sufficient practice on correct responses. More self-correcting instructional materials programmed for individual use, together with auto-instructional devices ("teaching machines"), are making it possible for teachers to provide for this essential of learning. We return to a discussion of such devices in the next section.

Note that we have been talking here about "doing something" in the limited sense of giving the right answer to a question. "Doing something," the reader will recall, means, in the Piagetian sense, restructuring knowledge as a result of information assimilated. "Doing something" involves making transformations upon data; it means carrying on mental operations that will result in what the learning theorists call a "response." Piaget is concerned with what goes on inside the organism between reception of the stimulus and output of the response. The suggestions above are directed toward handling what the child says or does, rather than what is happening internally.

Reinforcement

Reinforcement is essential to ensure repetition of a particular response. Skinner (1954) in particular has emphasized reinforcement as essential to the learning of correct responses. He has been extremely critical of the way in which schools handle reinforcement, pointing out that after fifty years of supposed reforms, schools still rely more upon aversive control of the learning process than upon positive control. The child is kept working at such tasks as filling in his workbook primarily to avoid a series of minor punishments—the teacher's displeasure, the criticism of his classmates, low marks, a trip to the principal's office.

Skinner has also been concerned with how the contingencies of reinforcement are arranged; that is, with what the reinforcement follows or is contingent upon. He finds that the contingencies provided by the teacher are far from optimal:

> It can easily be demonstrated that, unless explicit mediating behavior has been set up, the lapse of only a few seconds between response and reinforcement destroys most of the effect. In a typical classroom, nevertheless, long periods of time customarily elapse. The teacher may walk up and down the aisle, for example, while the class is working on a sheet of problems, pausing here and there to say right or wrong. Many seconds or minutes intervene between the child's response and the teacher's reinforcement. . . . It is surprising that this system has any effect whatsoever. (p. 91)

Behavior Modification

Skinner's persistent emphasis upon reinforcement has begun to bear fruit in the number of researches being reported using behavior modification. The two psychologists who have made the greatest contribution to the use of reinforcement techniques to changing behavior are Bijou and Baer; their book, *Child Development: A Systematic and Empirical*

Theory, Volume II (1965), presents the principles and techniques that they have found effective. These authors insist that the reinforcement contingency is central to education. Pupils *are* being reinforced for making certain responses, though often without the teacher's awareness that reinforcement has occurred. At the same time, teachers tend to be stingy in doling out positive reinforcers, so the very responses that should be strengthened are not.

What constitutes positive reinforcement? According to Bijou and Baer, overt acts might consist of the teacher's praise, approving glance, smile, a pat, or any other sign of teacher approval. In shaping behavior in experimental situations, the teacher is most generous with such reinforcements when the correct response first appears. After an initial period where each response is immediately reinforced with a raisin or some other food, there follows a period where the child receives a token instead of a raisin, with the tokens to be cashed in for raisins or some other prize at the end of the session. Gradually the period of waiting for his reward is lengthened, so the child learns to postpone immediate gratification. Eventually material rewards taper off and other types of reinforcement, such as praise or attention, are substituted.

In addition to using reinforcement techniques to help children learn subject matter, reinforcement is also used in the classroom to help shape behavior. As Bear (in Hess and Bear, 1968) points out, teachers are already using reinforcement to shape behavior, but using it without any sophistication. Experimental programs have helped to make explicit the principles a teacher might follow. Such programs make extensive use of positive reinforcement, and no physical punishment or cross words are used as negative reinforcers. For example, in a classroom composed of young children with such severe behavior problems that they cannot learn, an initially unmanageable child might be removed from the situation and kept in isolation for a time that is specified in the prearranged schedule. In one such special class, a five-year-old who could not be kept in a regular classroom because of his violent temper tantrums works with a tutor on reading-readiness tasks. After working for five minutes with the tutor, he throws the book at her and lies down on the floor, screaming and banging head and feet. The tutor picks him up without scolding and puts him in an isolation room. When the screaming subsides, she waits a minute by her watch and then opens the door saying, "Shall we continue with the lesson now?" The lesson continues until the end of the period—or another tantrum. With this same boy, the tutor looks for positive behaviors and immediately reinforces them, both with an enthusiastic "Good boy!" and a token. Over a period of time, the boy's behavior is gradually shaped and it becomes possible for him to reenter a regular classroom.

The above is an account of experimental work in shaping behavior. Most teachers cannot (if they would) follow the same procedure. However, application of operant conditioning is being made to the classroom. In particular, the importance of *what* the teacher pays attention to is being emphasized, as well as what she praises (Becker et al., 1967).

Most of the experimental work in shaping behavior has been done with individual children. Application to the regular elementary classroom is now being studied. Some very interesting work by Becker and his associates (1967) is showing the importance of the factor of the teacher's attention and praise. A number of studies (Harris et al., 1964) have pointed out that when the teacher pays attention to the deviant behavior of a pupil, that behavior is likely to appear again. Teachers note the same thing; as one teacher put it, "If I had planned it, I could not have reinforced (his) negative behavior more, for I caught him in every deviant act possible and often before it occurred" (Becker et al., 1967, p. 294).

In the early history of most children, attention from an adult serves to get rid of unpleasant stimuli. When a baby is cold or hungry or uncomfortable for some other reason, the discomfort is removed when an adult attends to him; thus adult attention in almost any form acquires reinforcement value. Becker attempted to use teacher attention and praise *selectively* to manage classroom behavior problems. The general rules teachers were to follow for a nine-week experimental program were as follows:

1. Make explicit rules as to what is expected of children for each period. [Remind children of rules when needed.]
2. Ignore [do not attend to] behaviors which interfere with learning or teaching, unless a child is being hurt by another. Use punishment which seems appropriate, preferably withdrawal of some positive reinforcement.
3. Give praise and attention to behaviors which facilitate learning. Tell child what he is being praised for. Try to reinforce behaviors incompatible with those you wish to decrease.

   Examples of how to praise: "I like the way you're working quietly." "That's the way I like to see you work." "Good job, you are doing fine."

   Transition period: "I see Johnny is ready to work." "I'm calling on you because you raised your hand." "I wish everyone were working as nicely as X," etc. Use variety and expression.

   In general, give praise for achievement, prosocial behavior and following the group rules. (Becker, 1967, p. 292)

In addition, there were special rules devised for certain children directed toward change in observed behaviors. In these special cases, the teachers were given a list of behaviors to praise—using hands for things other than sucking, concentrating on work, paying attention to teacher directions, and so on. Observations were made of the teachers' behavior and pupils' response to that behavior. One teacher was observed to change from 90 percent negative rewards to a child to 90 percent positive. Changes in the children followed as the following account shows:

> Elmer (6 years, 10 months) scored 97 on a group I.Q. test. He apparently started out the school year working well, but his work deteriorated. He seemed "nervous," hyperactive and would not work. He threw several tantrums and would cry if his work was criticized. His twin sister was also in the class and was doing well. By comparison Elmer often lost out. The parents expected as much of Elmer as of his sister. During baseline he was rated as showing inappropriate gross motor behaviors as much as 70% of the time. Talking was as high as 50% at times. Noise and turning in seat were at about 10% each. Initially our observers thought he was brain damaged.
>
> Elmer's rapid response to positive reinforcement and a better structured classroom made it possible for him to stay on task longer. However, he did not improve greatly in his reading group. When the children were silently reading, he would at times clown and make noises. More work on reading will be necessary for academic progress.
>
> Elmer's father came to work as a teacher's aide in one of our other classes just after the shift off baseline. His work with Mrs. C and changes in Elmer led slowly to his accepting the value of a positive rather than a punitive approach. Very likely father's attempt to be more rewarding with Elmer contributed to the maintenance of Elmer's improved classroom behavior. More to the point, however, is the fact that Elmer's improved classroom behavior (we showed father the graph during Week 9) served to reinforce father's acceptance of a positive approach. (Becker et al., 1967, pp. 306–307)

Becker concludes that much can be done by the classroom teacher to eliminate behaviors that interfere with learning. Setting up rules alone is not effective nor is ignoring deviant behavior. But praising a child for an appropriate response, particularly when another child is misbehaving, *is* effective.

Readers will do well to keep in mind the old adage about catching more flies with honey than with vinegar, but with contemporary modifications derived from Skinnerian principles. Behavior *can* be shaped; teachers *can* be effective in the shaping; habits that interfere with learning *can* be weakened; habits that promote learning *can* be strengthened. And to those who contend that modern operant conditioning techniques smack of Aldous Huxley's *Brave New World*, behavioral psychologists in the Skinner tradition point out that teachers are presently using operant techniques, but often to strengthen deviant behavior. Awareness of how operant conditioning works can help a teacher change pupil behavior in a constructive direction. The techniques in and of themselves are neutral; that is, they have no value loading. Depending upon the teacher's values, they could be used to shape pupil behavior in the direction of an over-conforming, uncreative individual, or a free, creative individual who can learn more freely and creatively because behaviors that interfere with learning have been eliminated. Behavior modification is not a substitute for psychotherapy, but it can serve as a useful adjunct.

Educational Technology

Teaching Machines

The 1960s saw increasing use of technology applied to learning prob-lems, and so-called teaching machines proliferated. These machines have two great virtues: they provide for self-teaching and for immediate feedback. The learner knows instantly if he has made a mistake, and so he does not practice the wrong response. They are best used on drill-type materials like arithmetic combinations. To solve the problem of ensuring correct responses, Skinner early advocated automatic teaching devices to provide immediate reinforcement. These devices would be programmed to present materials in a sequence such that each succeeding problem would be contingent upon the answer to the preceding problem. Skin-ner's first device was simple and ingenious: a small box containing a window through which a question printed on a paper tape could be seen. The child moved sliders underneath the window to what he thought was the correct response. He then turned a knob to move the paper tape to the next problem. If his answer was right, the knob turned freely, thus providing immediate feedback; if it was wrong, the knob would not turn.

The teaching machine described above is at least twenty years old. With the help of modern electronics, contemporary machines can do a great deal more than merely inform a child if he has given the correct response. Perhaps the most elaborate (and expensive) of the machines commercially available (in 1970) is the so-called talking typewriter or Edison Responsive Environment. This machine through its voice box can do many things: it can give the user the name and/or the phonetic value of the key that he has struck; it can name a letter and direct the user to strike the appropriate key, the only key that can be activated; it can spell a word, which the user is then asked to type, and only those keys capable of being depressed will print the letters in order. In addition to teaching letter-sound combinations, the machine can also be programmed to monitor the typing of sentences. A visual stimulus is also possible; a screen attached to the keyboard permits pictures of objects with printed words or sentences to be flashed, the child reads what he sees, and the voice box corrects him if he makes an error. Such a responsive device has enormous possibilities for helping the child acquire responses formerly only possible through adult-child interaction. At present the Edison Responsive Environment is used largely in experimental programs where possibilities for its use continue to be researched.

A less elaborate auto-instructional device for teaching reading, language, and arithmetic skills is the Bell and Howell Language Master. This is a two-track recording device that records and plays on short pieces of magnetic tape attached to $3\frac{1}{2}'' \times 9''$ cards. The cards have printed on them letter combinations, words, arithmetic combinations, or whatever responses are to be drilled on. The child feeds these cards into the machine. He presses the recording bar and reads out loud what he sees printed on the card. He then presses the listening bar which activates the instructor's voice. He can also listen to himself and the instructor alternately and compare the two responses.

Deutsch and his colleagues (1967) at the Institute for Developmental Studies report that the Language Master has been received enthusiastically by teachers and children in primary grades. The machine lends itself nicely to teacher-constructed materials, so that individual drill on skills and abilities can be quickly and easily provided. Children spend prolonged periods on the machine, concentrating closely on the task at hand.

The tape recorder is also finding its way into classrooms as an auto-instructional device. Stories can be taped, then played, and a child can follow along in a book the printed version of what he hears. An automatic slide projector can be synchronized with the tape; while the directions recorded on the tape tell the child what to do, a visual display provides him with a model.

Preschools and primary grades in particular are making increasing use of teaching machines. In fact, it is not uncommon to see in a classroom a row of individual carrels, or booths, similar to the open telephone booths one sees in air terminals. A child can sit in one of the booths, don large well-padded earphones that block out classroom sounds, and proceed to teach himself a lesson in phonics, spelling, classification, or addition. He can move at his own speed, repeating drills as he sees fit, consistently receiving feedback on correctness of responses and working without fear of a scolding for errors he may make. Teaching machines intelligently programmed and used can help children learn certain responses efficiently, thus freeing the teacher for those teaching activities that only a human teacher can do. They can be especially effective in open, informal classrooms.

In a category separate from teaching machines is an application of technology still in the research stage—that of computer-assisted instruction. Computers can be used to provide drill on certain reading or arithmetic skills in a highly individualized fashion. They can also be used to help the child acquire knowledge in a more creative way. Since their use in the elementary school is presently confined to arithmetic, we leave this subject for further discussion in Chapter 11.

Programmed Teaching Materials

In addition to teaching machines, modern classrooms are making increasing use of auto-instructional, programmed teaching materials. Programs in reading and arithmetic in particular have been designed for self-teaching. The IPI (Individual Prescribed Instruction), a program developed at the University of Pittsburgh, is one example. Such programs are based upon a step-by-step analysis of the responses needed to

Learning arithmetic by computer. The children are doing arithmetic lessons. The PLATO (Programmed Logic for Automatic Teaching Operation) arithmetic program during the past year was developed in three major directions: drill, concept development, and strategy games. Standard drill exercises were kept to a minimum, and major emphasis was on a games approach. Courtesy of Computer-Based Education Research Laboratory, University of Illinois at Champaign-Urbana.

build certain skills; these are the "behavioral objectives." A student moves along in the program to each succeeding step at his own speed, completing individual worksheets. He may use a check sheet for self-correcting, or the teacher may correct his work. Such materials are useful in that they enable pupils to work with a minimum of supervision, again freeing the teacher for other phases of instruction. Like all other learning aids such materials can be badly misused. There is hardly a more depressing educational sight than a classroom where children spend 50 percent of the school day working mindlessly like ants, routinely filling in blanks on individual worksheets.

Individual Learning Styles

That learning is affected by personality factors has long been known in a general way, but we are now beginning to have the relationships defined more precisely. We are beginning to see that there are certain "nonintellective" characteristics involved in the successful application of intelligence to problem solution. The terms *learning styles, cognitive styles,* or *conceptual styles* are used, quite often interchangeably, to refer to these nonintellective characteristics. It appears that children develop "preferred ways of organizing and interpreting stimuli, and some of these conceptual preferences are consistent over a wide variety of situations" (Kagan & Moss, 1962, p. 281). All the dimensions of these styles have yet to be identified, but terms such as *compulsivity, impulsivity,* and *reflectivity* have been found to characterize some approaches to learning. For example, an impulsive child may be a classroom wriggler who finds it hard to listen carefully to teacher directions and to reflect before he does an assignment. In a testing situation, when asked to respond to a task, Draw-a-Line, and then to Draw-a-Line Slowly, he may draw both lines at about the same speed. Classroom learning, test performances, and social adaptation all point to acting upon impulse.

Hayweiser et al. (1967) describe the impulsive child in this fashion:

> In descriptive terms, the impulsive child seems to respond to stimulus situations at a too rapid rate in order to process the information presented. Components of the stimuli may be missed altogether or responses may be made only to the most dominant or familiar features of the stimuli. There is the additional possibility that the child does not even consider the stimulus characteristics of the problem but responds on some totally irrelevant basis unique to the child. Impulsive children, whether the antecedents are biological, environmental, or a combination of both, find complex tasks, which require processing time, more difficult.

Impulsivity and intelligence-test performance appear to be related. Underachievers with superior intelligence were found to be more impulsive on impulsivity tests than successful students who were equally bright (Levine & Spivack, 1963). Most of the studies of the relationship between impulsivity and intelligence have used adolescents as subjects. While being able to delay a response may not become fully functional until adolescence, individual differences in impulse control appear in early childhood and appear to persist into adulthood.

Conversely, it may be that dramatic changes in I.Q. reflect changes in some aspects of the child's personality, and particularly in motivation (Zigler, 1966). Perhaps children may be more motivated to emit responses, and hence to do well on the tests, if they know that they are expected to perform, and if they have had enough positive encounters with adults to want to please those adults.

How do we make impulsive children more reflective? Investigators are seeking to find out. In one study some first-grade girls (but not boys) showed longer response tendencies in training sessions with a tutor who first persuaded the children that he and the subjects had interests and certain characteristics in common. It may be that perceived similarity between teacher and child by the child is one factor in making girls stay longer with a task.

Wetzel (1969) is finding that reinforcement of responses by the use of material rewards will also accomplish the same end. The use of M & M's and other material rewards will keep the impulsive child, *in the field,* working for a longer period of time on a task than when no rewards are used. Perhaps the only conclusion to be drawn at this point is to say that a teacher whom the child perceives as sympathetic and empathetic with him and who also uses material rewards liberally stands a good chance of helping an impulsive child become a more reflective learner.

Discovery Methods as an Aid to Learning

Discovery methods of teaching are based upon the premise that children learn to solve problems and acquire concepts on the basis of inductive reasoning from empirical data. Instead of *telling* the child that air exerts pressure, for example, the child may engage in some activities from which he can *discover* that air does indeed exert pressure. Instead of having pupils read what the prerequisites are for the location of large cities, pupils can discover through map study and other activities certain features common to the location of metropolitan areas.

Discovery methods of teaching have engendered tremendous enthu-

siasm among devoted followers who advocate their use in teaching all
school subjects, but particularly in concept-oriented subjects like mathematics, science, social studies, and grammar. Their use has been argued
on the basis of effectiveness; pupils retain more of what is to be learned
if they participate actively in discovering the knowledge. Furthermore,
the actual process of discovery forces pupils to use logical operations and
thus has the effect of making children better thinkers.

Some writers, however, think that the claims for discovery methods
have been exaggerated, and that the methods have only a limited use in
classrooms. Ausubel (1964) criticizes them as much too time-consuming
and inefficient. He points out that, particularly at the high school and
college level, students could not progress much beyond the rudiments of
any discipline if they had to discover for themselves every principle or
even the major principles in the subject. Furthermore, he maintains that
problem solving via discovery can be just as deadening, formalistic, and
mechanical as the worst form of verbal exposition. Those who have
observed classroom procedures and have seen the misuse of discovery
methods, in situations where a principle or concept could be more effectively explained to children or where the concept to be discovered was
trivial or where the teacher's lack of skill in questioning only muddied
the waters, could not agree more.

On the other hand learning by discovery can enhance learning, retention, and transferability, particularly when self-activity is emphasized.
Bruner's (1964, 1966, 1967) discussion of the importance of self-activity
sheds additional light on the problem. He sees the child, as he carries on
an activity or experiment, building inside himself a mental image of the
process. Bruner reports on an experiment in which he attempted to teach
children quadratic functions in such a way that children would be able
to use their knowledge in the solution of problems. In the first task
children were to lay out cubic blocks in different ways and to see how
many ways would be possible for a given number of blocks. From their
activity, the children grasped the notion of factoring—that three rows of
three cubes made nine, that three such layers had the dimensions of
$3 \times 3 \times 3$. Later a balance beam was introduced, the task being to discover the different combinations of rings that could be put on one side of
the balance beam to balance a single ring placed on the opposite side.

Additional activities with building materials were also carried on, in
which the child marked off squares on a large flat square with strips of
wood and little squares. He was asked in each case to record how long
and how wide the square was. His first descriptions are very concrete:
"an X-square, (X, the child is told, is an unknown), two X-strips, and a
one square." He can check each written description by going back to his
construction. As Bruner puts it (p. 326), "The syntactical insights . . . are

matched by perceptual-manipulated insights about the material referents." Here it is not the discovery method per se that is at work, but the
use of concrete materials as well (Bruner, 1966).

Obviously, the child should not continue to lean on visible, manipulable materials; even in discovery methods, he must be able to deal with
abstractions or symbols. Given direct, physical experience, he will assimilate enough data to build a mental representation of the essence of those
experiences. A variety of ways of dealing with the concept would seem to
be called for. For example, only one experience with twirling an object
on the end of a string may not free the child from the restricting influence of a single sensorimotor act, but a number of activities in which the
child "feels" the outward pull of a projectile will enable him to develop a
preferred way of thinking about projectile problems. He will not rely
upon one image based upon one act, but will have built an image that
has abstracted the properties of many acts, an image essential to his
discovery of the principles of projective motion.

The Danger of Overreliance upon Linguistic Transmission

Piaget has written of the dangers of premature verbalization. Children can be taught to parrot responses, they can learn a formal explanation of the workings of a pendulum or memorize a formula for lever
problems, but without concrete referents they will encounter problems of
transfer when asked to perform tasks in a slightly altered form. For
Piaget (1964) logic is not a derivative of language; it is "an experience of
the actions of the subject, and not an experience of objects themselves. It
is an experience which is necessary before there can be operations. Once
the operations have been attained this experience is no longer needed
and the coordination of actions can take place by themselves in the form
of deduction and construction of abstract structures." Piaget does not
deny the importance of linguistic transmission, but he maintains that the
child can receive valuable information via language only if he is in a
state to understand the information. In elementary school subjects, direct
physical experience either through demonstration or experimentation is
essential to readiness for many concepts in the curriculum.

Discovery and Exposition

Atkin and Karplus (1962) differentiate two different types of lessons
in teaching science. In one type, an *invention* lesson, a new concept is
presented both verbally and by demonstration. The new concept (melt-

ing point, for example) is called a *conceptual invention* because it was once invented by a scientist. It is not expected that children will also invent the concept; obviously, reinvention by definition of "invention" is impossible. The concept is explained and then followed by laboratory experiences to build concrete referents for the term.

For example, in a lesson involving *invention of thermal equilibrium*, the teacher might begin with questions about measuring the temperature of a cup of hot water. The teacher might ask, "How can you tell when the thermometer and the hot water come to the same temperature? When we put the thermometer into the water, the temperature of the thermometer changes rapidly at first, but gradually it stops changing. At that point, we say that the thermometer and the warm water have come to the same temperature and are in *thermal equilibrium* with each other." Thus the teacher explains and names the concept.

Discovery in art. By offering children the freedom and the means to make their own experiments, allowing them to spill, pour, smear paint, and to rub or scrape to their hearts' content, they come to discover for themselves the meaning and the processes behind the formation of shapes and relations between them. Both these methods of education depend on the free play of the child's imagination, on his own or in a group. From Réalités, *March 1971, p. 20. Photo J. Ph. Charbonnier—Réalités.*

Discovery lessons follow the verbal presentation of thermal equilibrium. The children carry out a number of experiments in which a thermometer interacts with various media, and they plot the change in temperature over a period of time. They come to see how the thermometer gradually enters into equilibrium with a medium and how the rate of change slows down and almost stops when equilibrium is reached. They discover applications of the scientist's invention of thermal equilibrium.

As Karplus and Thier (1967) point out, children form stable concepts only when they have a verbal label to focus on the concept. Atkin and Karplus (1962) call lessons in which children are given a verbal label, *invention* lessons, and the laboratory lessons, *discovery* lessons. However, the terms may be a bit unfortunate, since many teachers associate *discovery* not with the application of a concept but with its initial formation, and think of *invention* as synonymous with discovery.

In this text we will reserve the term *discovery* for those lessons where children are to abstract the concept from a variety of experiences, and *exposition* for those lessons where the teacher explains a concept by verbal transmission. The lesson described above, where children discover *for themselves* the meaning of thermal equilibrium, is a *discovery* lesson; the initial lesson in this example, where the teacher presents the concept, is *exposition. Both* types of teaching are important, and as we examine more specifically how children acquire knowledge in different subjects, we will try to present good examples of each method.

We have covered a number of different facets in this chapter—the components of learning, operant conditioning, learning styles, and discovery methods—all tied together by the common thread of the learner and the teaching-learning process. We hope that we have helped the reader to see the enormous complexity of the process. In interacting with the child, the teacher must make a decision, often on the spot, as to how to respond to a child or deal with his behavior. "Is this the kind of behavior that I want to see strengthened, and if so, what type of positive reinforcement can I use? Does this child's response tell me that he has missed an important cue, and how can I best make it clear to him? How can I handle this particular behavior so as to make the child stay longer with the task? What kind of feedback can I supply to show the child he's on the right track?" With lightninglike speed, the brain must process information and arrive at an answer. It is the teacher's responsibility to see that the brain is programmed with up-to-date knowledge about learning and about the individual learner so that the answer will be the best possible one for the child.

Summary

Behavioral psychologists have identified components of learning—drive, cue, response, reinforcement—which are helpful for teachers to keep in mind in guiding the learning process. The *drive* or motivation to learn is strengthened in various ways—by the rewarding of a response by associating it with an already present drive, and by involving the student in goal setting. It is also strengthened in a circular reaction where intellectual stimulation leads to a desire for more intellectual stimulation. Motivation to succeed in school tasks is weak in lower socioeconomic groups, a factor that contributes to lower I.Q. scores.

It is important in learning that the child notice the right *cues*. Teachers should stress these cues by means of auditory and visual stimuli.

With respect to *response*, emphasis should be placed on practicing the correct response, rather than the incorrect, which can be effected by the use of auto-instructional devices, including teaching machines and programmed teaching materials.

Skinnerians place considerable emphasis upon *reinforcement*, and point out that teachers are too sparing in their use of rewards. Considerable research shows that operant conditioning is effective in changing certain kinds of behavior.

Investigators note that the use of certain teaching techniques will help in making impulsive children more reflective and thus more efficient learners.

Discovery methods, particularly when they involve discovery of a principle through manipulation of materials, appear to be effective. Teachers must beware of overreliance upon the verbal; merely giving an explanation to students is not necessarily effective. Atkin and Karplus propose that the teacher explain a particular principle that man has invented, and then give children an opportunity to discover applications of the principle.

READING LIST 3

Anderson, R. C., & Ausubel, D. P. *Readings in the psychology of cognition.* New York: Holt, Rinehart and Winston, 1965. A collection of papers on a variety of topics by psychologists primarily interested in cognition. Papers by Ausubel, Bruner, and Guilford are especially relevant to the content of this chapter.

Becker, W., Thomas, D., & Carnine, D. *Reducing behavior problems. An operant conditioning guide for teachers.* Urbana, Ill.: ERIC, Early Childhood Education, 1969. A very useful document for the teacher who wishes to use operant conditioning techniques in the classroom.

Bruner, J. S. *Toward a theory of instruction.* Cambridge, Mass.: Harvard University Press, 1966. A collection of essays in which the author examines the ways in which teaching can be adapted to the course of mental growth.

Bruner, J. S., Olver, R. R., Greenfield, P. M., et al. *Studies in cognitive growth.* New York: John Wiley & Sons, 1966. A report and discussion of a series of experiments on the maturing of various cognitive operations in children.

Gagné, R. *The conditions of learning.* New York: Holt, Rinehart and Winston, 1965. Gagné considers here the circumstances under which learning takes place. He describes eight types of learning: signal learning, stimulus-response learning, chaining, verbal association, multiple-discrimination learning, concept learning, principle learning, problem solving. He presents an excellent discussion of the application of principles of learning to the management of instruction.

National Society for the Study of Education. *Theories of learning and instruction.* Sixty-third Yearbook. Chicago: University of Chicago Press, 1964. Chapter 1 by F. J. McDonald ("The Influence of Learning Theories on Education, 1900–1950") and Chapter 13 by J. S. Bruner ("Some Theorems on Instruction Illustrated with Reference to Mathematics") are particularly relevant to the discussion in this chapter.

Ripple, R. E., & Rockcastle, V. N. (Eds.) *Piaget rediscovered.* Ithaca, N.Y.: School of Education, Cornell University, 1964. Papers delivered by Piaget in person at a conference on cognitive studies, together with reports on American cognitive studies and application to curriculum.

Smith, B. O. *A study in the logic of teaching.* Urbana: University of Illinois Press, 1970. A provocative thinker analyzes protocols of teacher-student interaction in a clear, insightful way.

Professional Journals To Become Acquainted With

Review of Educational Research. American Educational Research Association, 1201 Sixteenth St., N.W., Washington, D.C. 20036.

Exemplars of Curriculum Theory

The Need for Curriculum Theory

Etymologically, the term *curriculum* is derived from Latin roots meaning a chariot course—a kind of route over which the learner travels. Metaphorically speaking, the conception of the curriculum as a route is still a rather satisfying one: a seasoned traveler, the teacher, guides inexperienced travelers over a path he is familiar with, pointing out the major features of the landscape as they go. In more concrete terms, however, the school curriculum comprises a selection of certain resources of a culture organized for the purpose of teaching.

Any society develops mechanisms, formal and informal, conscious and unconscious, by which its culture is transmitted to future generations. In some societies, special institutions designed to accomplish some part of the task of socialization are developed. As Stephens (1967) has argued, the task of the school is often not related to those cultural elements that have the highest survival value for the individual. High survival functions tend to be performed by the family. Rather than dealing with the immediate and pressing tasks of survival, according to Stephens, the typical school curriculum embodies those resources of a culture which are relatively playful rather than serious—in which the members of the society evidence a "general permissive, supportive interest" rather than a "daily, urgent, and continuing concern" (p. 7). As such, the school curriculum in our society characteristically comprises such playful intellectual resources as mathematics, science, and literature. Paradoxically, these playful intellectual resources may, in the long run, assume great social importance, but their significance for the individual in terms of his daily survival is limited. Even within these broad guidelines, however, decisions must be made as to which of the resources of a culture ought to constitute the content of the curriculum and what form they shall take.

As such, it would be impossible for us to conceive of a school in the sense that we know it without a curriculum of some kind, even in cases where the curriculum is not explicitly set down. One must always teach some*thing* to some*one*; one cannot just teach in general, and, consequently, every teacher is in some measure a curriculum planner. Moreover, in a very important sense, the decisions that a teacher makes are the most important of all curriculum decisions since it is the teacher whose decisions regarding the selection and organization of subject matter most closely affect what actually goes on in the classroom. One study has shown that even when teachers are directed to teach the same thing, they tend to vary widely in how they actually organize and present subject matter (Bellack et al., 1966).

While curriculum decisions are inevitable in the practice of teaching, they are not always taken with due consideration of the various alternatives and the possible consequences. The field of curriculum is devoted to the study and examination of the decisions that go into the selection and organization of what is taught. Implied in such a study is the notion that a curriculum may be planned with basic principles in mind. These principles, when they are reasonably consistent and coherent, constitute the essence of curriculum theory. Curriculum theory, in other words, attempts to consider in a *systematic* way the question of how the curriculum should be developed with due regard for the salient factors that impinge on that question. This means that the field of curriculum is concerned to some extent with such factors as the role and function of the school as a social institution, the nature of the school population, and the process of teaching itself. What follows are a few exemplars illustrating attempts to treat principal problems of curriculum development from the perspective of some kind of central theoretical position.

The Early Development of Curriculum Thought in the United States

The Theory of Mental Discipline

The first coherent way of viewing curriculum decisions to become popular in this country is frequently represented by the term *mental discipline*. Although much maligned and caricatured in curriculum textbooks today, mental discipline was a vigorous and widespread curriculum theory throughout most of the nineteenth century whose influence on modern educational thought is frequently unrecognized, or at least unacknowledged. Advocates of the theory of mental discipline saw the primary role of the schools as one of developing mental functioning or habits of thought. The purpose of schooling, in other words, was to *discipline* the mind and thereby improve it. As one major document early in the mental discipline era put it, "The two great points to be gained in intellectual culture are the *discipline* and the *furniture* of the mind; expanding its powers and storing it with knowledge" ("Original Papers in Relation to a Cause of Liberal Education," 1829). The former of these two functions, however, was the most important, and subjects would be selected mainly with a view toward improving mental functioning (discipline) rather than acquiring factual knowledge and skills (furniture).

Disciplining the Faculties of the Mind. Much of the educational literature of the mental discipline period was devoted to an explication of the various functions of the mind, often referred to as *faculties*. These were usually represented in such terms as perception, observation, imagination, memory, and reasoning although there was no absolute agreement as to what these mental powers were. In addition, much attention was given to making the case for various subjects such as mathematics and Latin as the most efficacious means of developing those processes. Such subjects were regarded as having disciplinary value (in the sense of disciplining the mind) rather than being merely informational.

Mental discipline as a curriculum theory is closely tied to a popular psychological theory of the time, *faculty psychology*. Although these two theories have common elements and are certainly compatible with each other, one may be regarded as a way of making decisions about what to teach and how to organize it, and the other as a conception of mind and how it functions. Like the mental disciplinarians, faculty psychologists were concerned with powers of the mind, which they called faculties; but it is quite possible to see the primary role of the school as developing desirable habits of thought, such as keen observation and critical thinking, without also adhering to the doctrine of faculty psychology per se. Historically, it is likely that one of the contributing factors in the demise of mental discipline was its close association with the discredited theory of faculty psychology. Another factor may have been that some popularizers of mental discipline interpreted such terms as *exercising the faculties* or *exercising the mind* in a literal sense and actually put forth the notion of mental discipline as a form of exercise whereby the mind would be strengthened in the same way that a muscle would be strengthened by exercise, a rather vulnerable interpretation of the theory. It is doubtful that the principal exponents of mental discipline literally thought of the mind as a muscle to be strengthened by virtually any sort of vigorous mental activity, but this is the popular image we have today of that theory.

Mental discipline is now associated with such classroom practices as monotonous drill and the memorization of Latin declensions even though some of the chief spokesmen for the theory specifically argued against such routine activities. At the end of the nineteenth century, for example, President Charles W. Eliot of Harvard University argued in favor of interest as a critical factor in developing the powers of the mind and supported an elective system in the Harvard College curriculum. By permitting students to choose what subjects they were to study, desirable habits of thought would be encouraged to a greater extent than if the curriculum were rigidly prescribed. In extending this theory, Eliot was to recommend a form of the elective system for students as young as ten or eleven. His principal criterion apart from interest was that the subject be suitable for sustained study.

The Decline of Mental Discipline as a Curriculum Theory. When such eminent psychologists as William James and Edward L. Thorndike conducted experiments designed to test the validity of faculty psychology and found it deficient, mental discipline was challenged and lost favor in the educational world. James's experiments, for example, led him to conclude that the faculty of memory was not improved when one practiced "exercising" one's memory (James, 1892, pp. 287–301). Thorndike carried these conclusions a step further not only by challenging the notion of faculties or broad mental powers but trying to determine whether the study of such subjects as Latin or mathematics had any more "disciplinary" value than other subjects. Thorndike (1924) concluded that no subject could be said to improve the mind more than any other subject in any significant way.

Perhaps more than anything else, the decline in mental discipline as a curriculum theory may be attributed to a changing social and intellectual climate. The mental disciplinarian saw the school essentially as a place where intellectual activity and intellectual development were paramount. Practical subjects, the mere acquiring of information or preparation for a career, simply represented a lower order of activity. The school existed in large measure to keep alive a certain intellectual tradition, one where the life of the mind was central. Over and against such a conception, the school in this country was becoming a place where one prepared to fulfill a certain role in life. Influential social theorists saw the schools as a vehicle of social control and social betterment, where, for example, crime would be reduced and good citizenship promoted. School was conceived of as the place where one learned to perform the myriad explicit functions that society expected of one. After a period of ferment around the turn of the century, this became the dominant conception of schooling, and the curriculum became the means by which social functions were defined and learned.

Social Efficiency and Scientific Curriculum Making

Under the influence of the doctrine of social efficiency, the dominant conception of curriculum shifted radically. Instead of the means by which one developed desirable habits of thought in the intellectual sense, the curriculum became a kind of repository of socially desirable abilities and behaviors along with the means by which one acquired them. Since curriculum emerged as an identifiable field of specialization during the period when social efficiency was particularly vigorous and popular, much of our curriculum thinking today and our approach to curriculum problems is strongly influenced by that doctrine although, perhaps, unconsciously so. The 1920s in particular was a period when curriculum literature was full of attempts to set forth in great detail and with great precision exactly what would be expected of people in their adult lives. These expectations became the objectives of the curriculum.

Probably the most influential figure of this period in curriculum, and the man who set the tone for much of our curriculum thinking today, was Franklin Bobbitt. In the first book ever written on the curriculum, Bobbitt set forth his basic conception:

> The central theory is simple. Human life, however varied, consists in the performance of specific activities. Education that prepares for life is one that prepares definitely and adequately for these specific activities. However numerous and diverse they may be for any social class, they can be discovered. This requires only that one go out into the world of affairs and discover the particulars of which these affairs consist. These will show the abilities, attitudes, habits, appreciations, and forms of knowledge that men need. These will be the objectives of the curriculum. They will be numerous, definite, and particularized. The curriculum will then be that series of experiences which children and youth must have by way of attaining those objectives. (Bobbitt, 1918, p. 42)

Activity Analysis. The procedure by which one set about "discovering" the objectives of the curriculum came to be known as *activity analysis*. Activity analysis was advertised as a scientific way of determining curriculum objectives, thereby, presumably, cutting through the maze of vague philosophical argument and counterargument about the purposes of schooling. It consisted essentially of going "out into the world of affairs" and noting in minute detail what actual activities were being performed by adults in a given community. The ability to perform these activities efficiently became the objective. Bobbitt's influential curriculum study in Los Angeles was perhaps the major instance of such an analysis although the actual objectives seemed to reflect the judgment of the teachers involved rather than direct observation (Bobbitt, 1922). Hundreds of curricular objectives were set forth in ten major categories: Social Intercommunication, Physical Efficiency, Unspecialized Practical Labors, Occupational Objectives, Efficient Citizenship, General Social Contacts and Relationships, Leisure Occupations, General Mental Efficiency, Religious Attitudes and Activities, and Parental Responsibilities.

While mental discipline as a curriculum theory focused on mental and intellectual development, social efficiency encompassed the full range of life's activities as its domain. Bobbitt's ten categories, in other words, comprised a kind of classification system under which all of life's activities could be subsumed. The objectives included under Bobbitt's categories included such wide-ranging activities and abilities as Ability to converse easily, agreeably, and effectively; Physical strength and endurance sufficient for all of one's necessary or desirable activities, within limits of normality fixed in heredity; Ability to control sex functions in the interests of physical and social well-being; The making of lawn swings and simple porch furniture; and Ability to substitute intelligence for physical force as the method of adjusting social differences. The curriculum consisted essentially of objectives such as these along with the means by which they could be efficiently achieved.

The Appeal of Social Efficiency Theory. The appeal of such a conception of curriculum was obvious. It promised a scientific way of developing a school program that dealt in a directly functional way with the actual lives of future citizens. It was supremely utilitarian in nature and provided a mechanism by which dry rot in the curriculum—Latin, higher mathematics, history—could be eliminated or minimized since these subjects could not easily demonstrate a functional relationship to man's actual activities. It directly performed the social function of producing an adult population equipped with all the socially acceptable skills, beliefs, and attitudes. It prepared youth to fit neatly into the proper slot in the social order.

It is primarily with respect to this last feature of the social efficiency doctrine that much attention was given to curriculum differentiation. If the curriculum was the means by which one prepared for a future social role, it became important to predict what that social role would be and to differentiate the curriculum along the lines of probable destination. Hence elementary school teachers were continually exhorted to predict a child's probable line of development and future career. It would be important to know, for example, whether a child was likely to become a plumber, a lawyer, or a steeplejack if the curriculum was to be properly designed. This was in sharp contrast to the basic notions of mental discipline. In the famous Report of the Committee of Ten published in 1894 (National Education Association, 1894), for example, Charles W. Eliot and his colleagues proposed four "programmes" or courses of study, but these were not differentiated along lines of probable destination. Each of the four curricula was considered to be suitable either for college or for "life." The conventional labels for modern curricula such as college preparatory, noncollege preparatory, vocational, commercial, and so forth basically reflect the social efficiency orientation toward prediction and differentiation rather than the mental disciplinarian orientation toward the improvement of mental powers irrespective of destination or future social role.

Provision for Individual Differences in the Social Efficiency Curriculum. In addition, the social efficiency doctrine embodied a basic change in how one viewed the phenomenon of individual differences in the school population. While the mental disciplinarians recognized the obvious differences in ability among school children, they did not interpret those differences as dictating radically different programs of study. Under the new "scientific" curriculum, measured differences in ability as well as other differences such as social class became determining factors in the kind of curriculum one followed. One of the major figures in the social efficiency movement, David Snedden (1923), for example, proposed that children be placed in "case groups" based on the child's unique biographical data with differentiated curricula expressly designed for such groups. Most spokesmen of the period, however, settled for labeling children as belonging in one or another category of the school population. A leading sociologist of education of the period, Ross Finney, divided the school population into future followers and future leaders, the former to be taught by drill to follow the appropriate catchwords and slogans, and the latter also to be taught the *why* of those slogans. Finney chided Dewey for spreading the foolish notion that all children should be taught to think, arguing the "I.Q.'s below .99+ are not likely to secrete cogitations of any great social fruitfulness" (Finney, 1929, p. 388).

The Value of School Subjects. Perhaps the most important difference between mental discipline and the scientific curriculum making of the social efficiency period was one with respect to the value of school subjects. Mental disciplinarians saw school subjects as having the power to discipline the mind, that is, to make one think better. Advocates of social efficiency emphasized the content of the subjects rather than their disciplinary value. Subjects were primarily bodies of useful knowledge and skills to be imparted to the young and immature in the society. Content was selected not primarily with reference to developing intellectual habits of thought, but because it represented what was good to know. Concomitants of this basic conception were the distinctively "scientific" means by which the curriculum would be determined (activity analysis), and curriculum differentiation as the means by which students were routed along different paths to socially useful adulthood.

Culture Epochs and the Progressive Organization of Subject Matter

The decline of mental discipline as a curriculum theory coincided with the rise of other conceptions of the curriculum, although they were not destined to have quite the lasting impact of social efficiency's scientific emphasis. One of the most intriguing and popular conceptions of curriculum theory was developed just before the turn of this century by the American followers of the German philosopher Johann Friedrich Herbart. Some of the Herbartians, as they were called, had actually studied with Herbart's major disciples in Germany, Stoy and Rein at Jena and Ziller at the University of Leipzig. Herbart himself died in 1841, but his philosophy strongly influenced the course of American curriculum thought in the late nineteenth and early twentieth centuries through the work of Charles and Frank McMurry, C. C. Van Liew, Charles De Garmo, and other articulate and energetic interpreters.

The Contribution of J. F. Herbart. Herbart's conception of the mind was quite different from that of the faculty psychologists. Rather than considering that it consisted of innate faculties, Herbart conceived of the mind (soul) as "a tabula rasa without any form of life or presentation: consequently, there are in it neither primitive ideas, nor any predispositions to form them. All ideas, without exception, are a product of time and experience" (Herbart, 1932, p. 360). Rather than intellectual virtues, Herbart stressed moral character itself as the great goal of education, and he hoped to achieve that goal in part through the application of two major concepts: *interest* and *apperception.* Through developing many-sided interests, Herbart sought to provide direction to learning that was "morally good and true." He also thought of a mind as an *apperceptive mass* consisting of knowledge and experience already gained. Learning occurred when new ideas found some unity with the apperceptive mass and were assimilated into it. In curriculum terms, this would mean that new content must be deliberately organized so as to be related to what the child already knew.

One of the most appealing aspects of Herbart's theories for American educators, particularly the pioneer child psychologist G. Stanley Hall, was the attempt to take into account child study as a major element in curriculum development. One of the major deficiencies of the older education, they felt, was its failure to incorporate scientific knowledge about child growth and development into school programs. In Herbartian theory, a child's stage of development would dictate, at least to some extent, the kind of curriculum that would be designed. The notion of the concentration of subjects around a single unifying theme, largely developed by Ziller, was an effort to unify external knowledge as reflected in the curriculum in the child's mind.

The most conspicuous manifestation of the effort to concentrate school studies around a unifying theme was the culture epochs curriculum. As a curriculum theory, culture epochs was based on the assumption that a child's individual development recapitulates the stages in the development of mankind. The process of curriculum development, then, became essentially a process of matching a given stage in the development of an individual child with a stage in the development of Western man. One version of such a scheme appeared in the Second Yearbook of the National Herbart Society (Seeley, 1896, p. 73):

Age of the Individual, Relatively Indicated	Psychical Epochs in the Individual	Epoch in Race Development
From infancy to about the eighth year	The intuitive epoch, sense-perception, as the beginning of intellectual culture	The mythical and heroic epoch
From the sixth to the tenth year	The imaginative epoch, development of imagination and memory	The intermediate epoch
After the tenth year	The logical epoch, thinking and reasoning, receiving prominence	The epoch of freedom, self-government, and recognition of the individual

In one Detroit school in 1896, the culture epochs theory was translated into the study of Longfellow's "Song of Hiawatha" as the unifying theme of the first grade; Hiawatha was representative of the heroic epoch. When a rabbit begged Hiawatha not to shoot him with his newly fashioned bow and arrow, rabbits then became the center around which the day's activities were concentrated (Buck, 1896, pp. 376–384). Robinson Crusoe was also a favorite theme around the second grade, being generally regarded as representative of the historical epoch when man was beginning to gain control of his natural environment. Although quaint at best to the modern educator, the Herbartian theory of culture epochs was a daring and imaginative attempt to combine in one conception the nature of the child and his interests, on one hand, with the external subjects of study on the other.

Dewey's Conception of Curriculum. Such a systematic way of viewing the curriculum was undoubtedly among the most appealing aspects of Herbartian theory to one of the prominent members of the National Herbart Society, John Dewey. Although Dewey was known primarily as a critic of some key elements in Herbartian doctrine, the influence of the

Herbartians on Dewey's thinking in education is apparent, particularly in his curriculum theory. One of the first expressions of Dewey's curriculum theory, which appeared in 1897, is also an attempt to synthesize the subjects of study with the life of the child, but in a manner different from the Herbartians. Dewey saw no inherent conflict between these basic elements and attempted to illustrate the potential for unity through the teaching of geography to a young child:

> The primary point of concern in education is beyond question with the subject as a special mode of personal experience, rather than with the subject as a body of wrought-out facts and scientifically tested principles. To the child, simply because he is a child, geography is not, and cannot be, what it is to the one who writes a scientific treatise on geography. The latter has had exactly the experience which it is the problem of instruction to induce on the part of the former. To identify geography as it is to the pupil of seven or fifteen with geography as it is to Humboldt or Ritter is a flagrant case of putting the cart before the horse. With the child, instruction must take the standpoint not of the accomplished results, but of the crude beginnings. We must discover what there is lying within the child's present sphere of experience (or within the scope of experiences which he can easily get) which deserves to be called geographical. It is not the question of *how* to teach the child geography, but first of all the question of *what geography is for the child*. (Dewey, 1897, p. 361)

It is clear that Dewey is not ruling out geography, nor any other subject of study, as appropriate for the curriculum in favor of some loosely defined play activity. The latter is probably the image that Dewey's educational ideas have in the popular mind. Instead, Dewey is looking within the child's present experience for those elements of geography that will eventuate in the highly organized and abstract geography of a Humboldt or a Ritter. According to Dewey, although this highly organized form of geography is perfectly appropriate as an end point, it is inappropriate as a beginning.

This conception of curriculum is even more clearly developed in Dewey's most famous essay on curriculum, "The Child and the Curriculum," which he published in 1902. The essence of his curriculum theory can be represented as a continuum defined by the child's present experience on one end and the experience of the human race (organized knowledge) on the other: "Just as two points define a straight line, so the present standpoint of the child and the facts and truths of studies define instruction. It is continuous reconstruction, moving from the child's present experience out into that represented by the organized bodies of truths that we call studies (Archambault, 1964, p. 344). Dewey insisted that there was no difference of kind, only of degree, between the present experience of the child, his seemingly random and impulsive behavior, and the experience of mankind, the systematic, highly organized disciplines of knowledge. He was, in other words, denying any fundamental opposition between the psychological and the logical. As Dewey put it, they are "the initial and final terms of one reality" (Archambault, 1964, p. 345). The teacher had to know both the nature of the child and the nature of subject matter, and, armed with such knowledge, she was given the critical task of perceiving what in the child's present experience gave the most promise of moving in the direction of the systematized experience of the human race, the "organized bodies of truth."

During his lifetime, Dewey made one major attempt to translate his theory of curriculum and other educational ideas into practice. This was the Laboratory School at the University of Chicago, which he founded, together with his wife, in 1896 and which lasted until 1903. From the accounts available to us, the Dewey school, as it is commonly known, was one of the most exciting and daring educational experiments ever undertaken. Even among schools today, it is rare if not impossible to find school practice actually arising out of a carefully articulated educational philosophy. Educational experiments today usually involve merely testing the efficiency of a narrow hypothesis.

The problem of education, as Dewey saw it, was "the harmonizing of individual traits with social ends and values," (Mayhew & Edwards, 1965, p. 465). The question was, in essence, how education could contribute to the maximum development of the individual and still be consistent with social values and purposes. In his formulation, Dewey explicitly rejected the notion of "social adjustment" in the sense of fitting the individual to the existing social pattern. Instead, he saw the school as an "embryonic" social community in which ideal forms of the integration of the individual and society would be constantly evolving. Dewey, for example, did not make a fetish of so-called individualized instruction whereby individual pupils race through prepackaged standard units of work. Education, according to Dewey, was primarily a social activity. Insofar as the curriculum was concerned, this meant in part an emphasis on what Dewey called *occupations*, not in Froebel's mystical sense but in terms of the basic activities of human beings, involving such things as food, clothing, and shelter. In the Dewey school, therefore, one could observe children engaged in such primary occupations as cooking, sewing and weaving, and woodworking.

Misconceptions about Dewey's Curriculum Theory. Possibly, the very prominence of these activities led to at least two major misconceptions about the curriculum of the Laboratory School. One misconception probably arose from the unusual physical activity that one could observe or imagine in connection with the occupations—the noise and the bustle —which led people to believe that the children were engaging in a kind of free play; that is, that the curriculum for Dewey was simply a collection of unstructured or random activities arising strictly out of children's immediate interests and impulses. (In point of fact, the curriculum in the Dewey school was scrupulously planned.)

A second misconception was probably based on the assumption that the children in the Dewey school were being trained in manual and household skills because of their utilitarian value. Dewey explicitly rejected both of these interpretations. The occupations were the basis of the curriculum because they represented a means by which the child could make the connection between the basic activities of mankind and the highly refined intellectual resources of the culture such as history, science, mathematics, and literature. In a sense, Dewey was attempting to trace the development of the organized fields of knowledge from their origins in ordinary human activity. The organized fields of knowledge would not be presented to the child in their finished and refined form, but as evolving out of the human predicament itself. This presentation was psychologically sound, according to Dewey, in that it corresponded to the child's, not the adult's, way of viewing the world and also to his natural impulses; and, at the same time, it served as a living illustration of the vital connection between knowledge and human affairs. Knowledge, in this sense, was being restored to its role *in* life rather than being presented to the child as abstracted from life, an approach alien to the child's own way of making sense out of his experience. Unlike its position in the "scientific" curriculum making of Bobbitt, education was not viewed as a preparation for a specific anticipated adult role, but as a process of continuous growth. Dewey's curriculum theory would not set education apart from living, but treat it as coincidental with living.

The Disciplines in Dewey's Progressive Organization of Subject Matter. In a sense, then, Dewey's theory of curriculum, like that of the Herbartians, was a theory of recapitulation. But, whereas the Herbartian theory of culture epochs was based on the notion that the development of the individual recapitulates the development of the human race from, let us say, an age of savagery to an age of civilization, Dewey's version recapitulates the evolution of the disciplines of knowledge from their origins in the fundamental occupations and experiences of mankind to their present abstract and theoretical state.

In the last book he wrote on education, in 1938, Dewey reiterated and refined his central curriculum theory calling it *the progressive organization of subject matter.* "Anything which can be called a study," he said, "whether arithmetic, history, geography, or one of the natural sciences, must be derived from materials which at the outset fall within the scope of ordinary life-experience" (Dewey, 1938, pp. 86–87). Dewey meant this not simply in the sense of making school activity interesting and meaningful to the child by relating it to his own experiences, but in the sense that these studies are in fact outgrowths of human experiences and purposes. One of the problems for the teacher and the curriculum maker is that, in their present refined and abstract states, these studies are not easily recognized as such outgrowths. A critical job in curriculum planning, therefore, is one of recapitulating the evolution of knowledge from its beginnings in human occupations and human activity to its present logical form.

Dewey was especially critical of the Progressive Education movement for its overemphasis on the present experience of the child and its relative neglect of the direction such experience should take. ". . . Finding the material for learning within experience is only the first step," he said. "The next step is the progressive development of what is already experienced into a fuller and richer and also more organized form, a form that gradually approximates that in which subject matter is presented to the skilled mature person" (Dewey, 1938, p. 87). In the concept of the progressive organization of subject matter, Dewey wove together what he had identified earlier as the fundamental factors in the education process, the child, on one hand, and the curriculum, the subjects of study, on the other.

Contemporary Manifestations of Curriculum Theory

A Behavioral Objectives Approach to Curriculum

Our myopic viewpoint on contemporary events in education makes it difficult to isolate and identify current curriculum theories in the same way that theories can be examined in the light of historical perspective. In any case, the few illustrations of curriculum theory presented here are not intended to exhaust the full range of curriculum theories even in the United States. Much of what is going on in the field of curriculum today, however, seems to be a kind of amalgam of previously articulated curriculum theories along with some modern modifications and an extensive new rhetoric. Prominent in the field, for example, is the dictum that one begins the process of curriculum planning by developing an extensive list of *behaviorally stated objectives*, sometimes called specific performance objectives. These objectives are, in effect, a blueprint drawn in minute detail for how children will behave once they are processed through the instructional program (an idea which, of course, would have been entirely repugnant to Dewey). The second step in curriculum development would be to find the combination of films, programmed instruction, live teaching, computer-assisted instruction, and so on by which the desired behaviors can be most efficiently produced. The third step would be the evaluation of the program by matching the anticipated outcomes with the behaviors that children actually manifest. The rhetoric of legitimation for such an approach frequently involves such terms as *competency based curriculum, accountability,* and *individualized instruction.* Its psychological kin is behavior modification theory, discussed in Chapter 3; not only does the teacher teach a specific fact or skill, or have the child learn it through programmed instruction, but she may also reinforce the child's response when it is correct.

The most immediate ancestor of such a conception of curriculum is probably the 1950 formulation by Ralph Tyler, widely known as the Tyler rationale (Tyler, 1950). Tyler built his rationale around four major questions, which may be conceived as steps in curriculum development:

1. What educational purposes should the school seek to attain?
2. What educational experiences can be provided that are likely to attain these purposes?
3. How can these educational experiences be effectively organized?
4. How can we determine whether these purposes are being attained?

Tyler also emphasized the need to state objectives in behavioral language as a way of putting vaguely stated goals of education into operational terms. Tyler's formulation was, in turn, only a reworking of the theoretical core of the curriculum doctrines of Franklin Bobbitt and other leading figures in the social efficiency movement, such as W. W. Charters and David Snedden. One can, therefore, trace a line of theoretical development in curriculum thinking from the early formulations in the social efficiency period through the refinements advocated by Tyler to the present emphasis on precision and particularity with respect to the stated objectives and modern technology as the means of achieving them. In each case, the curricular objective represents a terminal state to which the child must conform.

Criticisms of the Behavioral Objectives Model

Although the behavioral objectives model of curriculum development seems relatively simple and straightforward, certain critical problems present themselves when we attempt to translate it into practice. One problem involves the identification of learning with observed changes in behavior. Some kinds of learning, it is true, are likely to be manifested in modified behavior; but some learning may represent only a potential for change or even something as elusive as a deeper understanding of or sensitivity toward certain phenomena. The very real problems associated with measuring such subtle forms of learning need not lead us to the position that the forms are relatively unimportant. The most important outcomes of education may not be associated with the short-term production of immediately observable and easily measurable behaviors, but the long-term development of intellectual patterns of thought. If a mature adult were to measure the success of his education by comparing the "input" of thousands of hours of instruction with a directly produced "output" of specific facts and skills that are or could be manifested in his behavior, his education would almost certainly be counted a failure. Broudy has argued that close adherence to the doctrine of behaviorally stated objectives leads us to put "a high premium on the replicative use of learning which asks the learner to reinstate the original learning pretty much as learned in response to definite cues." This has made researchers in the field "loath to seek answers to educational questions about broad outcomes of schooling as well as long-range outcomes of a course of instruction" (Broudy, 170, p. 44). There is, in other words, something more to becoming educated than the ability to reproduce on cue the specific facts and skills typically imbedded in statements of behavioral objectives. That "something more" in fact may be what is significant and lasting in one's education.

Another problem that arises is the extent to which a teacher or curriculum maker can or ought to anticipate in precise terms what "terminal behaviors" are to be associated with a given educational experience. In other words, is the educational activity an outgrowth of, and instrumental toward the achievement of, a given curricular objective? Or, is the objective an outgrowth of the activity itself which cannot be anticipated in precise terms? Dewey took the latter position. Goals, he said, "are ways of defining and deepening the meaning of an activity . . . an end or aim is thus a characteristic of *present* activity." Objectives give us "merely the *present direction* of activity." Since objectives find their context *within* activity, they are not to be defined as terminal states or ends of activity. "An end-in-view is a *means* in present action; present action is not a means to a remote end," (Dewey, 1950 [1922], p. 226). Dewey, therefore, saw objectives or ends-in-view as arising out of activity, giving that activity a richer meaning and direction. Objectives do not precede activity, with activities then designed to bring about the efficient achievement of the prespecified objectives.

A further problem that arises out of the currently popular model of curriculum development is that it leads to a rather simplistic view of evaluation. A program of instruction is generally considered successful when the measured outcomes match prespecified objectives. But the most important outcomes of an activity may not have been anticipated at all. Programmed instruction, for example, may with relentless precision infuse into a child's behavior pattern all the objectives that have been specified in advance, and on those terms would be judged a huge success. As Newmann (1965, p. 295) has pointed out, however, the child may also learn the following:

1. Questions have clearly correct and incorrect answers.
2. Knowledge consists in the accumulation of a fund of correct responses.
3. Learning occurs while attending to relatively small amounts of material.
4. Learning occurs when one makes responses that consist of only a few words at a time.
5. Whenever you make a response, you will receive information about the correctness of your answer.
6. Learning is easy; i.e., without much mental effort one can almost always make correct responses.
7. The most efficient way to gain knowledge is through interaction with controlled and constant stimuli like the printed word, pre-recorded material, etc.

These possibly undesirable, albeit unanticipated, outcomes must also be considered when one attempts to assess a program of instruction. Rigid prespecification of curricular objectives, therefore, may lead to the development of a kind of "tunnel vision" in evaluation whereby the most significant outcomes go unnoticed.

The Open Curriculum

A second, currently popular, approach to curriculum is that of the open curriculum, originating in British Infant Schools (discussed in Chapter 1). Seen in historical perspective, this, too, is a kind of amalgam of previously articulated curriculum theories, although for its philosophy it borrows most heavily from Dewey. On both sides of the Atlantic, those who write about informal education, as it is sometimes called, maintain that learning is problem solving, that it initiates with the learner, and that the learner continually evaluates experiences in the light of their consequences, a belief that is basically like that of Dewey. And, like Dewey's, the philosophy behind this movement emphasizes that the child in essence constructs his own subject matter and learns through his own doing; the emphasis is upon his experiencing.

But Dewey gave education not only a philosophy, but also a psychology, of learning. A key concept in that psychology is the notion of interest. For Dewey, interest on the part of the learner is the basic motivation that moves the learner to become absorbed in subject matter. Interest formed one of the cornerstones of the Progressive Education movement, *the* dominant movement in education in the 1920s and 1930s. In its most distorted form, the notion of child interest led to statements like "The child must decide what it interests him to learn; the school must be child-centered and not subject-centered." Dewey (1930) himself deplored "The absence of intellectual control through significant subject-matter," as well as the intellectual flabbiness that developed as a result of misinterpretations of his philosophy.

The error of the progressivists in ignoring the cognitive domain is one that open-education advocates hope to avoid. They recognize with Dewey that schools must be concerned not only with freeing the child to learn, but also with *what* the child is learning, with the intellectual disciplines of language, arithmetic, science, and other subjects. For a theory of how children acquire knowledge in the intellectual disciplines, British educators lean upon Piaget, whose work we have discussed in Chapter 2. Not only does Piaget's equilibration model, encompassing assimilation and accommodation, fit the general approach of these educators, but his analysis of how children acquire logical classification structures, those underlying number, measurement and space, as well as structures in other cognitive domains (see pp. 51–53, 259–265), give teachers powerful tools to use in their planning for children's experiences. Teachers in open education today can avoid some of the errors of the earlier progressivists because there is now available a more completely developed psychology of how children acquire knowledge than was true fifty years ago.

Summary

As one reviews some of the efforts to consider curriculum questions in terms of a coherent theoretical framework, one is confronted with problems of enormous complexity, problems that have not only widely different possible solutions, but that may be formulated in radically different ways. The mental disciplinarians saw the curriculum in terms of facilitating a process of mental training whereby certain desirable habits of thought were developed. Partly in reaction to the vagueness of such a doctrine, the "scientific" curriculum makers of the social efficiency period brought particularity, standardization, and a product orientation into curriculum discourse. The Herbartians and Dewey tried to incorporate the child's own developmental pattern into the process of curriculum theorizing. Current efforts attempt to combine a theory of behaviorism with an older emphasis on specificity and predetermination.

The story of curriculum theory in modern times is not one of unbroken progress toward a clearer conceptualization of curriculum decisions. The record of these efforts, nevertheless, serves to provide a perspective on the kinds of problems one faces in curriculum development. Although we must frequently resort to simple common sense, broad theoretical questions continually intrude when we try to make practical decisions about what to teach. The development of curriculum theory is, at least in part, the effort to bring these theoretical questions into focus and to see them in relationship to each other.

READING LIST 4

Archambault, R. D., (Ed.). *John Dewey on education.* New York: The Modern Library, 1964. A compilation of Dewey's major writing in the field of education, including his most significant work in curriculum.

Bobbitt, F. *How to make a curriculum.* Boston: Houghton Mifflin Company, 1924. A curriculum "classic" written during the height of the social efficiency period. It embodies the major features of "scientific" curriculum development including the careful specification of curriculum objectives.

Broudy, H. S., Smith, B. O., & Burnett, J. R. *Democracy and excellence in American secondary education.* Chicago: Rand McNally, 1964. Chapter III, "Reassessment of the Uses of Schooling," and Chapter IV, "Schooling as Used by the Specialist and Nonspecialist," in particular attempt to develop alternatives to replicative outcomes of schooling.

Kolesnick, W. B. *Mental discipline in modern education.* Madison: University of Wisconsin Press, 1962. A reinterpretation of the impact of the theory of mental discipline on modern educational thinking.

Mayhew, K. C., & Edwards, A. C. *The Dewey School.* New York: Atherton Press, 1966. (Originally published by D. Appleton-Century in 1936.) A fascinating account of the actual workings of the Dewey Laboratory School in Chicago written by two former teachers in the school.

Peters, R. S. *Education as initiation.* London: George G. Harrap & Co. Ltd., 1964. Strongly influenced by Dewey, an English philosopher makes a brilliant attempt to reconceptualize ends and means in education.

Stephens, J. M. *The process of schooling.* New York: Holt, Rinehart and Winston, 1967. An intriguing and original theory, attempting to account for the effects of schooling and some persistent and puzzling outcomes of educational research.

Professional Journals To Become Acquainted With

Curriculum Theory Network. The Ontario Institute for Studies in Education, 102 Bloor Street West, Toronto 5, Ontario, Canada.

Educational Theory. Education Building, University of Illinois, Urbana, Illinois 61801.

Journal of Curriculum Studies. Wm. Collins Sons & Co. Ltd., 144 Cathedral Street, Glasgow C.4., England.

CHAPTER 5

Selection of Content

In Chapter 4, we examined principles underlying decisions about what should be taught in the schools—principles such as mental discipline, social efficiency, progressive organization of subject matter, behavioral objectives, and the open curriculum. All of these principles are of interest not only historically, but also because they underlie contemporary decisions about selection and organization of content, a problem we turn to next. By "organization" we mean putting the content into some kind of form for use with children.

Content is selected from basic disciplines of science, mathematics, the social studies, language arts, the arts, and health. Someone has to say, in each discipline, "Of what we know about this subject, what is important for children to learn?"

Who Selects Content?

First of all, we should recognize that, operationally, content selection takes place at two levels. Curriculum developers, with the aid of research grants, plan curricula for either a national group of pupils or a group within a state or school district and are concerned with selecting content for a large number of classrooms. They have only very general perceptions of the children who will be dealing with the content, and so usually plan a curriculum that fits their notion of how children learn. Most of our innovative programs begin in this way. On the other hand, the individual classroom teacher also carries on content selection in deciding what to teach a given group of pupils. Because the group has unique characteristics and is not specifically like any other group, the teacher makes decisions that require that the material be teachable with regard to a specific group of individuals. Content selection, then, for the teacher means making use of the best and most effectively organized materials available. In fact, the use of a variety of sources might be best in constructing an effective program. In addition, the classroom teacher must be assessment-oriented in assuring herself that the content selected has meaning and is effective for the specific learners to be educated in her classroom.

Research has repeatedly shown that, regardless of the size of the school unit, patterns of responsibility in the determination of content and the selection of materials have remained remarkably consistent. Whereas prior to and in the early 1950s principals were charged mainly with recommending instructional materials as well as content modifications and changes, a decade later found these individuals passing on recommendations made by teachers, supervisors, and others on the staff. Individually, and as a member of a group, the teacher has become the main recommender of those elements with which she works, despite the fact that there have been such obstacles as lack of funds in many school situations, failure to provide time for teachers for choosing and planning the use of materials, failure to provide the resources to assist in locating, evaluating, and acquiring materials (and organizing them so that their use is facilitated), and failure to provide required space for materials.

In discharging this responsibility that she has now accepted, the teacher is frequently at a loss to find what she needs or would consider useful in classroom situations. She has had to ask herself such questions as these: What are the purposes or objectives that are sought in programs designed for the elementary grades? Are the purposes being served by the programs we find? How well are these purposes being served? Problems of scope and sequence have been causes for grave concern. How can the teacher in any grade find out about the level her students have attained in both concept and skill development? How much responsibility, if any, does the teacher at any level have in preparing his students for the next higher level? Who sees to it that the work of the elementary school is related to the work of the secondary school, the work of the secondary school level to that of the elementary school and of college, the work in college to that of the high school and the graduate school?

That the teacher has become the central figure in content matters and in the selection of materials is not disputed, nor is the fact that she requires education or perhaps reeducation because of the complex nature of the problems faced. To whom may the teacher turn for needed aid? How can teachers who want to change find out about new programs?

How New Curricula Become Operational

Some states, through the state office of public instruction, have demonstrated a continuing concern with curriculum improvement. They have provided consultative assistance and materials for local curriculum studies; they have initiated in local school systems experimental projects designed to improve teaching and instructional services; they have conducted workshops in order to bring school and lay people together for work on school programs; they have prepared and distributed curriculum bulletins and have assisted other educational organizations and agencies without duplicating their efforts. North Dakota in particular might be mentioned here. North Dakota schools are gradually being remodeled along the lines of open education as the result of a state-wide study carried out by the state department of public instruction, the University of North Dakota, the U.S. Office of Education, and other agencies.

The U.S. Office of Education is also providing aid in a variety of ways to the teacher who wants to change. Under a grant from this agency, the University of New Hampshire, for example, has set up Learning Centers throughout the state, demonstration primary classrooms where teachers may see different curriculum models in action and have a chance to study new curriculum materials. The Centers reach teachers in some of the isolated rural communities where the population consists mainly of French-Canadian Americans, one of our several neglected minorities. In the Follow-Through Project, set up to continue compensatory education through the primary grades, teachers in all fifty states can see ten different curriculum models, some of which will be described later in this chapter.

There are also provisions for disseminating written reports of programs.

Chapter 1 of this book includes an extensive treatment of the Elementary and Secondary Education Act of 1965 and attempts to make some assessment of the legislation's impact on schools. With the passage of time, it became quite clear that the country-wide dissemination of the reports compiled in the various project centers was of such importance as to warrant a topmost priority. In 1968 the U.S. Office of Education embarked upon a special program to inform the nation's schools about these new projects. That office commissioned the Southern Education Reporting Service to undertake the task of reporting, and in 1970 this organization produced *Improving Education through ESEA: 12 Stories*.

In this work, Campbell presents seven articles covering Title III projects that are concerned with innovative programs designed to advance creativity in education. They range from an experimental approach to teaching American history at the eighth-grade level to a new program for dropouts and potential dropouts, from a science center to a central city-community project, from a theater program and a creative teaching center to an aerospace curriculum. Three programs described were supported under Title I. They cover a teacher's aide project, a reading center, and a program for handicapped children. The titles of the twelve stories are most revealing: "Teaching in the Inner City," "Creative Teaching Center," "Science Interpretive Program," "Slow Readers Move Ahead," "Aerospace Program," "Stand Up and Walk," "Individually Prescribed Instruction," "Project Discovery," "A Chance to Succeed," "Planning a Rural Program," "Teacher Aides Link School and Community," and "Interpreting American History."

In 1970 the U.S. Office of Education published a series of monographs under the general title of *It Works*. These reported exemplary programs for the education of disadvantaged children, and the studies were compiled for the agency by the American Institute for Research in the Behavioral Sciences, Stanford University. Grouped under the headings, Preschool Programs in Compensatory Education, Elementary Programs in Compensatory Education, Elementary-Secondary Programs in Compensatory Education, and Secondary Programs in Compensatory Education, all of these studies, thirty or more in number, described successful "models" for emulation by communities and schools interested in this phase of education.

In a variety of ways, then, in workshops and seminars, through demonstration and participation, through reading and audiovisual materials, teachers are acquiring information about new programs and how to change their ways of teaching.

Changes have usually come about slowly and in a rather orderly fashion. They come about from feelings of dissatisfaction in various schools that result from the use of existing techniques, content, or materials. To provide practical solutions for these problems, research studies have been instituted in universities and research centers connected with public schools. In addition, much valuable information has been discovered by teacher-planned and teacher-executed research in classrooms. Various techniques have been tried out, and teachers have learned much from comparing their own results with those obtained by teaching according to other and perhaps older methods.

As research findings have become available, a trend is often apparent. Articles are written in professional journals; papers are read at gatherings of teachers and administrators and others. These articles and speeches help to stir interest in the newer developments that have been suggested as improvements over the old. A few schools try out the newer methods or materials. Their results are, in turn, reported to an ever-enlarging circle of educators. Thus, after tryout and evaluation, certain changes may seem to be in order. The reading program may evolve in this way, or a program in the social studies. The process is a gradual one; few educators would espouse the "earthquake" type of change, for, while it may bring about immediate benefits, it may likewise generate unanticipated and unwanted changes.

What Content Is Appropriate for Elementary School Children?

The Problem of Definition and Dimensions

One approach to deciding what content in a given field is appropriate for children is to consider first the problem of definition and dimensions of that field. Defining a content field is not the simple task that it was once viewed as being. Nor are skills ably and aptly described. This last observation perhaps requires elaboration. One notices a tendency of a researcher to make his own definition rather than entertain all the possible definitions provided by various authorities in a given skill, say, reading. A good researcher may do this and then endeavor to use his definition in a reliable and valid manner. The trouble is that others do the same thing, and the result is confusion that makes it virtually impossible to compare pieces of research.

That this is very much the case in *reading*, an extremely important language art, is quite clear to Jenkinson (1970). She observes that the whole field of reading is plagued by a lack of acceptable definitions and suggests that the profession is indeed in a bad way when agreement cannot be reached with respect to a comprehensive definition of reading. Some would define reading very narrowly, equating it with the ability to sound out words. Others, almost as narrowly, define the skill in grade-equivalency scores. That is, a second-grade child after three months in school should achieve a score of 2.3 on a standardized reading test in order to be "reading" satisfactorily. Still others would argue for more inclusive definitions to include taste and development of a reading habit.

Jenkinson calls for flexibility, believing that definitions must be capable of changing in base and in content as new ideas emerge.

The Role of Educational Objectives

An important contribution to the problem of defining appropriate content and stating its dimensions emerged in 1953 when the Midcentury Committee on Outcomes in Education published a document known as *Elementary School Objectives*. This committee observed that parents and those interested in the education of children ask each other and elementary classroom teachers a great variety of pertinent questions about schools and schooling. If a condensed summary were made of these queries, it might look something like this:

1. What is not done that should be done?
2. What is done that should not be done?
3. What is not known that can and should be found out?
4. How can I know for sure what is now being planned and done?

These questions were applied to nine curriculum areas: physical development, health, and body care; individual, social, and emotional development; ethical behavior, standards, and values; social relations; the social world; the physical world; esthetic development; communication; quantitative relationships.

Each of the foregoing areas represents a major category of the educational goals that schools may strive to attain. In each area, in addition to the questions posed above, the *Elementary School Objectives* study would additionally pose these as subquestions in a realm, say, of *quantitative relationships*:

1. What should children know, remember, understand?
2. What skills should they perfect to the point of performance with little pause for thought?
3. What competencies should they have in the way of solving problems, thinking clearly on the basis of reliable evidence?
4. What attitudes and interests are most valuable?
5. What values should children have?
6. What general habit patterns and what methods of attack on problems should be developed?
7. What are the limitations set by nature and culture that the schools (and the children) cannot be expected to overcome?

It was for the purpose of providing answers to some of the questions listed, and of helping teachers and parents to find answers to others, that the Midcentury Committee on Outcomes in Elementary Education undertook the survey and presented the report from which the above list has been abstracted. And it is in the pattern of the questions posed above that the recommended goals of the elementary school were organized. In reflecting on these, we direct our attention in this section of the chapter to the area of *quantitative relationships*, but emphasize that this aspect is illustrative of the kind of analysis that might be made in any of the nine areas with which the committee dealt.

Within the quantitative relationships area, as in all the other curricular areas referred to in the *Elementary School Objectives* report, four types of student behavioral patterns were stressed: knowledge and understanding, skills and competencies, attitudes and interests, and, finally, action patterns. Objectives were derived for each of the behavioral patterns to conform with what might be expected of a pupil at the end of the third-grade period, at the end of the intermediate- or sixth-grade period, and at the end of the upper-grade period, roughly the ninth grade. Note that the thinking was very much in terms of grade standards, that is, in terms of what an average child should have accomplished at the end of a specified grade, but also note the beginnings of a more flexible approach. Whereas, earlier, objectives were specified for each grade, now there is a three-year time span for the accomplishment of behavioral patterns.

In the broad area of quantitative relationships, *knowledge and understanding* refer to those things that average children should *know* and *understand*. These words refer to things that are memorized or that are understood so well that they can be easily recalled. *Skills and competencies* refer to the intellectual abilities that children should be able to exercise in making decisions and judgments, in being resourceful, in meeting difficult problems, in examining new and difficult data, and so on. A third category provides for items concerned with the basic needs and drives of human beings—the exercise of will, the play of emotion— as these are shown in *interests and attitudes*. *Action patterns* refer to broad generalized ways of behaving, such as ways of responding to problem situations through the union of intelligence with good working habits and scientific methods of thinking. In addition to these behavioral patterns, the Midcentury Committee found it necessary to add an additional consideration. This they called *determining conditions*. They put it this way: The factors mentioned in this category cannot properly be called outcomes in the sense that the schools and society strive to bring them about, for only occasionally and over long periods of time may some of them be indirectly affected by what goes on in the schools or the community. Their purpose is to suggest the complexity and variability of the forces that play constantly upon the child.

A further development in the task of defining objectives came with the work of Bloom et al. (1971), who developed a classification system for dealing with objectives. Their taxonomy is discussed in Chapter 14; very briefly, we point out here that the *cognitive domain* was seen by Bloom as composed of six subdivisions, of which knowledge is the first. *Knowledge* involves the recall of specifics and universals, the recall of methods and processes, or the recall of a pattern, structure, or setting. The other subdivisions, subsumed under the heading *intellectual abilities and skills*, consist of comprehension, application, analysis, synthesis, and evaluation. These five sometimes have been referred to as *understanding*. If the cognitive domain is viewed in this manner, then it is obvious that it can be helpful in analyzing and interpreting educational objectives. Related also are the facets of the *affective domain*: receiving, responding, valuing, organizing, and characterizing by a value or value complex.

One of the persistent issues identified by Kliebard (1970) is the role of curricular objectives. As can be seen from this brief review of their recent past, objectives can be broadly defined as in the *Elementary School Objectives* study. They can also be stated as "particularized" objectives, resulting in curriculum content described in behavioral or operational terminology.

The Behavioral Objectives "Movement"

Hoetker (1970) believes that it is imperative that this question be dealt with: Why has the insistence upon behavioral objectives continued to grow more urgent? He recounts the efforts of Eisner, who sought to answer this question by tracing the concern with microscopic specifications of objectives back fifty years, to the "scientific movement in education," and to Franklin Bobbitt, "the father of curriculum theory." Hoetker observes that the early specificationist emphasis lapsed after the 1930s and was revived in the late 1940s and early 1950s by Tyler, Herrick, and Bloom. Hoetker thinks

> . . . there are three sorts of behaviors that educators are concerned with. I am going to call these "can-do" behaviors, "may-do" behaviors, and "will-do" behaviors. "Can-do" behaviors are those specific things that a student can do at the end of a particular unit of his education that he could not do at the beginning of it; in terms of Bloom's *Taxonomy*, the "can-do" behaviors include knowledge, comprehension, and the application of knowledge in familiar situations. "May-do" behaviors are things a student may be able to do in a novel or unfamiliar situation because he has mastered certain "can-do" behaviors. These would include, among cognitive behaviors, the application of abstractions in novel situations, analysis, synthesis, and evaluation; plus, among affective behaviors, attending, responding, valuing, and, in some cases, organizing. "Will-do" behaviors are the choices and preferences that describe the quality of an adult's life, and which are present only fractionally during the school years. The affective *Taxonomy* refers to "will-do" behaviors as "characterization by a value or a value complex." (Hoetker, 1970, p. 49)

Hoetker believes that "traditional" education is concerned with the "can-do" behaviors—skills and knowledge; that "progressive" educators are more concerned with "may-do" behaviors, but

> . . . all educators profess to believe that the can-do and may-do behaviors they shape from day to day lead to the development of desirable patterns of will-do behaviors—patterns which describe good citizens, free men, cultured gentlemen, or whatever. Unfortunately, will-do behaviors are, by definition, exhibited in times and places far removed from the training situation, so teachers seldom know whether their efforts have borne fruit. These elements of time and distance also make it unlikely that behavioral scientists will ever be able to establish empirical relationships between particular can-do or may-do behaviors and particular patterns of will-do behaviors. (Hoetker, 1970, p. 50)

Hoetker does maintain, however, that the habit of thinking about educational objectives in behavioral terms can provide positive contributions in improving instructional practices. The views of Hoetker are not those shared or accepted by all curriculum workers, needless to say. Some educators in the early 1970s seemingly would wash their hands of the whole behavioral objectives "movement." They are critical of the fact that some elementary school teachers and indeed whole staffs are being *required* to write behavioral objectives for courses in content areas, and they are raising questions as to what kinds of behavioral objectives teachers are being required to write. There is a temptation to write only those objectives that can easily be stated in very precise behavioral terms. For the beginner in arithmetic, for example, it is easiest to compose objectives stating, "The learner can count to twenty without help" or "The learner knows his addition facts through the tens," than it is to define in terms of child behavior the concept of a set, and it becomes still harder to behaviorally define attitude, taste, mathematical aptitude, and other important categories where we would hope to influence development. Atkin (1968), whose criticism we have mentioned in Chapter 4, writes along this same line.

> A child who is learning about meal worm behavior by blowing against the animal through a straw is probably learning much more than how this insect responds to a gentle stream of warm air. Let's assume for the moment that we can specify "behaviorally" all that he might learn about meal worm *behavior*. (An arduous and never-ending task.) In addition, in this "simple" activity, he is probably finding out something about interaction of objects, forces, humane treatment of animals, his own ability to manipulate the environment, structural characteristics of the larval form of certain insects, equilibrium, the results of doing an experiment at the suggestion of the teacher, the rewards of independent experimentation, the judgment of the curriculum developers in suggesting that children engage in such an exercise, possible uses of a plastic straw, and the length of time for which one individual might be engaged in a learning activity and still display a high degree of interest. When any piece of curriculum is used with real people, there are important learning outcomes that cannot have been anticipated when the objectives were formulated. And of the relatively few outcomes that can be identified at all, a smaller number still are translatable readily in terms of student behavior. (p. 4)

As Atkin points out, stated objectives determine the emphasis the teacher will give to certain learnings; she is very likely to use the time alloted to a particular topic on those readily identifiable learnings to which her attention has been directed.

A very different approach to selection of content is that employed in the curriculum reform movement that was dominant in the 1960s. We turn to this approach next.

The "New" Discipline-Centered Curricula

Long before Sputnik, curriculum people had given thoughtful atten-tion to the so-called subject curriculum that dominated the scene and had begun efforts to direct reform toward a more discipline-centered curriculum. At about the time the *Elementary Evaluative Criteria* (1953) and *Elementary School Objectives* committees were at work, the development of a Curriculum Laboratory at the University of Illinois was taking place. At first, the work of the University of Illinois Commit-tee on School Mathematics (1952) commanded the attention of individ-uals interested in and involved in curricular reform in the realm of mathematics.

In the next ten years, the same close scrutiny that was afforded mathematics was extended to science and foreign language instruction. In each discipline, the emphasis was upon *structure*, upon a body of content selected by scholars in that discipline as being the critical con-tent. One observer, Goodlad (1966), stated:

> . . . If previous eras of curriculum development can be described as child-centered or society-centered, this one can be designated as subject- or discipline-centered. The ends and means of schooling are derived from organized bodies of knowledge. Further, the curriculum is planned by physicists, mathematicians, and historians, and students are encouraged to think like these scholars. The word "structure" has replaced "the whole child" in curriculum jargon. . . . Many curriculum builders seek to orga-nize their fields around the primary structural elements of each discipline: the concepts, key ideas, principles, and modes of inquiry. It is assumed that understanding these elements (rather than merely possessing the facts) gives the student the intellectual power to attack unfamiliar prob-lems and enables him to grasp intuitively the relationship of new phe-nomena not previously encountered to phenomena already experienced. Ability to think inductively becomes a built-in goal, and teachers are encouraged to let students discover meanings for themselves.

Curriculum reform in the late fifties and in the sixties was dominated by university professors of physics, chemistry, biology, mathematics, and foreign languages. At first, reform concentrated on the secondary schools, but it spread to the elementary, resulting in the "new" curricula we will be discussing in separate chapters on different subject-matter areas.

However, it was soon evident that the development of individual subject-matter curricula in isolation, more or less, presented problems for school administrators who endeavored to implement curricular find-ings into coherent school programs. In addition, certain very significant portions of the school curriculum were receiving little or no attention

from the special projects that continued to mushroom. Music, art, indus-
trial arts, vocational education, physical education, and a number of
other important areas in the school were little affected by the reform
movement.

It also became painfully clear that the problem of curriculum reform
was not going to be solved simply by reorganizing the subject matter in a
particular discipline and teaching it to teachers. Silberman (1970) points
out two errors of the reform movement. One was the failure to involve
classroom teachers in the creation and modification of new curricula, a
mistake that later projects to be organized (SCIS, for example) avoided,
and the second error was the failure to ask: What kind of human beings
and what kind of society do we want to produce? In the late sixties, this
concern came to dominate curriculum reform; it was a concern expressed
first in early childhood education.

Some Fresh Directions for Selection of Content for Early Childhood Education

Out of the many innovative programs for children in early childhood
education (ages three to eight), we can find some fresh approaches to
content selection. These innovative programs derive from Head Start, set
up in 1964 to help disadvantaged children overcome some of the effects
of cultural deprivation. The guidelines for Head Start included

1. Improving the child's physical health and physical abilities.
2. Helping the emotional and social development of the child by encouraging self-confidence, spontaneity, curiosity, and self-discipline.
3. Improving the child's mental processes and skills with particular attention to conceptual and verbal skills.
4. Establishing patterns and expectations of success for the child that will
   create a climate of confidence for his future learning efforts.
5. Increasing the child's capacity to relate positively to family members
   and others, while at the same time strengthening the family's ability
   to relate positively to the child and his problems.
6. Developing in the child and his family a responsible attitude toward
   society, and fostering constructive opportunities for society to work
   together with the poor in solving their problems.
7. Increasing the sense of dignity and self-worth within the child and his
   family.

Note that the second guideline has to do with cognitive processes
that might directly affect the child's ability to succeed academically in
elementary school. Middle-class children typically enter school already

familiar with books and school-related objects (pencils, crayons, and so on). Furthermore, as we shall see in Chapter 8, they are accustomed to using language to follow directions, respond to questions, and so forth. Lower-class children, on the other hand, frequently lack such experiences and are therefore at a disadvantage in school learning. Experiences with school-related equipment, therefore, and opportunities to hear stories and look at books were planned in most Head Start programs.

In the conventional middle-class nursery school, teachers assume that both concept and language development are furthered through social play. For example, in building with blocks, playing in the doll house, and in other social play situations, children can acquire notions of space, number, classification, and seriation, using language freely as they play. If play benefited the middle-class child, then why not the lower? Accordingly, many Head Start programs included, as a major part of the day, time for free play.

Evaluation of the impact of Head Start was made by measuring the extent to which children in the first, second, and third grades who had attended Head Start differed in academic and social development from comparable children who did not attend. The Metropolitan Readiness Test, the Stanford Achievement Test, and a number of tests of self-esteem and achievement were used in the assessment. In one such nation-wide assessment, no significant differences were found between the two groups, except on the Metropolitan Readiness Test—which showed that Head Start children who had attended preschool for a full year were superior by a small margin (*New York Times*, 1969). The cry went up that compensatory education had been tried and had failed. However, Evans (1971) points out some defects in evaluation procedures:

> The most basic question (regardless of stated objectives) is whether subsequent and reliable differences can be observed in children who attend Head Start programs as compared with those who do not. A meaningful answer to this question assumes, among other things, that comparisons are made with children of similar ethnic and socioeconomic backgrounds. This assumption is not always met in practice. In many cases, children in one Head Start program may be compared to those in another or to children not in a program. Group composition may be influenced by race, ethnicity, and other variables. . . . This situation is further complicated by the frequently unproved validity of evaluation instruments and the frequently tacit assumption that something universal defines a Head Start program. (p. 69)

While acknowledging the defects in evaluation procedures, many early childhood education specialists thought Head Start programs should be changed, that the typical play-oriented nursery school was not enough to overcome the deficit from early deprivation, and that, in fact, it might not be challenging enough even for middle-class children. Most recognized the value of play both for social and cognitive development, but many pointed out that not all children make marvelous discoveries about the world as they play, and that the language used in play is often stereotyped. They argued that there should be structure in the preschool program, with the degree of structure ranging from a loosely to a completely structured program according to the views of the particular educator. At the same time, they also argued for continuing compensatory education at least through the primary grades; they pointed out that two months of school (which was all that some children had in Head Start) or even a full year was not enough to compensate for the effects of several years of deprivation.

A number of innovative programs were developed, and ten of them were selected for trial in a Follow-Through program financed by the U.S. Office of Education. Some of the programs were academically oriented; the Engelmann-Becker (E-B), formerly Bereiter-Engelmann, is based upon the premise that disadvantaged children must learn at a faster rate than middle-class children in order to catch up. The way to accomplish this is by direct teaching of reading, arithmetic, and language skills, with language seen as the key to academic success in all subjects. Objectives are very clearly specified, as the following, to be attained by the time of first-grade entrance, reveal:

1. Ability to use both affirmative and *not* statements in reply to the question, "What is this?" "This is a ball. This is not a book."
2. Ability to use the following prepositions correctly in statements describing arrangements of objects: *on, in, under, over, between*, "Where is the pencil?" "The pencil is under the book."
3. Ability to recognize and name the vowels and at least 15 consonants.
4. Ability to rhyme in some fashion, to produce a word that rhymes with a given word, to tell whether two words do or do not rhyme, or to complete unfamiliar rhyming jingles like "I had a dog, and his name is Abel; I found him hiding under the _____." (Bereiter & Engelmann, 1966)

Selection of curriculum content is based upon these objectives, and lessons are planned for direct, unambiguous teaching. (The reader will find an example of a lesson on pp. 239–240.) Engelmann believes that teachers must be told and shown exactly what to do. Begun originally for the preschool, the program has been extended to include a structural curriculum for the primary grades as well.

A quite different curriculum model is that based upon a "Continuing Growth" concept developed by the Education Development Center. This curriculum draws heavily upon the philosophy of the British Infant School, where there is no prescribed curriculum, but where school personnel have freedom to carry on open classrooms with the emphasis upon learning rather than teaching. An important feature of the EDC approach is an advisory service that may provide seminars, curriculum materials, resource centers, and so on, to help the teacher in setting up an open classroom. Considerable use is made of the structure, activities, and materials developed in new mathematics and science curricula, and creativity in these areas as well as in writing and the arts is encouraged.

A third curriculum model, developed at Bank Street, is based upon a concept of teacher adaptation to the needs of individual children. Curriculum in the primary grades includes certain community themes such as food marketing, sources of water, traffic control, and certain personal themes such as pet and plant care. There is also a strong emphasis upon language development through reading, discussion, and social activities. The contribution of play to cognitive development is recognized, and, through play, cooperative group projects are initiated. The teacher's role is to provide a stable, ordered environment where learning can take place. She is trained to be a close observer of children, to diagnose their needs, and to plan for each individual child. While the curriculum is not prescribed, it is expected that the teacher will introduce new skills and materials and provide for mastery of skills as the child's progress warrants. More than other programs, the Bank Street approach emphasizes the affective aspects of development; the concern is with developing children with sensitivity to sights, sounds, and feelings, children who are increasingly able to come to grips with reality and to deal with frustrations.

The other seven models in Project Follow-Through show the same range in degree of prescription of curriculum content and view of the role of the teacher. Maccoby and Zellner (1970) analyze the differences as follows. These are

1. Programs oriented toward behavior modification. Performance on intellectual tasks is thought of as a class of behavior subject to the same laws that govern other kinds of behavior. *Education is, or should be, a process of reinforcing children for the desired behavior.*
2. Programs oriented toward cognitive growth. Performance on intellectual tasks is thought of as reflecting the level of development of mental structures and operations. *Education is, or should be, a process of facilitating the normal stage-wise growth of these processes.*
3. Programs oriented toward self-actualization. Performance on intellectual tasks reflects whether a child has chosen to master the tested-for contents in pursuit of his goals. *Education is, or should be, a process of stimulating the child's intellectual curiosity, providing him with a range of experiences and materials appropriate to his existing skills, so*

that he can learn to become competent in his own physical and social environment.

4. There is a fourth kind of program which emphasizes changing the locus of control over the schools . . . *The educational system must be responsive to the needs and wishes of the community being served. If this condition is met, any of the three educational approaches listed above will work.* (pp. 25–26)

While an evaluation of the project is not yet completed, one can make certain predictions about the outcomes. In terms of achievement in the basic skills as measured by standardized tests, there will probably be little difference in children's progress; we come back to this point later in Chapter 14. Outcomes in the affective area are much more difficult to predict and to measure; advocates of flexibility in classrooms maintain that it is only as schools become humane—where provision is made for growth and exploration, and where the curriculum is designed to enhance feelings of dignity and worth—that society can itself become humane.

Suggested Approaches to Improving Instructional Programs

A key question now being raised by many individuals and groups is aimed at the degree to which the curricular and instructional programs offered by schools, colleges, and universities are relevant to the students in attendance and, in certain instances, to the communities from which the students come. Students are raising the question; so are parents, teachers, and laymen (*Educational Research and Development in the United States*, 1969, p. 35). The report referred to observes that a special but important case of this concern for the relevance of instruction and education can be found in the emerging interest in the development of educational programs expressive of and contributive to the special cultural needs and backgrounds of children attending certain schools. Demands for black studies in lower and higher education are being made, and they are being responded to by educators. Attention is being paid to the inclusion of materials, curricula, and approaches that respect the interests or desires of cultural minorities in the country.

As one examines the issues confronting education in this country, one has to be drawn to the preeminence of one question: How do we go about improving education? From a perusal of the report referred to (*Educational Research and Development in the United States*, 1970, p. 37), certain approaches, not necessarily mutually exclusive, can be identified:

1. One approach argues that what schools and colleges really need is simply a greater supply of money. If the schools could obtain more, they would be able to install the kinds of programs they already know would represent improvement in American education.

2. Another approach to improvement moves from a political rather than from a financial base. Political approaches to improvement hold that alteration in the governmental structures for the support or administration of education will produce significant improvement. Often, together with this approach, there is strong emphasis on the accountability of professional personnel to lay political leadership or to the public. School decentralization, provisions for student participation in the governance of higher education, and the release of achievement scores school by school are typical suggestions.

3. A third approach finds the source of improvement in alterations in the organizational structure of educational institutions, alterations that are designed to help those institutions better accomplish their instructional missions. Nongrading, team teaching, and flexible or modular scheduling are examples of these kinds of organizationally based innovations in education, justified in terms of real improvements that will result.

4. A fourth way to school improvement might be characterized in terms of its emphasis on professional role. Under this approach particular attention is paid to the labor-intensive character of contemporary schools and to the different roles played by education personnel. Improvement is sought through the redirection of the programs created to train such people.

5. Finally, a fifth approach: People who support this view hold that the improvement of education rests ultimately on the expansion of the knowledge base in such areas as human learning, the manner in which teacher role affects student achievement; the operations, support, and political structure of schools and universities; and the social factors affecting learning and the maintenance, support, and [goals of education. On the basis of that knowledge, instructional systems and organizations, curriculum materials and the like must then be carefully designed, tested, and validated. When this has been done, the alternatives thus developed can be made available to school and university officials, practitioners, and policy makers as live options for installation and adoption in operating settings.

These, then, are some of the positions identified. They represent different kinds of starting points for discussion about paths to educational improvement. They have been used in the past, and we will undoubtedly encounter them again in the future.

Summary

In this chapter, we have taken a closer look at how curriculum content is selected. The tendency over the years has been to begin with a statement of educational objectives and to try to determine content in the light of these objectives. Perhaps the ultimate in stating specific objectives is to be found in the behavioral objectives movement.

The field of early childhood education has been particularly fertile in the development of innovative curriculum models. Three of these are reviewed here: the Engelmann-Becker, the Education Development Center, and the Bank Street model.

Five possible avenues leading to the improvement of education are presented, from an approach that calls for more money for schools to one that argues for more knowledge about learning, teacher role, effect of political institutions, and social factors.

READING LIST 5

Armstrong, R. J., Cornell, T. D., Kranert, E., & Roberson, E. W. *The development and evaluation of behavioral objectives.* Worthing, Ohio: Charles A. Jones, 1970. States that one of the most critical aspects of an instructional program is that of identifying, defining, and measuring outcomes expected from that program, and provides through examples a consideration of approaches to evaluation, a rationale for such, and a consideration of several measurement factors.

Bloom, B. S., Hasting, J. T., & Madaus, G. F. *Handbook on formative and summative evaluation of student learning.* New York: McGraw-Hill, 1971. Presents a broad view of evaluation and its place in education and is primarily concerned with its use to improve teaching and learning. Part I deals with procedures in a general way, and Part II provides the teacher of selected subjects and programs with illustrations of those procedures and techniques which are likely to have the greatest practical value in each subject field or program.

Evans, E. D. *Contemporary influences in early childhood education.* New York: Holt, Rinehart and Winston, 1971. The subject of this book is the pre-primary educational program; the focus is upon broad educational strategies variously applicable to children ages three to six. One of the Early Childhood Education Series which presents in readable fashion what the state of the art is with respect to some of the continuing problems.

Levit, M. (Ed.). *Curriculum.* In H. Broudy (General Ed.), Readings in the philosophy of education series. Urbana: University of Illinois Press, 1971. A series of essays organized around curriculum problems: determination of objectives, selection of subject matter and experiences, reconceptualization of ways of studying the curriculum.

Maccoby, E. E., & Zellner, M. *Experiments in primary education: Aspects of Project Follow-Through.* New York: Harcourt Brace Jovanovich, 1970. This book deals with some of the experimental programs in Project Follow-Through, a nationwide effort to improve the grade school education provided for children from impoverished environments. Describes how ten different Follow-Through programs have tried to bring about educational reform.

Putnam, J. F., & Chismore, W. D. (Comp. and Ed.) *Standard terminology for curriculum and instruction in local and state school systems.* State Educational Records and Report Series, Handbook VI. Washington: U.S. Government Printing Office, 1970 (OE-23052). Classifies and defines specific items of information about the organization, administration, content, resources, and processes of curriculum development and instruction and includes additional related terminology.

Wright, B. A., Camp, L. T., Stosberg, W. K., & Fleming, B. L. *Elementary school curriculum: Better teaching now.* New York: The Macmillan Company, 1971. This book is broad in scope. It introduces the reader to theory, research, and practice to stimulate his thinking and to help develop clear concepts about children and their educational programs.

Professional Journals To Become Acquainted With

Educational Leadership. The Association of Supervision and Curriculum Development, NEA, 1201 Sixteenth Street, N.W., Washington, D.C. 20036.

The Elementary School Journal. University of Chicago Press, 5750 Ellis Avenue, Chicago, Illinois 60637.

School and Society. Society for the Advancement of Education, Inc., 1834 Broadway, New York, New York 10023.

CHAPTER 6

Grouping
Children

As an issue, the grouping of children has concerned educators for many years, and it appears that it is here to stay for as long as there are more children than there are teachers. Although a great amount of writing, research, and experimentation related to grouping has taken place during the last fifty years, grouping children still remains a vital and controversial issue. The reason for this is clearly evident in the following statement (Yates, 1967): "In arguments about grouping policies one can usually find evidence to support any point of view that one chooses to adopt—enough evidence to discomfort one's opponent but never enough to overwhelm him."

There is a tendency in the literature to classify the practices of grouping into vertical and horizontal types of organization. An example of vertical organization would be the graded system in which the children are divided in groups mainly on the basis of their age. Horizontal organization results when a cluster of students, such as all second graders or all children in the first, second, and third grades, are randomly divided into a number of groups, all of which have equal and similar standing.

Vertical and horizontal types of grouping have usually been associated with grouping practices within a particular school—practices that have been initiated mainly for the purpose of facilitating instruction. Recent developments, however, require that grouping practices be viewed not only from the point of view of what is happening within a particular school, but from the point of view, as well, of what is happening within the educational system as a whole. By design or by accident children have been grouped in separate schools by social class or color, thus contributing to the perpetuation and even worsening of undesirable social conditions. As a result, new dimensions have been added to the phenomenon of grouping children, and interschool grouping has become a concern as vital as intraschool grouping has been for many years.

The intent of this chapter is to deal with both intraschool and interschool grouping practices. While the first category is important because of changes resulting from the emergence of a new definition of intelligence, the development of new teaching materials and devices, and the design of new strategies of teaching, the second category is also important because of its social implications and its relevance to the present conditions of our society.

Intraschool Grouping

There have been a number of criteria in the past on the basis of which children have been grouped within a particular school—among them are age, intelligence, achievement, aptitude, interests, motivation, and special needs. Educational history is full of terms signifying grouping designs. People in education are familiar with such terminology as heterogeneous grouping, homogeneous grouping, xyz grouping, vestibule groups, Winnetka Plan grouping, Dalton Plan grouping, platoon grouping, multiple-track grouping, departmental grouping, intraclass grouping, family grouping, and several others.

Some of the grouping designs mentioned were intended to individualize instruction, while others tried to make group instruction easier by reducing the range of individual differences. From a theoretical point of view, individualizing instruction appears to be a noble purpose and the solution to most problems associated with the task of educating children. But most attempts to individualize instruction are contrary to the ever-present need for economizing in the areas of personnel, facilities, and materials. In the typical school, to pay adequate attention to individual differences the teacher must have a reduced class size and must be freed of all peripheral responsibilities. The situation is different in British Infant Schools with as many as forty in a class; there, the child regulates his own learning. The teacher's role is to assist in the process by creating an environment that makes it possible for children to work alone, in pairs, or in a group. Materials and a variety of special purpose facilities make his role an easier one.

Because most plans to individualize instruction call for constant teacher-pupil interaction and therefore necessitate a smaller teacher-pupil ratio, they have never in the past been implemented on a wide scale. So long as the unit of instruction was the class and teaching conceived of as what went on when the teacher was in front of the class, attention to individual differences could only be accomplished if class size were small. Since that was not possible financially, *ability grouping* emerged as a popular plan and dominated the scene for a rather long period of time.

Ability Grouping

Ability grouping was intended to produce homogeneity in classes; the chief criterion was mental ability, and this was rated according to the

Intelligence Quotient (I.Q.) of children and by their performance in standardized achievement tests. Though rigid homogeneous grouping, based only on I.Q. and achievement, is not at the present considered a sound practice, in the past the terms *homogeneous grouping* and *ability grouping* were often used interchangeably.

The advantages claimed for ability grouping, as stated by Maurie Hillson (1965), are that

> Each child is challenged at his own level and therefore has a real chance to succeed.
>
> Enrichment fails in heterogeneous grouping because the teachers do not have time for the one or two really bright students, but in homogeneous grouping the teacher is able to care more adequately for all individuals since the total range of the class is somewhat reduced.
>
> Children have an opportunity to successfully compete, academically and socially, and the average and slow students have a chance to become leaders in their own groups.
>
> It is easier for the teacher to teach successfully since there will be fewer groups within the class for skill subjects, and the groups themselves will be made up of students of nearly equal ability.
>
> Children naturally make friends with others who have similar intellectual ability.
>
> In real life situations we do not find the barber competing with the chemist, but rather with the other barbers, and consequently it seems more true to life to have children compete with those somewhere near their own level.
>
> Because the teacher has less groups to prepare she does a better job.

Ability grouping continues to be widely practiced in the United States, but not all claims made in its favor have proved to be valid. Rigid and permanent ability grouping made on the basis of I.Q. and achievement test scores disregards other emotional and intellectual factors affecting a child's potential. Furthermore, rigid ability grouping gives rise to conditions that are undemocratic in nature and have a tendency to perpetuate and even aggravate existing social ills. As Thelen (1967) has pointed out, "Homogeneous ability grouping roughly approximates socioeconomic class grouping and therefore may produce social stratification of the student body."

Blacks, too, speak vigorously against ability grouping; they point out that conditions of poverty and racism result all too often in the black child being placed in the lower ability groups. As a result, neither the teacher nor the child himself has high expectations for learning. "If no one expects," say Brookover and Erickson (1969), "or considers it appropriate for students to learn well, and all evaluate them as unable to learn, it is unlikely that many will perform at high levels."

Current research evidence indicates that children in the elementary school do not necessarily profit from ability grouping. Goldberg, Passow, and Justman (1966) were led through their experimentation to believe that ". . . narrowing the ability range in the classroom on the basis of some measure of general academic aptitude will, by itself, in the absence of carefully planned adaptations of content and method, produce little positive change in the academic achievement of pupils at any ability level." As a matter of fact, evidence supports the notion that children in the average and lower ability groups suffer deprivation of intellectual stimulation when brighter children are removed from classes.

Usually, children in the lower groups are aware of their status to the detriment of their self-concept. Parents often refuse to have their children in the lower ability groups, while teachers find it difficult to work with slow children and prefer not to.

In spite of the apparent deficiencies of ability grouping, a review of research on grouping since 1930 led Goodlad (1960) to conclude that "Teachers tend to react more favorably to teaching groups in which the heterogeneity has been somewhat reduced, than to teaching groups selected at random." This is an interesting conclusion, because it leads one to believe that teaching and learning are perceived as a process in which the teacher offers and the pupils receive as a group. Apparently, the fact that children can learn by themselves and from each other is overlooked.

Obviously, rigid and permanent ability grouping has not proved to be the answer to the problem of meeting the individual differences of pupils. In fact, such grouping may lead to *less* attention to individual differences, since teachers assume that grouping has taken care of the problem. On the other hand, falling back to teaching children under the conditions imposed by the graded system and the traditional heterogeneous self-contained classroom based on grade standards would be retreating from the problem.

The Nongraded School

As a reaction to the failure of rigid ability grouping to combat the inadequacies of the graded system, and in view of the fact that ability grouping generated additional problems, a new type, or types, of intraschool organization emerged. For lack of a better term, this organizational form came to be known as the *ungraded* or *nongraded school*. In the words of Maurie Hillson (1967), "Nongraded schools represent an attempt at organizational plans which embrace the scientific findings about the learner and how he learns. There are attempts to deal with the problem of inflexibility in the education of the child. The nongraded school gears the school's administrative structure to the intellectual development of the child. It is a practical means for making it possible for teachers to personalize instruction for every pupil."

John Goodlad (1970) defines the nongraded school from another point of view: "It is not," he says, "simply the school we have known with grade labels removed. Nor is it a return to the one-room schoolhouse, as is sometimes suggested. There are no models from the past that do justice to the concept involved." According to Champlin (1969), "Nongradedness is a spirit, a frame of mind. It requires technical, logical and administrative support and understanding."

Some of the major differences between the graded and nongraded schools could be charted as follows:

Traditional Graded School	Nongraded School
1. It is assumed that all children will meet certain standards of achievement in a given period of time.	It is assumed that each child has his own pattern and rate of growth and that children of the same age will vary greatly in their ability and rate of growth.
2. If a child fails to meet the standards, he is required to repeat the grade in which he did not meet the standards.	A child never repeats a grade. He may progress more slowly than others in the group, and spend four years rather than three in the primary unit, but efforts are made to keep his growth continuous.
3. Grade placement is based mainly on academic achievement.	Placement is flexible and theoretically is based on physical, mental, social, and emotional factors.
4. Fixed standards of achievement to be met within a set time put pressures upon teachers and pupils that cause emotional tensions and tend to inhibit learning.	Tensions are minimized when each student works at his own rate and tries to meet standards determined on the basis of his potential and experiential background.
5. Each teacher works independently.	Teachers often work in teams and receive assistance from paraprofessionals.

While theoretically nongrading seems like a sound plan, research evidence produced thus far falls short of giving it adequate support. After a thorough review of related studies, McLoughlin (1968) concluded that "Taken at face value, current research on the nongraded school seems to say that its contribution to academic, social, and emotional development of children is marginal." He goes on to point out, however, that this rather pessimistic picture is probably based on the possibility that some experimental schools purporting to be nongraded are not truly nongraded.

Probably one of the biggest criticisms of the nongraded school is that it does not live up to its name by completely departing from the concept of the graded school. In most cases grades have disappeared only to be replaced by levels. In other words, the typical six-grade elementary school has, in a sense, modified its vertical organization by reducing the six grades to a smaller number of units, usually the primary and intermediate units, each of which is then subdivided into levels: Level 1, Level 2, Level 3, for the first year in school, and so on. And, unfortunately, placement in each level is too often determined on the basis of scores on reading achievement tests; Level 1 becomes the "slow" group, spending most of the first year on reading readiness activities, Level 2, the preprimer, and so on, so that nongraded becomes a euphemism for ability grouping based upon reading.

It is true that, as compared with the average graded school, each one of the nongraded levels is characterized by more flexibility and concern for the individual. This does not mean, however, that these two qualities cannot be achieved within the framework of the graded school as well. "If teachers believe in a learner-centered approach," the National Education Association (1963) reported, "and act in harmony with their belief, it is necessary for them to modify some of the standard practices associated with grade structure. They use grade designation only as group labels for convenience in keeping records, locating pupils, transferring data and pupils to other schools, and so on. Literally, they destroy the meaning of 'grade,' and a truly nongraded school emerges although it is still called 'graded.'"

In order for a school to succeed along the lines of the concept of nongradedness, there is a need for changes more basic than the elimination of the grade labels. The most fundamental of these is undoubtedly the designing of a suitable curriculum. As Stuart Dean (1967) emphasized, "The greatest potential of nongradedness may lie in the realm of curriculum development and breakthrough." Unfortunately, many schools overlooked this and attempted to establish a nongraded organization while maintaining traditional curricula.

Multigrade Grouping

It was hinted earlier that one of the most promising trends in terms of improving the teaching-learning process is the realization that children can learn by themselves and from each other. In order to promote the idea of children teaching children, a new type of grouping emerged known as *multiage* or *multigrade grouping*.

Multigrade grouping, as compared to ability grouping, is more realistic, for it allows for the formation of groups that resemble those outside the school. Such groups are more challenging than the artificial groups found in schools using grades or ability grouping.

Warren Hamilton and Walter Rehwoldt (1965), encouraged by their research, give the following description and assessment of the multiage group. "The group will be composed of children of different ages, different interests, different abilities, and different accomplishments. . . . Those who excel in one quality will contribute to the enlightenment of others. Thus the diversities of the various members of the group can enrich and extend the learning experiences and opportunities of all the members of the group."

According to reports from England, multiage grouping appears to be catching the imagination of educators and even politicians of that country. It has been implemented successfully in a number of infant schools (these schools take children from age five to seven), and it is usually known as *family grouping* due to the expectancy that the groups will function in many ways like brothers and sisters living and growing up together. This type of grouping is also known as vertical grouping.

In those infant schools in which family grouping is practiced ". . . each class," says Joseph Featherstone (1967), "is a cross-section of the whole school's population, all ages mixed together. This seems particularly successful," Featherstone continues, "in the early school years, when newcomers are easily absorbed, and other children help teach the young ones to clean up and take first steps in reading."

One particular British teacher (Brown, 1967) describes her class, made up of five-, six-, and seven-year-olds, as follows:

> Already my particular group is functioning as a family. The qualities of each are realized and accepted by the rest of the group far more easily than in segregated age-groups. Some of the young five-year-olds are more mature and confident that some of the six- to seven-year-olds. A little five-year-old reception girl called Tina will always be there to help an older child in difficulty over a lost possession, and Jill, who is just six, is one of the accepted good "shoe-tiers" for the older boys who can tie but not really tight enough. This, of course, works the other way round, but it is not on age-basis at all, just on an individual level of capabilities, and also applies in the classroom situation where the children learn and are helped by each other irrespective of age.

It is a fact that the British innovations in grouping have attracted worldwide attention. Family grouping appears to be working. It should be noted, however, that it is not grouping practices alone that were changed in the British schools. Objectives, curriculum, and methods of teaching changed, as well, with the adoption of the concept of the "integrated day." This concept is defined as follows by a British educator (Sealey, 1966):

An integrated day is one in which there are no class lessons as such. Instead, each child makes a unique synthesis of his learning experiences. The classroom is subdivided into specially-equipped working areas. Normally, one area is associated with science and mathematics, another with reading and the language arts, a third with work in the visual arts; and a fourth serves as a general purpose area. In addition, certain classroom space is devoted to programmed learning or other special purposes.

Within this type of classroom children move about freely and work according to their interests and capabilities. Spontaneous groups are formed so that children may read to one another, each from a different book, work on science or math problems together, or engage in dramatic play. The teacher has an eye on everything and everyone, but serves only as a guide, particularly when individual children or groups of children seek his or her assistance.

Will multiage grouping, in the British or any other similar form, be adopted by the American elementary school on a wide scale? No one can predict the degree to which this might happen, but the pressure to move in that direction is indeed overwhelming. As a matter of fact, a number of schools in the country are already experimenting with multiage grouping and flexible teaching, and they serve as models for many educators visiting from all over the country.

We ought to remember, however, that multiage grouping or family grouping—whatever one may wish to call it—will not succeed without changes in the basic philosophy about learning, in the curricula, the learning resources, the teaching strategies, and the parental outlook toward school. Ignoring these important factors will definitely lead to great disappointment.

Other Types of Intraschool Grouping

There are other types of intraschool grouping patterns that have emerged as solutions to the problems of individual differences. One such pattern is the *dual progress plan*, which "bears its name," Glen Heathers (1960) writes, "because, within it, students progress in language arts, social studies, and physical education according to the usual grade system, while they progress in science, mathematics, and the arts on a nongrade-level basis." Obviously, the nature of the dual progress plan demonstrates an attempt to take advantage of some of the qualities of the flexible plans without at the same time entirely destroying the self-contained classroom. It is based on the assumption that language arts, social studies, and physical education are "cultural imperatives" that should be mastered by all children, and that the only way children can achieve the mastery of these "cultural imperatives" is by being subjected to the graded system with its inherent grade standards. On the other hand, it is assumed that science, mathematics, and the arts are "cultural electives" that need not be mastered at any level of proficiency by all children. Each child can proceed in the electives at his own pace and according to his own interests.

The dual progress plan is also known as the *semidepartmentalized plan* due to the fact that in the morning the children meet with their homeroom teacher to be taught the "cultural imperatives," while in the afternoon they meet with different specialists for the "cultural electives."

Among the main advantages of the departmentalized plan is that each teacher is presumably well qualified in the subject she teaches and has more time for planning. In the self-contained classroom teachers often neglect the subjects in which they are not interested or for which they feel they are inadequately prepared. In the departmentalized situation all subjects are equally emphasized because they are taught by different teachers convinced of and committed to the importance of their own subjects.

On the other hand, some of the disadvantages of departmentalization for the elementary school are quite obvious. The children do not identify with any particular group and the schedule becomes rigid. The program is subject-centered and the needs of the children become less important. Evaluation of pupil progress in terms of overall behavior development becomes very difficult.

There is still another important intraschool grouping scheme that resulted not from the persistent general effort to meet the children's individual differences, but from a new way of organizing the teachers to instruct cooperatively. This rather interesting venture, known as *team teaching*, has been described (Shaplin, 1963) as an ". . . organization where teachers will share in planning but will carry out their plans not as individuals but as a team in which different teachers assume different degrees of responsibility within the group. At the same time," the same source continues, "the grouping of children becomes more flexible. Classes may vary widely in age range, intelligence, and size according to the various needs of the individual children within them. A single child might well participate in subgroups ranging from three to a hundred children and receive instruction from five or six different teachers during a school day."

The team approach to teaching is based on the assumption that not all students learn in the same way. It is also based on the expectation that better utilization of instructional personnel will result. Teachers bring with them a variety of backgrounds, interests, talents, and specializations. Team teaching, it is argued, gives them an opportunity to capitalize on these qualities and, in so doing, strengthen the entire program.

Team teaching is not a precise set of procedures and practices to be followed. It is an idea for grouping children, the implementation of which varies from school to school. It is interesting to note that in addition to regular teachers, the team usually includes other individuals. In Claremont, California (Dean, 1965), for instance, each team includes five to seven classroom teachers, an auxiliary teacher, a teacher aide, citizens with special skills and knowledge, and intern teachers. Each team has a leader who is either elected or appointed. All of these individuals are collectively responsible for the instruction of 150 to 200 pupils. While one teacher makes a presentation to a large group of children, the other team members may plan for or work with those children with special needs. The presence of the auxiliary teacher and the intern teachers makes it possible for all regular teacher members of the team to get together often in order to plan for instruction and evaluate pupil progress. At the same time, the teacher aide relieves the regular teachers from a variety of clerical chores that ordinarily take so much of their time.

Like all other innovative organizational plans, team teaching cannot succeed in meeting individual differences without at the same time changing the concept of teacher-role and the learning process. We have been too prone in the past to rely upon administrative devices with catchy names—nongraded, team teaching, ungraded—to section students into instructional groups, and then to carry on the same teacher-centered program under a new name. When the child is viewed as the chief instrument of his own learning, the teacher is no longer viewed as one whose duty it is to impart knowledge, and more haphazard grouping arrangements become possible.

Interschool Grouping

Systematic efforts to practice interschool grouping at the elementary school level are not as prevalent in the United States as they are in other countries, especially in a number of European countries. In England and Sweden, for example, where the secondary schools are divided into academic and vocational, children at eleven years of age are separated so that they can be educated according to the type of high school for which, supposedly, they are suited. The criterion for determining suitability is usually academic ability as evidenced through achievement scores. This pattern is changing, although not as fast as some educators and parents would like. The comprehensive nature of the American secondary school does not require any such specialization at the elementary level.

In the United States the only form of interschool grouping based on mental ability is that for the retarded children who definitely cannot profit from the regular classroom situation. School systems often establish a unit within the system to provide a special type of education for the slow learners. Attending special units are also children with severe physical handicaps.

There is little argument against special schools for children who cannot profit from the regular classroom situation. The inability, however, of a child to cope with a normal learning environment should be determined very carefully to avoid the phenomenon of special schools or classes becoming the dumping ground for children who are often educable, but who create a variety of problems for the regular teacher.

Another type of interschool grouping emerged recently within the ranks of the public school as a result of the *middle school* movement. The middle school is a new school unit that draws the sixth graders from several elementary schools and puts them together with seventh and eighth graders. "The main argument in favor of the middle school of grades five through eight," says Neil Nickerson (1966), "is that there is evidence that kids mature earlier now than they used to." Sixth graders, therefore, are too sophisticated to be grouped with children in the lower grades, while ninth graders are mature enough to join the upper grades of the secondary school.

It is too early to determine whether the middle school really makes any sense. Presently there is a considerable amount of excitement about it around the country, but there are those who look at this organizational scheme as no more than a reshuffling of grades. Responding to enthusiastic advocates of the middle school, Wayne Jennings (1967) made this point: "The key to better education is not slicing the pie differently, but in altering classroom practices, developing a curriculum significant for life and preparing competent staff." Another educator (Popper, 1970) said that the ". . . reasons for a 5–8 or a 6–8 middle school organization run the gamut from vulgar opportunism to claims of an earlier adolescent onset in the United States. Stubborn empirical evidence indicates, however, that claims of an earlier adolescent onset should be taken *cum grano salis*. Vulgar opportunism deserves to be treated as vulgar opportunism, and professional groups who take seriously their value commitment to client welfare should always treat it with contempt."

Looking at American education from a general perspective, one may recognize a form of interschool grouping in the existence of private schools. There is a 14 percent segment of the American student population that does not attend the public schools to which these children would normally belong; 95 percent of this segment of students attend parochial schools. The few remaining private schools exist for a variety of other reasons, such as homogeneity in terms of socioeconomic status and emphasis on college-oriented education.

Most of the religious schools are under the auspices of the Catholic Church—and the fate of Catholic education will, to a great extent, determine the fate of private education. In talking about the Catholic schools, Daniel McGarry (1965) wrote: "To put it simply, secularistic public education is constantly spreading, and by virtue of a tax-monopoly and resultant economic compulsion, it is forcing private education out of existence." Then McGarry goes on to point out that in the Catholic schools "Kindergarten is regularly abandoned, and there is talk all over the country of giving up the primary grades, perhaps all grades in the elementary level in our schools." Since 1965, McGarry has been proven to be correct; more and more parochial schools have limited their offerings or closed their doors altogether.

Undoubtedly the most significant, and certainly the most provocative, aspect of interschool grouping in American education has been the result of race differences and race relations in American communities. For hundreds of years black children, for example, have often been deprived of a good education by attending separate schools; as we pointed out in Chapter 1, the Supreme Court ruling of 1964 declared that separate education is *not* equal education. In the southern states there was *de jure* segregation while in the northern states there was *de facto* segregation. Both types of segregation are bad. "Whether it be blatant in the South or subtle in the North," wrote Francis Keppel (1964), "it saps and diminishes democracy and justice. Whether it exists by law or by custom, by edict or by tradition, by patterns of unemployment or patterns of housing, segregation hurts all children, Negro and white alike."

As part of the civil rights movement, during the last few years serious attempts were made to reduce school segregation. Thus far, the main objective of these efforts has been to bring together black and white children under the same roof and under the influence of the same educational conditions. As a result, two new types of interschool grouping emerged; on the one hand, children from the ghettos were bused to all-white neighborhood schools. On the other hand, new large schools were established in locations where they could attract students from a variety of racial and socioeconomic backgrounds. The latter plan became known as the "education park."

In writing about the education park concept as conceived in Pittsburgh, S. P. Marland, Jr. (1967) pointed out that "It addressed itself to the problems of racial, social, and economic integration by embracing a larger than conventional school service area, thereby reaching across historical boundaries that have separated children in disparate subcommunities."

In 1971, as the result of a Supreme Court ruling (see p. 7) busing began on a very large scale, with whites being bused to black schools and blacks to white. The suburbs, incidentally, have been little touched. As we pointed out in Chapter 1, parents, whether black or white, do not like the idea of their child being taken away from his neighborhood school to go to somebody else's neighborhood school. On the other hand, both groups, for the most part, recognize the benefits in terms of better social relations that integration can bring. As one white parent put it, "I want my child to be in touch with reality. All-white schools are artificial." The education park appears to be a promising solution to some problems of segregation; it involves busing large numbers of children, but to neutral territory. However, since present school plants will continue to function, it is only a limited solution for those systems needing to expand.

Parallel to this general effort to eliminate, or at least to reduce, school segregation there is a tendency on the part of the larger minority groups to seek out the establishment of separate schools that would be controlled entirely by them. Minorities such as the black, Hispanic, Chinese, and Indian feel that they have a culture of their own that ought to be preserved. They also feel that they have special needs that ought to be met through the schools which their children attend. One example of a separate minority school is the Rough Rock Demonstration School in the state of Arizona. Sanctioned by the United States government, this school is controlled and administered by a Navajo school board. One of the board members (Dick, 1968) characterized the school as follows: "In our school we are teaching two cultures. We are offering a choice between the modern way of life and the way of the Navajos in the years past and at the present time. We want to have the children make a choice from both sides. We're not saying, 'You must stay in the reservation and be as Navajos always have been before.' We are saying, 'We have the choice. You can learn both ways and be strong in both ways.' We're not saying, as in the past the government has said, that you can completely change into the way of the modern society."

Another plan for a school oriented toward the needs and the subculture of the people living in the inner-city was recently proposed in Seattle, Washington. The proposal envisions the development of a 3,000-student "Seattle Academy" that would help underachievers and enhance the educational opportunities for all youths from three years to twenty years of age. As the education editor (Angelos, 1968) of the *Seattle Times* wrote, "The proposal suggests: Development of specific academic, vocational, and academic-vocational goals, student-parent-community participation in teaching, strong home-school relations, including teachers visiting homes, teachers sensitive to inner-city problems." Even temporary living accommodations were recommended as a part of this plan for students "who cannot function in their home environment."

Suggestions for separate schools and more local community control are not free of criticism. As was stated recently in *The Journal of Negro Education* (Morsell, 1969), "The principal danger presented by proposals for 'community control' is that it may result in the 'balkanization' of a city system under such rigid conditions that integration becomes more, rather than less, difficult. This imposes a special and demanding responsibility upon those working to improve the schools by decentralization to see to it that integration prospects are *maximized*, not reduced, by whatever community district lines or overall criteria are adopted."

Apparently interschool grouping of children is a very sensitive and controversial topic at the present time. It is also one that deserves much attention because this country can no longer afford the inequalities that have existed up to this time.

Summary

For many years schools attempted to solve the problem posed by the individual differences of children through the implementation of a variety of grouping practices. Most of these practices are classified into two basic organizational schemata, the vertical and the horizontal. In the vertical organization the children are classified in groups on the basis of a high-low continuum, with the criterion usually being age, mental ability, or achievement. Horizontal grouping, usually, is done on the basis of interest and consists of forming subgroups that tend to be similar to the parent group from which they originate.

Included among the vertical types of grouping are ability grouping and the graded system. The graded system has been in practice for over one hundred years, but educators now realize that age is a very limited criterion for grouping children. Ability grouping is proving to be unsatisfactory because it stigmatizes the children in the lower ability groups and it tends to perpetuate existing unfair social stratifications.

A promising form of horizontal grouping is the multiage or multigrade grouping. In England, where it is known as family grouping, it has been advanced successfully to the point that it is receiving worldwide attention. The groups in school resemble natural groups of children outside of school, and the children learn by themselves and from each other under the guidance of the teacher.

A horizontal type of organization—with some elements of vertical organization—is the nongraded school. In many of the schools that have become nongraded, the grades have been reduced to two units, the primary and the intermediate. The concept of nongradedness has appealed to American educators, but it is not an easy concept to implement. As a result, there is difficulty in measuring how successful the nongraded school has been or will be.

Most of the grouping practices are of the intraschool type, but there are also interschool grouping practices, most of which have religious or racial bases. Various religious groups enroll children from the various neighborhood schools to which they would normally belong to teach them in a religious atmosphere. But parochial schools are being threatened because of inadequate finances; many have had to close. Communities across the nation are attempting to eliminate segregation and racism in education by bringing children of various races from all over the community to study together. The education park is one solution.

READING LIST 6

Beggs, D. W., III, & Buffie, E. G. (Eds.) *Nongraded schools in action.* Bloomington: Indiana University Press, 1967. The first part of this book is a discussion of the nongraded school from a theoretical point of view. The second part consists of reports from individual schools that use varying forms of nongraded organization.

Morgenstern, A. (Ed.) *Grouping in the elementary school.* New York: Pitman Publishing Corporation, 1966. A collection of articles dealing with ability grouping, team teaching, and nongraded grouping. The last part of the booklet includes articles dealing with the implications of grouping practices to the learner.

Rogers, V. R. (Ed.) *Teaching in the British primary school.* New York: The Macmillan Company, 1970. An anthology of papers written by British educators about their schools, including a paper by M. A. Mycock, "Vertical grouping in the primary school," and one by D. Skinner, "Cooperative and team teaching."

Westby-Gibson, D. *Grouping students for improved instruction.* Englewood Cliffs, N.J.: Prentice-Hall, 1966. This booklet briefly describes and discusses most of the grouping practices in the elementary school. It ends with practical suggestions for the implementation of these practices.

CHAPTER 7

Social Studies: The Subject in Transition

The United States of America, the country that has often been referred to as the Great Democracy of recent times, during the last few years has been experiencing serious difficulties, domestically as well as internationally. For a long time the multigroup character of American society was considered to be a blessing, but it is obvious now that it has become the source of almost uncontrollable friction and conflict. As is evidenced by the riots and other forms of violence that occur everyday, the tensions between various ethnic and social-class groups have reached a point that is alarming. In the international scene, the United States has done for, and has given to, the rest of the world more than any other country. Yet, what Americans receive in return is dislike, mistrust, and suspicion.

There is no doubt that as a nation we have failed somewhere in some respects. As educators involved to a great extent in the upbringing and education of the younger generation, we cannot help asking ourselves: Are we responsible in any way for the situation in which our society finds itself? Regardless of what the answer to this question may be, should we not do something to make our communities, our nation, the world a better, or even safer, place in which to live? How can we improve relationships among men?

Traditionally, social studies has been that part of the school program which was supposed to develop good citizens. As a matter of fact, until very recently *citizenship education* and *social studies* were used synonymously by many school systems across the nation, as if all other subjects or school experiences had nothing to do with the development of those human qualities that are necessary for good citizenship. But in view of the difficulties with which our society is plagued, it cannot be claimed that social studies has been effective. Indeed there are those who say that if our schools did not teach social studies at all, it would probably make no difference whatsoever as far as the quality of the behavior of those graduating from our schools is concerned.

The ineffectiveness of the social studies programs that were inherited from the past is also evident in the children's perception of this subject. A number of subject preference studies with elementary school children (Greenbladt, 1962; Herman, 1963; and Curry, 1963) find social studies ranking the lowest, or very low, as compared with all other subjects taught in the elementary school. The findings in these studies present an interesting phenomenon when contrasted with the findings in studies dealing with children's interests expressed in the form of spontaneous questions. While the youngsters indicated a dislike for the subject of social studies, the majority of their questions were related to topics and issues that normally fall within the domain of social studies. Rudman (1955), for example, discovered that children enrolled in grades four through eight were strongly concerned with fundamental problems of values, ethics, and behavior. They felt that they needed to find their place in the world in social, vocational, and spiritual terms.

Obviously, there is a need for a better social studies program. This need is being felt today in many responsible circles in our society, to the point that a movement of national dimensions has been initiated to bring about changes. Whatever the changes may be, their promise for the new generations will not be felt unless the classroom teachers cooperate with enthusiasm and a strong sense of mission. The main purpose of this chapter is to motivate the young teacher, as well as the older one, to become a missionary in the design and application of new social studies programs that will inspire hope for a better society. In order to accomplish this purpose, the status of traditional social studies programs will be described and critically evaluated. Major efforts to improve social studies will then be presented and contrasted. Finally, practical suggestions will be offered for the teacher.

Traditional Programs

Social studies programs can be identified through an examination of courses of study, curriculum bulletins, and teachers' guides. Systematic examinations of such sources reveal that social studies has not changed through the years. Richard F. Burns and Alexander Frazier (1957) found that during the 1950s, twenty-three large-city school systems in various parts of the country included the following general topics in their kindergarten through grade six social studies program;

Living in home and school
Living in the neighborhood
Living in the large community
Types of community life

Study of the local community
Study of the local state
Geographic or climatic regions of the world
United States history
United States geography
Then-and-now studies
Current history studies
American neighbors
Eurasia and Africa
Global geography

The first five of the above topics comprised the program of the first three grades in practically every city. The rest of the topics were included in the program of the three upper grades.

Another survey conducted later by D. L. Barnes (1960) listed the following topics as the ones more frequently taught in the various grades of the elementary school:

Grade 1: Family, Home, School
Grade 2: Community, Neighborhood, Community Helpers
Grade 3: Indians, Pioneers, Food, Shelter, Clothing, Transportation, Communication, Our City
Grade 4: The Local State or Regions
Grade 5: United States of America, Western Hemisphere
Grade 6: Old World, Other Nations, Eastern Hemisphere

More recent surveys are lacking, but one will not have to visit many schools to be convinced that the traditional scope and sequence is still with us.

In regard to the method of teaching social studies, one would be very safe to assume that in the majority of instances it is done through the use of one textbook. Needless to say, many textbooks leave much to be desired. As John Palmer (1965) wrote, "Too often, geography consists of 'learning inert facts about climate, topography and resources,' United States history includes a 'strong dose of patriotic indoctrination,' and civics deals with the structure of government but very little with the process." Another educator (Rogers, 1970) points out that "the majority of elementary classrooms (despite decades of criticism from Montessori to Dewey to Holt) are still dreadfully lacking in what might be called the raw materials of learning, i.e., things of all kinds that can be touched, examined, felt, handled, arranged, and rearranged."

Traditional Programs and Innovations

The social studies programs outlined above have been with us for a long time. Recently, however, they have been challenged—new trends and new programs have emerged that hopefully will change the present scene drastically, and for the better. It is difficult to predict how long this will take because the new programs are still in experimental stages and their implementation is limited. It will require a considerable amount of effort to bring them from the halls of innovation to the nation's class-rooms. How to accomplish change is one of the biggest problems facing professional educators today. Although they realize that the new trends in social studies must reach the classroom as soon as possible, they have not yet found the necessary detailed procedures.

Within this uncertainty, the only bright hope appears to be, as we have already mentioned, the teacher and the role she can play in the improvement of social studies. It does not make any difference how excited college professors may get about innovations and how many articles they may write (which are usually read by other professors). The final hope for spreading innovations rests with the teacher's willing-ness to accept them and her capability to implement them.

In order for teachers to develop this desire for change, they must become aware of and sensitive to the many deficiencies of the traditional programs. Teachers who have a feeling of dissatisfaction with the status quo most likely will be those who will reach out and try to benefit from innovations.

The Deficiencies of Traditional Programs

One of the major deficiencies of the traditional programs is the vagueness with which the objectives are stated. Usually they are flowery statements remotely related to what is being taught and almost impossi-ble to evaluate. Here are examples of such objectives: Makes worthy use of leisure time; develops democratic qualities; acquires sensitivity to the values of his (the child's) society; and there are others just as vague. Learning has been defined by psychologists as changes in behavior, but in the past there has often been no effort to pose general statements of objectives more specifically. What are the "democratic qualities" to be developed? Both the extreme right and the extreme left in this country argue for their own brand of "democratic qualities." And in some class-rooms, developing democratic attitudes has been equated with having the children vote on any classroom issues that arise.

Another important deficiency is related to the selection of specific content. Most study guides list topics to be studied. In some cases spe-cific suggestions are included in regard to the content of each topic, but in the majority of cases, it is expected that the content be determined by the teacher. No specific philosophy is stated as to the approach that should be used in the selection of this content. As a result the specifics represent a random collection of factual information that very often is not related to any broader concepts or ideas. For instance, there is an infinite number of facts that a child can learn about the policeman, a favorite topic for study in the first grade. Unless the teachers have some criteria on the basis of which to select a limited number of these facts, much time can be wasted. What difference does it make, as far as the child's behavior is concerned, to know the color of the policeman's uniform or the way in which he hangs his whistle or his gun? Whether the policeman is friend (as the schools teach) or foe (as some children feel) does make a difference and is an issue that should be dealt with. Facts are important, but their teaching should be justified in terms of their relationship to some major understanding.

A third deficiency is the oversimplified nature of the content, especially in the primary grades. Several studies (Kaltsounis, 1964; Smith and Cardinell, 1964; and Foster, 1965) have shown that most of the things taught to children are already known to them prior to instruction. The reason for this deficiency appears to be the widespread use of the *expanding horizons* or *expanding environment* approach in the selection and grade placement of social studies content. In an attempt to have children proceed from the nearest to the farthest and from the known to the unknown, the expanding environment approach put geographic limits to the primary grades program and discouraged depth studies. Children are expected to study the local community in isolation from the rest of the world and in an oversimplified descriptive manner.

Still another deficiency of the present programs is their nonrealistic character, well reflected in a popular song for which the lyrics were written by Tom Paxton, "That's What I Learned in School," (1962). When a little boy is asked what he learned in school today, he replies that he has been told about the existence of truth, justice, freedom, and plenty in America. We can no longer continue ignoring the conditions of our society or misrepresenting it to children in this way. It is true, for example, that this country is an affluent one, but it is also true that millions of people in this country are very poor and thousands of children go to bed hungry. Until very recently textbook writers portrayed their characters living in Cape Cod–style houses even though not all children in our society are fortunate enough to live in such houses.

It is rather obvious at the present time that our society has problems, but we keep on teaching in school as if nothing is wrong. Apparently the values that people hold are in conflict with one another, but we do not talk about such things in our schools. Teachers acting under pressure avoid any topic or issue that in any way might touch upon values. As Bruce Joyce (1967) pointed out, " 'Race relations' are not found in the index, nor are 'strike' or 'air pollution' or 'aid to dependent children.' The language in these books does not include the language of the streets [or black English], and the people do not include prostitutes, drunkards, or dope addicts."

One reason for the deficiency just presented may be found in a fifth deficiency of the present social studies programs. Traditionally, social studies has been and still continues to be history-oriented. As a result, the past received and is receiving more emphasis than the present under what appears to be a false pretense. As Clegg and Schomberg (1968) pointed out, "The often professed purpose of history is its assumed relationship to the task of training for citizenship." These writers challenge this assumption, however, by following it with the observation that "the teaching of it [history] continues to be, for the most part, the recitation of the narrative of the American past with little or no connection with the current or the future tasks expected of the citizen." There is no doubt that our world is a different world from that of the past. In order for children to understand it, they need information and insights from all social science disciplines along with those they get from history. And they need a history that is relevant to contemporary problems.

A sixth deficiency of social studies, as practiced in the past and as is still practiced in many elementary schools, is its tendency to be centered too much around America and the Western world. It is true there are a number of cultural imperatives that children in any society should acquire, but in these times of close interdependence the rest of the world should not be ignored.

Still another deficiency is the inadequate development in children of those intellectual powers needed to perceive and understand today's world—its conditions, problems, and issues. "The chief criticism of current social studies teaching is," wrote the late Hilda Taba (1967a), "that it is descriptive, that it is concerned exclusively with the accumulation of descriptive facts which are highly obsolescent, are not readily retained, and if retained, are retained only for a short period." The accumulation of knowledge alone is not enough, because knowledge changes. Mere description of social phenomena is not adequate, because it is the understanding of the causes of these phenomena and a commitment to play a positive role in the society that stimulate action.

There is definitely a need for emphasis on the development of the creative abilities of the youngsters. Analysis of actual social studies teaching situations and careful examination of social studies instructional materials leave no doubt that this is not being done adequately at the present. The blame for this situation cannot be thrown entirely on the teachers' shoulders, but, we say again, they are the ones who can make the difference. Are they equipped to cope with what is logically expected of them? One study (Weber, 1965) attempted to find out the extent to which teachers understand learning theory. One hundred and fifty-six teachers from twenty different schools were asked: "What is your understanding of the nature of the learning process; how, in your opinion, do children learn?" The answers (single answers in the majority) fell into six major categories as follows: (1) by drill and repetition, 45 percent; (2) by imitating others, 38 percent; (3) do not know, had not thought about it, 33 percent; (4) by hard work, 26 percent; (5) by following teachers' directions, 21 percent; and (6) by trial and error, 17 percent. There was very little mention, if any, of motivation, goals, transfer of learning, meaningful experiences, discovery, and similar concepts most popular in modern learning theory.

Finally, it must be stressed that in the past social studies fell short because it ignored the affective domain of the child. The emphasis has been on the accumulation of knowledge without any regard for the values of the child that dictate how he perceives reality and how he uses the knowledge he has accumulated. What values children possess is not clear; as a matter of fact it is not quite clear what values *are*. Social studies programs have been lacking in opportunities that would enable children to explore and evaluate their own inner world.

Projects That Have Marked New Directions

The deficiencies of the traditional social studies programs have been spelled out in considerable detail not to present a gloomy picture but, as we have stressed, to convince the preservice and the in-service teachers that there is a need and time for change. The purpose of this section is to demonstrate that the change has already started and that the new directions are quite visible on the horizon. For those who wish to move ahead there is plenty of inspiration and support.

Many have said that social studies today is in a status of ferment. In the sixties, forward-looking school people, social scientists, and learning psychologists joined forces and moved forward with unprecedented determination to stamp out deficiencies and bring about improvement in the social studies programs. Private organizations and the federal government spent considerable amounts of money to support innovative projects in social studies. Professional organizations such as the American Economic Association, The American Association of Geographers and National Council of Geographic Education, the American Anthropological Association, and others sponsored projects for the betterment of the social studies programs in all of the precollege levels of the educative process as they had never done in the past. Social studies was very much a part of the curriculum reform movement in which subject-matter specialists and professional educators joined forces to strengthen the scholarly content of the curriculum.

There were all kinds of projects under way. Some of them designed comprehensive programs for grades kindergarten through twelve. Others were limited to a fewer number of grades, and still others concentrated on only one discipline. According to John Goodlad (1966), the most outstanding of these projects had been planned to accomplish the following:

1. To redefine the scope and goals of the social studies curriculum.
2. To develop techniques and materials to achieve these goals.
3. To submit newly created materials to a sequence of experimentation, evaluation, and revision.
4. To disseminate the materials and relevant information.

The projects in operation in the seventies that appear to be the most promising for the elementary school, and the individuals who have directed them or are still directing them, are included in the list below:

1. Raymond English, The Greater Cleveland Social Science Program, Educational Research Council of Greater Cleveland, Rockefeller Building, 614 W. Superior Avenue, Cleveland, Ohio (to be referred to from here on as the Greater Cleveland Project).
2. Lawrence Senesh, Elkhart, Indiana, Experiment in Economic Education (1–12), Department of Economics, Purdue University, Lafayette, Indiana (Senesh Project). Professor Senesh recently moved to the University of Colorado.
3. The late Hilda Taba, Curriculum Development Project, San Francisco State College, 1600 Holloway Avenue, San Francisco, California (Taba Project).
4. Edith West, Preparation and Evaluation of Social Studies Curriculum, College of Education, University of Minnesota, Minneapolis, Minnesota (Minnesota Project).
5. Ronald Lippitt, Robert Fox, and Lucille Schaible, Behavioral Science Project. Developed at the University of Michigan and distributed commercially by Science Research Associates (Lippitt and Fox Project).
6. Jerome Bruner, Man: A Course of Study, Educational Development Center, Newton, Massachusetts (EDC Project).

With the exception of the Lippitt and Fox and the EDC projects, all of the above have developed or are in the process of completing the development of materials for grades kindergarten through six. The Lippitt and Fox Project consists of seven units. These were designed to be used as a one-year program or they may be plugged in at any time during the third- to seventh-grade programs with the exception of the first unit, which is the introduction to the methods of social sciences and should be taught first. The EDC Project appears to have started as a sequential program for grades one through twelve, but it ended as a one-year program for the fifth or sixth grade of the elementary school. Occasionally it is being used in the fourth grade as well as in the junior high school grades.

All of the programs are being tried out experimentally throughout the nation. Some of them are being produced commercially. Specifically, the Greater Cleveland Project is being published by Allyn & Bacon. The Senesh and the Lippitt and Fox projects are available through Science Research Associates. The Taba Project is published by Addison-Wesley Publishing Company. For more details on these and other newly developed programs the reader should refer to a special review in the April 1970 issue of *Social Education*.

The chart on pages 144–147 provides a comparative view of the scope and sequence of the six projects mentioned and points out the differences between these new programs and the traditional social studies program.

The common characteristics of the new programs will be identified and elaborated on in the section that follows. Certain procedures, however, used by all projects should be mentioned at this point. As a rule, all of them relied on social scientists to decide what is worth teaching. They all consider the use of one textbook inadequate and they are producing a variety of materials to be used with the children. Learning psychologists and media experts have been consulted systematically in the production of the instructional materials. Finally, the materials developed are or will be field-tested and revised on the basis of the feedback received.

The Trends in Elementary Social Studies As Dictated by the Projects

An examination of the comparative chart of the scope and sequence of the projects reveals that there are differences from one project to the other. Regardless of these apparent differences, however, a close examination of all the projects verifies the existence of a number of underlying common characteristics. These characteristics actually represent the majority of the trends in elementary social studies education today, and

A Comparative Chart of the Scope and Sequence of the Traditional
Elementary Social Studies Program and the Programs Produced by
Six Major Current Social Studies Projects

Grade	Traditional Program	Minnesota Program	Greater Cleveland Program
K	Home School	The Earth as the home of man A world of many people Our global earth A home of varied resources Man changes the earth	Learning about our world Children in other lands
1	Our families, home, and schools Work and play Pets Farm Holidays	Families around the world Hopi family Chippewa family Quechua family Japanese family	Learning about our country Explorers and dis- coverers: Balboa, Byrd, Columbus, Cook, Cousteau, DeSoto, Glenn, and others
2	Helpers in the community The Post Office Firemen, Dairy, Bakery, Gro- cery store	Families around the world Boston family in early 18th century Soviet family in urban Moscow Hausa family in Nigeria Kibbutz family in Israel Urban family in Paris	Communities at home and abroad Our community The aborigines of Central Australia The Eskimos of Barrow, Alaska A historical community (Williamsburg, Va.) A military community (Fort Bragg, N.C.) An apple-growing com- munity (Yakima, Wash.) A forest-products com- munity (Crossett, Ark.) A steelmaking commu- nity (Pittsburgh, Pa.) A rural community (Webster City, Iowa)
3	The town or local community Food, clothing, shelter, com- munication, transporta- tion, Indians, pioneers	Communities around the world Rural and urban communities An American frontier community Paris community Manus community	The making of Anglo- America The metropolitan commu- nity (Historical study of an imaginary city) Cleveland: A metropolitan community Boston and Brockton: A metropolitan com- munity

Taba Program	Senesh Program	Lippitt and Fox and EDC Programs

Our school
  School plant, friends,
    school workers, trans-
    portation, activities,
    composition
Family living
  Structure, composition,
    work, income, values,
    transportation
	Families at work
	  Getting to know the
	    family
	  Families are alike
	  Families are different
	  How do families pro-
	    duce, etc.	

Services in the super-
  market
Construction workers and
  materials, utilities,
  suppliers, store
  workers
Services in our community
  Business, government,
  other community
  workers
	Neighbors at work
	  What is a neighbor-
	    hood?
	  Types of neighborhoods
	  Institutions guided by
	    prices and profit
	  Institutions guided by
	    general welfare
	  Dynamics of the neigh-
	    borhood
	  School: Threshold to
	    the world
		The Lippitt and Fox Pro-
		gram, designed for
		one year or as a
		supplementary pro-
		gram throughout
		Grades 3 to 7,
		includes the follow-
		ing seven units:
		1. Learning to use
		   social sciences
		2. Discovering differ-
		   ences
		3. Friendly and un-
		   friendly behavior
		4. Being and becoming
		5. Individual & group
		6. Deciding & doing
		7. Influencing each
		   other

Nonliterate of Africa
People of the hot dry lands
The boat people of
    Hong Kong
The people of Switzerland
	Cities at work
	  The problems of the
	    city and other as-
	    pects of city life.
	    What can be done to
	    solve these problems
	    through individual
	    groups, and through
	    the political process	

A Comparative Chart of the Scope and Sequence of the Traditional
Elementary Social Studies Program and the Programs Produced by
Six Major Current Social Studies Projects

Grade	Traditional Program	Minnesota Program	Greater Cleveland Program

4	Our State
	Type regions
	Contrasting
	  communities
	  in the U.S.
	Exploration and
	  pioneer days
		Our own community
		A community in the
		  Soviet Union
		A Trobriand Islander
		  community
		Indian village south of
		  Himalayas
			The story of agriculture
			The story of industry
			India: a society in
			  transition

5	United States—
	  past & present
	Western Hemi-
	  sphere
		The U.S. of America
		  Overview
		  Sequent occupance
		  Local area
		  Representative
		    cities
		Canada
		  Overview
		  Case studies of
		    regions
		Latin America
		  Overview
		  Sequent occupance
		  Buenos Aires
		  Cuzco
		  Etc.
			Human Adventure
			  Part I—Ancient
			    Civilization
			  Part II—Four World
			    Views (China, India,
			    Israel, Greece)
			  Part III—The Classical
			    World of Greece and
			    Rome
			  Part IV—Medieval
			    Civilization
			  The Middle East

6	Old World
	Western Hemi-
	  sphere
	Eastern Hemi-
	  sphere
		Indian America
		Colonization of North
		  America
		Revolutionary America
		Westward expansion
		Civil War and recon-
		  struction
			Part V—Rise of
			  Modern Civilization
			  in the West
			Part VI—New World
			  and Eurasian Cultures
			Part VII—Empires
			  and Revolutions
			Part VIII—The Coming
			  of World Civilization
			Latin America

they can serve as guidelines in the development, evaluation, or revision
of a social studies program. We do not mean to give the impression, of
course, that all questions and problems in social studies have been resolved by the projects presented.

Taba Program	Senesh Program	Lippitt and Fox and EDC Programs
California		
An interdisciplinary treatment of California at the present time		
		The EDC Program, known as Man: A Course of Study, is a one-year program suitable for the fifth or sixth grade. There are occasions in which it has been used in the fourth as well as in the junior high school grades. The program attempts to answer the following general questions:
Anglo-America		
The dynamic character of America through the study of history, her people, and social, political and economic conditions today		
	Professor Senesh is in the process of developing the program for the fourth, fifth, and sixth grades.	1. What is human about human beings? 2. How did they get that way? 3. How can they be made more so?
		These fundamental questions about the nature of man are introduced by way of animal contrasts.
Latin America		
Generalizations such as the following are developed:		Units include the life cycle of the salmon, the herring gull, and baboon behavior. The last unit investigates the concept of culture through a study of the Netsilik Eskimo.
Civilizations change when they meet a new culture.		
The types of people a country has give a nation its unique features.		
Change in one important aspect of a country's way of life usually brings about other changes, etc.		

The common characteristics of the various projects, identified and classified according to their relevancy to the objectives, content, teaching strategies, evaluation, and in-service education for teachers, are as follows:

Objectives

1. *There is an attempt to bring about a balance between cognitive, affective, and skills areas.* Programs in the past have been mostly oriented toward the cognitive domain of the individual and particularly toward the accumulation of factual information. As we have already pointed out, value-loaded topics and issues were avoided. The new projects, though still favoring the cognitive domain, include the treatment of important controversial issues and the development in children of such important qualities as sensitivity to human problems, objectivity in the examination of social conditions, and a desire to arrive rationally at the acceptance or development of a number of values. Skills are also important in the new projects, especially those needed to acquire new knowledge as well as to apply knowledge already possessed.

2. *There is an emphasis on autonomous thinking, creativity, and the method of inquiry.* We live in a complex civilization in which it is difficult for the individual to find his place. Preparing oneself for participation in the life of the present society is a long effort that requires a considerable amount of concentration. Many changes are taking place in the society, and an abundance of new knowledge becomes available and necessary for effective life while much of the old knowledge becomes outdated. It has been said that half of what man knew fifty years ago is now obsolete, while half of what he knows now will be obsolete a few years from now. The individual should be able to acquire new knowledge, discard that which becomes useless, and come up with new cognitive syntheses with which to direct his behavior and adjust himself to the rapid changes. In other words, the individual needs to develop into a good decision maker. To do this, he must be creative and capable of exercising autonomous thinking and the skills of inquiry.

3. *Purposes of all activities in the program are clearly defined.* Some units and some activities have become, for many teachers, so sacred that they are continued in the social studies program regardless of the fact that the purpose for which they were originally initiated is no longer valid. In teaching about the grocery store, for example, teachers used to build a corner grocery store to familiarize children with the general arrangement of the store. In some classrooms this practice still continues in spite of the fact that today the family car makes it possible for the child to study the arrangement of a real grocery store (probably a supermarket) at least once or twice a week, and over a period of several years prior to going to school.

The new projects attempted to achieve clarity in objectives by stating them in terms of observable behaviors to be achieved by the children. Not all projects, of course, achieved this goal to the same degree.

Experiences such as the one pictured here, where children are seeing a metal sculptor at work, provide the "raw materials of learning" so lacking in many classrooms. The experience is one that will give children perspective not only on new art media, but also on ways in which creative young people are making a living and building a life style that offers an alternative to the mainstream of American culture. It is living the "social studies." Photo by Zita Lichtenberg, State Office of Public Instruction, Olympia, Washington.

Map making in the new social studies is no longer related only to geography; economics and ecology also play a part. Plotting the natural resources of a region is the first step toward finding out how man is using—and misusing—those resources. Photo by Zita Lichtenberg, State Office of Public Instruction, Olympia, Washington.

Content

4. *The social studies content is dictated by the structure of the disciplines.* Every social science discipline, like any discipline, has a number of logically interrelated fundamental ideas that represent the cutting edge of knowledge. These ideas in a discipline constitute what is referred to as the *structure* of that discipline. (All new curricula developed in the sixties emphasized structure, a key idea in curriculum reform.) Not all social scientists necessarily agree on the exact number or the exact nature of the basic ideas, but in order for the structure to be sound, a good number of them should accept the same ideas as being the most basic ones in their discipline. The following ideas represent, for example, the structure of sociology as seen by a number of sociologists (Senesh, 1967):

1. Values and norms are the main sources of energy to individuals and society.
2. Societies' values and norms shape social institutions, which are embodied in organizations and groups where people occupy positions and roles.
3. People's positions and roles affect their attitudes toward society's values and norms and result either in support of the existing values and norms or in demands for modification of them, and the circle starts again.

The structure of the social science disciplines is proving to be very valuable in curriculum development. It serves as the basic source from which the social studies content is drawn. Furthermore, it is useful in judging the value of any learning experience in terms of the contributions it makes to the development of some basic idea. Facts to be taught are no longer selected indiscriminately; they are selected on the basis of their relatedness to a particular idea.

The new social studies projects claim that programs built around the structure of the disciplines are less superficial, and, therefore, more challenging to the children. The program assumes more continuity from grade to grade, because the same basic concepts and generalizations are developed spirally as the child becomes familiar with more settings from which he draws illustrations for the concepts and generalizations. In addition, emphasizing the basic elements of an area of knowledge makes that area become more comprehensible for children. Finally, the structuring of factual information around basic ideas facilitates the retention of that information for a longer period of time.

Needless to say, as a result of the importance placed upon the structure of the disciplines, social scientists played an active role in the determination of the content included in the new projects.

5. *The social studies content is interdisciplinary or multidisciplinary.* The main purpose of the social studies in the elementary school is not to make all children little social scientists, but to give them a comprehensive understanding of their society, and to assist them to become well-functioning members of that society. Neither history nor geography alone can accomplish this. Political science, anthropology, sociology, economics, social psychology, and even philosophy are needed to make whatever contributions they can so that the children will gain insights into the conditions, issues, and problems of the present society.

It is obvious from the new projects that it is not necessary to stress all disciplines equally at all times. Some topics call for the emphasis of one discipline more than others. The Minnesota Project, for example, emphasizes geography in kindergarten and fifth grade, anthropology in the first, second, and third grades, economics in the fourth grade, and history in the sixth grade. In the Senesh Project this phenomenon is referred to as the "orchestrated curriculum." Depending upon the nature of the topic under consideration, one discipline plays the solo while the others fill in from the background.

6. *The content of the new programs is social-reality oriented.* The need for a realistic treatment of our society has been expressed earlier in this chapter. It is most encouraging that the new projects have already moved in this direction. As a result, the case study approach and the problems approach have become very popular. An examination of the materials of the new projects reveals that the purpose of the new social studies is not to idealize our society, but to analyze it and understand it. One particular project went so far as to use the lives of actual people living in the city of Chicago in order to describe life in the big city.

Fractions of the public object to this approach, because they apparently feel that romanticizing our society builds devotion and love for it. On the other hand, they feel that realistic and critical evaluation of the society might undermine the children's confidence in qualities traditionally considered superior. The spirit of the projects contradicts this position and supports the view that our society can stand and should undergo critical analysis. Our youngsters should know the real nature of the society in which they live, if they are to develop into members contributing toward the perpetuation and improvement of that society.

7. *Values and value-loaded issues and topics are a part of the social studies content.* The American society is a pluralistic one and each group has its own interests and values. Traditionally, values were considered to be a private matter and they were not included in the school program. As we have pointed out, however, one of the fundamental ideas of sociology claims that "values and norms are the main sources of energy to individuals and society." As such, they cannot be ignored. The Minnesota Project goes so far as to give a list of values to be developed. Other projects deal systematically with value-loaded issues and topics in order to develop in children the valuing process rather than any specific set of values.

8. *The new programs provide for a world view with more emphasis on the non-Western world than previously.* In selecting their content, the new projects have not been limited by such concepts as the expanding environment approach. Even at the kindergarten and first-grade levels the children go far beyond their own immediate environment—for instance, children study the concept of family by comparing the nature of their own families with that of selected families around the world and at different times. Usually families from cultures much different from our own are selected. The same approach is used when the children study the community in the third grade.

A quick look at the scope and sequence chart of the various projects verifies that elementary school children are exposed to a worldwide view, not only through the comparative study approach in the lower grades, but also through the systematic study of various cultural regions in the fourth, fifth, and sixth grades. The Greater Cleveland Project, for example, introduces the study of India in the fourth grade and the study of such diverse civilizations as the Chinese, Judaic, and Greek in the fifth grade.

Teaching Strategies

9. *There is an emphasis on learning through reflection.* "Learning through reflection" is a term opposite to "learning through rote memory" and encompasses a number of approaches to teaching as well as a number of skills and abilities to be developed in children. By *reflection* is meant going beyond the simple awareness of social phenomena and situations into the task of formulating hypotheses and theories on the basis of observable data and then discovering relationships between these data.

Among the teaching approaches emphasizing learning through reflection are inductive teaching, problem-solving approach, discovery approach, pupil-oriented teaching, inquiry, and others. Chapter 3 discusses such approaches in some detail. The skills and abilities involved in all of these approaches are several and have been organized and classified in many different ways. Hilda Taba (1967b) grouped them in three major cognitive tasks, as she called them, as follows:

Task I: Concept formation:
  1. Enumerating and listing, differentiating
  2. Grouping by identifying common properties
  3. Labeling and categorizing
Task II: Interpretation of data:
  1. Identifying points
  2. Explaining items of information, relating points to each other
  3. Making inferences, going beyond what is given
Task III: Application of principles:
  1. Predicting consequences, explaining unfamiliar phenomena, hypothesizing
  2. Explaining, supporting the predictions and hypotheses
  3. Verifying the predictions

The reader will be interested in comparing the Taba point of view of how children acquire knowledge with that of Piaget presented in Chapter 2.

10. *The textbook is being replaced by a variety of materials and teaching techniques.* A social studies lesson is no longer expected to consist of a textbook reading session. The classroom is now becoming exciting. The superficial, uninteresting, too often boring textbook is being replaced by real-life persistent social problems that concern everyone and make the news of the day. Films, filmstrips, still pictures, records, models, plays, dances, maps, stories, games, and visits to appropriate parts of the community are used to provide the supporting data for the development of concepts and generalizations. In an attempt to stimulate children's higher levels of thinking, questioning has become a highly sophisticated matter. Case study and independent study are prevalent in the new projects and provide stimulation and challenge, especially for the advanced student. "Using inquiry approaches . . ." says Turner (1970), "implies, at least to some, the use of rather extensive information, resource banks as well as a wide variety of multi-media."

11. *The valuing process is stressed along with the cognitive processes.* If social studies instruction is to have any effect upon the child's behavior, the development of attitudes, commitments, and values is just as important as the development of the cognitive processes. As Raths, Harmin, and Simon (1966) pointed out, values were developed in the past by setting an example, by persuading and convincing, by limiting choices, by inspiring via dramatic or emotional pleas, by rules and regulations, by cultural and religious dogma, and by appeals to conscience. But, as two of the staff members of the Minnesota Project (West & Gardner, n.d.) wrote, "It is unwise to develop an unthinking acceptance of values; lack of understanding of the implications of values may lead both to rejection of them completely when they are in temporary conflict or to retention of them when they may no longer be useful because of changes in society."

The most accepted trend today as far as values are concerned is not to develop in children a particular set of values, but to apply a process through which the children will be able to clarify, reorganize, and develop their own values. In order to understand this process, one must realize that each topic chosen to be studied in social studies consists of two elements that could be labeled as *cognitive* and *affective*. The cognitive element consists of the concepts and generalizations that can be developed through an appeal to actual data. The affective element of a topic consists of the controversial issues related to that topic. Resolution of these issues depends only partly on actual data. What is in the minds and hearts of people is just as important if the issue is to be resolved in any way. In some cases individuals are not aware of what it is that makes them take a particular position. The forces that direct them could be in the subconscious.

During the past, social studies ignored controversial issues, but such avoidance does not make sense if the function of social studies is to prepare individuals to make rational decisions as members of the society. Recently, a process dealing with controversial issues emerged that helps children bring out their feelings and values, examine them in the light of evidence, reorganize them, and sometimes reject them. The steps involved in this process are as follows:

1. State the issue in the form of an unresolved, open-ended question. Example: What should be done about poverty in our community, city, country?
2. Have the children suggest alternative solutions.
3. List and carefully examine with the children the consequences of each alternative.
4. Now that the children have examined all possible consequences, ask them to make and defend individual decisions as to the best way to resolve the issue. Obviously, there are no right or wrong answers in this type of deliberation.

It should be emphasized that the most significant reward in dealing with controversial issues, as suggested above, is not the answers at which the children arrive, but the opportunities that they get to bring out their feelings about a particular issue and evaluate those feelings in light of the facts surrounding the issue. The more we deliberately encourage this process in schools, the more chance there is to move toward decisions that are based on reason rather than on emotions and narrow interests.

Evaluation

12. *The new projects provide (though not all of them adequately) for the evaluation of pupil progress as well as the continuous evaluation of the programs themselves.* The teaching act involves a constant interaction between pupils, the teacher, and the program. The teacher attempts to affect the pupils, and the pupils react by changing their behavior or by resisting change in an active or a passive way. The program, which consists of the content, its organization, and the way of presenting it, is good only if it helps the teacher to effect in children predetermined changes. If the program falls short of this, it should be revised and revised again until it accomplishes exactly what it is supposed to accomplish.

Obviously, the clear definition of the changes to be achieved is very important. Without clear objectives neither is evaluation of pupil progress possible nor can meaningful feedback for the evaluation of the program be obtained. We should point out that not all new projects fare equally in this respect. Some of them have delineated their objectives much more clearly than others.

The testing or evaluation of the new projects has not yet been completed. Actually, no project has been perfected to the point that it can be recommended for wholesale adoption by school systems across the country. Testing and evaluation of the designs and materials developed by the projects should continue.

In-Service

13. *The implementation of all new programs requires extensive in-service work on the part of the teacher.* This is necessary because both the content and methodology of the new programs are quite different from those of the past. The Taba and EDC projects in particular demand a systematic in-service program prior to implementation. In-service at the initial stages should consist of two parts: (1) the development in teachers of a desire for change; and (2) an understanding of what the new program is or ought to be.

14. *In-service should be thought of as a regular and continuous program.* A new program might initially appear to be suitable for a particular school or district from a theoretical point of view, but its actual quality cannot be determined until it is possible to view the program in the light of feedback from the classroom. The teachers who are involved in the implementation of the program should meet regularly to iron out difficulties and consider ways to improve the program.

Change and the Role of the Teacher

A group of experts in social studies education and the social sciences (Sowards, 1963) agreed, early in the sixties, that "The upgrading of the social studies curriculum is ultimately dependent on teachers who can bring intelligence, human values, literacy in the content fields of history and the social sciences and a lively inventiveness to the act of teaching." The various social studies projects gave rise to the numerous trends that were presented in the preceding section of this chapter, but it is only the teacher who can bring these trends into the classroom and make their impact felt on the social studies programs now practiced.

At the same time, however, we should recognize that it is not easy for the teacher to jump on the bandwagon of change. As we have earlier pointed out, the change has been of considerable proportions and it came too fast. Teachers are asked to teach anthropological concepts, but they never had a course in anthropology. They are asked to help children analyze contemporary society, but all they had when they went to college were some introductory courses in history and physical geography. They are asked to implement complicated learning theories, but all they have been exposed to were some abstract definitions on the process of how human beings learn.

It is obvious that at this particular stage of transition, and even considerable confusion, the teacher needs assistance at the preservice as well as the in-service stages. The purpose of the last section of this chapter is to provide some concrete suggestions on how a teacher can implement the new trends in the classroom.

In the first place a teacher should develop a philosophical point of view as to what social studies should be and what function it should serve. The Committee on National Assessment of American Education (Campbell and Nichols, 1968) made the proposal that seventeen-year-old pupils should have reached the following objectives:

1. Show concern for the welfare and dignity of others
2. Support constitutional rights and liberties of all individuals
3. Help maintain law and order
4. Know the main structure and functions of our governments
5. Seek school and community improvement through active democratic participation
6. Understand problems of international relations
7. Support rationality in communication, thought, and action on school and community problems
8. Take responsibility for their own personal development and excellence

A teacher should be able to evaluate intelligently a statement of objectives like this, and to defend it or reject it in its totality or in part on the basis of her own views on social studies. Furthermore, she should be able to interpret such objectives into more specific behaviors.

Having a philosophical point of view will provide direction for the teacher in other, more specific, tasks that she usually has to undertake.

Most likely a teacher will have to follow the framework of a program already adopted or developed by her district or school. As a result, her first step will be to determine what general area is to be taught during a particular year. Whether this area of study is the community, the United States, South America, or Africa south of the Sahara, the teacher must study it thoroughly in order to be able to divide it into five or six major units that will provide a comprehensive coverage of the entire area. Unit topics related to current conditions, problems, and issues are usually preferred, because they deal with situations in which the children will be called upon in the future, as citizens, to make decisions.

The next step will be to select for each unit a limited number of fundamental ideas or generalizations that can serve as the basic elements around which the units will be developed. The generalizations are usually borrowed from the social sciences and they are statements of relationship that have broad applicability. Social scientists and educators have made available a number of sources in which the teachers can find generalizations; among these sources are:

1. Bernard Berelson and Gary A. Steiner. *Human behavior: An inventory of scientific findings.* New York: Harcourt Brace Jovanovich, 1964.
2. John Jarolimek. *Social studies in elementary education,* 3d ed. New York: The Macmillan Company, 1967, pp. 444–447.
3. John U. Michaelis and A. Montgomery Johnston (Eds.). *The social sciences: Foundations of the social studies.* Boston: Allyn & Bacon, 1965.
4. Raymond H. Muessig and Vincent R. Rogers (Eds.). *Social science seminar series,* six volumes. Columbus, Ohio: Charles E. Merrill Publishing Co., 1965.

Along with the generalizations, the teacher should also attempt to identify the controversial issues related to each unit. These issues, usually ignored in the past, need to be dealt with just as much as the generalizations. Experience shows that the treatment of controversial issues brings the teaching of a social studies unit to life.

In order to provide an illustration for the suggestions made thus far, let us assume that a fifth-grade teacher is expected by her district to teach about the United States. After a considerable amount of reading on the subject, she decides to deal with the following units: (1) Family Development in the United States, (2) Social Structure in the United States, (3) Economic Development in the United States, (4) Political Development in the United States, and (5) United States and the World. Her next step will be to find a number of appropriate generalizations and controversial issues to serve as the basic structural elements for each one of the units.

The following are some generalizations that she could borrow from one of the sources above (Berelson & Steiner) to provide the structure for the first unit, Family Development in the United States:

> Across societies the father is more likely to provide material support and at least *de jure* authority within the family and the mother is more likely to provide affection and moral support. (Berelson and Steiner, p. 314) [However, in the case of poor black families where the existing,

still racist structure of society makes it impossible for the father to function in the traditional role, the mother assumes the burden of both functions.]

The greater the social heterogeneity to which the family is subjected, the weaker its own internal integrations, especially with regard to the extended family. (Berelson and Steiner, p. 315)

The more social movement by family members—geographical, occupational, socioeconomic, educational, religious—the weaker the family ties and the less the family's contributions to the maintenance of social positions. (Berelson and Steiner, p. 315)

The rise of industrialization affects the family: it undermines and finally disintegrates relatively tight and large groupings in simple societies, shifts the distribution of power within the nuclear family, and changes marital patterns. (Berelson and Steiner, p. 397)

The controversial issues could include such questions as the following:

1. Should the state or the family have more to say on the kind and amount of education a child should get?
2. Should the state guarantee a basic income for each family?
3. Whose responsibility is it to care for the aged? for the poor? for the unemployed?
4. Should parents be held responsible for the delinquency of their children?

Of course the generalizations and the controversial questions stated are too abstract, too general, and certainly too difficult for the fifth graders to grasp, as they are. The next step, therefore, should be to reduce the generalizations and controversies to more specific objectives related to three of the child's domains: the cognitive, the affective, and skills. The cognitive objectives will be in the form of concepts—words or phrases that represent a group of objects or ideas with common characteristics—as well as in the form of subgeneralizations—small-order relationships related specifically to the development of the family in the United States. The affective objectives will include attitudes, interests, values, and the like. The skills will consist of intellectual as well as social skills.

Continuing the illustration, we suggest some of the subgeneralizations to which the above generalizations can be reduced.

While theoretically the father continues to be the head of the family, the plurality of the American society has created a variety of family types.

The rise of industrialization in the United States caused the extended family, with its close ties between the members, to break down, and subsequently created the nuclear family, now under attack for its failure to produce emotionally stable offspring.

The important concepts in the same unit would include extended family, nuclear family, family of orientation, family of procreation, kinship, and other concepts present in the subgeneralizations and unfamiliar to the children. Alternatives to the nuclear family as represented by the Israeli Kibbutz, the Chinese Commune, and American Communes would be examined. Among the affective objectives the following could be included: an opportunity will be provided for the child to express his feelings about the institution of family; the child will be guided to accept certain roles and responsibilities as a member of a family; the child will be guided to exhibit a desire to know more about what makes a secure family, and will be given opportunities to express his feelings about the family as a basic socializing unit. Finally, the skills could consist of getting along with others, and the various intellectual and study skills.

With the suggestions made to this point, the teacher will be able to plan for a year's program that will be based on the social sciences, and one that will stress the affective and skill areas as well as the cognitive one. The next big step should be to develop the learning experiences that will enable the children to reach the specific objectives. For this the teacher will turn to the children's experiences and to a variety of resources and activities such as the community, reading materials, current events, films and filmstrips, recordings, maps and globes, and dramatic and rhythmic exercises. A knowledge, on the part of the teacher, of the different methods of inquiry used by the various social scientists could also open the way to some imaginative activities in which the children could be involved.

In order to avoid random activities, the teacher, guided by the generalizations and the controversial issues identified, should formulate a number of basic questions that require specific activities in order to be resolved. For example, some of the questions that might be asked in connection with the unit on Family Development in the United States are these: What have been the critical periods in the development of the American family, and what factors caused important changes in the composition of the family? Is the institution of family important in our culture and, if so, why? How many types of families do we have in our culture today and why? What does a family offer to an individual? Who should be the head of the family? Why do some children become delinquent? Who is normally and even legally responsible for the care of the old people?

The questions and activities approach is a very convenient one for the promotion of reflective thinking. It is an approach that assists in the development of such intellectual skills as observing, differentiating, analyzing, evaluating, synthesizing, hypothesizing, and, ultimately, discovering relationships. It is also a highly workable way to provide for individual differences without having to set different objectives for children at different intellectual levels, or of different reading abilities or experiential backgrounds. The questions that are derived from the objectives of the unit are usually the same for all children. The only thing that differs are the activities through which the children will collectively resolve the questions. While all children might enjoy viewing a film to gain information in connection with a question, some of them might choose to read a related book. Others, less able to deal with abstract sources, might engage in activity of a more concrete nature, such as observing or even experiencing an actual situation. It is important for a class of children, actually a form of a community, to be striving together toward the same goals. Every child should feel that he is making contributions for the achievement of these common goals.

We have attempted, in this last section, to provide a way of planning for and teaching social studies on the basis of the current trends in social studies education. What we discussed is actually a step-by-step substitute for the traditional unit plan as it is indicated on page 162.

Social Studies Is Still Changing

Change in social studies was long overdue. The deficiencies of the traditional programs and the emerging needs of the society could no longer tolerate the status quo—a new direction was needed. With the financial assistance of the federal government and other funding agencies, educators, social scientists, and learning psychologists joined and marked this direction. A great number of social studies projects have been initiated and have stirred up enthusiasm and generated hope all across the nation. Publishers already feel the impact of the new movement and have begun to develop materials that are in line with the new trends.

The outlook is optimistic, and nothing should probably be said that might give a different impression. We should remind the reader, however, that there is much still to be done. Most of the new projects have not yet been completed. All of them need to be field-tested in many parts of the country and then be improved on the basis of feedback from the classroom. The shortcomings of the new social studies projects must not be overlooked. Their most serious shortcoming is the fact that their designers ignored the various subcultures in the United States; black studies for whites as well as for blacks have attempted to fill this need for one group, but the Chicanos, the Chinese, the French-Canadians,

Traditional Unit Plan	*Modified Plan To Implement Current Trends*
1. *Title*—traditionally popular topics, in many cases not all of them related to each other.	*Title*—area of study unified by a common theme and related to the contemporary scene of society.
2. *General objectives*—broad flowery statements, in many cases impossible to reduce to specific behaviors.	*Generalizations and issues from the social sciences*—capable of providing structure for a particular area of study.
3. *Specific objectives*—mostly content statements to be mastered.	*Specific behaviors to be achieved by children*—all of them derived from the generalizations and issues, and stated as subgeneralizations, concepts, social and intellectual skills, interests, attitudes, and values. Decision-making skills, as objectives, are of extreme importance.
4. *Content*—an outline of subject matter; an expansion of the content statements listed as specific objectives.	*Basic questions*—will stimulate the children to look for evidence, analyze it, and discover relationships. Questions calling for assessment of values are included as well.
5. *Activities*—an account of types of activities that could be used; rarely specific enough to give adequate direction to the teacher.	*Learning experiences*—specific activities for each one of the basic questions. They can actually represent the procedure of specific lesson plans. They are of a wide variety and provide for individual differences. Many activities are inspired by the methods of inquiry used by the social scientists.
6. *Culminating activity*—an activity or activities to help summarize the unit.	*Culminating activity*—serves the same purpose.
7. *Evaluation*—a variety of methods to evaluate pupil progress; overemphasis on pencil-and-paper tests; too often objectives not clear.	*Evaluation*—since instruction is directed toward the development of specific behaviors, evaluation is more precise and more techniques are used. Activities, programs, and teaching procedures are evaluated along with pupil progress.
8. *Resources used*—mostly children's books and commercially developed units. Some audiovisual aids and field trips are used.	*Resources used*—social science resources for teachers have become a must along with all kinds of resources for children such as the community, reading materials, audiovisual aids, current events, and others. Much emphasis is placed on raw data.

and other groups have had no representation in the curriculum, and studies of the Indian make no mention of the plight of the Indian today. The programs teach a few cursory facts about the subcultures, but not all of them are designed to be *used* by all subcultures as a way of developing better human relations through understanding. "If the new social studies or any successive movements for rational reform are to have the impact they deserve," states Hazel Hertzberg (1970), "they must be modified to take account of a factor largely neglected: the subculture of students themselves."

There are those who feel that in an effort to solidify the content of social studies, the projects overemphasized the social sciences at the expense of important humanistic elements. If the focus of the social studies is the development of the child, there is probably too much emphasis placed on inquiry, concepts, and generalizations from the social sciences. ". . . The social studies classroom," Richard Whittemore (1970) writes, "should be . . . a place where the rational and the romantic can exist side by side as equally valid categories of understandings, where the two cultures of science and art find common ground."

Black Studies and the Social Studies

The study of the culture of various minorities has become a concern for the new social studies. The various minorities welcomed their belated presence in social studies textbooks and in teacher-prepared materials. But, while textbook writers began to allocate space, or more of it, to the contributions of minorities to the development of this nation, minority group leaders definitely felt that this was not enough. Blacks, American Indians, Chicanos, and Orientals have started and are presently heavily involved in the search for an identity, and they want the schools attended by their children to join in this struggle and play a significant role. This demand on the part of the minority groups is a strong one and has given rise to a number of special programs such as black studies.

". . . Two functions of black studies," stated a black educator (Black Studies in Schools, 1970, p. 3), "are building ego-identity and ethnic confidence for the black student. . . . The major motivation of black studies is to entice black students (conditioned to exclusion) to greater involvement in the educational process. Black studies is, above all, a pedagogical device." Concerned white parents are also anxious that their children learn about the culture of the blacks; they have been instrumental in introducing the study of African history, art, music, and the dance into the curriculum. Contributions of blacks in America as well—to poetry in the work of writers like James Weldon Johnson, to music in the rise of new musical forms like spirituals and jazz, to civil rights in the leadership of Martin Luther King—are also included in black studies.

The programs designed to meet the objectives of black studies vary widely. Some reflect genuine attempts to deal with the black experience in realistic terms, while others represent hurried responses intended to appease black militants. Most programs were developed locally at the district level. Publishers introduced elements in their textbooks that tended to project black studies as a unified national movement, but as Professor James Banks (1971, p. 2) points out, "Most of the 'integrated' materials now on the market are little more than old wine in new bottles. . . ." Professor Banks goes on to say that these materials ". . . contain white characters painted brown, and the success stories of 'safe' blacks such as Crispus Attucks and Booker T. Washington. The problems which powerless ethnic groups experience in America are deemphasized or ignored." Minority studies films are perhaps more realistic, although most of these are for upper elementary and high school students. Films produced by BFA Educational Media (Santa Monica, California), for example, center around the young Chicano, American Indian, Japanese-American, and the black, and explore such issues as growing up in two cultures, the manifestations of bias, and the myths that perpetuate prejudice.

It is quite obvious that the educational institutions of this country can no longer afford to ignore the blacks and the other minorities existing within our society. As Armstead L. Robinson (1969, p. ix) wrote, "Students can no longer be given a myopic vision of America as a homogeneous, placid and idyllic land of the free and home of the brave." It remains to be seen, however, whether the present programs on black studies or other minority studies are what they should be. In the words of Professor Banks (1971, p. 2), ". . . few of them are sound because the goals of black studies remain confused, ambiguous and conflicting." Also, it is not clear whether the best way to deal with black and other minority studies is on a separate subject basis or to integrate them within the existing curricula.

As the efforts for the formation of sound black and other minority studies programs continue, teachers should approach social studies with an open mind and try to present and reflect on society as it really is rather than as one group, any group, wants it to be. This is a multigroup society, and everyone should realize it. Long ago a promise was made by our forefathers that all groups and individuals would live under the umbrella of equality and justice. It is about time that this promise became a reality; social studies teachers have a responsibility to work toward this end.

Summary

The ultimate objective of social studies appears to be to create rational decision makers who will be able to function in a diverse society that is in a period of transition resulting from a penetrating self-examination of its structure, composition, and values.

The traditional social studies, characterized by its biased and descriptive content and by its exposition method, is being pushed aside in favor of a new social studies that reflects the following characteristics:

1. There is a balance between cognitive, affective, and skills areas.
2. Those skills and processes which foster decision making are emphasized. Included among them are autonomous thinking, creativity, and the method of inquiry.
3. Purposes for all learning experiences are clearly defined.
4. The content is dictated by the structure of the disciplines and it is interdisciplinary in nature.
5. The content is social-reality oriented and includes values and value-related issues and topics.
6. The new programs provide for a world view with more emphasis on the non-Western world than previously.
7. The teaching strategies are investigation-oriented.
8. The textbook is replaced by a variety of materials and media that attempt to bring the child face to face with raw data.
9. The valuing process and the method of dealing with controversial issues are stressed with the same emphasis as the cognitive processes.
10. Evaluation of pupil progress on the basis of clearly predetermined behavioral objectives is considered essential. Programs are constantly revised on the basis of continuous feedback from evaluations of pupil progress.

The new social studies is far from reaching all classrooms in the nation, but things look brighter every day. Publishers are replacing their traditional social studies materials, and colleges and universities move prospective teachers in the new direction. At the same time, a concentrated effort must be made to reach the teachers on the job at all levels in order to provide them with the stimulation and the knowledge needed to teach social studies differently. And, finally, curriculum makers must keep abreast of changes in the world in order to ensure relevancy of content.

READING LIST 7

Estvan, F. J. *Social studies in a changing world: Curriculum and instruction.* New York: Harcourt Brace Jovanovich, 1968. Dr. Estvan attempts to provide direction for improving social studies practice through the identification and consideration of related basic questions.

Fair, J., & Shaftel, F. R. (Eds.) *Effective thinking in the social studies.* The 37th Yearbook of the National Council for the Social Studies. Washington, D.C.: National Council for the Social Studies, 1967. This is a good source for those interested to study in detail about inquiry and related thinking processes.

Fraser, D. McC. (Ed.) *Social studies curriculum development: Prospects and problems.* The 39th Yearbook of the National Council for the Social Studies. Washington, D.C.: National Council for the Social Studies, 1969. This publication presents a good overview of elementary social studies with emphasis on the curriculum as reflected in the new trends.

Jarolimek, J. *Social studies in elementary education,* 4th ed. New York: The Macmillan Company, 1971. This has been a very popular book in elementary social studies for many years. The new edition emphasizes inquiry and environmental education.

Kaltsounis, T. *Teaching elementary social studies.* West Nyack, N.Y.: Parker Publishing Company, 1969. A main selection by the Educators Book Club and the Grade Teacher Book Club, this is a practical book, mainly for the teacher on the job. It assists the teacher to bridge the gap between the old and the new social studies.

Michaelis, J. U. *Social studies for children in a democracy,* 4th ed. Englewood Cliffs, N.J.: Prentice-Hall, Inc., 1968. This has been a basic book in elementary social studies for many years. It is about to be revised again to include the latest developments.

Professional Journals To Become Acquainted With

Social Education. National Council for the Social Studies in collaboration with the American Historical Association, 1201 Sixteenth St., N.W., Washington, D.C. 20036.

Social Studies. McKinley Publishing Co., 112 S. New Broadway, Brooklawn, N.J. 08030.

Journal of Negro Education. Bureau of Educational Research, Howard University, Washington, D.C. 20001.

CHAPTER 8

The Language Arts Curriculum

One hears everywhere such terms as *the new math* and, though less frequently, *the new science*. Such terms refer to the developments that have occurred in mathematics and science curricula as a result of co-operative efforts of subject-matter specialists and professional educators. One does not hear the term *the "new" English*, but there have been significant developments in the language arts[1] curriculum also. Efforts here stem from several sources. One is that of psycholinguists who, in studying the structure of the language and particularly its grammar, have helped to identify what elements ought to be part of the curriculum. Another is that of psychologists and sociologists who have been interested in the language problems of disadvantaged children and have developed experimental programs to overcome their language deficit. Other sources are professional organizations like the National Council of Teachers of English and that branch of our national information retrieval system, ERIC,[2] that deals with the language arts. Such sources seek to disseminate information about newer developments in the teaching of English. We draw upon all three kinds of sources in the material to follow.

The Process of Language Acquisition

A noted authority on the study of language has said, "The ability to learn language is so deeply rooted in man that children learn it even in the face of dramatic handicaps." Their grammar may be substandard, but they use all parts of speech—noun, verb, pronoun, adjective, adverb, preposition, and so on—and use them in a functionally correct way. They construct sentences with parts of speech in the right order by the

---

[1] *Language arts* typically includes reading, but in this text we consider reading in a separate chapter.
[2] The ERIC Clearinghouse on the Teaching of English is located at the University of Illinois at Champaign-Urbana.

time they are five, beginning the typical sentence with a noun subject followed by a verb predicate and a noun object. They do not use the word *candy*, for example, as the action word in a sentence; they use it only as subject or object. They do not, of course, know the technical labels for parts of speech and parts of a sentence, but they have a functional command of them.

While mastery of a major portion of syntax is accomplished during the preschool years, recent research provides evidence of some significant differences between child and adult grammar. C. Chomsky (1969) has identified relatively complex constructions that appear to be acquired later. Consider these sentences:

(a) The doll is eager to see.
(b) The doll is easy to see.

In (a) the doll does the seeing, whereas in (b) someone else does. The implied subject of *see* is different in the two cases, with (b) being the more difficult construction.

The verbs *ask* and *tell* also present difficulties. Here are two sentences:

(c) The girl told the boy what to paint.
(d) The girl asked the boy what to paint.

The sentences appear to have the same structure, but the subject of *to paint* is different in each case. In (c) it is the boy who will do the painting, whereas in (d) the girl herself clearly expects to do the painting. Chomsky found surprisingly late acquisition of certain structures, with (d) being imperfectly understood by some children even at age ten.

The exploration of syntactical development after age six is a fairly new research activity, and further work in the area may reveal additional late acquisitions.

Linguists study a language and language acquisition in terms of properties common to all the several thousand languages of the world, namely, a lexicon, a grammar, and a phonology. The *lexicon* of any Indo-European language is the total number of words in the dictionary, together with the inflexional affixes used to denote number and tense, such as *s, es, ed*. The *grammar* of a language refers to the set of rules specifying the manner in which sentences are to be constructed; it is also used to refer to the constructions themselves. A linguist, in studying the grammar of a child, collects all the constructions used by the child and analyzes them for underlying rules. The rules include how relationships are to be expressed among subject, verb, and object, of how transformations[3] of declarative sentences change them into negative sentences, questions, or commands. *Phonology* refers to the phonetics or rules of pronunciation and intonation in a language.

The statement that *all* normal children have mastered the fundamentals of language by five years may come as surprise to some readers. There are writers who have argued that black children from culturally disadvantaged homes have *no* language by five years, that they come to school with so-called giant words, like "Dasawabbit," and that they lack even the simplest rudiments of grammar. The psycholinguist, however, would point out that even the most disadvantaged child can say many different things about a "wabbit"; he can take the word and put it together with other words to talk about "a big wabbit," "A li'l ole wabbit," or make other statements about a rabbit, *none of which he may have heard before.* This is the essence of human language—the ability to put words together in a meaningful relationship to communicate an idea. A parrot can imitate a sentence he has heard, but not assemble the words in a different way to express a new idea. The language of the disadvantaged may not obey the rules of standard English, but it does obey grammatical rules with respect to what part of speech will be used as a subject, predicate, and object, and in what order the various parts of the sentence will be presented. The fundamentals of language are there.

In the thirties, forties, and early fifties, studies of language acquisition centered for the most part on inventories of the parts of speech used by children at different age levels, the kinds of sentences they put together, and the length of their sentences. From these studies have come a tremendous amount of data, not only with respect to development of language itself, but also with respect to factors associated with individual and class differences in language development. We know, for example, that "only" children are more advanced in development than children from multichild families. More recently, under the impact of psycholinguistics, attention has centered on a *theory* of language acquisition with several hypotheses being proposed.

Imitation as a Theory of Language Acquisition

One theory is that the child acquires language by imitation. It might seem at first glance that this is true. The young child does indeed hear utterances and repeat what he hears, but more often he reduces the utterance to what has been called "telegraphic" utterances. In a longi-

[3] Such transformations are governed by rules of usage rarely verbalized yet practiced in the standard dialect. The proper answer to the question, "Would you like some?" is, "No, I don't want *any*," while we respond to "Have you had *any* of this?" with, "Yes, I've had *some*."

tudinal study done at Harvard (Brown, Cazden & Bellugi-Klima, 1971), it was found that the child might hear, "No, you can't write on Mr. Cramer's shoe," but repeat, "Write Cramer's shoe." This particular "imitation" preserved the word order but omitted everything except the verb and two nouns. A few months later, in analyzing the same child's language, the investigators found a marked independence from the adult's model in certain respects. Here are examples (Bellugi-Klima, 1967):

1. CHILD: I don't have no paint.
   MOTHER: Can't you find any paint?
   CHILD: No, I don't find no paint.
2. MOTHER: Can't you find any shoes?
   CHILD: No, why I can't find my shoes?

It is clear here that the child is not imitating the adult, but is composing original utterances. And, where elicited imitation has been used as a research tool (Slobin & Welch, 1971), further information with respect to the role of imitation in language development is obtained. It appears that children process the utterances they are asked to imitate, deforming the utterances in certain regular ways. They may substitute one word for another, or encode the meaning in a new form, or invert order in compound sentences, or change the utterance so as to use whatever linguistic forms they already have in their repertoire. Examples are

E: The owl who eats candy runs fast.
s: Owl eat a candy and he runs fast (2 yrs. 4 mo.).
E: This one is the giant, but this one is little.
s: Dis one little, annot one big (2 yrs. 4 mo.).

The child in each case has retrieved the underlying meaning of the sentence, and is encoding that meaning in a new form. From these and other studies, it would appear that imitation does not explain the chief way in which language is acquired and that a theory of encoding and decoding, of processing speech and abstracting rules, more nearly describes the process.

Language Acquisition as Rule-Processing

According to one widely accepted view (Chomsky, 1957), the conditions for language learning require only that the child grow up in an environment where language is used with him. The rules are not taught in any direct way; the child abstracts the underlying regularities from the sentences he hears. He listens to scattered examples of various forms of syntax and synthesizes these in his own speech. He does not memorize particular strings of words or word forms, but he figures out the rules for generating strings of words. A four-year-old says, "Mommy, the bird flied away," and then upon reflection corrects himself to say, "The bird flewed away." He has never been taught the rule for forming the past tense by adding *ed* to the present tense of a verb, but he shows by his two errors, consistently in the same wrong direction, that he has abstracted the rule by himself—a truly remarkable, quiet achievement, marred only by his ignorance of exceptions to the rules.

While many experts are in agreement with respect to a theory of language acquisition by a processing of rules, testing of the theory has only just begun. The Harvard study, to which reference has already been made, provides excellent longitudinal data. The sample included only three children, but investigators collected two hours of speech every two weeks over several years, recording conversations between mother and child in the home. The sessions were tape-recorded, so a tremendous volume of data was gathered, and several interesting developmental studies completed by analyzing the data. Studies of how the child learns to say "no" and to ask questions are particularly revealing. In using negatives Bellugi (in press) points out that we have definite rules with respect to where to put the negative marker (early in the sentence), and how to use negatives with auxiliary verbs. To negate "He did it," we say, "He didn't do it"; we do not say, "He not did it" or "He didn't it." The negative element is not attached to the main verb nor does it stand in place of the auxiliary. Such sophistication grows gradually in the child's speech; at first he negates by beginning each sentence with *no*, as in "No wipe finger; no play that; no a boy bed." In the next stage he uses *can't* and *don't*, but appears to have learned these as separate lexical forms rather than to have composed them out of two separate elements. In the final stage, mastery of the negative is complete. In most English sentences, changing the location of the negative changes the meaning (*That means you don't like it*, compared with, *That doesn't mean you like it*). By five years of age the children in the Harvard study understood each of these two utterances. The research data show the astonishingly fast rate at which language acquisition takes place and attest to man's capacity for acquiring language.

Socioeconomic Differences in Language Development

Despite the child's phenomenal background in language acquisition the elementary curriculum rightfully places strong emphasis upon language training. Recently, that training in kindergarten and primary grades has concentrated on improvement of the language skills of children from disadvantaged homes. Studies of language development show that a significant relationship exists between the child's linguistic development in standard English and the socioeconomic status of his family. The results are strikingly in favor of the upper-socioeconomic levels in all indicators of language: vocabulary, standard syntax, sentence length, use of complex sentences, and articulation. Differences also appear when relationships between language and thought are studied. Disadvantaged children have more difficulty than middle-class ones in holding to a formal subject through a speech sequence; they more frequently confound reason and conclusion to produce categoric statements; they have trouble in talking about things or events that are not in the immediate present (Moore, 1971). These differences in usages of language do not arise out of any deficiencies in the speaker's understanding of the linguistic system, but, rather, out of cultural constraints that affect the speakers' communicative intent. The difference is at the level of performance, not competence (Gahagan & Gahagan, 1970).

It has been rather generally assumed that dialectal differences, both those involving pronunciation and those involving syntax, affect the learning of black disadvantaged children. This assumption, however, is being seriously questioned by linguistic experts. They point out that the typical black dialect has its own grammar, and that difficulty arises chiefly out of a social-class prejudice which has the effect of turning off the teacher's efforts to understand the child. Schools in England for children of West Indian origin have a problem comparable to ours. Some educators there take the position that, no matter how you try to disguise it, to suggest an alternative way of speaking implies a criticism of what was said in the first place. Bernstein has strong words to say about the teacher's role in dealing with dialects:

> There is nothing, but nothing, in the dialect as such, which prevents a child from internalizing and learning to use universalistic meanings. But if the contexts of learning, the examples, the reading books are not contexts which are triggers for the child's imaginings, are not triggers on the child's curiosity and explorations in his family and community, then the child is not at home in the educational world. If the teacher has to say continuously, "Say it again, darling, I didn't understand you," then in the end the child may say nothing. If the culture of the teacher is to become part of the consciousness of the child, then the culture of the child must first be in the consciousness of the teacher. This may mean that the teacher must be able to understand the child's dialect, rather than deliberately attempting to change it. (Bernstein, 1969, pp. 15–16)

Black English

Labov & Cohen (1967) have made interesting observations about use of the dialect. One investigation showed that, in tests involving imitation, the black child would take a sentence spoken to him in standard English, "I asked Harry if he wanted to go," and give back, "I axed Harry do he want to go." What the child does is to decode what the speaker has said, and encode its meaning into his own dialect, no small feat, to be sure.

In an effort to eliminate any possible difficulty in learning to read standard English, some beginning readers have been prepared that are written in both standard and black English. The child might read in one column, "He go to the store," while in the other column, in so-called "school English," he reads, "He goes to the store." The approach is an interesting one, although highly controversial. There are black leaders who speak out strongly against such an approach; they want black children to learn standard English, for they know the stigma attached to dialect. As The Barbiana School (1970) put it,

> Languages are created by the poor, who then go on renewing them forever. The rich crystallize them in order to put on the spot anybody who speaks in a different way. Or in order to fail him at exams.

At the present time, perhaps the best advice one can give a teacher is to treat the child's language with respect, at the same time giving parents of the children and community leaders a chance to participate in goal setting. Where this has been done (Cazden, Bryant & Tillman, 1970), black parents have felt that black English has no place in the school. Children will learn it anyway they say, but the job of the school is to teach in, and teach, standard English. Community leaders, on the other hand, are resentful that it is always the blacks who have to change. Furthermore, they feel that language is important for black solidarity and reject the notion that to get ahead one must speak standard English. With the increasing amount of black English spoken on television and by white college youth, the dilemma may in time be resolved.

Cazden (1970) has reported consideration of the inclusion of black English pronunciations as standard English at a conference at the Center for Applied Linguistics in Washington, D.C. Such a move might help to dispel the special prejudice against black dialects, although there still remains the question of social-class prejudice against all dialects. This prejudice is often stated as a reason for changing dialectal grammars to make them conform to standard English. The argument is advanced that if a person is going to participate in the fullest possible sense in American society, he must be able to speak standard English. Many experts think that while children may retain their dialect for use at home and with peers, children should also have available to them standard English. Schools need not take drastic measures to stamp out the dialect, but they can take steps to see that children make steady progress in growth of standard English.

Using Language to Meet Cognitive Demands

What is more likely to interfere with school learning than a dialect—and there is a growing conviction on this point—is the disadvantaged child's inability to use language to meet the demands of the school. When he is asked to follow directions, participate in discussion, compare two objects or events and make discriminations between them, classify or draw inferences, he is often at a loss to do so. In a word, he does not know how to use language to meet cognitive demands.

A number of writers have theorized about the antecedents of this specific disability. Bernstein (1961) in several provocative papers noted that lower-class parents tend to use a "restricted" code in talking to their children, in contrast to the "elaborated" one used by middle-class parents. In the restricted code, only short, grammatically simple sentences are used, with little use of subordinate clauses, limited use of adjectives and adverbs, frequent instances of illogical statements, and few specific referents, with the speaker often taking it for granted that the listener knows what he's talking about. Some of the characteristics of the restricted code are[4]

1. Short, grammatically simple, often unfinished sentences with a poor syntactical form stressing the active voice.
2. Simple and repetitive use of conjunctions (*so, then, because*).
3. Little use of subordinate clauses to break down the initial categories of the dominant subject.
4. Inability to hold a formal subject through a speech sequence; thus a dislocated informational content is facilitated.
5. Rigid and limited use of adjectives and adverbs.
6. Infrequent use of impersonal pronouns as subjects of conditional clauses.
7. Frequent use of statements where the reason and conclusion are confounded to produce a categoric statement.
8. A large number of statements/phrases which signal a requirement for the previous speech sequence to be reinforced: "Wouldn't it? You see? You know?" etc. This process is termed "sympathetic circularity."
9. Individual selection from a group of idiomatic phrases or sequences.
10. Individual qualification implicit in the sentence organization: it is a language of implicit meaning.

[4] It should be noted here that Bernstein (1970) emphatically denounces the equating of the concept of "restricted code" with the nonverbal child. He points out that the restriction is on contexts and conditions that help develop a universal range of meanings, but that the child can still produce elaborated speech in particular contexts. See Weber (1971) for a fuller discussion.

Note that these characteristics are indeed likely to create difficulties for the child in meeting the cognitive demands of the school. Note especially items numbered 4, 7, and 10, which involve clear communication of ideas and for which special provision should be made in a training program.

Improving Speaking Skills: Primary Grades

One of the widely publicized approaches to improving language development is that in which English is taught as if children were learning a second language. In parts of large metropolitan areas populated by Puerto Ricans, and in the Southwest with large populations of Spanish-American or Indian children, English may indeed be a second language. Even where it is not, however, some investigators maintain that the children's handicap is sufficiently great to warrant a drastic new approach to language teaching, an approach that is patterned after contemporary methods of teaching foreign languages.

The Patterned Drill

Two educational psychologists, Bereiter and Engelmann (1966), developed a preschool program for disadvantaged four-year-old children that relies solely upon patterned drill. The program, which has since been extended into primary grades, has been so widely publicized that it will not be described in detail here (the reader can find a discussion of certain other aspects of the program in Chapter 5). To review briefly, fifteen subjects received three periods of twenty-minute instruction a day in subject-matter areas—language, arithmetic, and reading. All three subjects were taught by the same method, that of having children repeat statement patterns; all instruction was verbal and no toys or other concrete objects were used. For example, language instruction began by teaching children basic identity patterns by verbatim repetition:

1. *Verbatim repetition:*
   TEACHER: This block is red. Say it . . .
   CHILDREN: This block is red.
2. *Yes-no questions:*
   TEACHER: Is this block red?
   CHILDREN: No, this block is not red.
3. *Location tasks:*
   TEACHER: Show me a block that is red.
   CHILDREN: This block is red.

4. *Statement production:*
   TEACHER: Tell me about this piece of chalk.
   CHILDREN: This piece of chalk is red.
   TEACHER: Tell me about what this piece of chalk is *not.*
   CHILDREN: (ad lib) this piece of chalk is not green . . . not blue, etc.
5. *Deduction problems:*
   TEACHER: (With piece of chalk hidden in hand) This piece of chalk
   is not red. Do you know what color it is?
   CHILDREN: No. Maybe it is blue . . . maybe it is yellow . . . (Bereiter &
   Engelmann, 1967, p. 134)

Bereiter reports that it takes four-year-old children considerable time to
learn these statement patterns with their plural variations and subclass
nouns (for example, "This animal is a tiger"). The length of time varies
considerably—from six or seven months for those who came in with
practically no spoken language to two or three months for those of near
normal language competence, at the end of which time the children can
recite such statements as "If it's a hammer, then it's a tool," which purportedly illustrates proficiency in class inclusion (knowing that "hammer" is a subclass in the more general class, "tool") and in inferencing
(knowing that *if* something is true, *then* we can infer that something else
is true). The approach has been somewhat modified in the Engelmann-
Becker *Distar* version, but the basic principles remain.

Critics of such an approach to language training argue that the
grammatical sentences children give are evidence of response learning;
they doubt that patterned drill affects language and thought processes
any more effectively than memorizing nursery rhymes and learning to
respond, "Dickory comes after Hickory," and, "The mouse ran down the
clock; the mouse did not run up the clock."

Critics of patterned drill also contend that it is too limited a program. In language lessons, for example, the children in patterned drill
classes are exposed to a very limited variety of syntactical forms including a limited number of verbs, mostly in the present tense. Yet we know
that human beings have a natural capacity for language and acquire it
often in the face of great difficulties. With sufficient exposure to a rich
vocabulary and a complex syntax in interactions with adults, children
can process data and put together utterances that they have never heard
themselves. If a mother says to her three-year-old, "Find Daddy and tell
him supper is ready," the child does not find his father and say, "Find
Daddy and tell him supper is ready," as a child might parrot in patterned
drill. Instead he says to his father, "Daddy, Mommy says supper's ready."
Young children acquire the structure of the language by listening to
what is said to them, processing the information, figuring out the rules,
and *using in reply what they have figured out.*

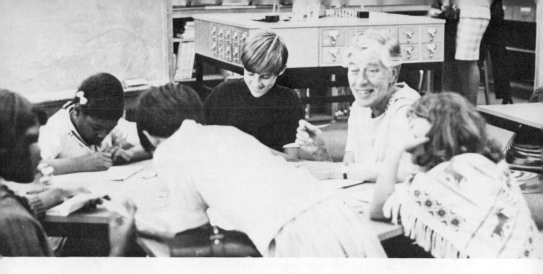

Carefully selected volunteers can enormously enrich the language arts curriculum. Here a free-lance journalist teaches the rudiments of good journalistic reporting to a group of sixth-grade students.

Some schools maintain a file with names of local citizens who can be called upon to furnish information in such diverse areas as the life of a migratory worker and the arts. Children have much more to say in discussions and in their writing as a result of such experiences. Photo by Zita Lichtenberg, State Office of Public Instruction, Olympia, Washington.

The "Natural" Method

Some support for the "natural" method of language training is to be found in Cazden's research. Cazden (1965) exposed a small group of preschool children to a treatment she called "modeling"; that is, a tutor would reply to a child's utterances in a conversational manner, modeling as she did so a rich variety of syntactical forms. While differences between modeling and a second treatment were not significant, results favored modeling.

But the natural method of acquiring language is only effective if the child has sufficient chance to *interact* with adults who use language effectively. Jensen (1968), who has been a major investigator in the area of language learning, states, "The degree of subtlety, diversity, and complexity of the verbal environment will determine the nature of the syntactical processes incorporated by the developing child. The extent to which these structures become incorporated is a function of the frequency with which they are experienced in the environment, the degree to which the social environment reinforces their overt manifestation, and the individual's basic capacity for learning."

To provide opportunity for interaction, small-group work must replace the teacher-whole-class instruction that still prevails in many elementary schools. Schools do not have to be joyless places where children must sit and listen for most of the day. Whether the subject is science, social studies, or arithmetic, children can carry on their work in groups, in ways described in appropriate chapters in this text. And, as the teacher works with small groups, regardless of what the subject is, the teacher can use the opportunity to teach English as well. She can work to extend the speaking skills of all children, posing questions for individual children that demand thoughtful answers, listening to responses, and modeling good language patterns for children to process.

Exposing Children to Syntactical Structures

Granted that language training should take place in small groups so that there is considerable adult-child interaction; granted that in the training the child should be exposed to a rich variety of syntactical forms and particularly those that might conceivably aid logical development: How can such training be systematized so as to make sure that what is known about language is fully utilized? In the area of syntactical structures we can turn to the field of developmental psycholinguistics for an analysis of syntax and how syntactical forms emerge. From this relatively new but fascinating field we can identify the syntactical forms children are likely to need help on. Some of those identified to date and their relevance for education include (Bellugi-Klima & Hass, 1971):

1. *Inflections* denoting plurals, past tense endings, and third person singular present indicative. Example: The bead*s* are round. We pour*ed* the water. The number of pennies match*es* the number of bottles.
2. *Prepositions* such as "behind," "in," "on," "over," etc. The precise meaning of these "little" words which nevertheless encode considerable information is often lost on the young child.
3. *Auxiliary verbs.* Studies show that "helping" verbs like the "has" in "has gone" are often missing in the speech of disadvantaged children; yet, like inflections, such verb forms add more information to a sentence. "He gone" might mean "He has gone," "He will have gone," or any number of other meanings.
4. *Coordinators* such as "and" that connect two grammatical elements in a conjoining transformation. Here the difficulty may be in short-term memory. If the teacher says, "Put the red beads here," even the very young child can do it. If the teacher next says, "Put the blue beads here also," the child can also follow the directions. But when the teacher connects the two ideas, "Put the red beads here and the blue beads here," the very young child may bring only the blue. Older primary children may not be able to follow more complicated statements involving coordination such as, "Finish cleaning up your table and then go along to the bathroom."

5. *Adversatives* where one idea is the opposite or the antithesis of another. "But" is an adversative conjunction, as in the sentence, "It's small but heavy." We expect small objects to be light, and when an opposing idea is added instead, the "heavy" may be lost.
6. *Disjoint* where a class may be taken apart and the elements making up the class separated from one another. An example of a disjoint is the statement, "Show me the beads that are red and not square."
7. *Comparatives.* "More," "less"; "lighter," "darker"; "shorter," "taller," are examples of comparative forms which are essential for putting objects in some kind of order.
8. *Complex noun phrases.* The use of modifiers such as "the short narrow piece"; "jagged, rough, uneven objects" aids in precise description and definition of properties of objects.
9. *Relative clauses.* Directions of teachers often include such modifying clauses as "Whatever beads you can't sort, you can put to one side." The construction is a useful one in describing an object precisely.
10. *Temporal connectives.* Connectives such as *when, after, until, as soon as* which indicate time appear late in language development. Teachers of young children know that a statement such as, "When you have finished, you can get ready for juice," is usually the signal for children to move in on the juice.
11. *Conditional statements.* "If–then" type statements as expressed in, "If you put the longer one here, then where should the shorter one go?"

It is possible to model each of these forms systematically in the course of the small-group lessons. For example, the teacher might model a complex noun phrase such as, "Find a picture of a large, furry animal"; "Show me a small, white, baby shoe," and then elicit by a question ("What is it? Tell me about it.") a statement from a child requiring that he use such a grammatical construction.

This modeling and eliciting procedure demands that children listen to the statement, process the input, and construct a verbal response. Constructing a verbal response is much more difficult than decoding meaning from a spoken statement. If one is studying French, it is much easier to figure out the meaning of the statement, "On peut étudier la perception de nombreux points de vue, dont le plus classique est le point de vue psycho-physiologique," than to state in French, "One can study perception from a number of points of view, of which the most classic is the psychophysiological."

Caution must be exerted that eliciting occurs in a warm, friendly, supportive manner. Sharp insistence upon repeating exactly what the teacher said or correcting every response that the child makes will make verbal communication distasteful to the child, and, indeed, turn him off. Dr. Mowrer some years ago worked with birds to discover the conditions under which parrots, mynah birds, and other talking birds learned to talk. He found that a bird learned best when the caretaker acted as a good "mother" to the bird, talking to the bird as he fed it, so the bird learned to associate talking with the good things of life. A child who hears language continually directed to him in a critical, rejecting way is not going to be motivated to change speech patterns.

Perhaps one of the most useful activities in which a teacher can engage is to listen to children's talk in their peer groups and to study their writing from the standpoint of language structure. Primary teachers often set up play centers or interest centers in the classroom to encourage free play and language activity in that play. They also use "Show-and-Tell" periods, where a child brings in an object from home to show to the class and to tell about it, as a way of stimulating child language. However, teachers are generally concerned not merely with whether children talk, but also with the quality of their talk. Cazden (1971) reports that Bernstein eavesdropped on children's conversations in Wendy houses (play centers) in England and concluded that language in that setting is highly routinized, with children making more or less routine comments and responses to one another. One hears the same kind of conversation on this side of the Atlantic. In a third-grade classroom where an Indian unit was in progress, children had set up a tepee and were engaged in free play. Their conversation rarely got beyond the, "You be the chief and I'll be a brave." "You grind the corn." "I want to be the hunter." There was little evidence of language extension in terms of vocabulary or sentence structure.

The Tucson Early Education Model

A unique and promising model for language training has been developed in the primary grades of the Tucson, Arizona, public schools, under the direction of Dr. Marie Hughes. The children in the program are Mexican-American children, one-third of whom typically were not ready for first grade after a year in traditional schools.

In initiating the project, researchers noted that in these special classes there were infrequent opportunities for language practice. Few individuals talked but the teacher; when the teacher asked a question, the children all answered in a chorus. There was little opportunity for using language to express ideas. A description of the remedial program follows (Lavatelli, 1971).

The Tucson model for language training might be described as the "natural" method systematized and accelerated. It is based upon a conviction that to acquire language competence a child must interact with an adult who uses models of many syntactical elements in his speech, and who responds to the child's remarks in such a way as to extend the child's language. The adult also, ideally, reinforces the child continuously for his attempts to practice new syntactical discoveries.

To stimulate language, children in the Tucson program engage in many varied activities including trips, cooking, observation of animals, and physical science experiments. A child's remarks about these experiences are recorded *verbatim*, with all errors and deficiencies included, by the teacher, an assistant, or the child himself. A program assistant who serves as a resource person or agent of change helps the teacher to analyze the sample and plan next steps. When the child's story is reread, the teacher, in conversation directed toward the child, includes utterances to serve as a model of the next higher level of language sophistication, asks questions to elicit the more sophisticated phrasing, and praises the child for his accomplishments.

Let us see how the program might look in action. The children in a first grade immersed a sponge in water and observed the bubbles of air coming out of the sponge. "Coming bubbles out of the sponge," Bertha said excitedly. Her classmates' remarks and Bertha's were recorded by the teaching assistant. The program assistant and the teacher decided in conference that the next language level for Bertha might be beginning a sentence with the subject and using a participle to describe the bubbles. Accordingly the teacher planned to model this type of construction for Bertha the next day.

Six-by-eight cards were prepared, with each child's remarks printed on an individual card, and with such phrases as, "Bertha said," or "Angie remarked," prefacing what the child had said. The plan was to have the teacher read the cards verbatim and then model the correct structure for Bertha. The teacher might say, "I saw bubbles coming out of the sponge also," and then proceed, by questioning, to elicit the use of the correct structure for the child. The same kind of language mediation is used in all aspects of curriculum work, and classrooms are full of "talking" murals with pictures and accompanying comments, individual books children have made containing pictures and their spontaneous remarks about a particular experience, and collections of stories by the whole class about a common experience. Thus the children are living in a language environment where their products are held in high esteem and form the basis of the work in reading and development of intellectual skills—all of which serves to reinforce for the child the importance of improving his clarity of expression.

Growth in language control by the child is paralleled by his ability to think in increasingly discriminating ways, especially if his environment provides for language growth and intellectual development to be mutually stimulating. For example, certain forms of speech like the past tense are best learned if the adult reminisces with the child about an earlier experience such as a trip to the park; if the experiences were stimulating to the senses, there is also a chance to acquire adjectives or adjectival phrases. Such verbalization of recall provokes a variety of sentence transformations and provides practice in remembering, a skill disadvantaged Mexican-Americans lack.

If the remembering practice is directed systematically by a discriminating adult, it will also involve the skills of sequencing, associating, and categorizing, to mention a few. Children are helped to recall details in chronological order and record them in sequence—a skill highly important in learning to read, where anticipation of what might happen next helps one to figure out new words. It is a skill that also helps in making predictions. Children in the second grade peeled avocado, ate the fruit, and planted the seed. Not only was there deliberate retrieval of the experience by rereading their books, but along with the recall, a discussion about what was going to happen—what changes might occur in the avocado, recording of predictions, and playing them back during the next few weeks to check predictions.

Much use is made also of categorizing and associating. Children are asked to describe the characteristics of objects they are observing in terms of shape, color, and size. There are many opportunities for comparison: "It's bigger than my hand," or "It's smaller than my fingernail." Questions about the origin of an object, its relation to other objects, and its sensory characteristics—how it smells, tastes or feels—also provoke language.

Of paramount importance is the teacher's consciousness of her role as a modeler of language and her increasing awareness of what language is, syntactically. She chooses to model patterns in order to evoke these same patterns from the child and to arrange for the child to practice them within a meaningful context. The analysis of language is based upon a grammatical analysis developed by John Carroll (1964).

Carroll lists certain sentence-types that are basic English expressions. One such type is the *there* + verb phrase + a nominal (a noun, or a word used as a noun). This type of expression simply asserts the existence of something: "There is a rabbit." Another basic type is the *predication* type, where the basic pattern includes a subject and predicate. The constructions include (1) linking verb + nominal ("It was Tuesday"); (2) linking verb + adjective ("Her mother is sick"); (3) linking verb + adverbial telling where, when, etc. ("He's home"); (4) intransitive verb taking no object ("He's swimming"); or (5) transitive verb + object ("He killed a rabbit").

In the Tucson study, the program assistant and the teacher analyze the child's stories to assess the level of sophistication at which the child is operating, and to determine next steps. The predication types in particular are useful in studying the varieties of language control demonstrated in the children's stories. These types form the basis of variations of language patterns, and lead eventually to greater language control. They are used in "kernel" sentences which are then transformed by adding, deleting, transposing word order, or negating.

In addition to analyzing how children are putting sentences together, and what help they may need in transforming kernels to the negative or other forms, the program assistant and the teacher also look to see how various parts of speech are used. Does the child use articles like "a" or "the"? Does he use nouns alone (snake), or does he attach adjective modifiers (long, skinny, green snake)? Does he use prepositions correctly to denote relations of space, time, or logical position? Does he use auxiliary verbs?

As the reader can see, the grammatical analysis is not a difficult or complicated one to make. As a result of making such analyses, the teacher becomes aware in a very specific way of children's language difficulties, and concerned with doing something about them. The grammatical analysis also helps the teacher to know what grammatical forms to model for the child. Teachers become sophisticated in determining what might be done further to provide a "language lift," that is, to increase the complexity of language and to use more transformations. Becoming aware of the discrepancy between how the child is performing, and how he should be performing through analyses of his language expression, is a necessary first step in teacher modification of behavior.

To summarize, the Tucson model may be described as based upon the following premises:

1. Mexican-American lower-class children entering school at six years of age are handicapped in language; they speak neither Spanish nor English well and are reluctant to express themselves freely.
2. Interesting curriculum activities, like trips and experiences with food, can provide the stimulus to get children to talk.
3. Under conditions of positive reinforcement, children will increase their use of the English language.
4. The child's own language output in the form of stories dictated to the teacher or to a tape recorder can serve to stimulate the child to talk, and also serve as a source of feedback to the child on how well he is doing.
5. Teachers will be more aware of specific needs in language training if they have a knowledge of how language is structured.
6. Teachers can use their knowledge of how language is structured to make diagnoses of pupil needs and plan specific activities to improve language.

Extending Writing Skills through Literature

Teachers often have children begin writing by having each child compose a "story" about a picture he has made. Thus the child draws a picture and composes a one-sentence story, "This is a house and a tree." All primary teachers will recognize the sentence pattern: *This is a Z*. As Cazden (1971) points out, when a picture is drawn first and a sentence then composed about the picture, the child is constrained toward use of the *This is a* Z pattern.

In upper grades, too, the setting for writing can result in stereotyped composition. Witness the stories children write in response to the assignment on "How I spent my summer vacation." Such an assignment produces a sentence structure of *I* + verb repeated over and over again: "I went to my grandmother's. I met some new kids. We went swimming almost every day. I got sunburned the first day and then I couldn't go anymore till I peeled."

Expression and communication are spoiled also by the use of trite phrases or clichés. In describing his frightened hero, for example, the child says, "He was as white as a ghost." Contrast this with the way in which Mark Twain has Huck Finn describe the whiteness of his father's face:

> There warn't no color in his face, where his face showed; it was white; not like another man's white, but a white to make a body sick, a white to make a body's flesh crawl—a tree-toad white, a fish-belly white. (*The Adventures of Huckleberry Finn*)

The images that the words "fish-belly white" conjure up in the reader's mind are much more vivid than those suggested by the child's more hackneyed phrase. Occasional structured lessons on effective imagery are helpful here.

Reading poetry and stories aloud to children is very much a part of the language arts curriculum and is used by many teachers to improve written expression. Thus, children may listen to the teacher read a story like *Charlotte's Web* by E. B. White, and then discuss some of the effective ways in which White uses words. Or a teacher can use verse so that students can learn how powerfully ideas can be expressed in this medium. Shakespeare might have told his readers directly how it feels to be forgotten or slighted by a friend. But what could express his feeling more effectively than Amiens' song:

> Blow, blow, thou winter wind.
> > Thou art not so unkind
> > As man's ingratitude.
> Thy tooth is not so keen,
> Because thou art not seen,
> > Although thy breath be rude.
> Heigh-ho! Sing, heigh-ho! unto the green holly.

>Most friendship is feigning, most loving mere folly.
>Then, heigh-ho, the holly!
>This life is most jolly.
>(*As You Like It*, act II, scene vii)

In listening to such poetry, the older student learns that he often can communicate his feelings in this medium far more economically of words than in direct discourse.

Many children are limited in their use of language. They look at the thick snowflakes falling during a storm and are helpless to express their feelings. "It looks nice," they might say, "It's so pretty." A child who is freer in expressing himself might say, "Look! It makes everything so soft and cozy, but mysterious too." Only a rare child can become a Mark Twain or a Shakespeare or a Millay, but the language arts curriculum can help all children to communicate their perceptions with clarity, in-

A place to write also helps to encourage writing. The modern classroom has been geared to "togetherness," with children seated at tables in groups of four or more. A recent trend has been the introduction of carrels, made possible by the simple addition of a sheet of plywood between desks. The children have a feeling of privacy, distractions are minimized, and concentration on the writing task is improved. Photo by Zita Lichtenberg, State Office of Public Instruction, Olympia, Washington.

terest, and freshness. Stories and verse read by the teacher or pupils can serve as a springboard to written expression. Ideas gleaned from literature may spark a creative note, and, given time and encouragement, children take off on creative writing "binges."

British primary schools also use literature as an aid to writing, though not necessarily as a starting point. They emphasize direct sensory experiences that nurture the imagination of children, that prompt speech which is allowed freedom, that in turn allows writing "that is rich and full of the child" (Clegg, 1966). "Feeding is from the great stories of literature, poems, legends, and folk tales from Genesis and Homer and Dylan Thomas and Ted Hughes."

Textbook series suggest ways of using the literature included in the texts as a springboard to writing. However, teachers who are most successful in stimulating writing efforts are those who rely upon their own ingenuity to provide the stimulus for writing, and rely upon the texts, if there are texts, for remedial needs.

Improving Writing Skills

In order to communicate what he wishes to say in his writing, the child must learn to put his ideas into acceptable form. He must learn to punctuate and capitalize properly, to spell correctly, and to write legibly.

Punctuation and Capitalization

It is not difficult to help children see the need for correct punctuation and capitalization. A paragraph or two written on the board without benefit of either is very difficult for them to read. They can appreciate how correct punctuation and capitalization directly aid the process of communication.

Punctuation skills in classrooms where children do a great deal of writing are taught early and informally. In the first grade, when the pupil dictates to the teacher, the teacher comments on the use of the period: "Let's put a period here to show that you've finished with that idea." As the child learns to write his own stories, the teacher helps him to see that the period tells his reader when to stop. Other marks of punctuation are introduced as they are needed. In schools where young children do a great deal of original writing, this need may come early. It is not unusual for second-graders in modern schools to be using quotation marks.

The first drafts of children's stories and reports are often very poorly written from the standpoint of punctuation and capitalization. The teacher goes over these written efforts with the child, and together they work out the corrections for the first sentence or two. The teacher says, "How should this sentence begin? Read the sentence to me and tell me where the stop comes. What do we put there? How does the next word begin?" Once she is sure that the pupil understands the nature of the corrections, the teacher urges him to proofread for himself and find as many of his own errors as he can. The teacher also checks the final draft, points out errors to the pupil, and notes persistent errors for special attention during the next writing activity.

If it appears that certain errors are common to the class, the teacher should plan special lessons. During these lessons she may reteach the rules to make sure that the pupils understand them, and then provide practice exercises, based, if possible, on actual errors that the children have made. In the language of learning theory, pupils are more highly motivated to learn when they see a need for the learning; they must then be helped to notice the right cues, and they should be given the chance to practice the correct response under supervision so that reinforcement will occur.

Spelling

Spelling has long been the *bête noire* of the English-speaking world. Unlike that of many other languages, English spelling is not simply a defective system where words are not spelled the way they are pronounced. As Venezky (1970) has pointed out, there is a regular set of patterns for spelling English words, but the set is complex and involves both phonemic and morphemic elements. Research findings from linguistics are helpful here, for both the relationship of sound to letters *and* grammatical units are involved. Venezky suggests that it might be well to stress, in teaching, morphemic patterns such as noun-plural markers, *es* and *s*, and how such patterns are pronounced in different words. For example, in noun-plural markers, there are three distinct phonemes: /s/ in *cats*; /z/ in *dogs*; and /iz/ in *judges*, although the singular noun in each case is made plural by adding the letter *s*. As Venezky points out, if a student were taught only the so-called regular spelling for each significant sound in English, he could be expected to spell correctly less than 41 percent of all English words. Teaching him predictable patterns, as the newer spelling approaches do, may be more profitable.

It is interesting that many of these predictable sound patterns are drawn from phonological theory (the sound pattern of the language), interesting because for so long it has been argued that English is not a phonetic language and that a phonetic approach to spelling is impractical. But recent research on phonology (Chomsky & Halle, 1968) has shown that spelling does relate closely to pronunciation, but not from a phonetic viewpoint. Take the words *photograph, photography,* and *photographic* (C. Chomsky, 1970). The pronunciation of the three words differs, as any native speaker of the language knows, and the root word *photo* is not evident in *photography.* If the child were to spell the three words phonetically, chances are he would make an error. However, if he puts what he knows about the sound system to work, then he can make the translation between pronunciation and spelling. C. Chomsky gives additional examples: "The child who misspells *president* as *presedent* needs to have pointed out that it is related to *preside.* The child who misspells *really* as *relly* needs to think of *reality* to get it right. *Upon* is more likely to be written as *upon* if the child realizes that it is a combination of *up* and *on.* . . ." (p. 16). And once children tumble to the principle, spelling becomes a game, and motivation to search out the root word becomes high, with a consequent decrease in spelling errors.

Incidental Learning

A great deal of spelling learning is incidental. Typically, schools in which pupils do a great deal of writing report gains in spelling. In some British Infant Schools, where all children are expected to write every day, each child has a wordbook containing commonly used words selected from the children's own writing. Each child adds to the alphabetical list those words that he finds useful to him. In classrooms where there is much creative writing, children bring stories to the teacher to look over and correct misspelled words, which are then written correctly in the student's wordbooks. Regularly scheduled class periods for spelling are eliminated, and instruction on spelling generalizations takes place in small groups in connection with writing activities.

A Linguistic Approach to Teaching Writing Skills

Several textbook series reflect the current interest of scholars in linguistics, and their authors have attempted to apply findings from this discipline to the improvement of children's writing skills. Content derived from linguistics has concentrated on teaching children in grades 3–6 sound and spelling relationships, and grammar. The assumption is made that, while many students are able to figure out the rules, there are many who cannot do it by themselves. The syntax in most series is based upon transformational grammar. Traditional grammar is pretty much a description of the Latin plan for putting sentences together, and as such has many drawbacks; also definitions are not functional (an adjective, for example, does not always modify a noun or a pronoun). Transformationalists view grammar as a small set of kernel sentences plus the rules for transforming the kernels into an infinite number of sentences. Beginning in the third grade in many school systems, the child is exposed to the structure of kernel sentences, to noun phrases and verb phrases. Study of structure becomes increasingly more complex, and by the time the child has finished the elementary school, he has studied "all the various complicated structures of which mature writing is composed." Indeed, a very respectable amount of grammar is taught to children, and critics of the schools who urged its restoration are no doubt pleased. In inspecting the texts, however, one would hardly conclude that linguistics has revolutionized the teaching of grammar. Technical terms like "marker" are used, and some definitions of parts of speech are changed; the generalizations about sound-spelling relationships are presented. Nor can one claim today any more than twenty years ago that the new grammar any more than the old will have an appreciable effect upon writing skills.

Dramatic Expression

Of all creative modes of expression, children's dramatic expression probably receives the least time and attention today. Formerly, putting on plays was an activity close to children's hearts. Today, television tends to make children passive receivers of entertainment. As Strickland put it,

> Children of earlier periods were their own entertainers. They put on circuses and shows of their own creation in their back yards and attics and charged a penny or some pins for admission. It took a great deal of ingenuity and family or neighborhood planning to make the show come off. Children made tickets, rigged up sheets or blankets on clotheslines for curtains, concocted costumes, and planned sequences of activity. It required an immense amount of thought and creative effort as well as real skill in working together for a common end. They found ways to include all who wished to participate and took care of the working out of democratic processes themselves.
>
> Now one finds little of this sort of activity in homes and neighborhoods. The children are sitting in the moving picture theater looking and listening or facing a television instrument soaking up what they see and hear. They are no longer the doers and creators. While the modern media undoubtedly have brought educational values, they have deprived children of other very important values. Children need many experiences in thinking, planning, carrying through plans, and evaluating outcomes. They need to use their own creative minds and develop them through use. What children plan and carry through, with or without adult guidance, is something suited to their level of development and meaningful to them.

The mass media bring them ideas and stimulation but often of an un-wholesome and unsuitable sort. People who are interested in the develop-ment of children need to give thought to this phase of their development and put forth some effort to bring it about. (Strickland, 1969, pp. 460–461)

Participation in dramatic activity has many important values. It can help to develop creativity in several areas—in art, music, and the use of language. It can give children practice in the organizing skills and in working with others. And it can also help children with individual prob-lems. The child whose love of clowning often disturbs the class learns, as he portrays a silly gosling in "The Seven Little Goslings," that there are times and places for his antics. The timid child feels much braver when he takes on the role of the fierce troll in "Three Billy Goats Gruff," and the approbation of the class for his good performance of a part gives a much needed boost to his self-confidence.

An overcrowded program, of course, keeps many a teacher from allotting time to this worthy activity. Yet, once given the stimulation, children can find their own time for dramatics. In some parts of the country, children must spend many recesses indoors during inclement weather. One fifth-grade teacher encouraged children to use such occa-sions to organize themselves into groups and plan plays based on stories that they had read. A costume box was kept in the room, filled with scarves, lengths of material, long skirts, discarded costume jewelry, old hats, and other odds and ends, like the attic trunk that so many of us knew and enjoyed in our childhood.

Time set aside during the week for individual or small-group activi-ties might also be used for dramatics. In planning with children for such periods, the teacher should make sure that play acting is listed as one of the activities for children to choose from. "How many would like time for dramatization?" the teacher might ask, and then assign a corner of the room for this activity.

At times the language arts work may be so organized that children are working in small groups on separate projects. Thus there may be a group working on the class newspaper, a dramatization group, and a group preparing a class book. Or, if the class is to take charge of a school assembly, several projects might be planned to make use of all the chil-dren's talents. One group may do a puppet show, another a play, and a third may dramatize a scene from a favorite book. If the teacher wishes to encourage dramatization, he will find both time and opportunity to.

Dramatization need not engage the whole class. Allowing children to choose among several small-group projects, all going on at the same time, gives them a chance to participate in an activity suited to their individual talents and interests. Not all children should be expected to be creative in the same way at the same time.

Verse Choir or Choral Speaking

Choral speaking is another language arts activity that contributes to creative expression in the grades. A verse choir is not simply a group of children reciting poetry together. Children are divided into groups according to the pitch of their voices, and speaking parts are assigned to each group. One or two children may do solo parts to add to the interpretive effect.

Poetry and other rhythmic literature are suitable for such choirs. In selecting material for choral speaking, the teacher will want to look for, or have children search out, a poem with marked rhythm, or one in which certain lines are repeated for effect, or one that lends itself to the assignment of different speaking parts. Nursery rhymes, of course, delight the kindergartner and first grader, and ballads are especially effective in the intermediate and upper grades.

One group of children in a first grade planned and carried out an effective rendition of "Hickory, Dickory, Dock" as follows:

MEDIUM VOICES:	Hickory, dickory, dock.
	The mouse ran up the clock.
LOW VOICES:	The clock struck one
	The mouse ran down.
SINGLE HIGH VOICE:	Squeak! Squeak!
MEDIUM VOICES:	Hickory, dickory, dock.

Choral speaking can be a delightful form of creative expression. It can also be so overdirected that it loses spontaneity. Children should be encouraged to suggest creative ways of interpreting the selection. If they are allowed to participate in the planning, if they are made to feel that the performance is their creation and not merely an exercise in following directions, the results will be satisfying to all concerned.

Listening Skills

For at least the last two decades, curriculum makers in the language arts have included instructions in listening. The reader can well understand the reasoning behind its inclusion. Nichols (1969) has argued that there is a relationship between listening and speaking and improved performance in reading and writing. He would have teachers include among the central objectives of schooling that of helping each child to become aware of the need for clear speaking and careful listening and to develop good listening and speaking habits. He points out that speech can improve language usage or degrade it, and that most people talk more than they write. He urges that listening and speaking be given equal status with reading and writing in the language arts program.

In traditional classrooms, much of the burden of instruction was placed upon the children's ability and willingness to take in information from what the teacher or other students said. In fact many teachers believed that children were learning primarily while the teacher was conducting a class. Of lesser value but not to be scorned was the possibility of learning while other children were speaking. Paying attention, therefore, was of first importance, so that one might take in information from what another was saying.

But children, like all human beings, have a way of tuning out what they don't want to hear. All of us listen selectively, fortunately. We make choices of what we will listen to attentively and what we will "close our ears to." To influence the listening process, to ensure that children listen to what the teacher considers important, some language arts curricula include instructional strategies for "teaching listening." These strategies include lessons with articulated motivational devices; the children may be asked to listen carefully to a story so that they can describe a particular character when the reader finishes. A game that Bernstein (1969) reports as effective in development of certain speaking skills is played by having a child on one side of a screen describe objects he is selecting from a box ("a large red square," "two small brown dogs") to a child on the other side. While Bernstein describes the game for its value in developing ability to use spoken language effectively, the game is also useful as a listening activity, since the hearer must select from a box on his side of a screen the objects he hears described.

However, there is no problem in getting children to listen under the circumstances described above. Children *do* listen when they are motivated to do so. The problem of the classroom teacher is to provide that motivation. Exhorting children to listen does not produce good listeners. Neither do lessons in listening, for their transfer value is doubtful.

The present trends in elementary classroom organization toward giving students more initiative in planning and selecting their own learning experiences may reduce the burden placed upon listening as an avenue to learning. In open classrooms where children more actively participate in learning, the problems associated with listening in the traditional classroom may not exist. With motivation to listen in order to carry on an activity, there is less tendency for attention to wander. Lessons on particular aspects of listening, like listening appreciatively to verse or stories, can be effective when they focus on how words can deepen awareness and sensitivity to the environment.

Modern Languages in the Elementary School

For one all too brief moment in educational history, the study of modern languages enjoyed its rightful place in the curriculum of the elementary school. As part of the discipline-centered, curriculum-reform movement of the early sixties, financed by grants administered through the National Defense Education Act, the teaching of foreign languages was introduced in the grades. Spanish and French were most commonly taught, although some schools also offered Russian or German in "enrichment" classes after school hours. But as the Vietnam war made increasing demands upon the American economy, and as public support for foreign-language teaching dwindled, many a fine Spanish or French curriculum disappeared from the schools.

For those school systems still offering a curriculum, there are, fortunately, many excellent teaching materials available. Publishing houses in the sixties developed "systems" for instruction, packages that included texts, tapes, records, and films. The main emphasis in these materials is upon conversational skills; typically, schools postponed reading and writing a language until a given level of conversational skill had been reached. The teaching method is the aural-oral: the child hears a phrase, repeats it, and learns to use it under the appropriate circumstances. Thus there might be a lesson on telling time where the child learns to ask, *"Quelle heure est-il?"* and to respond, *"Il est onze heures,"* if it is indeed eleven o'clock.

A commitment to foreign-language teaching has usually meant the hiring of a special teacher to present two or more lessons a week in each class. In the absence of a specialist, a teacher who is proficient in a language may team up with other teachers to share instruction in several subjects, with each teacher instructing in her specialty in an informal, departmentalized arrangement.

It is not difficult to justify the inclusion of modern languages in the elementary school. We live in an age in which Americans from all walks of life are traveling to Mexico and Europe, or working on jobs that demand some knowledge of another language. Furthermore, language learning is easier when one is young; introducing its study early in the grades provides the ear and voice training that will ensure comprehension and a good accent in later life. There is no research evidence on the exact time to begin instruction; many of the experimental programs commenced in the second grade, a decision made arbitrarily. The choice of what language to teach is usually a joint parent-school decision. Fortunately, the student who chooses to study a second foreign language in high school will find that study made easier by virtue of his previous work in the elementary school.

The seventies may see increased interest in modern-language learning in some early childhood education programs. There was a time not
too long ago when America did its best to stamp out languages other
than English and to make the children of immigrants ashamed of learning their parents' tongue. Some states even had laws on their books that
forbade the speaking of Spanish in public elementary schools. Then,
America, having done its best to wipe out the language in the young,
spent great sums of money to teach these same students the language in
high school.

Today, in some innovative early childhood programs enrolling Span-
ish- or French-speaking children, attempts are being made to teach
bilingually, to have a Spanish- or French-speaking teacher or aide who
can talk to the children in the language used in the child's own home.
Far from confusing the child as many had feared, the bilingual program
makes him feel more secure and aids in his adjustment to school. It is too
early to tell how effective such programs will be in preserving a second
language, but the possibilities are there.

In contrast to American schools, the Soviet schools have a real commitment to foreign-language teaching. Instruction in English as a second
language begins in the primary grades and continues through secondary
school. The quality of the instruction varies, as it would in any country,
with the availability of English-speaking teachers, but all students study
English as part of the curriculum. In the large cities like Leningrad,
there are individual schools specializing in just one language—French,
German, English, or Spanish—and there is even a boarding school where
children aged ten and older may learn Chinese and some African languages. While this writer is not urging the study of modern languages "to
beat the Russians," here is one area where we could take a leaf from
their book.

Summary

In this chapter we have considered the process of language acquisition, and particularly the acquisition of syntax. It appears that not imitation, as is commonly believed, but a processing of the speech the child
hears and an abstracting of the rules more nearly describes what goes on
in language acquisition.

There are social-class differences in language development, with recent investigators emphasizing that the lower-class child may have difficulty in using language to meet the cognitive demands of the school—in
holding to a given subject through a speech sequence, in talking about
things or events not in the immediate present, in making categoric state-

ments. Dialectal differences per se are not believed to affect school learning adversely, nor is the dialect an inferior, less complex form of language. Opinion is divided, among black leaders as well as white, as to whether children *ought* to have to learn standard English.

Research on ways to improve speaking skills favors a "natural" method in which the teacher and other adults furnish many opportunities in which the child interacts in one-to-one conversations, and in which the adults model a rich variety of syntactical forms. The Tucson language training model, which is based upon such a natural method, is reviewed in some detail.

READING LIST 8

Burrows, A., Ferebee, J., Jackson, D., & Saunders, D. *They all want to write: Written English in the elementary school*, 3d ed. New York: Holt, Rinehart and Winston, 1964. This book, which was originally published in 1939, probably constitutes the best single reference on the how-to-do-it aspects of teaching creative writing. It is a classic of its kind and should be read by all elementary school teachers. Chapters 4 and 5 are particularly helpful.

Cazden, C. *Child language and education*. New York: Holt, Rinehart and Winston, 1972. A comprehensive, highly readable, and fascinating account of the development of child language from a psycholinguistic point of view, environmental influences upon that development, issues involved in black English, and intervention programs in the schools.

Lavatelli, C. (Ed.) *Language training in early childhood education*. Urbana: University of Illinois Press, 1971. An anthology of papers on language development, language problems of the disadvantaged, some training models, and informal language testing.

Moffett, J. *A student-centered language arts curriculum, grades K–6. A handbook for teachers*. Boston: Houghton Mifflin, 1968. This handbook describes in detail Mr. Moffett's exciting, radical cumulative curriculum which places emphasis upon speaking, dramatic improvisation, and small-group discussion to develop speaking skills, and writing workshops for writing skills.

Professional Journals To Become Acquainted With

Elementary English. National Council of Teachers of English, 1111 Kenyon Road, Urbana, Illinois 61801.

CHAPTER 9

Reading

Of all the subjects taught in the elementary school, reading has provoked the greatest concern and the greatest controversy. Most of the American public is dedicated to the proposition that all children should learn to read, if not in the first grade, then certainly by the end of second grade. And whether or not the child has learned to read is assessed by his ability to attain a score on a standardized test commensurate with his grade level. The norm, then, for a second-grade student after five months of school would be 2.5. As Zigler (1966) pointed out, the goal of the classroom teacher is to have all children rate above the 50th percentile in reading scores, obviously a statistical impossibility.

Leaving aside for the moment how to assess reading progress, the fact remains that by any standard many children at the present time are not able to read by the time they leave elementary school. This fact was true in the 1950s. The Bestorites, the Tellers, and other self-styled education experts diagnosed for us why Johnny couldn't read: it was because the schools were neglecting phonics. The next ten years saw a great surge toward phonics teaching, yet reading problems persisted and, indeed, reports from inner-city schools and schools attended by the rural poor indicate reading failures today of staggering proportion.

In early 1970, the late James E. Allen, Jr., then U.S. Commissioner of Education, publicized the fact that the United States has 11 million crippled readers who suffer from significant reading deficiencies. He observed that the shocking presence of 11 million such individuals contaminates virtually every aspect of education. He pointed out that that is at the heart of our nation's inability to educate the deeply deprived child of the ghetto, the backwoods, or the isolated reservation. But it also strikes hard at the children of the privileged middle class. Allen stated that regardless of social or economic status, unless a child acquires essential reading skills by the end of the third grade, or is given intensive remedial reading instruction later, he will fall further and further behind his age group.

One might think that a reading problem of such proportions is due to lack of attention to reading in the early grades. Nothing could be farther from the truth. In a book entitled *Behind the Classroom Door*, the authors probe and analyze schools and classrooms today to provide a basis on which to design tomorrow's educational programs. One of the "instructional events" described in the schools visited follows:

> The activity observed most frequently and consistently at all grade levels, with the exception of the kindergarten, was reading. When one adds to this the scattering of related activities—instruction in phonics, writing, spelling, listening to stories, discussing library books, studying the elements of language—it becomes clear that the language arts, in one form or another, dominated formal instruction in our sample of classrooms. One significant difference between classes enrolling a predominance of disadvantaged children and so-called regular classes was a much greater incidence of reading among the former at the first-grade level, followed by a rapid decline in grades two and three. Whereas reading dominated in the disadvantaged first-grade classes by a two-to-one ratio over the regular classes, second-grade differences were negligible, and the ratio changed to about four-to-one dominance in the regular classes by the third grade. (Goodlad and Klein, 1970, pp. 43–44)

Despite the early emphasis upon reading, too many children fail to master essential reading skills. Some do not master decoding, and do not know, therefore, what individual words say. Some have problems of comprehension. Some lack the ability to understand the ideas that they are "reading." Some do not use reading as a source of enjoyment. Too few have a taste for reading material at a level higher than the comics. Fewer still can read analytically. But before we consider the reasons for reading problems, let us consider the question of what is involved in reading, of what it means to read.

What the Act of Reading Involves

For some writers the teaching of reading is basically a problem of visual perception. Buswell has stated:

> The first goal is to enable the child to derive meaning from the printed verbal symbols at the same level of functional efficiency that he has already attained in getting meanings from spoken words. The child has learned to interpret speech at a functional level before entering school. The first obligation of the reading class is to produce this same efficiency with respect to the visual perception of print. There is no substitute for this ability; this is a first obligation. The process of learning to read is the process of doing just this. (Buswell, 1959, p. 114)

Fries would have it this way:

> The process of learning to read in one's native language is learning to shift, or transfer from auditory signs for the language signals, which the child has already learned, to the new visual signs for the same signals. (Fries, 1963, p. 188)

This is the first stage of reading. The second stage is accomplished when the reader's responses to the visual patterns become so automatic that the significant identifying features of the graphic shapes themselves sink below the threshold of conscious attention. The last stage of reading is reached when the reading process has become so automatic that the reader can use reading with ease to acquire and assimilate new experience.

The concept of reading that has guided school practice recently conceives of reading *not* as a single unitary process relating primarily to word perception, but as a series of complex mental activities relating to all aspects of interpretation applied to written or printed symbols. As Gray has put it:

> The specific processes involved vary to a greater or less extent with the purposes of reading and the types and difficulty of material read. Stated differently, reading is recognized today as a vital form of experience, like seeing and listening, as an indispensable aid to study, and as an invaluable source of mental stimulation, enrichment, inspiration, and pleasure. (Gray, 1960, pp. 53–54)

While this broad concept of reading was evolving, numerous efforts were being made to identify the essential understandings, attitudes, and skills involved in all types of reading. Most of them, it was found, were an integral part of one or more of four interrelated components of reading: (1) word perception, (2) recognition and construing of meaning, (3) thoughtful reaction involving both critical evaluation and appreciative responses, and (4) assimilation, or the integration with previous experience of the ideas acquired through reading. It was deemed to be of great importance that all four of these basic aspects of reading be cultivated from the earliest grades on.

Obviously, thoughtful reaction involving both critical evaluation and appreciative responses, and assimilation, or the integration with previous experience of ideas acquired through reading, are levels of reading competence that do not emerge readily, but it is not necessary to believe that their arrival has to be as late as it generally has been, and still is. Reading in this creative way implies the capacity to deal constructively and imaginatively with the ideas read and things previously experienced. Thus the child who is immature with respect to age, but mature in his reading, gains new insights, new and illuminating ways of thinking about ideas. New solutions to his personal and social problems may evolve. When he is at this stage the reader is recognized as one who is using reading on a very high level, and his learning is efficient and effective.

It will be our purpose in this chapter to scrutinize closely what research has discovered about teaching reading that may ultimately produce programs for individuals known to be at varying levels of maturity. Very few adult agencies, colleges or universities, high schools, junior high schools, or elementary schools are presently involved in program development along lines that will ensure maximal learning through mature types of reading. We will take note of existing research and possible trends, but we wish to make plain from the outset that while research is able to give us quite clear pictures of creative, mature readers, and how they function, we have yet to discover precisely how such mature, creative performance may be taught.

From a consideration of research may emerge some notions as to how we may directly influence the potential possessed by young readers for mature performance. In short, we are at the speculative stage now, badly in need of direction—which can emerge only as dedicated teachers and researchers describe the techniques that they have developed to assist pupils in reading creatively, thereby enhancing effective and efficient learning. As these techniques are tested by well-designed research, definite suggestions for practice may emerge.

But one must not be deluded into thinking that the task is a simple one; it is fraught with the utmost complexities. As many writers have emphasized, for those who have learned to read the process seems simple, and many are the panaceas that have been advanced, all with the implied or actual promises that reading will come if only the formula is followed, the technique applied, or the material supplied. As was observed in an earlier chapter (Chapter 5) the matter of definition is crucial, and it is well to recall the dictum of Jenkinson (1970), who has called for flexibility because she believes that definitions must be capable of changing in base and in content as new ideas emerge.

What Reading Is: The Child's Point of View

As a teacher reflects upon the school's program and tries to implement it, she would be well advised to pause and devote some thought to her own expectations. An early study by Dady (1953) of a large number of first-grade teachers revealed that in far too many instances they expected a totally unrealistic development of skills in children entering school for the first time. The significant aspect of the study was that teachers, who should be conversant with the fact that individual differences do exist, were prone to expect mastery of nearly half of the skills studied before the child could perform satisfactorily. Another early study, that of Preston (1953), reaffirmed what discerning educators have long been aware of—a tendency of teachers to classify as retarded in reading certain children who actually are progressing in line with their ability. In many such instances, teachers exert a pressure upon the children that proves frustrating and destructive of wholesome attitudes toward reading. Preston called for a realization of the fact that a lagging reader's mental ability is a more reasonable standard for judging reading retardation than is the child's ability or inability to read material prepared for the grade in which he is placed.

On the other side of the coin is the fact that teachers have tended to accept substandard scores of inner-city children as the best that such children can do, and hence have believed that a teacher should not strive for higher standards. An interesting study that sheds light on how such attitudes affect learning is *Pygmalion in the Classroom* (Rosenthal & Jacobson, 1968). The investigators show that if teachers are made to believe that certain children have exceptional promise, the children will outperform classmates of equal or even greater talent. Rosenthal discovered some time ago that rats perform more intelligently if their human mentors, the researchers, are made to believe that the rats have been bred for special intelligence. When he put the same theory to the human test in classrooms, he found the effects to be the same. When teachers were told that certain children were likely, according to fictitious pretesting, to "spurt ahead," the children *did* spurt ahead.

What makes the experimental findings valuable is not that they tell something radically new but rather that they offer documented evidence of how teacher attitudes affect learning. Thus unnecessary failures may result from low expectations. In the "Pygmalion" experiments, children "falsely" labeled as potential "bloomers" tended to bloom with extraordinary frequency—without any special tutoring or crash programs. The tests on which the findings were based were externally administered to avoid the risk of bias. But it turned out that the teachers tended to grade their "special" children more severely than the others and to spend less time babying them. In other words, they respected them more and spoon-fed them less. Incidentally, the performance of the "ordinary" pupils in the same classroom tended to improve, too, although not as dramatically.

But what does the act of reading involve, insofar as the child is concerned? Over a decade ago, Edwards described what he termed "make-believe" reading, an activity known to primary teachers but not so often observed perhaps by parents, in which the child displayed an extreme degree of fluency. That investigator observed that if one were to turn to the make-believer,

> . . . you will notice a rapid rate of "reading" with few interruptions even for breathing. Why does the child seek speed and fluency? We can safely conclude that he is imitating others—his parents, older brothers and sisters, or other adults with whom he is acquainted. We can also be sure that in most instances parents or teachers will not discourage the child's

belief that "good" reading is characteristically "fast and not bumpy." On the contrary, this belief is encouraged in the beginner by many parents and teachers. (Edwards, 1958, p. 239)

Edwards' study had involved 66 retarded readers from second, third, and fourth grade who were remarkably consistent in characterizing "good" reading as follows: ". . . good reading is not bumpy," ". . . like on a smooth road," ". . . no stops and not jerky." For the child who is just learning to read, it is not illogical for him to decide that when he reads he should sound like an adult.

Denny and Weintraub (1966) declared that there was a dearth of studies relating to young children's concepts of the reading act and their feelings about themselves as potential readers. These investigators wanted to ascertain how the beginning reader sees himself, how he sees the reading act, how he feels about himself as a future reader, and what changes may occur in his concept of reading as a result of learning or failing to learn to read. Beginning first graders were asked such questions as

> Do you want to learn how to read? Why? What must you do to learn how to read in first grade? (p. 441)

Answers to the questions revealed that

> slightly more than a third of all responses given offered no meaningful explanation of what one must do to learn to read. Of the remaining responses, two-fifths indicated that a passive type of obedience was required to learn to read; slightly more than a fifth conveyed the notion that the teacher or someone else would show them how to read or gave some description of what the teacher would do in teaching reading; and less than two-fifths, 37 percent, were responses in which children saw themselves as taking some action in learning to read. (p. 446)

Moore (1970) in some unpublished research provides some interesting insights gleaned from querying young children about reading. On pages 202–204 are the responses made by pupils in the primary grades when asked: "What is reading?" The samples appear as they were given and remain unedited.

Present Approaches to the Teaching of Primary Reading

As the gravity of the reading problem came to be recognized by reading experts, it was inevitable that many panaceas would be advanced to deal with such a pressing matter. Commonly accepted defini-

What is Reading? Gr 2 (top)

It is a chalang.

It is a sport.
It can be a hobe.
It is very fun.
It is good for learing to read.
(boy)

What is Reading?
Reading is a favorite sport.
Reading is a hobby.
I think you should learn to Read.
So you will not have to wipe the dishes.
(girl)

What is reading?
Reading is fun.
Reading is a hobby of mine
You will Like it too.
(girl)
(girl)

tions of the reading act itself have been challenged and programs have
been advanced that seek to telescope or otherwise shorten the period
wherein the reader learns to operate at the so-called lower levels. Clearly
not all of the solutions offered possessed equal promise; indeed, some
possessed but little to commend them.

In a very thoughtful article published many years ago, the author
argued that

the beginning stages are of first importance in reading, because attitudes
and habits formed in the primary grades largely determine later develop-

What is Reading?   Or 2. (top)

Reading is fun!
I hope you like reading!
I dident at first,
But I do now! first, god
Do you? Reading is a sport!
            (Girl)

Reading is fun. I Like it. Sometimes it is hard. (Dan)

Reading is very   important.
Reading helps you   to learn.
I read Because sometimes the
Story is funny and   sometimes
it is long and short.   (girl)

Reading is very important.
If you did not know how to read you
would not know what word is what.
Reading is fun.
            (Girl)

ment. Ironically, it is this first level which seems to suffer most from oversimplification. Possibly this is because the children are young and their vocabularies small, but it is more likely the result of opportunism in accepting quick or easy answers to practical problems. Much of the inconsistent practice in teaching beginning reading should be eliminated by examination of the relationships between assumptions in philosophy, psychology and education. (Harding, 1951, p. 25)

Phonics

Over the years many types of beginning reading programs have emerged that do indeed differ in philosophical, psychological, and educational assumptions. One difference has to do with how phonics is treated, and here we find three principal approaches: the so-called syn-

What is Reading?   Gr 3.

Reading is skill it helps us alot.
Reading can be a lot of fun only if
you want to learn.

(boy)

Reading is something teachers
enjoy interrupting. Reading is
somthing I enjoy when I read to
myself (not aloud!) (girl)

Reading is looking and saying a bunch of words
aloud or silent. You can read many kinds of stories.

Reading is fun to me.
Reading is to read good
stories. Reading is to read
fairy tales.
        (girl)

thetic or "part" methods, analytic or "whole" methods, and "functional" methods. Among the "part" methods are the alphabet, phonic, and linguistic approaches. In the "whole" category are the word method, the phrase or sentence method, and the story method. The "functional" approach includes the natural, kinesthetic (through writing), and experience methods.

In the *synthetic* approach, children are taught letter-sound correspondences directly; that is, the children are shown a particular letter and taught the sound (or one of the sounds) of that letter. For *B* or *b*, for example, the children learn to give a *buh* sound, as in *bed*. Typically, they may learn vowel sounds first, then some consonants, at which point they begin combining to read words like *cat, mat, sat, bat*. In such an approach, the children do not necessarily learn the letters of the alphabet by name; *k* is not *kay* but, rather, *kuh*.

The *analytic* approach also teaches phonics, but starts with words that children already know by sight or sound. For example, the children may know such words as *see, Sam, sew, sore, sit.* The teacher may write the words on the board and have children find how all five words are alike. Following the discovery that *s* has a particular sound at the beginning of the word, the teacher has the children apply the generalization by naming other words that start the same way. In each case, the words are written for the children to see, so that auditory and visual discrimination proceed together.

The period of the 1950s and 1960s saw the development of many reading systems based upon phonics. The reader might well explore one or more of these. They include the Hay-Wingo system, *Reading with Phonics* (Lippincott); the Cordts system in *Readiness for Power in Reading,* and *I Can Read* (Beckly-Cardy); the Fillmore system in *Steps to Mastery of Words* (Education Service, Inc.); *The Phonovisual Method* of Schoolfield and Timberlake (Phonovisual Products, Inc.); The Herr System in *Improve Your Reading through Phonics* (Smith and Hoist); the *Phonetic Keys to Reading* system (Economy Publishing Company); the Daniels-Diack approach in the *Royal Road Readers* (Chatto and Windus); the Barnhart-Bloomfield technique in *Let's Read* (Wayne University Press). There are many others almost too numerous to mention or recall.

Reading through Writing

Both the synthetic and analytic approaches to reading place primary emphasis upon phonics. The *functional* approach does not. While a wide assortment of teaching practices are subsumed under the name, a functional approach is usually one in which reading is taught as it serves a useful and important purpose in the child's life, and phonics, either synthetic or analytic, is taught as needed. Reading and the child's own experiences are seen as related, so this type of approach is also referred to as an *experience* approach to reading. Writing plays a critical part. In British Infant Schools, for example, once children have learned how to form their letters, they begin writing—labels, directions, announcements, stories. They get the spelling of words from the teacher, keeping new words on small cards or in picture dictionaries. Over a period of time they build competence in spelling and are able to write longer and more complex stories. Since these are read to teacher, friends, and family, the child gains in ability to read, also. Reading is a highly individualized affair, however. The child reads to the teacher, but often two or three friends find a spot in the classroom where they can read in relative privacy to one another. And, since each child schedules his own day, such reading times may go on throughout the course of the day.

Reading through writing is by no means new to the American scene. Since the days of Progressive Education in the 1930s there have been many classrooms where children have directed their own reading programs by making their own reading materials based upon written experiences. The advantages of such individualization are obvious: motivation is high to read one's own products; there is pride in authorship; one's competence is not measured in comparison with others. All these advantages are in sharp contrast to too many classrooms where children are made to feel incompetent and worthless because they cannot learn to read in lockstep with their classmates.

Carol Chomsky, in a persuasive article entitled "Write First, Read Later" (1971), argues that all children ought to learn how to read by creating their own spellings for familiar words as a beginning. She would have them start first by learning the letters of the alphabet by *sounds*, not names, and by making words of their own choosing. They may use a set of plastic letters or alphabet blocks and lay out words for themselves to read. (Montessori used the same method, though in a highly ordered way.) Chomsky is not concerned with the correctness of the spelling to begin with; that comes later. She is interested in facilitating the process of sounding out words, and having the child first encode sounds and then decode them. When the child takes an actual part in the entire process, the difficult step of decoding is easier.

Sylvia Ashton-Warner's book, *Teacher* (1963), describes how she used an experience approach in teaching Maori children in New Zealand to read. The unique feature of her approach was the building up of stories out of words conveying a strong emotional message to the individual child. The result was that reading became a highly personal activity. The same technique is being used in innovative programs in this country in public and store-front schools. A black child may have among the words in his pack of cards "police" and "rat" as well as some with a more positive meaning for him.

Basal Reading

So-called basal reading programs are probably used in more schools to organize the teaching of reading than any other program. The basal reading approach is based upon a set of reading materials designed to take the child from the stage of reading readiness (kindergarten or grade 1) to a stage where complex study skills, reading tastes, and good reading habits are, hopefully, mastered. The program is developed sequentially, with increasingly difficult books prepared for each grade level. In the first books there is strict exercise of control over vocabulary, with only a limited number of words in a preprimer, for example 26 in one, and considerable and often inane repetition. Control is being relaxed, however, largely as a result of criticism of the *Look, look/We look and see/* school of highly restricted vocabulary.

Basal reading programs typically include instruction in phonics, the building of word recognition skills in ways other than the phonetic (syllabification, for example), and the building of comprehension skills that receives increasing attention once the child can read at about the third- or fourth-grade level.

Where basal reading programs are used, teachers are likely to divide the class into ability groups, with groups reading books that vary in difficulty. While one group reads in a circle with the teacher, the rest of the class reads and does workbook exercises independently of teacher supervision.

An examination of the ability-group system of teaching reading reveals many weaknesses of which the classroom teacher is only too well aware. First there are questions raised about the contribution of the workbook to the reading process, and whether filling in blanks in statements of fact (*Jack's coat was* _____ [*red, yellow, pink*]) really aids comprehension. Then there are questions of motivation, and of what dreary boredom—doing exercises day after day and sitting in a circle listening to others stumble over words—does to the young reader's desire to read. Also, the system does not provide enough practice in *oral* reading for the beginner. Often he reads orally for only a minute or two a day, yet oral reading for him *is* reading, is a way of testing himself.

Some teachers are adapting basal reading systems to provide for more flexibility and attention to individual differences. Team teaching and nongraded schools have been tried, but as we discussed in Chapter 6 ("Grouping Children"), they often are based upon a track system of ability grouping with all of its inherent weaknesses. A more creative adaptation is the use of a basal system in an individual reading program, with children selecting from basal readers or trade books (nontexts) for their reading materials.

How do the various systems work? Which approach is best to use? Some insight into the complexity of the question is revealed in the studies of first-grade reading sponsored by the U.S. Office of Education. These studies were made in different localities and represented a good geographic distribution. They were concerned with different problems in each instance and so designed as to avoid duplication of effort. Reports of these reading studies appeared in *The Reading Teacher*, vol. 19, no. 8

(May 1966), and in the same periodical vol. 20, no. 1 (October 1966); and later, the International Reading Association published the studies in *First Grade Reading Programs* (1967). There were, in effect, twenty-seven independent studies so well coordinated in research design, instruments of measurement, information gathered, and comparability of data collected that comparisons among the studies were possible in ways that had not previously existed. The project involved nearly 30,000 children and 1,000 teachers. A wide variety of teaching approaches were involved in the studies, and included among these were basal reader, language experience, phonic emphasis, linguistic emphasis, new alphabet, early letter, individualized reading, reading readiness, audiovisual, teacher supervisor, and approaches that for want of a better term were grouped under the heading of "reading for culturally different pupils."

But despite the high hopes for comparisons, they did not materialize, for it was observed by Stauffer that

> any attempt to compare method with method or study with study could easily produce misunderstandings and false conclusions. Each study must be examined on its own premises and results, and the reader must be careful that the conclusions he draws do not repass on the premises and results. (Stauffer, 1966a, p. 564)

Somewhat later on the same editor, in commenting on the U.S. Office of Education *First Grade Reading Studies*, pointed out that

> Regardless of the criterion used there is no one method and this is so in spite of the tragic consequences of the internal dynamism that some so-called methods have sought to advance—tragically, eccentrically, and captivatingly. Every method described used words, and phonics, and pictures, and comprehension, and teachers. True, they frequently used them differently, but they used them. There was no one phonics method that was pure or uncontaminated, if you wish, by other methods. There was no one linguistic method. i.t.a. is not a method but a medium. Basic readers claim everything.
>
> And where does all this leave us? All the malingering that reading instruction has endured for the past decade has not led to the golden era. No approach has overcome individual differences or eliminated reading disability. As I have said before, now that we have slashed around wildly in the mire of accusations let us remember that reading without comprehension is not reading. Let us focus our efforts on the eleven other years in school and make critical and creative reading our goal. Maturity in reading—that is the objective each child must seek and every teacher must help each child to attain. The thin crust we have punctured was just that and no more! (Stauffer, 1966b, p. 4)

Goodlad (1970) and his associates have viewed the current educational scene through visitations, observations, and interviews in 150 classrooms in 67 schools: 32 kindergartens, 45 first-grade, 26 second-grade, and 18 third-grade classes, and 29 classes at these levels classified as "special." Their purpose was to find out the degree to which frequently discussed ideas for schooling prevail in practice. Their expectations fell into ten categories, ten areas in which they felt that it was reasonable to expect that changes had been or were in the process of taking place. One of these was that the subject matter employed to teach children how to learn would evidence considerable intrinsic appeal for these pupils, and closely related to this was the assumption that the "golden age of instructional materials" would be almost everywhere evident in the schools.

Goodlad found that curricula were determined to a very great extent by guides prepared at the local, county, or perhaps state level, and these together with textbooks provided the major sources for learning. For example, in reading, the books of three companies—Ginn; Scott, Foresman; and Macmillan—predominated. Textbooks, virtually absent in the kindergarten, put in their appearance in grades 2 and 3 in rather large numbers after their introduction in grade 1.

> First-grade textbooks were predominantly "readers" but there were, as well, some science texts, spellers, mathematics texts of the "old" and "new" variety, health or safety textbooks, music texts, and language books other than readers. . . . Reference books were in short supply throughout; encyclopedias were visible in about a tenth of the classrooms and dictionaries in about one room in seven. Programmed materials were almost nonexistent. (Goodlad and Klein, 1970, p. 62)

These researchers were forced to conclude that the prime medium of instruction in their sampling was the textbook, supported by textbooklike related reading and workbooks. Few textbook series in what are referred to as the content subjects neglect grades 1 and 2 as was formerly the case: today almost all series provide books for these grades in science, social studies, mathematics, and English. Books or workbooks or programs packaged in other than book format are increasingly available for kindergarten children, but Goodlad sees the much-vaunted systems approach to instructional materials as perhaps materializing in the future, but hardly in the present day, in America's classrooms.

Beyond the Beginning Reading Stage

As children grow in their ability to read independently, they use reading more and more as a tool to get information. They need help in developing the necessary skills, including comprehension skills—the ability to take in or assimilate the meaning the author intends, and to accommodate it to information already stored in the cortex. The reader, in other words, must remake the information so that it makes sense to him. We ask the child to "put something in his own words," and by so doing, he finds out whether his level of comprehension is adequate.

In addition to translating into his own words what he reads on a particular subject, it is important that he learn study skills. The teacher must help the child learn how to locate answers to questions in reading materials: to use the table of contents and the index; to skim while keeping in mind what one is looking for; to keep up a running comparison between what one is looking for and what one is reading. The mental activities involved here are enormously complex, as anyone who has tried to program a computer to do the job knows. Modified outlining and note taking are also part of the reading-study-skills program. In addition, instruction in reading maps and graphs is necessary in social studies, science, and mathematics curricula.

Recreational reading also assumes an increasingly important role in the reading program as children advance in the elementary school. Reading for enjoyment and appreciation is one of the goals of the reading curriculum; so is the development of taste in choice of books. The difficult question of what constitutes good taste applies to any field where choice exists, and the question here is, "What are 'good' books?" How do we know when something has literary value? There are some adults whose reading is confined to confession magazines, pornography, or comics, while others think they would be stooping to a low intellectual level if they read such journals. In order to achieve the goal of developing taste in children, teachers need to establish some criteria for judging the worth of literature. They need to select books for the classroom that are well written, with well-knit, consistent plots, and with strong characterization. They need to be sure that nonfiction materials are reliable. Schools generally operate on the theory that sufficient exposure to books of good literary quality will develop reading tastes. Comics may answer the child's need for simple repetition of the same events; but after exposure to a rich diet of robust adventure stories, books that are genuinely humorous, or literature that has beauty and pathos, the child will eventually reject the easy thrill and demand more from his reading. Children, like most adults, will continue to choose some books that have value purely as escape literature, but by the time they leave the sixth grade, children should have sufficient acquaintance with books of quality to be able to recognize the difference between the two. Adequate school libraries together with easily available public libraries are essential if this goal is to be met.

Performance Contracting and Reading Instruction

As we move on through the decade of the 1970s the educational establishment in the United States is confronted with *performance contracting* (see pages 14–15) in education. The pioneer experiment in performance contracting, the Texarkana Project, developed an approach philosophically different from that taken by franchise-learning corporations in that it asked a contractor to establish a program on the local level and over time to integrate it into the local school system. Filgamo (1970) states that the paramount objective of the Texarkana Project was to remove the educational deficiencies of potential dropouts in grades 7 through 12. Thus, in Phase I of the program, efforts were concentrated on some 200 students in an endeavor to teach skills in mathematics and reading; in Phase II the instructional program was extended to include students from kindergarten through grade 6. Filgamo (1970, p. 305) says:

> This project is an attempt to demonstrate that there does exist at least one approach which can introduce quality control, so prominent in today's industry, and accountability into public education.

Unfortunately, while results initially announced were positive, an independent auditor concluded that pupils had been taught "to the test." The contractor admitted that the experiment had been "slightly contaminated" due to the "misguided efforts" of the head programmer, who turned out to be the contractor's sister!

The *Educational Researcher* (1970), the official newsletter of the American Educational Research Association, reported that in September 1970, hundreds of school districts across the country were either negotiating contracts or seriously considering the performance contract idea, which calls for private education-technology firms to be paid only if they produce, with the size of their payments scaled to how quickly and effectively they teach basic skills and raise the grade level of low-performing students. Earlier, in July 1970, the Office of Economic Opportunity had announced a $6.5 million, one-year experiment involving 28,000 disadvantaged students in sixteen states with teaching to be done by six private concerns.

The new program, unlike the Texarkana demonstration, is designed as a full experiment. The six private contractors selected by the Office of Economic Opportunity will apply different techniques in the experimental school districts. Some will use teaching machines; others will use incentive payments to teachers and students; others will use programmed learning methods. Still others will use a combination of methods. In at least one situation, children will work in special classrooms, learning from teaching machines at their own speed, guided by aides rather than certified teachers. In addition, there will be gifts for students, such as sports equipment, and higher pay for the aides. In time, it is said, through involvement of parents, family praise and encouragement are intended to replace gifts.

Cass, speaking editorially, sums up the situation thus:

> It is far from certain that the complexities of human aptitude, attitude, and motivation in the classroom will be any more susceptible to the innovative pragmatism of the behavioral scientist-businessman than to the philosophical dedication of the traditional schoolman. Students at Texarkana were given prizes for learning—free time to spend with friends, trading stamps, transistor radios, when a grade level in math or reading was completed—and reportedly these rewards provided stimulus, if not motivation for academic achievement. But the question remains whether, in the long run, immediate gratification can successfully replace the deferred rewards that traditionally have provided the motivation for learning. Perhaps at this age level it can, though school boards should remain skeptical until the evidence is in. In any case, we should find out. Fortunately, we have promise of a number of different laboratories in which to test the hypothesis that private educational agencies can succeed where the schools have failed. If they cannot, their disappearance is written into their contracts. If they can, the sooner we know it, the better. (Cass, 1970, p. 40)

The schools must watch closely to ascertain the impact of the performance contractors over time. Is this kind of program but a flash in the pan, or does it constitute a real breakthrough? And if it is a breakthrough, what aspects of the program contribute most to its success, or what combination of aspects?

Preschool Training and Reading Success

Concern for school failure, particularly among the disadvantaged, has led to a tremendous increase in compensatory preschool programs. The nursery school years (3–5 years of age) have traditionally been regarded as the period when educational intervention in the lives of children of the poor would be most effective. The child is old enough to bear separation from home, yet sufficiently plastic in development so that experiences to stimulate intellectual development can be effective. Build strong preschool programs, so the argument goes, and preschool children of the poor will no longer be at a disadvantage when they begin first grade. To that end, day-care centers, nursery schools, and Head Start programs proliferated, although not nearly fast enough to meet the need or the demand. A U.S. Office of Education 1968 survey (McLure and

Pence, 1971) showed that out of a total of 11,905,000 children aged three, four, and five, 3,929,000 children were enrolled in preprimary schools, whereas above 80 percent of five-year-olds were expected to be attending in 1970. These figures turned out to be highly accurate.

But what kind of preschool program will help the disadvantaged child to catch up to children who have been exposed to a "hidden curriculum" during the early years, a "curriculum" that includes experiences with books, stories, educational games and toys, and many social interactions that facilitate language development? The past ten years have seen many "answers" to the question, none of which is conclusive. The child-development-oriented nursery school has had many loyal followers who argue for a program that places greater emphasis upon social adjustment, personality development, and creativity than upon intellectual development. Theorists in this school of thought argue that play is and should be the main vehicle for intellectual development, and that mental structures develop as the child interacts with materials and other human beings in the environment. Others argue, however, that a relatively unstructured program is not enough to help the child overcome the effects of disadvantage; there must be something special about the preschool curriculum.

Some of the innovative curricula designed to fill the need have been described in Chapter 5, "Selection and Content of Materials." As we pointed out there, such models as the British Infant School and the Bereiter-Engelmann program take radically different approaches to educating the child. The tradition of the British Infant School at its best is to have trust in the child's ability to teach himself. The school provides the setting; the teacher and the peers, the nudge and the carrot; the teaching methods and materials, the pedagogical prompts. The philosophy of the Bereiter-Engelmann emphasizes an academic orientation; the disadvantaged child is virtually a *tabula rasa* when he comes to school and must master the fundamentals of language that would enable him to be taught. Teach the child a kind of Basic English, the argument went, and you could then teach him anything else you pleased (Bereiter, 1968). Teach him reading through generalizable rules for sounding out letters and words, with a minimum of irregularity at the beginning. Teach arithmetic the same way.

Which approach is more effective in teaching reading? Do reading skills develop more surely if they are not treated as academic exercises but are taught in a rich environment, with the child setting the pace? Or are children who master a systematized, structured approach to reading skills, beginning with association of sounds and letters and proceeding to more complex phonetic analysis, at an advantage? Evaluation in terms of test scores for Project Follow-Through is not yet completed, but we do have results from individual studies. These show that the innovative programs studied produced significant gains as measured at the end of the program, but that the gains tended to wither away in time so that by the end of second grade there are no significant differences in test performance of children exposed to special compensatory programs as compared with traditional nursery school children. Intensive follow-up studies by Karnes (1969) and Ogle (1971) reviewed progress of three groups of children at the end of first and second grades: a B–E group, a Karnes Ameliorative Group, and a Traditional Group. The complete California Achievement Test (CAT) battery was administered to the three groups. Children in both the B–E and Karnes treatment made significantly higher scores than did the Traditional Group at the end of first grade (see figure, opposite). However, at the end of second grade there were no significant differences between the three groups (see table below). These results hold true for reading scores as well as for tests of intelligence and achievement in other subjects.

California Achievement Test Scores at the End of First and Second Grades; Follow-Up of Three Preschool Programs[1]

| | | Grade Level Scores | | | | | |
| | | Reading | | Arithmetic | | Language | |
Group	N	1st	2nd	1st	2nd	1st	2nd
Traditional	25	1.69	2.48	1.49	2.29	1.77	2.36
Karnes	24	2.12	2.70	1.80	2.48	2.09	2.50
Bereiter-Engelmann	9	2.14	2.80	1.82	2.53	1.97	2.51

Results such as these might be looked upon as discouraging, but perhaps they only serve to highlight what a complex problem is involved in elementary reading failures. The problem has roots in the wider culture as well as in the school. When the poor had no hope, no aspirations for their children, success in school was meaningless. But more and more parents *want* their children to succeed in school, value school success, and communicate the value they place upon education to the child. Furthermore, social integration that frequently is the result of busing provides an opportunity for the values of different social classes to rub off on one another. The lower-class child develops a respect for and desire for school learning, and the middle-class child becomes less uptight about some traditional class values.

And schools are changing. More teachers and principals (though still

[1] The data used in compiling this table and the figure on p. 215 are from Dr. Merle Karnes' project #5–1181, Contract #OE 6–10–235, Bureau of Research, Office of Education, U.S. Department of Health, Education, and Welfare.

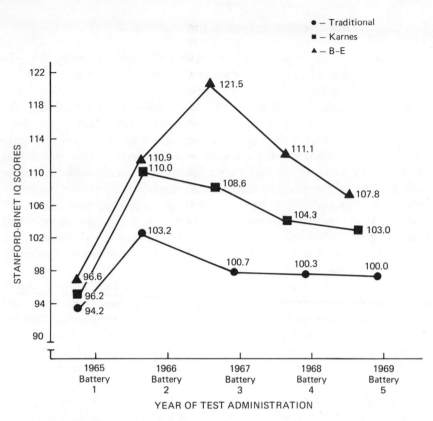

Mean Stanford-Binet IQ scores for children from three preschool intervention programs, tested at yearly intervals, 1965–1969. From R. Ogle, Long-Term Effects of Highly Structured Preschool Intervention Programs on Children's Personality Development. *Doctoral thesis, University of Illinois, 1971.*

not enough) are acknowledging their accountability for children's learning. They are looking at the lower-class child less as a person with low intelligence, incapable of normal achievement, and more as an individual whose potentiality cannot be assessed on a class basis but only after one has done his best to teach that child.

Perhaps in the end we will find that it is the teacher, after all, who holds the key. True, she will individualize teaching, and use some of the new technological teaching aides; true she will develop a strong word-attack program whether it be synthetic or analytic or functional; true she will use books of high literary quality to build taste in pupils; true she will teach reading-study skills following the directions of experts. But the teacher remains the chief factor contributing to reading success or failure. Some teachers can do all of the above and produce many failures. Fortunately more and more are producing successes.

Television and the Preschool Child

In March 1968, representatives of the Carnegie Corporation, the Ford Foundation, and the U.S. Office of Education created the Children's Television Workshop. Aware of the tremendous numbers of hours spent weekly in viewing television by children under six years of age, the workshop hoped to capitalize on the potential of television by teaching numbers, classic stories, the alphabet, language, and reasoning. The early thinking of the leaders involved in this project indicated a belief that numbers and letters of the alphabet might be offered through animation built around catchy jingles; that central characters in stories might be brought to life earlier by actors or through drawings; that games for children might be an instrument for identifying familiar objects and explaining how they are used and why. The games could encourage a child to try his skill at guessing and stretching his imagination. The result was the television program *Sesame Street*.

Sesame Street entered the world of children's television as a super-star, right from the beginning. The program was done with taste and verve, in sharp contrast to the cheapness and violence and lack of taste in regular programming. But *Sesame Street* was supposed to be more than simply a program of taste; it was supposed to help the disadvantaged prepare for school and particularly for learning both reading and arithmetic.

Sesame Street chose to concentrate on teaching names for letters of the alphabet and on teaching children to count. An evaluation by the Educational Testing Service of Princeton, New Jersey, based upon experimental data secured from 943 children, 741 coming from disadvantaged backgrounds in Boston, Philadelphia, North Carolina, Arizona, and California, as reported in the *New York Times* (November 5, 1970), showed that disadvantaged children who rarely watched *Sesame Street* improved from correctly answering about 8 percent of the questions requiring identification to about 13 percent. Those who watched more than five times a week improved from 19 to 53 percent. Similarly children were asked to name capital letters. Those who rarely saw *Sesame Street* answered 8 percent correctly in the fall and 14 percent in the spring. The children who had watched more than five times a week improved from 19 to 62 percent. While the children had learned their letters well, the program's indirect efforts to teach the many letter sounds were not too effective. The figures on pages 217 and 218 present these changes over the first-year "report card" period.

The basic question to be asked, however, is not whether children learn what we drill them on, but whether that learning has any significance in the real world, or whether it helps them to learn anything else

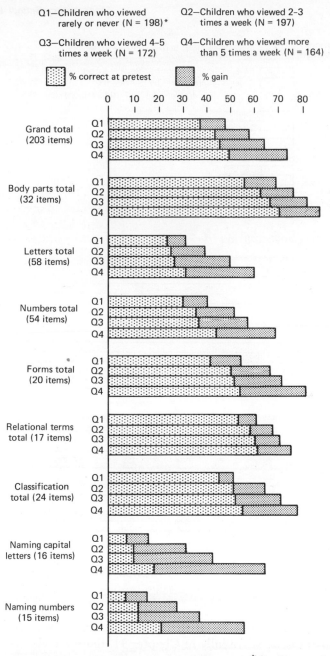

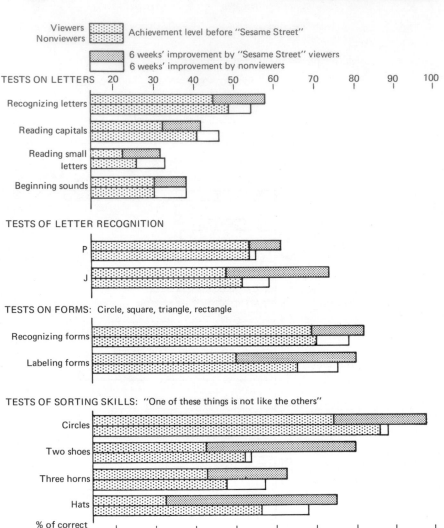

The impact of Sesame Street. © *1970 by The New York Times Company. Reprinted by permission.*

better. How important is it for the child to count to 20 or 200 or 2,000? As we shall discuss more fully in Chapter 11, there are children who can count beautifully but who do not have any conception of how to establish the equivalence of sets by one-to-one correspondence, and who will steadfastly assert that 8 does not equal 8 when one set of 8 objects is spread out in a row and one set of eight objects heaped together. And the only connection between knowing letters of the alphabet and success in learning to read was pointed out in studies showing that successful readers knew the alphabet when they came to school. The connection is not necessarily causal, we would remind the reader; mothers who teach children the alphabet undoubtedly do many other things to promote reading readiness. *Sesame Street* is a primary breakthrough in television programming, but at present is not likely to make any significant change in readiness for reading. But it and its companion production, *The Electric Company*, may produce tangential learning, which we cannot now accurately forecast.

This chapter has explored what the schools have been doing about reading in the recent past and in the present. It closes with a brief consideration of Chall's book, *Learning to Read: The Great Debate* (1967). In the period considered, one might suppose that some problems would have been solved and general agreement reached with respect to approaches and methodologies. As one reads Chall's book, one cannot escape the conclusion that over the years these approaches and methodologies have often been based on *a* philosophy, *a* psychology, *a* pedagogy, but one searches in vain for *one* that is based on all three! Many, many research studies have been quoted by individuals in support of their individual and different techniques—*identical* studies being cited as proof of the validity of *different* theories and techniques.

In her book, Chall shows quite convincingly that it is very difficult to find agreement on even the most basic questions. As she analyzes methods, these appear to fall into two groups: the so-called *code-emphasis* group, and the *meaning-emphasis* group. Chall sees the meaning-emphasis proponents as being in the ascendant at present, yet she personally believes that there is ample evidence to render the code-emphasis methods the more effective over time. She calls for a shift in beginning reading instruction from the meaning-emphasis to a code-emphasis approach. She is also quite concerned about the kind of content that should go into reading programs. She is convinced that there is no justification for restrictive vocabularies in children's materials and calls for more "advanced" readers for use by children in their early classroom exercises. Another recommendation calls for the development of better testing techniques and tests; and last, as throughout her book, she makes a strong appeal for improved reading research.

Much of the confusion that has prevailed in the "great debate" over reading could and would be dispelled if research, over time, were set up on such a framework as advocated earlier in this chapter. The elementary school has an obligation to go more deeply into the reading processes herein described than it has gone in the past. Research seems to indicate that mature reading performances can be developed in a child's early years in school, and many investigators are showing how this can be facilitated. What the elementary school must look for is the means for condensing not only the time but the effort usually expended in the development of recognition and of skills, in order that attention can be directed early at important tasks or areas that are usually now left for the junior and senior high school to develop. It is a truism that a method can be no more effective than its basic postulates, but nothing is more practical than getting one's theory straight!

A Summarizing Statement

Any reading development program is for *all* pupils regardless of grade level or place in school. Experts agree and emphasize that such a program should *not* be viewed as a remedial program for poor readers alone. The program must be teacher-guided and must make provision for a systematic, coordinated, step-by-step kind of development. It is not suggested that any one teacher attempt to do everything for everybody within the short span of a year. *But the individual teacher must be acutely aware of what reading is!* The teacher must know that reading is certainly more than perceiving or recognizing words, and comprehending their literal meanings. The teacher must see reading as a composite of recognizing and comprehending and evaluating and appreciating factors. These may not all be developed until late in the pupils' careers unless a studied effort is exerted at successive levels as pupils move through school. This *can* be done, but until it is, schools will continue to fall short of goals that might be attained.

There ought not to be much disagreement with the statement that the individual teacher, whatever the teaching level involved, is the key person in any program designed to develop readers who perform at the more mature levels. There is abundant research evidence to show that pupils do not come by higher reading abilities accidentally, nor do they come by them easily unless they are influenced by a home and a school which recognize and promote a realization of the significance of learning through reading.

READING LIST 9

Baratz, J. C., & Shuy, R. W. (Eds.) *Teaching black children to read.* Washington, D.C.: Center for Applied Linguistics, 1969. Presents a series of papers devoted to various problems and programs designed to alleviate severe cases of reading disability found in Negro children.

DeBoer, J. J., & Dallman, M. *The teaching of reading*, 3d ed. New York: Holt,

Rinehart and Winston, 1970. The basic dimensions of the reading process are treated in dual fashion—Part A of each chapter presents theoretical considerations while Part B gives a myriad of practical suggestions for the classroom teacher.

Goodlad, J. I., & Klein, M. F. *Behind the classroom door.* Worthington, Ohio: Charles M. Jones, 1970. Views the current educational scene through visitations, observations, and interviews in 150 classrooms in 67 schools: 32 kindergartens, 45 first-grade, 26 second-grade, and 18 third-grade classes, and 29 classes at these levels classified as "special."

Jennings, F. *This is reading.* New York: Bureau of Publications, Teachers College, Columbia University, 1965. Presents an inclusive inquiry into the nature and foundations of reading in all its ramifications—historical, sociological, psychological, educational—and endeavors to explain why we read, how we read, and how we can help others to read better.

Mathews, M. M. *Teaching children to read.* Chicago: University of Chicago Press, 1966. Focuses attention on the most significant events in the history of teaching children to read and discusses some of the experiments now being conducted to determine which of the two methods—the synthetic or the analytical—gives better results.

Stauffer, R. G. *The language-experience approach to the teaching of reading.* New York: Harper & Row, 1970. Provides teachers with a practical and detailed account of how the language-experience approach to reading instruction functions.

Professional Journals To Become Acquainted With

Journal of Reading. International Reading Association, 6 Tyre Avenue, Newark, Delaware 19711.

The Reading Teacher. International Reading Association, 6 Tyre Avenue, Newark, Delaware 19711.

Reading Research Quarterly. International Reading Association, 6 Tyre Avenue, Newark, Delaware 19711.

CHAPTER 10

The Science Curriculum

Like other subject-matter areas that have been under examination in this text, the science curriculum has felt the impact of curriculum revisions by subject-matter specialists that were carried on in the 1950s and 1960s. Most of the new curricula were concerned with the teaching of science at the secondary level. The Physical Science Study Committee (PSSC) was organized to revise the high school physics curriculum; a CHEM study project concerned itself with the teaching of basic chemical principles in high school chemistry; the Biological Sciences Study Committee (BSSC) worked to revise high school biology. In each case, the objectives were similar: to structure the curriculum around concepts considered important to modern scientists and to introduce the student to the processes of science, to the ways in which the scientist thinks about his subject and investigates problems.

There were also projects to revise the elementary school science curriculum. The criticisms of traditional curricula at the elementary level were similar to those at the secondary level: that there was too much emphasis upon knowledge of specific facts and not enough on concepts considered important by scientists, and that the actual inquiry process—how one sets about solving problems, which is an important aspect of curriculum—had been neglected in curricula to date.

Three Curriculum Reform Projects

Not all of the curriculum reform projects will be reviewed here. Selected for discussion are three, each of which has certain unique features and which are interesting to examine for their contributions to the teaching of elementary school science. Others are summarized briefly at the end of the chapter.

SCIS, Science Curriculum Improvement Study

This project, the most extensive of all the projects, was begun in 1962 under the direction of Dr. Robert Karplus, a physicist at the University of California, Berkeley. It is funded by the National Science Foundation.

The project differs from all other projects in its selection of content and in its development of teaching methods based upon contemporary cognitive theory of how children learn. Karplus and his associates have prepared ungraded sequential physical and life science units suitable for use in grades 1 through 6. The units were planned "to initiate threads of thought and inquiry" around such fundamental concepts as systems, relative position, relative motion and energy in the physical sciences, and life cycles, populations and ecosystems (the overall concept is that of the *ecosystem*) in the biological. The chart in the figure below shows the subject areas.

SCIS Final Edition program. The diagram shows all six levels of the SCIS program in Final Edition, along with the concepts introduced in each unit. Reprinted with permission from SCIS Newsletter *No. 21 written and published by the Science Curriculum Improvement Study. Copyright 1971 by the Regents of the University of California.*

Organisms		**Material Objects**	
organism	habitat	object	serial ordering
birth	food web	property	change
death	detritus	material	evidence
Life Cycles		**Interaction and Systems**	
growth	biotic potential	interaction	system
development	generation	evidence	interaction-at-a-
life cycle	plant and animal	of interaction	distance
genetic identity	metamorphosis		
		Subsystems and Variables	
Populations		subsystem	solution
population	plant eater	evaporation	variable
predator	animal eater	histogram	
prey	food chain		
community	food web	**Relative Position and Motion**	
		reference object	reference frame
Environments		relative position	polar coordinates
environment	range	relative motion	rectangular
environmental	optimum range		coordinates
factor			
		Energy Sources	
Communities		energy transfer	energy source
photosynthesis	producers	energy chain	energy receiver
community	consumers		
food transfer	decomposers		
	raw materials	**Models: Electric and Magnetic Interactions**	
Ecosystems			
ecosystem	oxygen-carbon	scientific model	electricity
water cycle	dioxide cycle	magnetic field	
food-mineral	pollutant		
cycle			

Basic to teaching methods in the SCIS program are two different types of lessons developed out of a conviction about how cognitive growth takes place. The lessons are called *discovery* and *invention*. Almy (1968) describes the rationale for these lessons as follows:

> Certain experimental and longitudinal studies (Almy, 1966, pp. 40–41, 126–127) suggest that the amount of new information children can incorporate into their understanding of a given phenomenon is dependent both on the knowledge they have already and on the way that knowledge is organized. Children who are becoming aware of logical contradictions may be less accurate in their predictions (presumably based on prior observations) as to the floating or sinking of objects when placed in water, than are children who are less systematic in their thinking. This finding highlights the importance of the lessons where the children are left somewhat on their own to explore and discover. These lessons also provide opportunities for the teacher to appraise the level of the children's thinking and to see to what extent the children are accommodating their ideas to those presented to them in the invention lessons.
>
> The SCIS program aims to nurture the ability to discover new relationships and to think imaginatively, at the same time as it facilitates the transition from preoperational to operational thought. Accordingly, it includes two kinds of lessons. One kind introduces or "invents" a new concept, while the other kind is designed to help the children discover the usefulness of the new concept. The invention lesson provides guided practice in using new labels and categories. It is clearly teacher-directed, and should provide an opportunity for each child to stretch his already acquired association of meanings for the objects in his world to include new meanings. In Piaget's term, the child "accommodates" his thought to that of the teacher, as he imitates her classifications. Such momentary accommodation may have little effect on the child's ability to use the classification, unless he can also try it out independently in new situations.
>
> The "discovery" lessons leave the children somewhat more on their own, in order to play with and eventually assimilate the new information. The latter kind of lesson also provides opportunities for children to make observations, perhaps paying attention to aspects of their world that have been highlighted for them in previous lessons, perhaps focusing their attention on aspects uniquely and personally of interest to them. If teachers are to assist young children in making the transition from preoperational to operational thinking as expeditiously as possible, they will carefully preserve the differences between the two kinds of lessons. (pp. 31–32)

Both types of lessons may make extensive use of laboratory methods. In fact, science lessons in the SCIS program are not the typical discussion-demonstration-discussion type, but are organized as laboratory sessions in which children work with actual materials to find solutions to problems. The written materials that children use are not texts but attractive laboratory manuals in which they record the results of their experimentation. For example, in a unit on temperature in a fourth-grade classroom, twelve laboratory "stations" were formed very simply by having two children who were to work as a pair push their desks together. The problem under investigation was to find the temperature of a slush mixture. From the student manual students learned what materials were needed; these were available in the classroom and children could help themselves. They proceeded to collect data as instructed by the manual and to record them in their manuals. They worked out difficulties with equipment as a team and checked one another's temperature readings. They also exchanged information with neighbors and commented on one another's work, which often resulted in students taking a second look at their findings. In the class session that followed, the teacher made a histogram on the blackboard, recording the temperature readings obtained and raising questions about the credibility of the extreme readings. The discussion that followed centered on what a thermometer actually measures (whatever it is in contact with), the meaning of thermal equilibrium, and, finally, the concept of melting point.

The laboratory method just described grows out of the project's foundation in contemporary cognitive theory. Instruction in science is organized so as to provide maximum self-activity on the part of the learner; children accumulate information from actual work with materials, information which more often than not results in disequilibrium in mental structures, followed by appropriate accommodation of those structures to encompass the new information. The curriculum is not open; lessons are structured in advance, but within that structure children are free to explore the problem, which is not of their making but in which genuine interest has been aroused, and through self-activity arrive at new knowledge.

SCIS is the most thoroughly tested and evaluated of all of the science projects. Each unit was tried out in several classrooms in very different school systems in various parts of the United States and revised several times before being put into its final form. Evaluation of growth in logical thinking under SCIS is discussed on pp. 230–231. Unfortunately no existing evaluation methods assess the zest, industriousness, inquisitiveness, and inventiveness of the children at work on SCIS lessons where the lessons are being carried out according to the philosophy in which they were planned.

AAAS Project: Science—A Process Approach

This program for grades 1 through 6 was developed by the Commission of Science Education under a grant from the National Science Foundation to the American Association for the Advancement of Science. The program is most often referred to as the AAAS curriculum

Observing and reporting. First graders observe and report changes in their aquaria in SCIS unit, Organisms. *Courtesy of SCIS.*

project. Curriculum content focuses on processes, rather than science subject matter. Science subject matter is brought in in a somewhat incidental way to teach the processes.

Processes identified for teaching in the primary grades are observation, number relations, measurement, space/time relations, classification, communication, prediction, and inference. Science content is drawn from the separate science areas, as Gagné (1966) point out.[1]

> A variety of content is used to support the learning of these skills. For example, observation exercises deal with colors, shapes, textures, and sounds, and involve such objects and events as magnets, plants, weather changes, rolling balls, animals in motion, seeds, and growing organisms. The exercises in each process grow increasingly complex, making use of what the child has learned before. For example, an early classification exercise treats the single-stage classification of sets of common objects (red-blue, rough-smooth). Successive exercises introduce more complicated classification problems, and an exercise in part 4 deals with a multistage classification schema applicable to collections of plants, animals, and other objects.

[1] From R. M. Gagné, "Elementary Science: A New Scheme of Instruction," *Science*, Vol. 151, pp. 49–53, 7 January 1966. Copyright 1966 by the American Association for the Advancement of Science.

In parts 5, 6, and 7 the exercises deal with the most highly integrated processes called Formulating Hypotheses, Making Operational Definitions, Controlling and Manipulating Variables, Experimenting, Formulating Models, and Interpreting Data. These more complex activities clearly build upon the simpler skills and knowledge acquired in parts 1–4. The exercises have a greater number of specific prerequisites which can readily be identified as having been taught in earlier lessons. Although process rather than content remains the focus of attention, the exercises in parts 5–7 cover a range of important topics from physical science, earth science, life science, and behavioral science. In the current edition, there is a trend toward grouping "blocks" of lessons dealing with particular science content. Quite possibly, this trend will be further emphasized in later editions. (p. 49)

The processes are not taught as separate and distinct processes. Measurement is related to prediction, to space/time, to inference, and so on. Gagné (1966) says:

The way in which these different intellectual processes build upon one another may be illustrated by beginning with an exercise from part 6 on "Control of Variables—Energy and Height" and tracing back the steps that prepared the children for it. In this exercise, fifth-grade children explore the meaning of the definition "Energy is the ability to do work," by systematically plotting the relation of one physical variable to another—the height of a cylinder on an inclined plane to the distance it pushes a block when it rolls down the plane. The children are led to formulate a method of measuring the energy of motion of a cylinder when it reaches the bottom of an inclined plane and pushes a block on the surface of a table. A piece of lined paper is used to measure the distance through which the block is pushed. The children try the effect of varying the slope of the plane, as well as the initial position of the cylinder, on the distance the block moves. They plot the results graphically. If students carry out this exercise with thorough understanding (and it is expected that they will), they are really doing some fairly advanced science. How is it they can do this?

First, they understand what is meant by "the property of being able to do work." They understand that in the operations they carry out they are actually defining the concept of energy. In other words, they have already gained the idea of the operational definition. In a most direct fashion, this has come from an immediately preceding exercise ("Operational Definitions—Force and Work Energy") in which they have learned that work is force times distance. It has also come from earlier exercises, with different subject matter, which deal with operational definition.

How do they know what is meant by a property of an object? By now this concept has been well established by means of a number of exercises which can readily be identified under the rubrics Observation, Classification, and Communication. (p. 51)

Similarly, the making of graphs, predicting height to distance pushed, relating height of cylinder to its energy are skills for which children have been prepared in earlier exercises. In fact, preparation for teaching difficult sequences of thought and action can be traced back to kindergarten and first grade.

Gagné points out that science education can be pursued through a content approach or through a creativity approach. According to the content approach, one would teach concepts such as force and energy directly, as does SCIS. But, Gagné emphasizes, one cannot teach the knowledge without the child's being able to deal with the process:

> One can't get very far with force and energy without teaching the child how to make systematic observations, measurements, and inferences. And if one proposes to do this in order to teach force and energy, the question naturally arises whether one might try to teach observation, measurement, and inference with reference to animal digestion, solutions of chemicals, and many other kinds of content. By this line of thinking, one is led back to a "process" view after all. (p. 52)

The creativity approach emphasizes the production of novel ideas, and would train children to be thoughtful and inventive in formulating new problems, restating a given problem in their own words, and generating ideas about the problem. The open curriculum probably comes closest to Gagné's description of a creativity approach. (In earlier days it would be described as child-centered, or following children's interests.)

The AAAS program, Gagné believes, has in it a little of both the content and creativity approaches. It rejects concentration on any particular science, but it does believe in teaching generalized ideas or concepts. It rejects the notion of a highly generalized trait of creativity, but adopts the idea that productive thinking can be encouraged in relation to the various processes of science that make up the AAAS curriculum.

University of Illinois Elementary School Science Project

This project (ESSP) focused on one domain of science, that of astronomy. A team of science educators, astronomers, and teachers, headed by Atkin and Wyatt, designed a series of units to teach students astronomy as an interdisciplinary field, drawing upon principles from many of the physical sciences and on the application of mathematics. Their objective was to move away from the typical astronomy units emphasizing only facts about the solar system and the universe, to a study of how the astronomer finds out those facts. The astronomer must study heavenly bodies at a distance. Elementary texts have long told children what the distances were to heavenly bodies like the sun and the planets. But how does the astronomer find out what these distances actually are? Traditional texts tell the student how big the sun and stars are. But how have astronomers found out their size? The fact that the sun like other stars is made of burning gases is known, but how do we know this to be true? As the investigators put it, concept development in this series helps the student not only to a better understanding of the universe but also to a more penetrating look at the methods by which astronomers uncover new knowledge about the universe. To achieve this result, the investigators drew heavily upon physics and chemistry and also upon applications of mathematics. In fact, this project has gone farther than any other in combining mathematics and science.

The scope of the series is as follows (Elementary School Science Project, 1966):

Book 1, *Charting the Universe*, deals chiefly with the measurement of size and distances of astronomical objects so that a static snapshot model of the universe can be developed. It includes

Measurement of angles and properties of triangles and scale drawings.
Triangulation to find distances on earth, to the moon, and to the stars.
Angular diameters to determine the sizes of moon, planets, and sun.
The inverse-square law of light as a tool for learning distances to stars and galaxies.

Book 2, *The Universe in Motion*, is concerned with how celestial bodies move in space and how these motions are observed by astronomers. It includes

Daily motions of sun, moon, and stars.
Planetary motions.
Moving models of the solar system.
Kepler's laws.
Motions of stars, star-pairs, and galaxies.

Book 3, *Gravitation*, investigates the causes of celestial motion and treats the laws that apply to all moving things in the universe. It includes

Basic ideas of speed, acceleration, force, and mass.
Gravity at the earth's surface.
Newton's universal law of gravitation.
Orbits near the earth.
Motions and masses of planets and stars.

Book 4, *The Message of Starlight*, turns to elements of spectroscopy and the analysis of light as an essential clue to understanding astronomical phenomena. It includes

Behaviors of light.
The wave model and the particle model of light.

The electromagnetic spectrum.

The role of spectra in determining stellar temperature, sizes, and chemical compositions.

The origin of light and the Bohr model of the atom.

Doppler effect as an aid to understanding much about stars and galaxies.

Book 5, *The Life Story of a Star*, treats the interiors of stars, their energy sources, and their evolution. It includes

Physical properties of the sun.

Models of the solar interior, using known physical laws as guides.

The source of solar energy.

Properties of other stars—their luminosities, temperatures, and masses.

Stellar models and evolution.

Birth and death of stars.

Book 6, *Galaxies and the Universe*, deals with the largest known units of matter astronomers have yet discovered and with the arrangement and motion of these units in the universe. It includes

The home galaxy: its contents, its overall architecture, the motion of stars within it.

Other galaxies and their types.

Arrangement of galaxies in space.

Motions of galaxies.

The expanding universe.

Like materials in other science projects, the ESSP units underwent extensive trials in the public schools and were revised accordingly before being published commercially as six separate books. No grade designation for the six books is given; they are described as "upper-elementary." Most fifth- or sixth-grade children could tackle *"Charting the Universe"* comfortably, following up with other books in the series in subsequent grades. The content is interesting enough and the activities challenging enough so that eighth and ninth graders not previously exposed could use the books profitably.

Evaluation of the Impact of Science Projects upon Logical Thinking

With the current emphasis upon inclusion of processes of science in science curricula, the question arises as to their possible impact upon development of logical thinking. Are children more logical as a result of studying the "new" science? Almy (1970) has been interested not only in possible impact of such study upon young children's thinking but also in the impact of mathematics study. She and her associates evaluated the effects of AAAS, SCIS, and GCMP (Greater Cleveland Math Program) upon the thinking of second-grade children, some of whom had begun their study of math and science in kindergarten, and some in grade 1. The children's performance on Piaget-type tasks of conservation, serial ordering, transitivity, and classification was compared with that of second-grade children who had not been exposed to an experimental curriculum. Results showed that children with no prescribed lessons performed about as well as did the children in the experimental curricula. However, children who began a prescribed curriculum in kindergarten and continued through grade 1 performed better on the tasks than children who began in grade 1 and had exposure for one year only.

In her discussion of the findings, Almy raises questions about whether instruction can *ever* facilitate cognitive development or whether such development is largely a matter of individual development, impervious to intervention. However, Almy also suggests some changes in instructional methods in line with Piaget's theory that might facilitate emergence of logical operations. These changes include more interchange among children themselves on the grounds that such interchange often provides cues to a child that he might have missed and that help him to clear up ambiguities; and more meaningful interchange between pupil and teacher on the grounds that when the teacher asks a child to explain his reasons, the teacher gets insight into how the child is thinking about a problem and is then better prepared to plan a strategy to aid cognitive processes.

Science Curricula Today

Has the curriculum revision movement had an impact upon the elementary school? Has the curriculum changed at all as a result of all of the experimental work? An examination of recently published courses of study and textbooks reveals some interesting trends that might conceivably be traced to the impact of science projects. The first trend is in the area of changes in curriculum content.

Changes in Curriculum Content

For one thing, elementary schools today teach more physical science than formerly. Units such as "Weather" are not new to elementary science, nor are "Magnetism and Electricity," "Sound and Light." But what is taught in each unit includes more basic science than was formerly taught, and the approach is different. Earlier the approach was through child interest: units were developed around persistent problems of living (riding the school bus or one's bike safely), and whatever science was involved in such problems was taught (facts about motion). As a result of the curriculum revision movement, science topics such as motion are taught as interesting and important in their own right, and the basic concepts in each topic, such as Newton's laws, are emphasized.

Perhaps the most important impact of the science-teaching projects is the latter: that elementary school science today is organized around key concepts identified by scientists in their respective disciplines as being significant. Furthermore, the concepts are selected and sequenced so that they build a structure of science. By the time the student finishes junior high school, he has been exposed to the major ideas making up a particular discipline, at least up to midcentury.

We can clarify the difference between old and new approaches by examining an area, "Livings Things," in one textbook series. The majority of pupils in elementary schools study living things, but past curricula taught such generalizations as "There are many different kinds of animals"; "Earthworms help to make the soil good for the farmer; they are our friends." The first generalization is so broad as to be meaningless, while the second is anthropomorphic; the worm is not working to help the farmer as the generalization implies, nor is he a "friend." Other learnings for pupils to master were highly specific: "The toad has a tough, dry skin." Few of the learnings sought to *explain*, to help the pupil grasp the underlying *structure* of the science of living things.

In contrast, the present trend in science teaching instigated by science-teaching projects is to emphasize *key concepts* rather than specific facts. Specific facts are included, but they are seen in relationship to key concepts. Granted, for example, that the toad has a tough, dry skin, the child is then asked to consider the function of that skin, and that leads to a consideration of the key concept of *adaptation*. Other specific facts such as "The eyes of the bat are adapted to night flying" lead to the key concept of interdependence of structure and function: that the eyes of nocturnal animals have more rods than the eyes of other animals, and so the nocturnal animals are able to use the available light to see in very dark places.

Barnard, Stendler, and Spock (1966) point out contrasts between old and new in the physical sciences also:[2]

> In the physical sciences also we can find a contrast between the "old" science and the "new" science taught to elementary school children. Let us take, for example, the topic of motion. In many programs, a pupil learns, "A wagon goes faster downhill because of gravity; gravity pulls things toward the center of the earth." But to tell a pupil that gravity makes something accelerate on a decline is only to give a name for the phenomenon; it does not really explain the phenomenon. For an explanation of any motion, the scientist turns to Newton's three laws. The scientist can predict from one of them that a constant force applied in the direction of the motion will make the object accelerate. This key concept of the effect

[2] From J. D. Barnard, C. Stendler, and B. Spock, *Science for Tomorrow's World.* Teacher's annotated ed. The Macmillan Science Series. © Copyright 1966 The Macmillan Company.

of a constant force can be used over and over again—to explain why a bicycle will accelerate even though the rider pedals with the same force or why an object falls faster as it nears the ground.

The scientist, using another of Newton's laws, can also predict that for any action in one direction there is an equal and opposite reaction. Again we find that this key concept can be used over and over. The frog is capable of a broad jump of several feet, but only by pushing backward against the mud or sand from which it springs. An inflated balloon released in the air will push forward rapidly as the air inside the balloon jets out, demonstrating the principle of movement of a jet airplane. (p. 12)

From a study of what scientists themselves consider important in science, key concepts have been identified to serve as the conceptual framework for an elementary science curriculum. It is interesting to note that these concepts are limited in number; the ten statements that follow encompass most of the principal achievements of science.

1. Events in the natural environment happen in an orderly rather than a haphazard way; man searches for laws to explain this order by observing, hypothesizing, checking his ideas, and rejecting those which do not square with reality.
2. Lawful change is characteristic of events in the natural environment; although living things tend to produce living things like themselves, over millions of years the earth and living things on the earth have changed, and diversified forms of life have evolved.
3. To find order in the natural environment, the scientist seeks basic units that can be put together in an almost infinite variety of ways; the cell and the atom are examples of such units.
4. All objects in the universe and all particles of matter are constantly in motion; man has discovered and stated the laws governing their motion.
5. The motion of particles helps to explain such phenomena as heat, light, electricity, magnetism, and chemical change.
6. There is a basic tendency toward stability or equilibrium in the universe; thus, energy and matter may be transformed, but the sum total of matter and energy is conserved.
7. When equilibrium is upset in organism-environment interactions, regulatory mechanisms go to work to restore equilibrium.
8. There is a relationship between structure and function; the structure of parts of living organisms determines the function of those parts.
9. The scientist has developed measures of space, time and matter so that he can communicate explanations that are reproducible and make predictions about events in the natural environment.
10. Man has changed and continues to change the natural environment, but because he is often ignorant of long-range consequences, his actions may have harmful effects for himself and for other living organisms. (Barnard, Stendler & Spock, 1966, pp. 12–18)

In curriculum building, the key concepts are broken down into elements and the elements arranged from the simple to the complex. Units on such topics as "Weather" and "Electricity and Magnetism" are then planned to cover several weeks' study at each grade level. Curriculum makers are mindful in selection of content and in planning sequence of the Bruner hypothesis that any subject can be taught effectively in some intellectually honest form to any child at any stage of development. Some cognitive psychologists would qualify the statement to specify that what is taught must include only those learnings appropriate to an individual child's stage of logical thinking. But with this qualification in mind Bruner's words have had a profound effect upon choice of subject matter to be taught, and textbooks today are full of learnings deemed respectable by the academicians.

Even a cursory comparison of current science curricula and texts with those of the early '60s will reveal considerable improvement in the quality of the subject matter included. Furthermore, subject matter is organized around major concepts, so that the kind of piecemeal learning found in earlier days has disappeared. But two things stand in the way of good science teaching: teacher background, first in science and second in development of logical thought processes. We come back to the second problem in the next section.

Teacher-training institutions have made some provision for instructing prospective teachers in some of the "new math" they are expected to teach, but one is hard put to find a single institution where future teachers are receiving adequate instruction in the sciences. This is particularly true in the physical sciences. Students do take courses in the biological sciences and feel fairly comfortable in teaching concepts drawn from botany and zoology. In physical science, however, most students will avoid courses taught in physics and chemistry departments as being difficult and irrelevant. Their criticism is partly justified in that the quantitative nature of physics makes it hard to do much in the subject without calculus, which few teachers-in-training have in their backgrounds. Also, teachers argue, and rightly so, that the course offerings in departments of physics and chemistry are not designed to meet their needs; in one midwestern university, teachers would have to take over forty credit hours to cover the subject matter required. Teachers need integrated short-term courses covering physics, chemistry, astronomy, and geology (not necessarily all in the same courses). Where such integrated courses exist, they are often taught by instructors whose own subject-matter background is inadequate. Despite all the hue and cry about strengthening the teaching of science and the tremendous amount of time and energy spent in government-financed workshops to update teachers' science background, only a dent has been made in preparing teachers-in-training, and we continue to pour out of teacher-training institutions teachers who will join the ranks of those unprepared in the physical sciences. It is past time when education departments and physical science departments joined forces to solve the problem.

Processes of Science

Curriculum changes as a result of science-teaching projects also include changes in a second curriculum thread: the processes of science. Formerly, curriculum makers talked about teaching the "scientific method." Students learned that scientists solved problems by observing, formulating hypotheses on the basis of observations, setting up controlled experiments, collecting and analyzing data, drawing conclusions, and evaluating results. However, as scientists themselves have made clear, no such tidy list of steps really describes the process of science. A committee of scientists and teachers appointed by the National Science Teachers Association identified the following five items as being important to the process. The statements might be described as articles of faith that scientists accept as basic to the way they work. They constitute a point of view toward the process of science that is one of the objects of the modern elementary science curriculum.

1. Science proceeds on the assumption, based on centuries of experience, that the universe is not capricious.
2. Scientific knowledge is based on observations of samples of matter that are accessible to public investigation in contrast to purely private inspection.
3. Science proceeds in piecemeal manner, even though it also aims at achieving a systematic and comprehensive understanding of various sectors or aspects of nature.
4. Science is not, and will probably never be, a finished enterprise, and there remains very much more to be discovered about how things in the universe behave and how they are interrelated.
5. Measurement is an important feature of most branches of modern science because the formulation as well as the establishment of laws is facilitated through the development of quantitative distinctions. (Barnard, Stendler & Spock, 1966, p. 19)

Piaget and the Science Curriculum

The two objectives of emphasizing the key concepts of science and the processes of science have more recently been expanded to include a third: teaching science in such a way as to develop logical thought processes. This particular objective derives from the developmental theory of Piaget. Science educators have reasoned that, knowing how children's thinking changes during the elementary school years, it should be possible to plan learning activities that will improve thinking processes. Classifying, ordering, inferring, identifying, combining variables and controlling them, formulating models, are all processes carried on by means of mental operations such as reversibility. The strategy is that of matching the timing of a particular learning experience to the developmental level of the child.

Classifying serves as an example. Piaget describes the young child's tendency to center on one variable in what he observes to the exclusion of other relevant variables and thus to arrive at an illogical conclusion. Asked to pick out long red objects, he may center on the redness and put both long and short objects in the same pile. He lacks the ability to do *multiple classification*, to see that an object can belong to *multiple* classes at the *same time by virtue of possessing more than one property*. Training in such an ability is provided in one series in a unit on "Properties" in which first graders discover the several factors or properties by which solids, liquids, and gases can be described. For example, children can experiment with plastic bags, filling them with air and compressing the air to form a bubble, and discovering in so doing that gases take up space, are compressible, and take the shape of their containers. They are not only learning about the properties of objects, but also *how to abstract the common elements* that distinguish a class of objects.

Training experiences are sequenced so that more complex classification activities are built upon the simpler. Following the step of abstracting common elements, children next classify objects by *two* properties. For example, they classify objects by *both* size and weight, thus developing readiness for the concept of *density*, in which weight and volume must be considered together. Still later in the sequence, there is training in class inclusion and in hierarchical classification.

Conservation is a second content category in which Piagetian training can be provided in the curriculum. The term *conservation* is often used in a specific sense to refer to the fact that number, length, area, and volume are conserved or remain the same in quantity even with a transformation in appearance, provided nothing has been added or taken away. The *principle* of conservation, however, has a much broader application. As Piaget uses the term, one comes to realize that conservation and rational activity are inextricably linked; he points out that conservation is a necessary condition of all experience and reasoning; that we can acquire concepts only when we recognize that they require a certain permanence in their definition; that certain properties of a concept retain their identity or are conserved even when used in new contexts. A magnet continues to exercise magnetic attraction even when it cannot be seen. Thus the acquisition of all concepts is only possible when the child can conserve.

The child can conserve when he has available to him certain logical thinking processes. These processes include ability to reverse an operation, to combine parts to make a whole, and to see that parts can be put together in various ways without changing the total quantity. Training in these thinking processes can be made part of the science curriculum. Children can carry out many activities in which quantity, weight, or volume can *apparently* change, but where appearance only is transformed.

Consider, for example, this activity: A boy has two cans, each containing an identical quantity of sand. He pours sand from one can into a tall, skinny container and from the other into a low, broad container. The tall, skinny container is filled to the top, while the low, flat container is not. Does one container have more sand than the other, or do both contain the same amount? The child who judges in terms of one factor only will look at the height of the sand in the tall, skinny container and think that it contains more "because the sand goes way up"; he fails to see that "taller than" is compensated for by "skinnier than." The teacher can help such a child appreciate the fact that quantity of sand is conserved not only by having the child physically reverse the pouring process, but also by teaching the logical proof, "If you don't add any sand and you don't take any away, the amount has to be the same; just pour it back and you'll see it's the same."

A third category of curriculum content, one that builds upon classification abilities and mental processes used to achieve conservation, deals with the concept of *model*, a concept that scientists find useful in their work. A model, as the term is used here, is an explanation of a particular phenomenon; it is an idea that one thinks up to explain the unknown. Before the existence of atoms was ever verified, scientists had invented their existence and proposed an atomic model to explain how matter is put together. Devising models is a very useful activity in solving science problems, but one that calls for high-level logical thinking. High-level operations, however, are built upon simpler operations; while eight-year-old children are not capable of devising models to explain complicated phenomena, they can begin to understand this abstract concept in a direct, concrete way.

The concept of model is first introduced in the science curriculum in connection with a "mystery box" out of the opposite sides of which there is a cord with a handle at the end. Held by the black handle the cord is longer than when held by the white handle. The problem is that the student must invent an idea to fit the facts. In this case, he can actually make a concrete, three-dimensional model of his idea to see if it really works. However, he does not have to reproduce what is inside the box; as is the case in formulating new scientific models or theories about the unknown, there is more than one explanation to fit the facts. The impor-

Models in science education. Sixth graders make their own minicell as part of their study of the SCIS unit, Models: Electric and Magnetic Interactions. *Courtesy of SCIS.*

tant thing is that the model must be able to account for *all* the facts. Children must list the facts to be accounted for, and then, by one-to-one correspondence, make sure their model takes care of each.

Once the *idea* of model is introduced, students can be encouraged to invent models to explain certain facts, or evaluate simple models. In connection with study of the chemistry of foods, for example, children might evaluate how well a nuts-and-bolts model would fit the fact that certain substances combine in certain ways with some substances, but in a different fashion with others. A simple model such as the nuts-and-bolts can prepare the way for a chemical-bond model to be introduced in a later grade.

The reader will recall that both SCIS and AAAS were also concerned with logical thinking. However, it is possible to go further than the projects in articulating the actual logical processes involved in specific lessons. Logical processes can be identified and nurtured in a systematic manner. With respect to classification, for example, the Piaget scheme can be described in detail for the teacher, and for each lesson the particular classification skill, like class inclusion, can be explained, as well as its place in the overall scheme. For all curricula, of course, the classroom teacher is the key to success. Whether objectives are accomplished or not depends upon her insight into logical thinking processes and her skill in directing pupils' thinking.

Typically, teachers lack background in how children learn and how children acquire knowledge. Below is a lesson on properties of objects taught in a first-grade classroom that illustrates how teachers miss out on opportunities to further logical thinking (asterisks indicate missed opportunities):

T: Today in science we're going to do a very exciting thing. It's very special. You will do it by yourself. Then we'll talk about it. I'll give you a tray and a very light wood. What is it called?

C: Balsa.

T: We weighed the plastic, too, and what did we find out?

C: Balsa is even lighter.

C: My dad made a boat out of balsa.

T: On your tray will be a piece of sandpaper, too. You can sand the wood. Let the shavings go onto the tray. Look at the pieces with your magnifier. See if the pieces are the same material as the big piece.

(Materials are distributed.)

T: Look at the balsa. What do you see?

C: Lines.

T: What do we call the lines?

C: Grain. Grain of the wood.

T: What can we say about the lines on the balsa?

C: Darker; straight.

T: Tell me something else about properties of this wood.

C: Smooth; soft; rectangle.

(Children begin sanding.)

T: What happens when you sand the wood?

C: Gets white.

T: Could you change the wood so it isn't a rectangle anymore?

*C: Yes, no.

T: What do you get in your tray?

C: Sand; dust; shavings.

(Child sands.) Look! It's round.

T: Now, put all the little pieces in a pile on the tray. Take your magnifier and see what you can tell me about it.

C: Looks kind of yellow.

C: Looks like cotton.

C: It looks like little pieces of wood.

T: Does it look like the wood?

C: No. Yes, it's the same kind.

*C: It's got dirt in it.

T: Where did the dirt come from?

C: It's from the wood.

C: It sticks to my finger.

C: It looks like dust.

T: What can you tell me about the properties of this? What kind of material is it made from?

C: Wood; balsa.

T: How do you know?

C: Because the wood was made out of that.

C: We just sanded it.

T: What did sanding do?

C: It made sand. Out of sandpaper.

T: Take your magnifiers. Look again. Where did the dust come from?

C: From the wood.

T: What did sanding do to the wood?

C: Changed the shape.

T: Is it the material?

C: Yes.

T: How do you know?

C: Same color.

T: And now is it a different material?

*C: Just because you sanded it, it didn't change it.

*C: It changed the shape into little pieces, but not anything else.

T: What property did it change?

*C: The wood property.

T: Is it still a rectangle?

C: No; changed its shape.

(Children sand again.)

T: What material is the dust?

C: It's balsa. It's the same color.

T: How is it different from the wood?

C: It's softer.

C: It's lighter.

*C: One is stiff and this one is just dust.

T: I'm going to shave off a piece from the wood. Is it the same material? How is it different?

C: One is smaller.

*C: It's the same 'cause you just cut off a piece.

T: I'm going to light these little pieces. Let's see if they are the same material. (T. burns one of the shavings.)

T: I'll take this around for you to look at. How is it different?

C: It's black.

T: Does it look like the same material?

C: No.

T: When you burn wood, what do you get?

*C: Ashes.

(Children sand some more.)

T: How has the material changed?

C: Different shape. Still balsa.

The asterisks indicate opportunities for teaching not only classification skills but also the conservation of certain properties that a teacher with a better background in Piaget might have successfully used. It is clear when some children say that sawdust is still a rectangle that they are not sure of the properties of a rectangle, and a few minutes spent on abstracting its common property would have been helpful here. In the same way children might have been helped to distinguish between *dirt* and *sawdust*, and given the proper name for the latter. Sharpening distinctions aids in clarity of communication and also of thinking. With respect to exactly *what* had changed in the sanding, questions like the following might have aided in developing conservation of quantity and weight and logical operations. The questions might follow the items with the asterisks.

> Suppose we put all the little pieces of sawdust back together again. Would we get the same shape? Why do you think so? Could we put them back into some shape other than a rectangle? Why do you think so?
>
> Do the little pieces have just as much stuff in them as the rectangle? Is there as much stuff after you sand it all as you had before? Why do you think so? How can you be sure? (Watch for identity, reversibility, and associativity in children's responses: You didn't add any or take any away, so it's got to be the same; just put all the pieces together again and it will be the same; the wood is made up of bits and pieces and they can go together any old way.)

Burning of the wood involved a chemical change that children were not cognitively ready for, and might better have been omitted.

Science and math both offer unique opportunities for furthering logical development. As teachers become more sophisticated about Piagetian theory, their teaching in these two subjects should be strengthened considerably.

Teaching Methods

Unfortunately, actual classroom procedures for teaching science still concentrate on textbook reading and answering of questions. In many classrooms, children read a chapter in the text and write out answers to questions in the book or on the board, which are then discussed in class. Such a deadening procedure certainly contributes to the joylessness of the classroom that Silberman (1970) decried.

Two innovations that have broken with the read-write-discuss procedure are notable. One is based upon the premise that children make knowledge for themselves, and the other, that the classroom should be organized so that there is opportunity to do so. In such classrooms there is a wide range of problems centering around a particular topic which children are free to explore according to their own interests and abilities. In a sixth-grade classroom, for example, in connection with a unit on astronomy, the teacher might organize the unit around such topics as

"Making Models of the Solar System"; "Finding Out about Parallax"; "Measuring Distances in Space." She prepares assignment cards, putting on each card some leading questions and suggestions for ways of finding solutions, including reading and experimenting. Materials are available so that children working in pairs or trios can assimilate information and make new accommodations, so that they transform what they take in and make it really theirs. Such a teaching procedure provides also for the development of the child's openness to learn from others as he takes as well as gives in the open learning situation. The teacher conducts class conferences several times a week for a pooling of mutual problems and discoveries and for planning for subsequent experiences. Other than these class conferences, there is no scheduled time labeled "science." Rather, within the large blocks of time provided relatively free of scheduling, a child is free to pursue his study of astronomy, in depth if he wishes, free from interruptions. He, with others, has a chance to get really excited by it and involved in it. Such a teaching method is especially suited to the teacher who feels the need for more control over curriculum than what is typical of the British Primary School.

Experimenting: A Laboratory Approach

Experiments ranging from simply trying things out to rigorously controlled comparisons have long been a part of the teaching of science in elementary schools. In fact, when a teacher announces, "Time for science," children will clap hands and give other signs of eager anticipation for they know that in science class, at least, things will happen. Actually, "experiments" are more often than not a demonstration rather than an experiment. A demonstration, as the name implies, demonstrates for the class a particular science phenomenon. Either the teacher does the activity herself, with the help of one or two pupils, or a committee of pupils will perform according to a plan made in advance. Other members of the class are spectators; some may be deeply involved but others not at all.

Conducting each science lesson as a laboratory lesson in which all students do the experiments either singly or with others can put greater demands upon self-activity than demonstration. Whether this method generates more learning than demonstration lessons depends, of course, upon the nature of the problem to be investigated and the students' involvement with it. Many an adult can remember high school or college laboratory sessions that were dull, deadly, and unrewarding. In British Primary Schools, where the importance of self-activity to learning is emphasized, teachers begin with children's curiosity about natural happenings in their environment, and encourage pupils to devise and carry out their own experiments (Schools Council, 1966):

Young children display a natural curiosity about their environment which provokes them to explore and to ask questions. The world they live in is unrestricted by subject barriers and the questions they ask concern nature study or science in its widest sense. Now science is not only a systematized body of knowledge but also a way of learning. It is this second aspect of science which makes it particularly appropriate for exploration by young children, since the keynote of the changes we have been considering is discovery by the children themselves. A question is asked (by the children or by the teacher), an experiment is devised, preferably by the children themselves, to find an answer to a problem that has arisen. The children observe and record the results for themselves and repeat the experiment as many times as they need in order to convince themselves, or for pure enjoyment.

· · · · ·

What is the right environment and what are the materials necessary to excite children's interest in science? The environment is the world in which they live, so the best advice a teacher can be given is: "Go out and see what is there." Materials for exploration are often the living plants and creatures in the children's environment. As for experiments, the homelier the apparatus the better. Young children are always ready to utilize the objects about them both in play and in their more serious investigations. But if children do not ask questions about the natural happenings in their environment the teacher must stimulate and provoke them to do so. In the first instance she may need to ask the questions which later, she hopes, will come from the children. (pp. 2–3)

Children as Tutors

The Roman proverb *Qui docet discit* (He who teaches learns) contains a great deal of truth, as every teacher knows. Many a teacher has added to her fund of science knowledge in the process of trying to explain to children a particular phenomenon. There is nothing mysterious about this result; it simply highlights the fact that the learner must be active, and that in order to be sure of what we teach, we must first take in information and restructure earlier concepts to accommodate to the new; we must be sure of our data, get feedback from students' expressions or queries as to what additional data are necessary, and in the process discover some missing bits and pieces that clarify the concept for us, the teachers.

Some innovative plans for the improvement of education include teaching by students. One such plan has been carried out in the field of science (Le Boeuf, 1968). Six pupils at a time from an eighth-grade class in Cambridge in the lowest track in science were chosen as resource persons for second-grade pupils in a neighboring community. With parental approval the "teachers" began their preparation. They used units developed at Educational Services, Incorporated, tried out experiments in pairs, made lesson plans, practiced on their peers and finally went out to teach. (We might note parenthetically that the use of children as tutors in other subjects is growing. See Gartner, Kohler, & Riessman, 1971). A number of positive results were reported at year's end in respect to motivation, self-concept, and growth in science knowledge. One student wrote as follows:

> This year has helped me to improve Science a lot. Last year I got D's and F's and this year I got A's and B's. Ever since I started taking Science I've hated it, but this year I learned to like it. It gave me a different outlook on Science. It isn't all facts like I thought it was. And it can be fun too. . . . (p. 56)

A project such as this one is no panacea, as the author points out. It would certainly not be advisable for every upper-grade class to engage in teaching lower grades. But vertical grouping in classrooms does provide a natural setting for such teaching-learning experiences, and, when combined with a laboratory approach, would seem to offer unique opportunities for science learning by both older and younger pupils.

In his criticisms of the schools, Silberman (1970) makes the point that the high school reform movement that swept the country following Sputnik "has been blunted on the classroom door" largely because the reformers, mostly university professors, concentrated on subject matter and paid little attention to how children learn. The reform movement of the early '70s may also be "blunted on the classroom door" if the reformers, mostly psychologists, teacher-trainers, and teachers, become romantics and assume that the child's nature can unerringly lead him to learnings that are good and true. Silberman tells the story of a cluster of children in one classroom who were examining a turtle with enormous fascination and intensity. The teacher told the children to put the turtle away and "get ready for science." Silberman argues that, in an open classroom, the children's interest in the turtle might have been used as a springboard into science, with the subject being pursued while the children's interest persisted, with each child being free to pursue ensuing interests as he pleased. But such a procedure might lead education back to the '30s, without capitalizing on educational progress since then. The turtle could all too easily become a project, or a unit of work, or a center of interest, and children involve themselves with busywork, individually or in small groups. However, under the guidance of a teacher who is aware of the contribution of structure in a discipline to cognitive growth and who also has confidence in children's capacity to learn by and for themselves, what happened next with respect to the turtle could be simultaneously child-centered and subject- or knowledge-centered, and what is good in both reform movements preserved.

Summary

The science curriculum in the elementary school has felt the impact of curriculum revisions by subject-matter specialists, resulting in a greater emphasis both upon *concepts* in science considered important by scholars in the appropriate discipline and upon the *processes* of science. A number of curriculum projects were undertaken to find out ways of effecting innovations. Three projects are reviewed here: SCIS (Science Curriculum Improvement Study); AAAS Project (American Association for the Advancement of Science): Science, a Process Approach; and ESSP (University of Illinois Elementary School Science Project). SCIS and ESSP emphasize a new approach to content as well as process, while the AAAS emphasizes process. Such projects have influenced curriculum content, as can be seen by examining current texts in elementary school science. In particular, the physical sciences play a larger role than formerly in the grades, a situation for which teachers are poorly prepared.

Piagetian theory has relevance for teaching science, and three categories of curriculum content where the theory can be effectively applied to the development of logical thinking are discussed.

Innovations in teaching methods include greater emphasis upon learner-directed activity and a laboratory approach. The open classroom is seen as a possibility for a less rigid approach to science teaching.

READING LIST 10

Almy, M. *Logical thinking in second grade.* New York: Teachers College, Columbia University, 1970. An exceptionally well-planned and executed study of the effects of new programs in mathematics and science upon the development of logical thinking. Dr. Almy worked within the framework of Piagetian theory and methods.

Jacobson, W., & Kondo, A. *SCIS Elementary science sourcebook.* Berkeley: Science Curriculum Improvement Study, University of California. Trial edition, 1968. A helpful sourcebook of fresh, challenging investigations that can be carried out by children regardless of whether they are following an SCIS curriculum or not.

Sullivan, J., & Taylor, C. *Learning and creativity, with special emphasis on science.* Washington, D.C.: National Science Teachers Association, 1967. Emphasizes the creative factor in teaching and learning science.

Victor, E., & Lerner, M. *Readings in science education for the elementary school*, 2d ed. New York: The Macmillan Company, 1971. A useful anthology of papers, particularly on the role of science in the elementary school, the teaching of science and evaluation of science teaching, the role of inquiry and process, and surveys of recent curriculum projects. NOTE: Readers will also find it profitable to examine as many as possible of the experimental science programs described on pp. 222–230.

Professional Journals To Become Acquainted With

The Science Teacher. National Science Teachers Association, 1201 Sixteenth St., N.W., Washington, D.C. 20036.

CHAPTER **11**

The Curriculum Revolution in Mathematics

A constantly recurring theme in this text is that there has been an extraordinary amount of ferment in the past ten years in various aspects of the curriculum. Revolution in the elementary school mathematics curriculum occurred first and certainly is the best known. "New math" has become a household term in the United States, and, indeed, in parts of the world including Japan, the USSR, Poland, Belgium, Switzerland, and England. In each country the movement in elementary school has been away from an arithmetic curriculum centered around computation (addition, subtraction, multiplication, division) to a curriculum including not only arithmetic number systems, but also algebraic systems, geometry and measurement, and functions.

Beginning in the 1950s, several teams headed by university mathematicians began serious work on the development of new content and new styles of teaching. Reform at first was confined to high school mathematics, as centers at the University of Illinois, University of Minnesota, and Yale University began consideration of modernizing content and teaching procedures that dated back more than a century and bringing the mathematics curriculum in line with the thinking of contemporary mathematicians. Gradually reform was extended to the elementary school, and school textbooks began to show the impact of the reform. By the late 1960s, there were twenty elementary textbook series and a number of other sets of materials out of which one could build an elementary school mathematics curriculum. There is still a great deal of reassessment of the new directions, with some experts taking the position that the "new math" is not yet a serious departure from the old, but new math in varying degrees of newness is here to stay.

The new math, however, as not-new as it might be, presented difficulties to elementary school teachers whose college training in mathematics left them ill-prepared to talk about "sets" and "set theory." Accordingly, pressures have been brought to bear upon universities and colleges to reform their own curricula so that teachers-in-training may take courses in modern mathematics. There has been improvement, but there is still a great deal to be done, particularly in the retraining of teachers who, too often, are being asked to teach content foreign to their own education. A hopeful sign: young teachers whose own education in the elementary and secondary schools included the new math are entering school systems in greater numbers every year.

One aspect of reform that is only just beginning is the integration of mathematics and science. Although mathematics is often claimed to be the language of science, and the dependence of the various sciences on mathematics is widely agreed upon, this dependence is usually ignored in curriculum design. Only a very few science projects, as we shall see, are making any serious attempt to integrate mathematics and science, and, at the teacher-training level, this badly needed reform has not yet begun. We examine some of the major mathematics projects next.

Selected Major Projects in Elementary School Mathematics[1]

P. Suppes, *Sets and Numbers*, Books K–6 (Syracuse, N.Y.: L. W. Singer Company, 1965)

This series of workbooks was the first to place almost complete dependence of addition and subtraction of integers on operations with disjoint sets in the very early grades. Because mathematical philosophers had identified set theory as the foundation of mathematics, sets were thought appropriate to introduce all major mathematical concepts. The union of sets is introduced early in the first grade. A strict but simple notation is used to keep concepts clear. Thus, $\{\bigcirc, \star\}$ is a set but $\bigcirc, \star$ is not. $N\{\triangle, \square\} = 2$ and $\{\triangle\} \cup \{\square\} = \{\triangle, \square\}$, so $N\{\triangle\} + N\{\square\} = 2$. In the second grade, variables are used; subsets and inequalities are discussed; multiplication and area are studied (a formula is given: "Width times length equals area").

Also in the second grade, solution of simultaneous conditions is undertaken. For example, the following problem is typical: $\{N:3 < N < 11$ and N is even$\} = ?$ The answer is: $\{4, 6, 8, 10\}$. Beginning with third grade, there is a decreasing emphasis on strict notation, and a transition to conventional notations with the workbook also becoming more conventional in content. The number line is introduced, field properties are named, variables are used frequently, and geometrical vocabulary is introduced (for example, isosceles, symmetry).

---

[1] The sections of this chapter treating specific materials were prepared by Anabeth Dobbins and James A. Barnard under the supervision of J. H. Easley, Jr., University of Illinois at Champaign-Urbana.

SMSG, *Mathematics for the Elementary School*
(New Haven: Yale University Press, 1965)

The grade placement of traditional subject matter in this set of texts is not much different from that in commercial texts of ten years ago. Some new content is introduced such as the following: Negative numbers are introduced via the thermometer in grade 2, then followed up by putting them on a number line, but there is no computation to be done with them. Much mathematical vocabulary is introduced. Congruence of angles and triangles appears in grade 2. Many geometric figures are discussed in kindergarten. The vocabulary of sets is used but there is not a great dependence on set notation such as in the Suppes materials described above.

Minnemast, *Coordinated Mathematics–Science Series*
(Minneapolis: University of Minnesota, 1969)

Mathematics and science are separated into different units. In 1969 there was a sequence of 22 mathematics units, some of which were published in 1967, beginning at the kindergarten level through grade 2. The approach used develops mathematical concepts such as set, number, and correspondence through stories, songs, and games. The impression conveyed is of a teacher-directed but very gently moving development. An early unit (Unit 4) spends a significant amount of time with counting. An earlier unit (Unit 1) uses words that many children would not be likely to understand, such as "parched desert."

A stated aim of the authors is to teach arithmetic geometrically and not to have students deliberately attempt to memorize number facts until after grade 3. Many approaches to addition are used, such as counting on a single number line, sliding a number line along a second one to find a sum, using a monogram or an addition table. At no time is a child requested to do problems without such aids.

Other topics included are map reading, symmetry, lattices and ordered pairs, and placeholders.

L. Rasmussen & R. Hightower,
Mathematics Laboratory Materials
(New York: Xerox Educational Division, 1964)

In these materials, there is a series of six pupil books that cover addition, subtraction, multiplication, and division in detail from a nonverbal point of view. There are few problems of the practical application type, but instead arithmetic drill. Basically, the problems are of the interesting, calculation types that involve the students in drill. Cuisenaire rods are used as manipulative materials. Some examples involve a code (children do problem, then decode answer according to given code to find a message); fill in $+$, $-$, $\times$, $($, or $)$ to make true sentences out of strings of symbols like 4 3 2 1 $=$ 11, and patterns that include connecting dots and clock arithmetic. Phrases like "If you care to, try these HARD problems" are used to challenge the student.

These books present no radical departure from other new math texts. Because the text provides basic drill, it is possibly the most thorough in providing training in sound mathematical ideas of all the new projects. It is also, possibly, the most demanding in terms of teacher competence.

B. Wirtz, M. Beberman & W. Sawyer, *Mathematics Workshop for Children* (Chicago: Encyclopaedia Britannica Press, 1964)

This series of texts is organized around nine "unifying ideas" (structure, sets, number and counting, numeration, addition and subtraction, multiplication and division, functions and relations, geometry, and measurement). The major emphasis for the teacher is that of teaching by discovery. The students are supposed to "think about relationships, to look for patterns and clues, and to draw logical conclusions for themselves" (*Teacher's Guide*. Level A, p. 3). The idea of "spiral curriculum" is followed closely. That is, students come across the same ideas again and again. Most pages present some sort of challenging situation. Major examples are games of "What's My Rule?" (teacher gives second number if student gives first; for example, STUDENT: 5, TEACHER: 4; STUDENT: 3, TEACHER: 2; STUDENT: 9, TEACHER: 8), noticing patterns, giving many names for numbers, cross number puzzles, problem solving (including problems that need a sketch or involve some thought before they can be finished).

AAAS, *Science—A Process Approach* (New York: Xerox Corporation, 1967)

Science—A Process Approach is a series of teachers' guides and worksheets organized in units in which subject matter is chosen to exemplify learning or inquiry processes such as observing, clarifying, measuring, using numbers, predicting, and communicating. This program, organized by the American Association for the Advancement of Science, differs from the usual science curriculum in which the emphasis is upon studying subject matter, and in which learning about processes of inquiry through such a study is more or less incidental. The mathematics taught in this program is closely related to the mathematics students need in the science experiments: measurement of liquids, ratios, dividing, scientific notation, descriptive statistics, and graphs. The description to follow concentrates on the mathematics content in the program, while Chapter 10, "The Science Curriculum," deals more fully with science content.

The curriculum is organized as follows. There is no text but only activities in kindergarten. Children make diagrams and are asked to arrange objects like the diagrams. In the first grade, children do not spend much time on addition. Pupils are evidently expected to know it from activities. Multiplication is treated as repeated addition on number lines. It is obvious that the mathematics contained was not intended to be the only mathematics studied.

Grades K–3 Processes: Observing, classifying, measuring, communicating, recognizing space-time relationships, recognizing and using number relationships, inferring, predicting. The materials use only the metric system, which raises a natural question: Where do children learn about inches, feet, and so on?

Grades 4–5 Processes: Formulating hypotheses, operational definitions, controlling and manipulating variables, experimenting, formulating models, interpreting data. Mathematical objects are used in the section on classifying.

Regarding Numbers: The study of sets provides a prelude to study of numbers. The number line is introduced early and used frequently. Negative integers are introduced in the first grade. Much use is made of graphs. Addition is done on the number line, and the addition of negative numbers is easily introduced quite early. Division is used frequently —averaging data, computing rates, ratios, proportions. The materials do not speak of a line as a set of points. The mathematical definition of angles is suggested after intuitive ideas (a corner, walking at an angle, bending wire at an angle) have been developed. The idea of measure of length, area, and volume is introduced; for example, sizes, choosing arbitrary units, adopting standard units, and so forth. Materials include treatment and use of scientific notation and negative exponents. Three-dimensional graphs are included. Descriptive statistics and vectors are developed slightly.

The Influence of New Curriculum Projects on Published Textbooks

The influences of the projects just described on the standard published textbook series are noticeable, if not profound. The changes described below in mathematics texts are typical but not by any means universal. Neither are these changes all that have occurred under the influence of new projects. They are presented to illustrate the character of the interaction between innovations and organized sources of curriculum material.

Some subject matter has been moved down in grade level, so that the point at which many topics are first introduced typically occurs a year earlier than before. For example, decimal fraction notation and some operations on decimal fractions have been moved from grade 6 to grade 5. Adding and subtracting common fractions has been moved from a first appearance in grade 5 to a first appearance in grade 4. Similarly, long division in which a two-place divisor occurs has been moved from grade 5 to grade 4. Roman numerals have been shifted in some series from grade 4 to grade 3.

Following are some specific changes in content to be found in arithmetic textbooks:

Science and math. Fifth graders experiment with rolling spheres in SCIS unit, Energy Sources. Experiments such as this one offer an opportunity for children to acquire math and science concepts together. Courtesy of SCIS.

Field Properties of Arithmetic. In newer texts the field properties of arithmetic (commutative, associative, and distributive laws especially) are studied and named explicitly, whereas formerly no attention was given to these properties. Some series as early as grades 2 and 3 name the commutative principle of addition, the associative principle of addition, and zero as the identity element. Also, the distributive principle is named as early as the fourth grade, and these phrases are used: "inverse of addition" for "subtraction," "inverse of multiplication" for "division," and "commutative and associative principles" for "multiplication."

Related to the attention given to field properties is the practice in some new books of introducing addition and subtraction almost simultaneously, and multiplication and division together, whereas the earlier books treated them as completely separate operations.

Sets. Another new topic that has received much attention is the language of sets. It is sometimes said that the new math books include or are based on set theory, but, in the literal sense of set theory, this does not appear to be true at the elementary level. Set theory refers to properties of operations on sets, such as the commutativity of union and intersection, and distributivity of union with respect to intersection. Addition of positive integers is done with these set properties in the Suppes material. What is used in almost all other cases is the language of union and intersection and the language that refers to disjoint sets in defining arithmetic operations, but not set theory per se. There is a consistent use of set notation throughout all six grades.

Geometry. Plane and solid geometry treated in an intuitive way have been introduced into the elementary school curriculum. Careful attention is paid to precise geometric definitions in many newer texts. For example, when a student is told to "color the circle blue" in one series, he is expected to distinguish between coloring points on the circle and points in the interior of the circle. Concepts such as point, line, curve, and plane are introduced, and a compass is used by students as early as grade 3. Experiences with the physical world are used to introduce such principles as symmetry, perpendicularity, parallelism, and congruence.

Algebra. Although some popular writers are fond of saying that algebra is now taught in grade 1, actually, the evident aspect of algebra that has been introduced into the grades is the mathematical sentence. There has been a noticeable shift in notation from the traditional vertical way of writing exercises to the horizontal format more characteristic of algebra. This presumably makes the algebraic properties more apparent and eases the transition to algebra by use of frames in writing equations. For example, $\Box + 6 = 12$ is equivalent to $x + 6 = 12$; that is, these equations have the same solutions in the set of integers. In rare instances, "solution set" is defined, but is not used extensively. Students are still told to "find the number for n" or "solve the equation," and are not expected to discuss a set of numbers that makes an equation or other statement true. Occasionally equations with two frames, that is, equations with two unknowns, are encountered in a supplementary exercise.

Additional Topics. Other topics not treated in earlier textbook series are inequalities, odd and even numbers, negative numbers, numeration systems, primes, and probability and statistics. Number patterns appear to have increasing importance. This is evidenced by problems of the type, "What are the next three numbers in the series: 5, 7, 6, 8, 7, 9, 8?" and also by the increased use of multiplication and addition tables at all levels. Students are asked to complete tables according to the number patterns they find and also to look for patterns in completed tables.

In earlier textbooks, percent problems were often treated in terms of three cases; that is, in the sentence, "x is y percent of z," finding an unknown in each position is treated as a separate problem, and one is taught the appropriate operations to use for that case. In the newer texts, percent is sometimes treated as a problem involving a proportion, that is, an equation of two fractions so that all three cases are covered by one procedure or case. This trend toward unification of the many different types of problems is certainly commendable.

Changes in Style and Language. Changes in style and language are quite noticeable. For example, developmental exercises that lead to the discovery of a principle tend to replace exposition of the method or principle for carrying through certain operations. That is, the student is expected to develop his own understanding with the help of questions and other hints rather than to learn through interpreting the language of the textbook. Another change in style and language is the way in which presentations of algorithms for operations—such as "cancelling" and "borrowing" in subtraction—are treated to include new terminology such as "renaming" and "regrouping" instead of "cancelling" and "borrowing." It is characteristic of the changes that a rather specific term like "borrowing" is dropped and a rather general term like "regrouping" is used instead.

Begle (1970) has pointed out that the new school mathematics differs little from the old in its subject matter; only a few old topics have been deemphasized and a few new ones added. The major difference, and this applies to texts as well as to projects materials, lies in the point of view toward mathematics. Computational skill is no longer the be-all of arithmetic learning; there is at least an equal emphasis upon concepts of mathematics and the structure of mathematics.

Changes in Teaching Methods

Along with changes in content of mathematics curricula have come changes in teaching methods. One of the most distressing evaluations of mathematics teaching, heard over and over again, is that children *hate* mathematics; when asked to name the subject actively disliked or liked the least, pupils almost invariably name mathematics. Such an attitude is in great contrast to attitudes found in Japan and the USSR, where mathematics is frequently named as the favorite subject. While it is our hope that the negative attitudes of American students will change as content and methods of teaching change, we have to point out that much of the curriculum and teaching in Japan and the USSR is highly traditional. There is a "new math" in both countries, but reform has not proceeded very far. Perhaps national likes or dislikes of a subject have cultural roots outside the classroom.

Teaching methods in connection with the new math have emphasized discovery methods and use of concrete materials. *Discovery method* is the term usually used to describe a teaching procedure in which the teacher presents a problem and leads pupils by judicious questioning to discover the rule or principle essential to the solution of the problem. The following descriptions of various classroom procedures in teaching subtraction with "regrouping" illustrate the difference between the "teacher-telling" and "pupil-discovery" methods of introducing new steps.

Teacher-Telling

A third-grade class has just finished a unit on subtraction in which no "regrouping" is required (such as $48 - 26$). The teacher begins the new unit on subtraction involving "regrouping" by having all the children look to the chalkboard. The teacher starts, "Everyone watch and I'll show you how to do subtraction that involves *regrouping. Regrouping* means I will need to regroup the number in the minuend in order to accomplish the subtraction easily. So for the problem $32 - 15$, I see I cannot subtract the units. That is, I cannot subtract 5 from 2, so I need to regroup 32. 32 is $30 + 2$, but another *name* for 30 is $20 + 10$. This means $30 + 2$ is $(20 + 10) + 2$, which I *regroup* to $20 + (10 + 2)$, which is $20 + 12$. Now I can subtract 5 from 12 and, of course, 10 from 20. So I have $(20 + 12) - (10 + 5)$, which is $(20 - 10) + (12 - 5)$ or $10 + 7$. And everyone knows this is a name for 17." (The example may be written vertically.) The teacher proceeds with several more examples, and then has the children attempt to work problems from their text. Notice that in this method of teaching, students rarely, if ever, contribute to the discussion.

Pupil-Discovery

As in the "teacher-telling" method of teaching, a third-grade class has finished a unit on subtraction in which no "regrouping" is required. The students have been using expanded notation in doing subtraction. For example, $48 - 26$ could be written as $(40 + 8) - (20 + 6)$, which is $(40 - 20) + (8 - 6)$, and a difference of $20 + 2$ or 22 is found. Also, the children may have used some manipulative or concrete materials, such as multibased blocks, to illustrate subtraction without "regrouping" before the abstract form is attempted as shown in the preceding example. Subtraction involving "regrouping" is then introduced through a problem situation. The teacher starts, "The table where John, Mary, and Joe are seated is longer than the table where Jane and Sue are seated. How much longer is John's table?" The children might proceed by measuring the tables with a "ruler"; they find John's table to be 23 units and Jane's table to be 15 units. The teacher asks, "Has someone found how much longer yet?" John replies, "I have! 8 units." The teacher asks, "How did you find your answer, John?" John states, "I measured Jane's table, marked off that much on my table and measured what was left over." (For this problem, John's solution is perfectly valid.) The teacher continues, "John has a way to find an answer by measuring; does anyone else have an answer by a different method?" Sue answers, "I have! I subtracted 15 from 23 and got 8!" (If no one has used subtraction, the teacher may need to make this suggestion.) The teacher would then continue by having Sue illustrate how she found her answer, and would then probably assign new problems. It should be noted that discovery is *not* constant in a classroom. Different children will discover different concepts at different rates. Also, students cannot discover such ideas as names, signs, or symbols. It is the teacher's job to provide such information and to *guide* the discovery process.

As the teacher assigns problems involving "regrouping" in subtraction, the students may find it helpful to use some manipulative materials. In the "teacher-telling" method of teaching, the materials tend to be toys, since the students expect to be told what to do. In the "pupil-discovery" method of teaching, the students tend to rely on their own knowledge once the teacher has given instruction as to the use of the materials. Following are descriptions of some manipulative materials and games.

Manipulative Materials and Games

With the development of new math, mathematics educators have found that manipulative materials and games can play an important part in the development of certain concepts and ideas for children. Manipulative materials should be concrete objects that children can manipulate easily and should have as a characteristic the concept or idea to be developed. Various objects, such as beads to represent points, or ice cream sticks bundled to represent a numeration system, can be made by the teacher. There are numerous commercially manufactured materials, three of which are described below.

Z. P. Dienes, *Multibase Arithmetic Blocks*
(Harlow, Essex, England: The Educational
Supply Association Limited)

Multibase Arithmetic Blocks are a type of manipulative material that can provide elementary students with a concrete model of certain mathematical concepts. A complete set of M.A.B. consists of one box each of base 5, base 6, and base 10 materials, and two boxes each of base 3 and base 4 materials. For example, a base 4 box would contain 100 three-eighths-inch cubes to be used as units, 40 longs which are each equivalent to 4 units placed end to end, 40 flats which are each equivalent to 4 longs placed side by side or 16 units, and 10 blocks which are each equivalent to 4 flats stacked or 64 units. These materials can be used to illustrate place-value, addition, subtraction, division, multiplication, translation from one numeration system to another, and problem solving, along with several games.

G. Gattegno, *Numbers in Color*
(New Rochelle, N. Y.: Cuisenaire
Corporation of America)

Colored centimeter rods (first used by George Cuisenaire of Belgium, after whom they are often called) are rods having a 1×1 centimeter cross section and lengths of integral centimeter values from 1 to 10. The method of teaching advocated by Gattegno is not the traditional one of having children play games with the rods. Instead, the rods are used to discover properties of arithmetic and geometry. The four basic operations of arithmetic are taught at the same time. Special abbreviations or notations are introduced for complex products, fractions, and exponents so that the rods provide a semiabstract manipulable material for a wide range of mathematical topics.

Z. P. Dienes, *Algebraic Experience Materials*
(London: The National Foundation
for Educational Research)

The A.E.M. materials are a manipulative material designed to enhance the elementary student's knowledge of multiplication. A set of
A.E.M. materials consists of one balance, one 12×12-hole pegboard,
together with numerous objects and geometric shapes to be used on the
balance and pegboard. Some of the concepts developed through these
materials are commutative and associative laws of multiplication, distributive law, and completing the square.

Games

Once a child understands a concept, a game can be used as a mode
of practice to develop skill. The criteria of a good game are (1) it must
be fun; (2) it must involve competition; (3) it must involve an element
of chance; (4) it must involve strategy to win; (5) it must provide
practice in some concept. In any game, the child must have predetermined rules that he understands in order for the game to provide practice. A game such as dominoes can provide practice in one-to-one correspondence if the teacher sets appropriate rules.

One commercially manufactured game is TUF (TUF, P.O. Box 173,
Rowayton, Connecticut 06853). A game suitable for almost any level
from grade 2 and up, TUF can involve from one to four players, all
playing at once. The game consists of 3 hourglass timers, and 64 cubes
with various numerals, operations, functions, and relations written on
them. The object of the game is to roll a predetermined set of blocks
within a time limit and then form a true mathematical sentence.

Manipulative materials and games can be used in either the traditional or open classroom. Children work in small groups consisting of one
to four students. One can identify three stages of learning—play, dawning awareness, repetition—and student activities with the materials are
directed along this line of thought.

Although commercial manufacturers sell numerous manipulative
materials and games, a creative teacher who has the time to do so will
find it less expensive—and possibly more educational—to make his own
materials. Number blocks (dice) and 1-inch cubes are particularly useful. The teacher need only keep in mind the *purposes* of both manipulative materials and games.

The Growth of Mathematical Thinking

Piaget's work on the development of logical thinking—and especially on the growth of concepts of number, geometry, and space—has implications for the mathematics curriculum. Piaget points out that children's thinking changes as they grow up, and that the ages of six or seven, and eleven or twelve, years are about when these changes occur. The early school years, through second grade for some children, are those in which the child's thinking is perceptual, when he centers on one variable, and when he lacks the ability to reverse operations, perform identity operations, and the like. He thinks *intuitively*, meaning that things are what they *seem* and not what they are. If it appears that there are more objects when the objects occupy more space, then there are more objects.

Piaget's insights suggest for the primary curriculum the inclusion of experiences that will enable the child to move into a stage at which logical necessity rather than perceptual judgments will guide thinking. His work is significant for both content and method. He has made us more aware of how the young child is thinking about number, geometry, and space; we know what "bugs" the child and can give more emphasis to concepts and experiences that will promote operational thinking.

The Development of Number Concepts
(Piaget, 1952)

Piaget and his co-workers have been interested in finding out how mathematical notions emerge in the thought of the child. Using the clinical method, the Geneva school has presented to children between four and eight years tasks that would reveal their underlying assumptions about the nature of number, measurement, and space. Piaget has not been interested in number readiness as defined by arithmetic readiness tests but, rather, in children's awareness of the fundamental properties of number, measurement, and space. For example, his primary concern is not with whether or not the child can add eight plus eight, but whether or not the child understands that a group of eight objects continues to be equal in number to a second group of eight objects, even with a transformation in the space occupied by the objects. For example, one can line up eight dolls in a row and ask a child to take out from a group of ten chairs enough chairs so that each doll has one to sit on. Most four- and five-year-olds do this, lining up a row of chairs, with each chair placed at the feet of a doll (children are told not to seat the dolls). However, some who lack visual correspondence will not stop at the eighth chair but will continue to give out chairs until all are exhausted.

With the child who is successful at Step 1, the experimenter next pushes the dolls together in a heap and asks the child if there are still as many chairs as dolls, one chair for each doll, or if there are more chairs or more dolls. The child who cannot conserve, who judges on the basis of how things look, will affirm that there are more chairs, because "they're spread out and the dolls are close together."

Interestingly enough, counting does not help; a child may count eight dolls and eight chairs, but still say that there are more chairs if the dolls are bunched together, even though he also says that the number was the same before the dolls were moved. Eight does not equal eight for the preoperational child. Number and space are confused in his mind, and number of objects changes with the amount of space the objects occupy. So does space change according to the objects occupying that space. A room becomes shorter in length when objects are placed in the space between the back and front of the room. Basic to our understanding of number, measurement, and space is the notion of conservation—that number and space are conserved, remain the same in quantity, even with a transformation in appearance, provided nothing has been added or taken away.

Two fundamental notions involved in number are *cardination* and *ordination*. In order to develop a concept of number, the child must understand that number is a class. The cardinal value of a class of ten objects is ten. This is its invariant property, a property that is conserved across changes in appearance. When we talk about a class of ten objects, we are, in effect, treating the objects as if they were all alike; we disregard object differences as well as object arrangements.

But number is not simply a class. In order to arrive at the name of the class (which is its cardinal value), we must count the objects one by one. The order in which we count makes no difference, but there must be an order so that we don't count an object twice. When order is considered, the objects counted are different from one another. They differ in ordinal position: first object counted, second object counted, and so on. Thus, number has an ordinal component as well as a cardinal one, and these two notions must be synthesized before the concept of number is logically achieved.

There is a way in which equivalence of sets can be established other than by counting, and that is by a one-to-one correspondence. This method is a mathematically certain way of establishing cardinal equivalence. Optical equivalence comes first. This occurs when the child recognizes equivalence by matching the objects one for one; equivalence is then apparent to the eye (by putting a spoon in a cup or lining up two rows of objects, for example). For the preoperational child, when optical equivalence is destroyed, equivalence is lost; it is only as the child can operate mentally upon the data, when he can move objects about in his

Conservation of number—that is, knowing that the total number of objects remains the same regardless of the way in which the objects are arranged—is a basic property of number. Arranging cubes in various ways and using pipe cleaners to make sure that for every cube in one row there is a cube in the other row results in interiorizing the actions and then combining them without needing any cubes. As Piaget points out, the mathematician no longer needs the concrete objects; the child in kindergarten–primary grades does. From A Piaget Preschool Program in Action, *"Number, Measurement and Space." Copyright 1971 Center for Media Development, Inc. Photo by Knowledge Tree Films, a division of Center for Media Development, Inc.*

mind, that he can retain equivalence in the face of a physical transformation.

For example, in the task already described, where the dolls were pushed together so that each was no longer directly opposite a chair, the child who is at the stage of concrete operations will say, "It's still the same number. Just put the dolls back the way they were and you can see there's just as many (as there are chairs)." Or, an occasional child will say, "There's still just as many. You didn't add any and you didn't take any away, so the number (of dolls and chairs) has got to be the same."

As has been pointed out in earlier chapters, logical operations develop out of the actions of the child in grouping, ordering, comparing, and so on. Thought arises out of action, Piaget says over and over again. Mathematical thinking is no exception; it becomes logical as the result of actions the child performs with objects. These actions lead the child to assimilate new data, which eventually transform existing structures of thought. It becomes possible for the child to go back in thought to the starting place and to make comparisons of the state of affairs before and after a transformation has taken place; to know the circumstances under which things remain the same or change; to put bits and pieces of ideas together in different ways; to combine parts to make a whole (Lavatelli, 1970).

The Development of Concepts of Measurement (Piaget, 1953)

The reader may think of measurement in terms of applying a yardstick to a length to be measured, or of putting an object on a scale and reading off a number from the scale, or of using some other instrument marked off in standard units. However, each standard unit has a long history in man's past, and it is the rediscovery by the child of the need, first for a unit and eventually for a standard unit, that concerns Piaget. Measuring involves first and foremost a change of position that may be effected by the moving eye comparing distant objects, or the movement may be that of a common unit of measure that links distant objects together. In fact, essential to measuring is the notion of unit-iteration, of deciding upon a unit and repeating it.

The task developed at Geneva to reveal concepts of measurement is one in which the child is asked to compose out of blocks of different sizes a "tower" equal in height to another "tower" already built. However, the second tower is to be built on another table lower or higher than the first. Piaget describes what happens:[2]

> Children's attempts to deal with this problem go through a fascinating evolution. The youngest children build up the second tower to the same visual level as the first, without worrying about the difference in height of the tables. They compare the towers by stepping back and sighting them. At a slightly more advanced stage a child lays a long rod across the tops of the two towers to make sure that they are level. Somewhat later he notices that the base of his tower is not at the same level as the model's. He then wants to place his tower next to the model on the same table to compare them. Reminded that the rules of the game forbid him to move his tower, he begins to look around for a measuring standard. Interestingly enough, the first that comes to his mind is his own body. He puts one hand on top of his tower and the other at its base, and then, trying to keep his hands at the same distance apart, he moves over to the other tower to compare it. Children of about the age of six often carry out this work in a

[2] From J. Piaget, "How Children Form Mathematical Concepts." Copyright © 1953 by Scientific American, Inc. All rights reserved.

most assured manner, as if their hands could not change position on the way! Soon they discover that the method is not reliable, and then they resort to reference points on the body. The child will line up his shoulder with the top of his tower, mark the spot opposite the base on his thigh with his hand and walk over to the model to see whether the distance is the same.

Eventually, the idea of an independent measuring tool occurs to the child. His first attempt in this direction is likely to be the building of a third tower next to and the same height as the one he has already erected. Having built it, he moves it over to the first table and matches it against the model; this is allowed by the rules. The child's arrival at this stage presupposes a process of logical reasoning. If we call the model tower A, the second tower C and the movable tower B, the child has reasoned that $B = C$ and $B = A$, therefore $A = C$. (pp. 78–79)

The experimenter proceeds at this point to show the child three rods: one longer than, one shorter than, and one just the same height as the model tower. The child is asked whether he can use one of the rods to see if his tower is the same height as the model. At first he thinks that the rod must be just the same length as the height of the tower, and he will place the rod alongside each to measure, although he may throw his measurement off by placing the base of the rod some distance away from the base of the tower so that the rod forms a diagonal to the tower rather than lying flat up against it. Later he conceives of the idea of using a longer rod and marking the tower height on it with his finger. Here, again, he may be inept in moving the position of his finger as he transfers the rod from one tower to another. Finally, he realizes that he can use a shorter rod and measure the height of the tower by applying the rod a certain number of times up the side. This is the beginning of true measurement.

Piaget analyzes the logic of the child's operation for us. He points out that one mental operation involved here is the process of division, which permits the child to conceive that the whole is composed of a number of parts added together. The second operation is that of substitution, which enables the child to conceive of one of the parts as a unit and to apply the unit upon other parts. The measurement concept develops later than does the number concept because it is more difficult to think of a whole as divided into equal parts than it is to deal with elements that are already separate (Lavatelli, 1970).

The Development of Concepts of Space
(Piaget & Inhelder, 1956)

A professor of physics who has taught thousands of physics students has observed, only partly facetiously, that the world seems to be divided into two kinds of people: geometers and nongeometers. It is certainly true that even among the very bright students there is great variability in the ability to deal with many aspects of geometry and, particularly, with space relations. There are those who relate to space very well and those who find it difficult to visualize what happens even in a simple 180° transformation of an object in space. To a certain extent, and perhaps to a very great extent, such differences are due to early experiences. It may be that children who engage in many play activities involving movement in space are more likely to be competent in this area than children who busy themselves with other kinds of activities.

According to Piaget, concepts of space begin to develop in the cradle. He cites some examples: by five or six weeks of age, the young baby is capable of recognizing a familiar face, despite changes in distance or the effects of perspective. During the four- to ten-month period, prehension and vision become coordinated, so it is possible for the infant not only to see objects in space, but to grasp what he sees within his reach. At nine months, given a long narrow object that will not fit a narrow space when held horizontally, the child can turn the object vertically so that it relates to space in a different way. Throughout the sensorimotor period, the child explores objects, begins to abstract shapes, reckon with distance, and form images of shapes and their relationship to space.

In studying how space becomes represented in thought, Piaget has been concerned with the development of concepts of open and closed figures, of geometrical shapes, of spatial perspective, and of objects in a plane. With respect to open and closed figures, Piaget found that recognition of such properties appears before that of geometrical shapes. Children three years of age were asked to match by manual exploration objects that they could not see; they could distinguish between objects open and closed (a washer and a disk, for example) before they could discriminate between a circle and a square. With respect to spatial perspective, children at the preoperational stage found it difficult to imagine how an object would appear from various points of view; for each task they were asked to do, they invariably performed it from their own perspective rather than that of another. Piaget finds this tendency to be yet another example of egocentrism, the tendency to see things always from one's own viewpoint and to find it impossible to assume the viewpoint of another. Finally, when it came to representing objects in a plane, as, for example, planting posts "nice and straight" on a model of a mountain and drawing the result, the preoperational child was inadequate to the task; his posts were always perpendicular to the slope of the mountain (Lavatelli, 1970).

American mathematics projects to date have been concerned with mathematical concepts almost to the exclusion of how children think about those concepts. As Begle (1970) has pointed out, the new school math differs little from the old. As a result, while the mathematics may be improved, the newer programs are no more challenging to children than the old. For a completely new approach, methods of teaching must also be changed. The present emphasis on the open curriculum is a step in that direction.

Mathematics in the Open Classroom

But inductive teaching and use of concrete materials to make discoveries are by no means new. They have been used by teachers before new math was heard of. What *is* new is that now they are being employed in classrooms so organized as to provide for greater independence on the part of the learner. The joy and creativity in connection with discovery when children *can* work independently are now being recognized.

In this newer type of classroom, (the arithmetic lesson as such has disappeared. A teacher no longer stands before a class to instruct children on a given concept, nor even to lead children to discover the concept as they work with concrete materials. Classwork in the sense of all of the children being involved in the same activity at the same time severely limits learning. Instead, the classroom is organized so that children work in pairs or in small groups. Lovell (1971) describes how a classroom might be organized for mathematics in an open school:

> . . . children are seated at small tables in twos, three, or fours per table. They are working at tasks provided by the teacher although sometimes chosen by themselves; but not all pupils seated at a table may be engaged on the same task. Moreover, pupils discuss their difficulties with one another and with the teacher; they also agree on their solutions. Pupils are also free to get up from their seats to fetch apparatus or to seek further information. The atmosphere is informal, and although the teacher still supplies the direction to the work of the classroom in the sense that she should know the precise purpose of each task which is set, she may also be regarded as an expert consultant.
>
> It is this third type of classroom situation which is most appropriate for learning mathematics, especially in the case of young children. It is not denied that the other forms of classroom organization have their place in some areas of the curriculum. But in mathematics, where the child has so often to derive his abstractions through reflecting upon actions which he carries out on materials, there is only a limited place for the teacher standing in front of the class, or sections of the class, and teaching through verbal exposition. Rather verbal dialogue or verbal explication must proceed between teacher and child, teacher and small group, or child and child. (p. 182)

In place of a syllabus outlining specifically what is to be covered in a year, a teacher uses general outlines of ideas and suggestions worked out jointly with other teachers in her school. How one headmaster got started in the beginning primary is described as follows:[3]

> To make a rough assessment of the level of mathematical readiness of the young children coming from the infant school I spent about a fortnight at the beginning of this school year giving each child an individual test. I sat down with each in my room, or some other quiet spot, and presented situations in a "practical" way—not a written test to be answered on paper. These involved such things as conservation of quantity, counting and recognizing patterns (seeing whether the children used "counting-on" or not), enumeration and knowledge of numerals, the ability to group objects and count in such situations, the ability to share (and cope if any objects were left over), the notion of ordinal number and the appreciation of quantitative order. From these tests it was possible to put the children into workable groups for number activities. Some appeared ready to use the Dienes' MAB, many required other activities with number strips, collections of objects for grouping and counting, finding patterns on number squares, ladders and strips for introducing ordinal number, and so on. In the practical discovery work on weights, measures, money, time, shapes, etc., some children required activities of an easier nature than those on the original set of work cards, and in these cases the instructions frequently were given orally by the teacher to a small group of children working together. In this second stage of the development of the work throughout the school a much bigger effort was also made with the older children. (Chambers & Murray, 1969, p. 53)

Textbooks are used to provide drill on computation as needed, but to stimulate the free spirit of inquiry, the assignment card is used.

> A card with a mathematical question on it, however simple or complex, is sometimes called a job card, a work card or an assignment card. In a sense these cards are a development from a sum card which was an early attempt to give a more individual flavor than was possible when all the children worked from the same sum book; for, on analysis, it appeared that sum cards frequently did no more than reproduce a page from a sum book. This situation must be guarded against when assignment cards are being considered. These cards must do more than suggest a problem involving some form of measurement or mental agility with numbers. These things are important, but the assignment card must also foster active thought, leading to the forming of judgments and the taking of decisions.
> A card for a young child might read: How many acorns balance the big pebble? It would be considerably enhanced by the additional instruction—Guess first. Later on an important addition might be: Comment on your results.

[3] From Nuffield Mathematics Project, *I Do, and I Understand*, John Wiley & Sons, Inc., and John Murray (Publishers) Ltd. and W. & R. Chambers Ltd.

In order to develop awareness and sensitivity, cards might contain the phrase: What do you notice? or What do you discover?

After some experience in this kind of work the suggested problem might be followed by such a question as: Can you see a pattern? or Is there a relationship?

It is when the child reaches this stage of his assignment that discussion with the teacher is most profitable. It is the teacher's skillful questions during this discussion which will lead the child to make the discovery—perceive the patterns and relationships within his recorded data—if he has not yet the ability or maturity to do this on his own. (Chambers & Murray, 1969, p. 36)

.   .   .   .   .

There are, of course, dangers inherent in the use of assignment cards. It would be possible for a teacher to prepare a selection of assignment cards at the beginning of the year, and for the rest of the year the children would systematically work through them. This would represent a tremendous advance in that the children would be actively involved with real materials. The danger would lie in the possibility that, in time, the situation might become overfamiliar and this approach might become as stereotyped as the old use of a textbook. There are probably three stages through which this kind of work might progress.

Stage 1

The introduction of the first assignment cards based on the ideas of the teacher. These ideas will have been culled from teachers' courses, from source books of mathematical ideas, or perhaps from the Nuffield teachers' guides.

Stage 2

The further development of the assignment cards in order to relate the work to the specific school environment and the particular interests of the children.

Stage 3

The partial or even total discarding of assignment cards as more and more of the work arises spontaneously within the framework of normal school activities. (Chambers & Murray, 1969, pp. 36–37)

Silberman and others have decried the "joylessness" of the all-too-typical classroom with its preoccupation with order, control, and routine for the sake of routine, where classes are taught in a uniform manner without regard to the individual child's understanding of or interest in a subject. One of the outcomes of education in open classrooms is that the student grows in his ability to think and act for himself. There is more time for learning, for there is less time spent for most children in waiting for the slow to catch up. And, from the informal evaluations of British schools, it would appear that "what children know, they know for sure."

The Nuffield Project

The Nuffield Mathematics project was set up in 1964 by the Nuffield Foundation of Nuffield, England, to develop new mathematical teaching for children. Its aim was to build on the lively activity in mathematics teaching in England at the time. In contrast to American endeavors, the British not only changed arithmetic to "maths," but also changed teaching methods drastically for the five- to thirteen-year-olds.

The central notion in the Nuffield program is that children must be set free to make their own discoveries and in this way to achieve understanding. In line with Piagetian theory, it is recognized that to achieve understanding children need concrete experiences. As Piaget has emphasized, they are typically not ready for abstractions in the primary school, but need to deal empirically with the environment, to solve real problems by using beads, globes, scales, and a host of other measuring devices. The title of the first volume in the Nuffield series of publications is appropriate for an approach that emphasizes learning by doing. It is *I Do, and I Understand*, a title derived from a Chinese proverb:

> I hear, and I forget;
> I see, and I remember;
> I do, and I understand.

An "Autumn Investigation" is illustrative of the type of challenging problems set for children. The problem was to figure out how one could find out how many leaves there might be on a particular tree. For some such problems, a hint might be given: that two children had counted 573 leaves to a pound. The emphasis was not on the answer, but on figuring out a way to solve the problem.

There are three main topics covered in the *Teachers' Guides*: computation and structure, shape and size, and graphs leading to algebra. The guides are built upon a spiral plan, with the same concepts included at each level but in different ways and with increasing difficulty. Each guide develops themes ranging in difficulty from easy to hard, so the teacher can help children progress at different paces.

Evaluation

Specially designed evaluation materials have been prepared to check on children's progress. These materials, developed by a team from the Institut des Sciences de l'Education in Geneva, consist of tests or tasks to be administered individually to children. They assess children's basic understanding of such concepts as size, shape, quantity, space, and geometry. They have been used by teachers to find out how an individual child is doing and to plan accordingly, rather than as a research tool to make comparisons between experimental and control groups.

As has been pointed out before, the British are not as keen on evaluation as are Americans, and comparative data on progress in informal and formal schools are not readily available. There are test data on children in matched pairs of formal and informal primary schools, on arithmetic as well as other subjects (Gardner, 1966). Results favored informal schools in English, drawing and painting, ingenuity, listening and remembering, neatness, care and skill, and breadth and depth of out-of-school interests. Formal schools were superior in arithmetic but since there have been no measures of achievement since the introduction of new curricula in "maths," the Gardner test results may no longer be relevant.

Summary

In this chapter we have reviewed the major curriculum projects devoted to the "new math" in the elementary school, a mathematics not quite as new or revolutionary as has been supposed. We have also examined the influence of curriculum reform upon textbooks: some topics are introduced earlier in the grades; the field properties of arithmetic are emphasized; the language of sets is used throughout all six grades, although little of set theory per se; geometry and algebra are introduced. Certain changes in style and language in the textbooks were noted.

Teaching methods in connection with the new math have emphasized discovery methods and use of concrete materials. Three commercially prepared materials are described: the Dienes Multibase Arithmetic Blocks, the Cuisenaire rods, and the Dienes Algebraic Experience Materials.

We owe to Piaget our insights into the growth of mathematical thinking in children. His theory with respect to growth of concepts of number and space is reviewed here. To date, curriculum projects have paid little attention to how children acquire notions of mathematics. In British Infant Schools, attempts are made to set children free to make their own discoveries and in this way to achieve understanding.

READING LIST 11

Begle, E. (Ed.) NSSE Sixty-Ninth Yearbook, *Part I, mathematics education.* Chicago: University of Chicago Press, 1970. Topics such as a comparison of new and old math, evaluation, and computer-assisted instruction are reviewed and discussed critically.

Grossnickle, F. E., Brueckener, L. J., & Reckzel, J. *Discovering meanings in elementary school mathematics.* New York: Holt, Rinehart and Winston, 1968. This text covers the basic topics taught in the elementary school in a more conventional way than the experimental programs we have been describing and is useful to study for contrast.

Lovell, K. *The growth of understanding in mathematics: Kindergarten through grade three.* New York: Holt, Rinehart and Winston, 1971. An excellent analysis, by a Piaget scholar who knows children and mathematics. Lovell presents mathematical ideas in terms of the thinking skills involved, together with a systematic, step-by-step presentation of how to teach eight main topics in modern math. There is also a useful chapter on how to organize the classroom for teaching mathematics.

The Nuffield Mathematics Project—A uniquely contemporary course of mathematics study for children aged five to thirteen. New York: John Wiley & Sons, 1970. The *Teachers' Guides* suggest many ways in which the change from conventional to modern math can be made in treating computation and structure, size and shape, and graphs leading to algebra.

NOTE: In addition, the reader will find it profitable to examine those new mathematics curricula materials available to him that are described on pp. 248–251.

Professional Journals To Become Acquainted With

The Arithmetic Teacher. National Council of Teachers of Math, 1201 Sixteenth St., N.W., Washington, D.C. 20036.

CHAPTER 12

Esthetic
Education

For decades, education has given lip service to the objective of educating people to "use leisure time wisely," but the seventies are likely to see some action with respect to this objective. We are entering a period where the four-day week is going to be in effect for many workers, whose three-day weekends must be filled. Some will use it to "moonlight" on another job, but others will seek activity more rewarding to the spirit. Women who have had the two babies they feel is their limit but who are not engaged in full-time work outside the home are already searching for self-fulfilling activities. And some young people today are increasingly rejecting materialistic values; they are not likely to seek the second job to pay for the second television set. Increasing numbers are turning to the arts for creative satisfaction, to drawing and painting classes, to drama clubs, to dance groups, to handicrafts. In this chapter we examine two curriculum areas, art and music, and consider the nature of creativity and how it can be fostered in the child.

The Art Curriculum

Education reflects the American value structure to a considerable degree, and in the past art has been held in low esteem. Witness the *New Yorker* cartoon in which an obviously well-heeled gentleman and his richly furred wife are pictured visiting an art museum. The husband is saying, "Sure, I've got a creative urge, but it's satisfied by knowing I could support ten of these guys on the kind of money I make." In other words, the husband is saying, practical people, successful people, people who really count in our society, do not have time to take art seriously. They may collect art for its prestige or investment value. Or they may dabble in it as did Churchill and Eisenhower, but their dabbling is accepted as the curious idiosyncrasy of successful men.

Eisner (1967) comments on how attitudes toward art are mirrored in art education:

By the time he leaves the first grade the student has learned what is important and what types of competencies are honored. Art, he learns, is a form of freetime activity. Children also learn that they may use art media as long as they and the media are not too "messy." And not on their desks because paint and desks are incompatible. And not during the heart of the school day because the real work of the classroom must be done first. And not as an independent study because art, to be justified in terms of time, needs to be related to something more important like social studies. And they should not come to expect instruction in art because the teacher usually cannot provide it. And should they come to feel inadequate in art by the end of the third grade, the talent myth can always be employed by teachers and parents alike to explain away the child's lack of competency—a lack fostered by little or no instruction with a curriculum that is concerned more with novelty than with learning. (p. 28)

We do have art education programs in both elementary and secondary schools, but often these exist not because we view art as an important part of the child's total development, but because art has served and continues to serve various goals. Goals influence program: the teacher who has certain child behaviors in mind as desirable outcomes is going to choose curriculum experiences appropriate to her objectives. We will review briefly what some of these goals are and how each has shaped art curricula.

In some classrooms art activities are selected in keeping with the teacher's ideal of the "good" child: one who is neat and tidy, who follows directions carefully, and who uses materials wisely. In such classrooms, children are given outlines to color, Easter bunny patterns to trace and cut out, dittoed sheets to be neatly filled in. When character building is the aim of art education, the most serious sin a child can commit is to color outside the lines, to use a color other than that which he was directed to use, or to turn out a smudged piece of work. The art materials are crayons and paper; occasionally, scissors and paste. Paints are too messy—except perhaps the neat little boxes of water color with small, tidy brushes. Plasticene is all right occasionally, but not clay.

Methods, too, are dictated by goals, and if art is to build character, then the child must be taught to draw properly so as not to waste time and materials in merely expressing himself or "messing around." He can be taught to draw a horse or a house; indeed, any teacher can, in a few easy lessons, learn how to draw trees, animals, and the human figure, and in turn teach the child. Then the child will be *learning* something and his time will be used to advantage.

It should be obvious from the way in which we have presented the above approaches that we are not in favor of a program in art education designed for the purpose of teaching neatness, care in following directions, and proper conservation of materials. Using patterns, coloring outlines, cutting out figures that someone else has drawn, copying pictures, or making a Christmas present for mother exactly like everyone else's are not art activities. It is hard to know what to call them, but surely they do not contribute to a child's esthetic development, and they have no place in the elementary school *art* curriculum. Occasionally a teacher tries to justify such activities on the grounds that the children like them. But a child's liking for a particular experience is no criterion of its worth. Children like many things that are bad for them as well as those that are good; it is the responsibility of the teacher to guide children to greater wisdom in their choices.

The second function that art has served in the schools has been to amuse or reward the child. As Eisner (1967) has pointed out, art has been something the child might do, say, on Friday afternoons from 2:00 to 3:00 P.M., for that time of day and week is of little use for serious study. Or, if the child should finish his other lessons before the rest of the class does, then he is permitted to go to the easel or to draw pictures at his seat. Where this is the philosophy of art education, obviously the program makes few demands upon the pupil. He can dabble in paints or in clay, make block prints or mobiles; what he does or even, indeed, the quality of work that he does is not so important. Working with one's hands is relaxing—gives the brain a rest so that the learner is better able to carry on the regular work of the school.

One outgrowth of this philosophy is that, in order to provide the maximum benefits, art activities must be varied, and even bizarre. Is the child bored with painting? Then let him paint to music. Have crayons palled? Then let him make pictures where he layers on the crayon and then scratches in a design. Is he tired of clay? Then let him sculpture with milk cartons. Where this philosophy prevails, the success of an art program is judged by the number and strangeness of the projects undertaken by children. Instead of seeking change in the maturing perceptions of the child, the teacher tries to provide change by faddish activities. The resulting products are often trite, shoddy, or contrived.

A more sophisticated version of this same philosophy is that art has mental hygiene values. According to this school of thought, the child who is overly aggressive or too tense or too withdrawn may be helped to release some of his hostilities or other tensions as he works, particularly with such media as finger paints or clay. Churchill's attitude toward art is in this vein. In *Painting as a Pastime* he says, "Many remedies are suggested for the avoidance of worry and mental overstrain by persons who, over prolonged periods, have to bear exceptional responsibilities and discharge duties upon a very large scale." He points out that *change* is the common element in all remedies, and that painting embodies this element. "Splash into the turpentine," he advises, "Wallop into the blue and white, frantic flourish on the palette and then several large fierce strokes and slashes of blue on the absolute cowering canvas."

Now it is true that pounding clay may help to make the aggressive child momentarily less hostile, just as socking a punching bag may rid him of his tensions. But no one (except extremists to whom everything is art) would call hitting a punching bag an artistic activity, nor would we say that merely because a child is working clay or "walloping into the blue and white" that he is having an artistic experience. An artistic experience may be very satisfying to the child, and because it is satisfying, may have beneficial effects upon his mental health, but such an effect is a fringe benefit and should not be regarded as the goal of art education.

A third and also limited interpretation of the function of art is that of self-expression. According to this interpretation, the artistic development of children follows certain natural laws with which the school must not interfere. It need only provide the child with the opportunity to express himself; guidance from the teacher not only is not necessary, but also is actually harmful.

The emphasis upon developmental stages is related to the function of self-expression. The concept of developmental stages in art expression may be an outgrowth of the theories of Gesell. Gesell, as the reader will recall, described in minute detail the changes that we might expect in children's behavior from four weeks of age to adolescence. His books are very comforting to the new mother who likes to know that at eight to ten weeks of age, the baby is interested in the pattern in wallpaper, that he may have a shy period at twenty-eight weeks, that at two-and-a-half years he will be extremely negative, that at three he will become a much pleasanter, more delightful being. Gesell attributed these changes to the gradual unfolding of a predetermined design; it is the nature of the six-year-old to be difficult and the nature of the preadolescent to conform to peer mores and to turn his back on adult standards.

The Gesell influence in art education is perhaps strongest in Viktor Lowenfeld (1957), who described in some detail the stages that children go through in their artistic development. These are the scribbling, the preschematic, and the schematic stages, the stage of dawning realism, and finally the stage of reasoning. From these stages, one of two types of individuals emerges: the visual-minded or the haptic-minded. The visual-minded child tends to reproduce how a thing looks, whereas the haptic-minded projects himself into the picture and determines size and space in terms of his emotional feelings.

Child art as an expression of innate perceptions is also reflected in Arnheim's (1966) explanation of children's artistic behavior. He de-

scribes the scribble of the young child as pure motor activity, springing
from an innate desire to make things. He believes that the child uses the
"primordial circle" as the basis for all objects in his preschool drawings:
heads are round; so are bodies, arms and fingers, so are flowers and the
sun. He relates the use of circles to the process of creation, "The shaping
of cosmic whirls and spheres from amorphous matter in the universe."

But in child development circles today, it is generally recognized
that if children resemble one another at any given age, it is at least as
much because they have experienced a common culture as because of the
unfolding of an innate design. Nor would students of child development
accept visual-mindedness or haptic-mindedness as due only to biology.
Whether children express themselves realistically or emotionally depends
not upon the child's being born with a particular response to the world,
but upon the nature of his early perceptual experiences. Consider this
example: Two families are crossing the George Washington Bridge by
car. In one car the father is pointing out the structural qualities of the
bridge—how it has been constructed, why it is so strong. In the second
car a parent is commenting on how small and insignificant he feels in
relation to this enormous structure, how antlike seem the cars crawling
along its roadway. Such differing experiences multiplied a thousand
times may contribute to visual-mindedness or haptic-mindedness. The
child *learns* to see the world in a particular way and to respond estheti-
cally to what he sees.

Nor is learning confined only to the type of one's responses to the
environment. A child's perception of color, proportion, and design is also
learned. One child grows up in a household where pictures are hung on
the walls in a very precise order—a large one in the center of the wall,
meticulously balanced by two small ones on each side. In another household balance may be achieved in a much more interesting but less conventional fashion. Each child learns to fill space in his pictures according to
the same principles. In terms of learning theory, the child is learning
certain *cues*. He is learning to notice the subtle distinctions between
what he will accept and what he will reject as artistic. And he accepts
and rejects in the way that significant people in his environment react
positively or negatively to certain forms of artistic expression.

By the time he enters school, the child has learned to notice certain
things in his environment and to exclude others from his attention. Depending upon what cues have been called to his attention, he will be
more or less sensitive to color, line, masses and shapes, textures, light and
shade. Some children never see a sunset; some never find imaginary
figures in cloud shapes; some never notice the contrast between the mass
of evergreens and the deciduous trees in the forest.

One of the chief functions of art education should be to increase the child's esthetic sensitivity to his environment; art should make him a better "noticer," should sharpen his perceptions. And as his perceptions are sharpened, he is better able to express what he notices in some medium. We do not give him lessons in perspective; we make him aware of how his perception of size varies with distance. We do not give him lessons in drawing trees; we call his attention to the tremendous variety of shapes and sizes in trees and to the anatomy of a tree. We let him make discoveries in color—discoveries not only of how to mix shades of color, but also of how color may be toned down or made more intense; of how the impact of a color upon the observer can be changed as the background against which it is seen is changed.

A second important function of art, the development of children's taste, is in part dependent upon esthetic sensitivity. Taste is developed as children notice more cues. Just as all new babies look alike to the uninitiated, so all abstract art, or all contemporary houses, or all flowered textiles may appear to be equally good from an artistic standpoint until

The child as a creator. Involving children in the work itself, as in Lygia Clark's communal plastic clothes, has proved an immensely stimulating way of teaching children the sensual and tactile as well as the specifically human content of art. Here, art becomes an activity, rather than a "subject" in the curriculum, and enables children to forget their inhibitions before this often intimidating phenomenon. From Réalités, *March 1971, p. 21. Photo, J. Ph. Charbonnier—Réalités.*

one has enough experience in noticing a great variety of objects in a particular category. Most children are limited in their exposure before they come to school. They ought to have the opportunity in school to sample a wide variety of art—some perhaps as color slides, some as inexpensive prints, some as photographs of outstanding examples of good design—both ancient and modern.

A more complete analysis of what is important and possible in and through art education has been provided by Tumin (1967). He is particularly concerned with the contributions of art education to the achievement of the more general goals of quality education:

1. Art education, if it is any good, is a model of real individuation in education. It is impossible, as I see it, to teach art successfully unless the uniqueness of every student, as an individual, in relation to what he is doing, is a central determinant of the relationship of the teacher to the student. To the extent that individuation of education is a *sine qua non* of quality education—to that extent art education provides us with a model of how to teach in general.

2. Experiences in art provide perhaps the only or at least the most persuasive path to self-discovery and sense of growth that is available anywhere in school or the rest of life. Most importantly, that growth and self-discovery have no meaning when they are matched competitively against the achievements of other students in these regards. They are meaningful only in comparison to oneself at a former condition of life, the day or week or year or moment before.

3. Art experiences—like those of love and play—can provide gratifications and pleasures to children that are distinctively characterized by their spontaneity, their lack of self-consciousness, and their yield of pleasure-in-process. It is process as much if not more than end-product that matters in art experience. . . . Such noninstrumental, noncontrived, nonmeasured rewards and gratifications constitute kinds of experiences not normally capable of being had elsewhere. It is no accident that even in science and mathematics, into which so much public money and effort have lately been poured, there is a continuous stress on creativity and its central significance for the entire scientific enterprise.

4. Experiences in art can convey important meanings of the terms "truth" and "integrity" that are not elsewhere to be found. One learns— if he has learned well—when he in his own work or others in theirs have resorted to contrivance, trickery, and sentimentality in order to achieve effects and how cheap and unsatisfying these effects can be. Once one has acquired a knowledge of what is real and what is artificial, what is solid and what is shabby, one can never again be as easily put off, or put on, nor can one ever again be satisfied with anything less than the real thing. Moreover, the capacity for discrimination, about oneself and others, is cumulative or can be, and has a power of asserting itself against all institutional pressures to the contrary.

5. Finally, and perhaps most important, art education, if properly

transacted, is an indispensable and perhaps uniquely effective way to enhance the enjoyment of life and the realization of human sense potentials. It is presently clear that without such education, we shall return to that state where though we have eyes, we do not see; though we have ears, we do not hear; though we can touch, we do not feel; though we have emotions, we know neither joy nor sorrow deeply. So, too, though we remain the effective agents responsible for the looks, sounds, and motions of our environments, and though we could make these increasingly pleasurable if not beautiful we have allowed them, out of apathy and ignorance, to be made mostly ugly and horrible. (pp. 9, 11)

Tumin's analysis of the potentiality of art experiences can serve as a foundation for the selection of content. We turn next to the problem of content.

The Content of Instruction in Art

What constitutes the art curriculum? What experiences is the teacher to provide that will lead to fulfillment of the goals that Tumin talks about? One writer (Chapman, 1967) argues for content that will extend the student's possibilities for creative action, and specifies the knowledge, skills, attitudes, and understandings required for such extension:

A. The variety of workers who might be called "artists," the variety of forms, products, and situations which might be called "art," and the variety of problems and situations in life that have "aesthetic" dimensions;

B. The variety of sources that artists have used as the beginning of their ideas and as cues from which to generate their visual studies—commemorative events, myths, dreams, fantasies, views of land, sea, sky, people, animals, technical possibilities of materials, functional purposes of objects;

C. The variety of ways artists interpret their ideas—reporting visually, as a camera might; with a humorous or satirical intent; dramatically, with built-in shock; ambiguously, with symbols which count for hidden meanings; poetically, with subtlety; with functional simplicity or ornamental complexity;

D. The variety of materials and processes that artists use to produce visual qualities such as fuzziness, thickness, roundness, brilliance, tallness;

E. The variety of ways artists improvise upon, study, extend, and refine their ideas to discover the particular organization of visual qualities which will embody their idea—shifting points of view, substituting a new part for an old one, rearranging locations of parts, creating "accidents" which modify an idea, eliminating or embellishing with detail, shifting media, borrowing ideas from prior work or the work of another;

F. The variety of feelings and meanings that different organizations of visual qualities can evoke in the viewer—lines that seem to be vigorous, a tree that seems to be lonely, a building that seems to be proud;

G. The variety of factors that influence the symbolic, technical, and formal character of works of art and the judgments that people make about them—social and cultural values, political and economic conditions, sheer geographic location;

H. The variety of points of view that one can use as criteria for determining the merit, worth, or significance of art—personal preference, technical control, formal organization, expressiveness, functionality, educational values; and

I. The requirements for logical justifications of judgments about art—identifying the points of view which will serve as criteria for judgment, describing features of the work and interpreting their relevance to the criteria, and drawing conclusions about the relative status of the work in relation to the criteria for judgment. (p. 21)

Were these "knowledge, skills, attitudes, and understandings" to be embodied in a curriculum for art in the elementary school, a new look in art education would result. Consider the all-too-typical lesson in today's elementary classroom. The teacher may provide materials and equipment, suggest subjects, "motivate" the children. She then steps aside so as not to interfere with the children's spontaneity, leaving many of the children with the very difficult decision of "what to draw." As Field (1970, p. 11) put it, ". . . the result has been that children throughout general education were, as the normal thing, asked in the art lesson to tackle a total problem—such as making a picture, with its incredibly complex organization . . . , its immense compromises, its endless uncertainties. Of course, young children are always doing this with gusto, unaware, without fear; but children do not remain in this unsophisticated state forever, and as they grow older the problems loom larger. By their belief [that drawing a picture is art], teachers were prevented from isolating a problem and enlarging it . . . Not until teachers realized that the artist himself was isolating and identifying his problems was it possible for the art teacher to do the same."

But suppose the teacher were to translate the ideas of Tumin into art experiences. Then, instead of suggesting to a fifth-grade class that they "draw a picture of a playground," the teacher might begin by having the class make studies of playground scenes, sketching bits and pieces of what they see—a child on a swing, two boys shooting baskets, a group of girls playing hopscotch. She, or a student, might take some Polaroid pictures; because these are instantly processed they could serve, as children begin work, as a way of refreshing memory about details otherwise blurred in memory. There might also be prints for the children to look at to illustrate the multitude of ways in which artists have portrayed such scenes—a Breughel, for example. Only after such preparation do children begin actual work. And, as they work, the teacher may encourage experimentation with materials and techniques that artists use to produce a sharp line or fuzziness, or to add brilliance to an area. Such a "lesson" obviously takes more than the hour typically allotted to art. But art experiences scheduled several times a week put art education in its proper perspective—as a serious curriculum experience that merits time and attention in its own right.[1]

The approach we have described above looks upon the art experience as a problem-solving experience, much as Dewey looked at it in his *Art as Experience* (1934). The general problem may be prescribed: making a playground scene. But how the problem is to be solved is up to the student; he must make decisions about the content of the product (what should actually be represented in the product), the media to be used (paints, crayon, clay, and so on), the nature of the product (a painting, a watercolor sketch, a collage, a three-dimensional tableau, a combination of any of these or all), the degree of representation or abstractness to be employed. Each successive problem must be identified by the student and tentative solutions tried and evaluated.

The question of how much control the teacher should exercise is a difficult one. The "father" of art education, Franz Czek, one of the first to recognize the importance of art education in the life of the child, exerted considerable control over the pupils in his art classes in Vienna. He urged pupils to outline each person to be drawn, as a first step, and even prescribed step-by-step procedures for some lessons. Yet Czek "liberated" children, as he claimed, and his children produced creative, imaginative products. Perhaps the lesson to be learned is that highly creative teachers work in many different ways, "without being aware that they [are] operating pedagogically within the limits of their own artistic vision" (Field, 1970, p. 63). For the classroom teacher in a school system where there is no specially trained teacher of art, perhaps control should be exercised only in a very general way—in setting the boundaries of the problem and in providing materials and cues that will help the child to understand and structure his experience. The teacher can also facilitate problem solving by encouraging experimentation, for example, on how to make a clay structure stronger, or how to make a purple redder. And sometimes the art class can be devoted to making a product by starting

---

[1] Two excellent teaching films that children as well as teachers could profit from are Edward Betts No. 1, *Abstract Design from Nature,* and Edward Betts No. 2, *The Modern Approach,* in *Masters Film Series on Watercolor Painting,* Electrographs Corporation, 305 E. 45th St., New York City. In these films, Mr. Betts talks about and demonstrates how an artist goes about painting a picture.

Building a groundwork of artistic language. What do Matisse's paper collages mean to most children? Probably nothing, is the answer given by Pierre Belvès. In his method of teaching, he instructs children in making their own collages, bearing in mind some elementary but crucial criteria—the need to make the plain patches as interesting as the colored ones. Thus, Belvès claims, when his pupils are confronted with the work of Matisse, they are fully conversant with the style and the problems involved in the handling of mass and form. Gradually, children can be led to acquire a wider vocabulary of artistic forms, but the starting point must be that which is closest to their own experience, or they are liable to lapse into boredom and incomprehension. From Réalités, *March 1971, p. 22. Photo, J. Ph. Charbonnier—*Réalités.

not with a subject, but with the media themselves—with "found" objects or with various materials for sculpting, or with combinations of paper and other substances to produce a desired effect. The teacher must be careful to avoid reinforcing only the visual artists—the students who can copy nature and reproduce a recognizable tree—and remember that the artistic process consists of the child's remaking the tree as he sees it.

The emphasis in the above appears to be on product, but product is only half of the art experience. *Process* is also important. There should be specific instruction in art with respect to the techniques of using certain media (how to keep clay moist between art sessions, for example), but there should also be time for children to use art in an exploratory way. In the exploration, with individual guidance from the teacher, the child should become aware of the raw data that the artist uses: concepts such as line, shape, color, mass, light, movement, contrast, direction. These are the elements that will make art available to the child as one of a number of modes of organizing and internalizing experience.

Esthetics and the Environment

One of the encouraging signs of a general esthetic awakening is the proliferation of good design in everyday objects. True, one has only to visit the gift "shoppes" attached to snack bars and gas stations along our new interstate highways to see hideous, tasteless examples of everyday objects and knickknacks. But at the same time, it is possible for families of average income in America to buy objects of good design. One doesn't *have* to buy even so mundane an article as a vacuum cleaner in an ugly design; it is possible to buy one that is both functional and pleasing to look at.

Unfortunately, while there has been improvement in the design and quality of many American products, the quality of the total environment has deteriorated. There are serious problems of pollution that are destroying the ecology, but there are also problems of what some authors have called *visual* pollution, or "sight blight" (Stone & Quinn, 1970). The teachers reading this book might consider their own communities and what the typical "Main Street" scene looks like, or the highway approach to their community.

Whether "envirionmental literacy" belongs in the science or social studies curriculum or in the arts or in all three is not important. But it *is* important that teachers help to develop sensitivity to the environment even in young children. Before-and-after photos (often shown in current periodicals) of ugly streams or alleys transformed into places of beauty are useful in developing such sensitivity in children. They learn to look more critically at their environment and to realize that it doesn't have to be ugly.

Stone and Quinn (1970) describe how children in one community were sensitized:

> In one community, Champaign-Urbana, Ill., a citizens' group became concerned with improving the quality of the community's environment. The Champaign County Development Council Foundation took a first step toward an environmental education program by sponsoring an "environment contest" for upper elementary school children. The purpose was to stimulate an awareness of the children's surroundings—the "good," the "bad," and possible alternatives. Pupils were asked to make a picture of a favorite place that they thought added beauty to the community, and they were asked to explain their choice. They were also given the option of drawing and describing a place they particularly disliked. The "environment contest" was voluntary, not an assignment.
>
> The range and depth of responses suggest that this is one approach to developing environmental literacy among children of any community. When asked to observe, the children really did get out and look, and they knew what they liked and disliked, although their analytical abilities varied:

"You can call this place anything you like except good!"
"This park is the only place where there are things to do."
"This place is on the beam. It gives our town a certain gleam."
"Help, help. Please! This summer. Please, somebody help this
    park!" (pp. 6–7)

There is little that young children can do to effect changes in their environment. (Older children can actually participate in clean-up drives.) But developing an environmental awareness in children will hopefully produce a generation motivated to and capable of rebuilding America.

The Music Curriculum

Throughout the ages, music has played an important part in the daily life of man. Even for primitive man, music was a definite part of every phase of life—courting and marrying, healing and invoking charms, worshiping, praying for rain, working, or waging war.

Man's daily life has changed, but music still performs many of these same services. Music is piped into many factories and offices to furnish a pleasant background for the workers; music is still part of courting and marrying, of worship, and, to some extent, of waging war. Today we shop at the supermarket to music, buy our plane tickets to music, are subjected to singing commercials, and, indeed, are so bombarded with musical stimuli that in self-protection many of us no longer listen. Music education for today's world needs to involve children as participants in singing, playing, dancing, and other musical activities in order to counteract the passive, consumer-type influences outside the classroom. And because the level of most popular music is so low, the school has a special responsibility for guiding pupils' musical preferences. The music program should also provide opportunities for children to create their own musical expression, both because creating their own music will heighten their appreciation for the efforts of others and because it will bring them satisfaction.

Developing Children's Esthetic Appreciation for Music

Perhaps the greatest contribution an elementary teacher can make to her pupils' musical education is to cultivate their capacity for musical enjoyment. It is the rare child who comes to school not liking to sing, run, march, or respond to music in some other physical way, to experiment with musical instruments, and to listen to some kinds of music, and who is not capable of some emotional response to it. The job of the school is to broaden and deepen these responses and to develop the child's musical discrimination. Like his tastes in art, the child's tastes in music are learned. Unfortunately, through repeated exposure to popular music, many American children today come to like a kind of music that demands little of them. Much popular music, particularly the "standards" written by Irving Berlin, George Gershwin, Richard Rodgers, and others, is inventive and tasteful, but most of it, particularly the musical fads, is repetitive and banal. Broudy (1957) has described some of the characteristics of the latter kind of popular music as follows:

> First, the piece is carefully constructed so that a minimum of self-reorganization is required from the learner. The melody, rhythm, and harmony are combined in a design already familiar to the consumer. Rhythmic and melodic habits are not jolted; they are pleasantly jostled. There are changes, but they are neither rapid nor radical.
>
> Further, the song is short enough, the melodic line clear enough, and the rhythmic pattern obvious enough for the bulk of listeners to recognize and to reproduce readily.
>
> Also, the subject matter is not only familiar, but the words and musical symbols it employs are no less so.
>
> Love, to take one of the standard themes of popular music, is couched in phrases nobody can mistake, and no variation of it is left unsounded: new love, old love; love lost, love found; love in June, love in December; love requited, love spurned.
>
> It is, however, love as experienced by the typical adolescent, and its musical expression is also guaranteed not to tax the intellectual and musical powers of the typical adolescent. (p. 135)

Serious music, on the other hand, which includes classical and non-classical, makes certain demands on the listener as well as the performer. The music has more variety in melody, harmony, and rhythm. It is more complex, more difficult to follow, but also more rewarding. Unlike the popular song, it cannot be comprehended all at once; repeated listenings yield fresh impressions of content not heard before. It offers potential esthetic satisfactions far beyond those of popular music. But the many children who do not have the opportunity to develop a liking for fine music may never realize this potential esthetic satisfaction.

We begin to build musical taste in children by carefully selecting the music to which they are exposed in school, including the music to which they will listen and the songs that they will sing. Children should have an opportunity to know many kinds of music. Popular music they hear continually; classical music is represented in some of the songs children sing and the records selected for classroom listening. But music of the Orient, the *Hausmusik* of the fourteenth, fifteenth, and sixteenth centuries (written for informal use and much of it eminently suitable for children), and contemporary music (including electronic) are largely neglected in the schools. Such music, particularly that of some contemporary composers, may sound strange to ears accustomed only to rock or to Western composers of the eighteenth and nineteenth centuries. When the teacher first presents it to children, she may find herself listening for certain kinds of melodies, harmonies, and instrumental colors. Not finding them, she may hear only a meaningless jumble of sounds, particularly if the music is not organized along the conventional tonal principles, and she may convey her rejection of the music to her pupils. It is important that teachers as well as children listen with fresh ears—not once, but many times. Not all contemporary music will survive the test of time, but it is an expression of the period in which we live and should be known to children.

Music selected for children must be suited to their level of maturity. First-graders are hardly prepared to listen to Stravinsky's *Agon* or to sing Handel's *Hallelujah Chorus*. But much ballet music and some program music is eminently suitable for listening in elementary classrooms. Tchaikovsky's *Nutcracker Suite* and Stravinsky's *Firebird*, for example, have been successfully used with primary children.

Many teachers tend to limit too narrowly the selections for children's listening. In selecting songs for children to sing, however, they tend to err in a different way: particularly in the lower grades, they choose songs for children that have been composed especially to correlate with other phases of school work. School music readers, for example, often provide songs about the postman for children to sing when they are studying the post office, and songs about Dutch children for use when pupils study Holland. Unfortunately, little can be said for most of these songs beyond the fact that they correlate in subject matter with other learnings; all too often the songs themselves lack sufficient imagination in words and complexity in music to challenge even kindergarten children. Ideally, of course, the teacher should choose songs for children that she herself would not be ashamed to sing. *Authentic* music materials both correlate with other learnings and have musical quality. Instead of songs about Indians, children can learn Indian chants; instead of songs about Holland, they can learn a real Dutch song, such as the beautiful "Prayer of Thanksgiving."

As with art, in order to develop children's tastes in music, the teacher must do more than expose children to it; she must give them certain knowledge and skills to deepen their esthetic response to good music. As children learn to understand the elements of music, and their relation to one another in a musical composition, as they become conscious of cues, they get more out of listening and performing. The discussion that follows is a brief overview of some of the elements of music that furnish the raw materials of perception. Embodied in these elements are the cues that children must notice if they are to deepen their esthetic response to music.

The Elements of Music

Rhythm, melody, harmony, and tone color are the main elements in music to which the teacher in the elementary school, consciously or unconsciously, turns his attention. Other elements, such as pitch, duration, and intensity, contribute to these main elements. Analyzing these elements may help the teacher who considers himself nonmusical, or does not feel secure in teaching music, to understand more clearly what his objectives should be in teaching music to children.

Rhythm. Although there are wide individual differences in sensitivity to rhythm as in all other areas, by the time they come to school most children have at least a rudimentary sense of rhythm. It is easy to understand why this is so. Rhythm is a natural element in life as in music. The heart beats with a definite rhythm; we breathe rhythmically; our working-sleeping patterns follow the rhythm of day and night. The babbling of the infant—"da-da, da-da"—the running, hopping, jumping, and leaping of the young child, the chants of children at play, are early expressions of rhythm. The school builds on these early responses. In the primary grades it encourages the child to skip to music in unison with others, to clap hands to the rhythmic patterns of a new song, to keep step to music, and to interpret rhythm in music through bodily movements in the dance. In the intermediate and upper grades the child's sense of rhythm is further developed as he learns to interpret the rhythmic pattern of a song in notation, as he folk-dances in figures and in sets, as he tries to express rhythm through the use of instruments. Rhythm is perhaps the easiest of all musical elements to develop in children; they have little difficulty in listening for rhythm and responding to it.

Melody. Melody refers to a succession of single tones in a musical composition. Just as most young children come to school with an already developed sense of rhythm, so most also have some grasp of melody. They can tell when a melodic line goes up or down; they can distinguish one melody from another; they can reproduce vocally many simple melodies that they have heard. The child's sensitivity to melodic sequences is further developed in his school experience. He may listen to short themes that leave the melodic line suspended and learn to recognize the kind of ending that will resolve the melody. The teacher may sing melodic themes as questions and have the child himself discover the secondary point of resolution. The child also learns to sing a variety of melodies, first by rote, and eventually from musical notation. He may create his own melodies vocally or on simple musical instruments.

Harmony. Children are accustomed to hearing melodies against a background of harmony, but they differ in sensitivity to this element of music. When a pianist plays the wrong chord to accompany his melody, some children are jolted; others do not recognize that anything is wrong. Children with little harmonic sensitivity also find it difficult to harmonize with others in part singing.

Harmony gives depth to music through the movement and relationship of chords. The most common chords in Western music are combinations of three tones, three steps apart, known as triads. There are three such chords in each scale, based, respectively, on the first (tonic), fifth (dominant), and fourth (subdominant) steps of the scale. Thus in the key of C major, for example, the three triads are C–E–G (1–3–5), G–B–D (5–7–9), and F–A–C (4–6–8). The movement of these and other chords is regulated according to principles evolved by musicians centuries ago. Certain chords in each scale are "active," seeking final resolution in the chord of rest (usually the 1–3–5 triad). We in the Western world are so accustomed to this movement in music that we do not feel that a composition is completed until we hear the tonic chord.

The teacher can help pupils to develop sensitivity to harmony by providing opportunities for individual children to play chords on the piano to accompany class singing. (Music readers suggest which chords to play.) Or the class may be sectioned to provide vocal chording while one group carries the melody.

Tone Color. By "tone color," the musician means the quality or timbre that distinguishes the tones produced by one instrument from those produced by another. The harp differs from the violin in the color of the tones it produces, and, similarly, the violin differs from the oboe. It is not difficult to help children learn to recognize the characteristic timbre of each instrument in a recording or live concert. Such selections as Prokofiev's *Peter and the Wolf* and Britten's *The Young Person's Guide to the Orchestra* provide invaluable aid. It is more difficult for pupils to appreciate how the composer must choose his timbres, blending and contrasting them to give a desired effect. Through careful listening, children can discover the capacities and limitations of different instruments and come to understand why the composer selects the piano when he wishes to produce one type of effect and the violin for another, and how the timbre of an instrument contributes to the unity he is trying to create.

An awareness of these four elements of music helps the teacher to deepen children's appreciation of music and to guide their performance. Some fortunate readers already know these elements, perhaps intuitively; others, whose natural musical sensitivity has not been developed by a rich background of musical experiences, must grasp them intellectually before they can experience them emotionally.

The fact that these four elements in music are discussed separately here is not meant to suggest that they be taught as separate elements to children. There are times, of course, when one element must be isolated for special attention. The teacher may have pupils listen carefully to the way in which a composer uses rhythm or harmony or melody or instrumental color in a particular composition. But the elements of music should not be isolated too frequently in the elementary school lest children fail to develop the ability to perceive the essential unity in musical compositions.

Music Activities

Music activities in the elementary classroom are planned in the light of the school's goals in music education. In the past, when the goal of music education was to teach the child to identify musical selections, to follow directions in keeping time, and to read notes, the program included formal "appreciation" sessions, rhythm bands drilled to perfection, and early emphasis on note reading and writing. Today, however, the teacher begins by stressing not technique but creative participation in singing, listening, playing, dancing, and other musical activities. Techniques are introduced at the time they are needed to increase the satisfaction the child derives from his musical experiences—when singing a song well, playing a piece with accuracy as well as verve, maintaining harmony in group singing, become important to the child.

The revolution that has affected other aspects of the curriculum has not evidenced itself in the music curriculum. Nor has the revolution in music that has occurred outside the classroom affected school music activities. Children's listening outside of school includes rock, country rock, black music, and other forms relevant to the social scene, while in school children hear and sing much more traditional music. Part of the difficulty may be that teachers are not knowledgeable about the revolution in popular music and tend to reject the good with the bad. Some of the history of this revolution and its relationship to the culture is contained in the following essay by Mark Lavatelli:

The revolution in popular music in America began with the creation of rock and roll in the mid-fifties. Rock was born of Rhythm and Blues, which is urban, electrified, black music. Its roots lie in the rural South, and the classic styles and songs of men like Mississippi John Hurt and Big Bill Broonzy come from the nineteenth century and still have currency today. Out of this rural tradition came urban rhythm and blues artists such as Muddy Waters and Sonny Boy Williamson. Blues rhythms are the basis of rock and roll, but rock is slicker and the content is different, as it is primarily a product of white culture.

This conscious revival of an American music style, combined with an electronic technology and the beginnings of a mobile, affluent youth culture, was responsible for the birth of rock. Radios, due to the miniaturization possibilities introduced by transistors and printed circuits, were portable and became common attributes of automobiles. Electronically produced music of simple rhythmic and harmonic structure could be satisfactorily reproduced on radio. It is interesting to note that with the increasing quality of sound-reproducing equipment available, the quality of rock music has also improved. Rock artists like Chuck Berry and Elvis Presley exemplify this late-fifties style, which had fast rhythm suitable for dancing, and, for the most part, lyrics about high school romance, the automobile-oriented culture (hot rods and drag-racing), and surfing.

In the early sixties, musical innovation was subordinated to the preoccupation with dances, the Twist, Frug, Watusi, and Swim to name a few. The Beatles, the Rolling Stones, and Bob Dylan shook rock out of this repetitive and relatively monotonous plateau. The Beatles and the Stones, in conscious imitation of Chuck Berry and other early rock artists, reinfused a dynamism into the music that had been lost. The Beatles soon began exploring the adaptability of rock to other musical forms such as the Indian *raga*, and, in general, they introduced new harmonies, melodies, and rhythms into the rock medium. The Stones, on the other hand, have remained with a heavy, blues-oriented, rock beat, and the power of the music makes them *the* classic rock band.

Bob Dylan first achieved fame as a folk singer in the tradition of Pete Seeger and Joan Baez. His change to an electric guitar and a rock back-up band scandalized the folk purists, because in rejecting the unamplified folk tradition, Dylan was also rejecting a political tradition of the protesting folk singer; he was in effect choosing life over politics. More significant is the music he created, which is called folk-rock. It is, when traced to its roots, a combining of rural and urban, white and black, and "light" and "heavy" music styles.

There have been many followers of this folk-rock tradition, notably The Band, which used to play many Dylan folk-rock songs. Elements from Country and Western music, particularly the use of the Hawaiian, or slide, steel guitar, have been included in the style of many country-rock groups. The love of nature and things natural—such as organic food and the life on a farm—is a sentiment that is often expressed by such groups, and I feel that this is one of the major cultural manifestations of a new Romanticism. In the history of ideas, periods of romanticism coincide with times of disaffection with the status quo, as is the case today. This tendency can be seen in many other art forms, particularly in films, and in popular music today the success of singers who use acoustic guitars may indicate a rejection of the loud, amplified, wall-of-sound music style in favor of a more natural one.

With the popularization of the blues by white groups such as the Paul Butterfield Blues Band (whose early lead guitarist was Mike Bloomfield, who also played on Dylan's early folk-rock albums), the now defunct Blues Project, singer Janis Joplin, and singer/guitarist Johnny Winters, there has been a revival of black blues artists whose city audience is dwindling because of the trend toward soul music—a slick, showy combination of gospel singing and big band blues in the Count Basie tradition—but who are now finding an audience among many college kids. Jazz, whose roots are black, has mixed with rock, as can be heard in the music of vibraphonist Gary Burton and guitarist Larry Coryell.

The Beatles, long hair, and drugs (primarily marijuana and hallucinogens) started happening at about the same time. From this point on, the growth of rock music and the drug culture are inextricably linked. Drugs and music are mutually compatible; drugs facilitate easy involvement with music. Although precisely how the drugs affect the music is impossible to determine, this factor, combined with the increasing possibility of sound and noise manipulation because of improved electric guitar and amplifier technology, has led to what is called acid rock, after LSD. This developed on the West Coast, where the drug culture began, and the combining of the loud, often screeching, and strongly rhythmic music with brightly colored swirling light patterns enhance the rock experience; the lightshow is an integral part of acid rock.

Drug use while listening to music receives reinforcement from the performers themselves, who use drugs and don't hide the fact. Furthermore, rock "superstars" are youth's culture heroes and have much influence, particularly in terms of life-style. The tragic nature of the involvement of music with drugs is evidenced in the early deaths of two such superstars, Janis Joplin and Jimi Hendrix, from drug overdoses.

Some rock music is bad, and the reason for this is that many rock musicians are quite young, and so is their audience—which is often not very demanding.

The tendency of rock performances to be theatrical is shown in the creation of two full-length rock operas by the Who. Because of this adaptability of rock to other musical and visual artforms, because of its dependence on electronic technology as its medium, and because of its close link with drugs and the contemporary life-style of our youth, we must conclude that the music cannot be considered apart from the culture it speaks of and to.

Special attention should be paid to the Negro spirituals, an art material regaining popularity first among blacks as they become conscious of their own cultural heritage, and then among whites. The spirituals were the "sorrow songs" of the slave, in which he described his oppressive environment and expressed his desire for freedom. Scholars think that spirituals originated in the 1750s and that they combined elements of Christian church services and African chants. Later the spirituals were used as secret messages; Nat Turner, for example, called together meetings of slaves with "Steal away, steal away,/Steal away to Jesus." Black Studies programs in elementary schools find rich material for study and appreciation in these spirituals, as well as in the newer gospel music that has been produced since the end of slavery.

Nonverbal Communication: Movement and the Dance

One of the underlying themes in music education is that understanding music can be facilitated by movement (Aronoff, 1969). Aronoff draws upon the work of Jaques-Dalcroze as a foundation for organizing music experiences. Jaques-Dalcroze evolved an approach to music education based upon the child's movement responses to music. His influence upon the curriculum is to be seen in the rhythm activities that form part of the curriculum in early childhood education. These activities first took the form of "doing what the music tells you to do": "elephant walk" music typically meant that young children used their bodies to imitate the heavy lumbering gait of the elephant, with hands clasped and arms dangling to represent a swaying trunk. The Dalcroze influence is still found in preschools and primary schools around the world; Japanese children and Soviet children, like their American counterparts, can be seen zestfully moving about as butterflies while their teacher plays appropriate music on the piano.

A contemporary approach to movement, however, does not begin with the music, but with expressing concepts within the individual. It starts with an idea that is to be communicated not with words but with the body, nonverbally. The dancer discovers, as he attempts to communicate his idea, what his body is capable of doing, and the discovery itself further liberates his freedom to communicate. Modern dance is one expression of such nonverbal communication.

At present, creative expression through the dance is confined to school systems in which a gym and a teacher or parent with some training in the dance are available. In some systems, music, art, and the dance are integrated as they are in contemporary festivals of art. In Philadelphia, three elementary schools have a "gymkraftics" program in which the children set themes, and choose music and lighting to carry out their ideas with bodily movement (Kies, 1971). America does not lack the talent for putting such programs into effect in the schools, nor is America a poor country; we seem to lack only a sense of priorities.

Summary

We have considered two facets of esthetic education in this chapter: the art and the music curricula.

We have pointed out that art education has suffered because it has been considered a "frill," or, at best, as important only as it contributes to some other goal, such as mental hygiene. But art education serves important functions in its own right: in the development of esthetic sensitivity, of taste; as a model of individuation in education; in inducing self-discovery, spontaneity, discrimination; and in enhancing the enjoyment of life. We have reviewed the knowledge, skills, and attitudes that make up the content of the art curriculum, and presented an approach to art as a problem-solving experience. Lastly, we have suggested "environmental literacy," the ecological implications of art, as part of the content of the art curriculum.

With respect to music, we have discussed the problems involved in developing an appreciation of music and have made a plea for extending the range of the present music curriculum to include contemporary and non-Western music. A brief section presents the elements of music that furnish the raw materials of perception. As to music activities, we have suggested that contemporary popular music be included in the curriculum, and have included—as background material—a survey of the history of such music and a description of the contemporary scene in music.

READING LIST 12

Gaitskell, C. *Children and their art*, 2d ed. New York: Harcourt Brace Jovanovich, 1971. A text for elementary school teachers which discusses both the theoretical and the practical aspects of rich and varied art programs. It contains detailed descriptions of art techniques useful for the classroom teacher who teaches her own art.

Pappas, G. (Ed.) *Concepts in art and education*. London: Macmillan, 1970. The chapter by I. Child, "The Problem of Objectivity in Aesthetic Value," includes some interesting data on children's esthetic judgments.

Smith, R. *Discovering music together: early childhood*. Chicago: Follett Educational Corporation, 1968. While written primarily for preschool and primary grades, this book offers delightful suggestions for music activities throughout the grades.

Smith, R. (Ed.) *Aesthetic concepts and education.* Urbana: University of Illinois Press, 1970. Greene's chapter, "Imagination," and Arnstein's, "Aesthetic Qualities in Experience and Learning," are thoughtful papers that will extend the reader's insights into esthetic development.

Professional Journals To Become Acquainted With

Journal of Aesthetic Education. National Association of Teachers of Art, 1201 Sixteenth St., N.W., Washington, D.C. 20036.

CHAPTER 13

Health and Physical Education

Health Education

Schools in general have had a relaxed attitude toward health and physical education for at least two decades. A rather smug attitude has prevailed that, after all, Americans are a pretty healthy people: we seem to be living longer, and, with the aid of antibiotics, to have eliminated many serious diseases. Furthermore, because teachers usually feel the pressures of an overcrowded curriculum (they worry about "covering" all the texts assigned to their grade), they devote little attention to health education as part of the curriculum. In fact, visitors to a classroom can observe that the health textbooks always show the least usage; and when the daily schedule becomes too full, it is the health lesson that is dropped or skimped. On the playground, when there are no special physical education personnel, tired teachers are glad of a break in their classroom activities and are likely to let the children engage in free play or stand around chatting with friends, rather than to attempt to direct the students' activities.

The Need for Health Education

In view of the foregoing remarks, there is a serious need for school programs to improve the health of the nation. UNESCO figures show that there has been a slippage in America's standing relative to other nations in average life expectancy and in infant mortality, two important indexes of a nation's health. Contributing to the statistical trend is the appalling lack of adequate health care for roughly one-third of the nation who live in poverty, subsist on substandard diets, have not been immunized against childhood diseases, live under unhygienic conditions, and are not receiving medical treatment for chronic ailments.

The facts with respect to the health status of the poor are well documented:

1. Prematurity of birth has an excessive representation among the disadvantaged, and especially among nonwhites. Baumgartner (1962) reports that the frequency of low birth weight is twice as great in nonwhite infants, a fact that she attributes to the greater poverty of this group. Prematurity is a matter of concern because an infant born early not only has less chance of surviving than the infant born at term, but also, if he does survive, has a higher risk of having a mental, sensory, or other handicapping condition. Consequently we find an excessive representation of prematures among mentally retarded children and other children identified as having minimal brain damage and subsequent learning difficulties. Where the premature is also poor, the likelihood of the handicap being minimized by good postnatal care is diminished. Of course, some prematures are the result of congenital anomalies, but the Aberdeen, Scotland, studies (see Walker, 1954, as a representative study), the most definitive of their kind, show that both prematurity and pregnancy complications are correlated with the mother's nutritional status, height, weight, illnesses during pregnancy, and social class. Most important, the findings show that the risk to the baby begins long before pregnancy, that the health care of the mother *during her childhood* is related to her status as a reproducer of healthy infants.

The girls in our elementary schools are the future mothers of America, and the kind of health care they are receiving *now* will affect the babies to be born in another decade or two. While the schools, unfortunately, cannot cure poverty, they can take advantage of federal lunch programs to see that children have at least one good meal a day. They can also see to it that health education is restored as an important subject in the curriculum. Wives of university students who feed their families on low-income budgets have been found, as a group, to provide diets more nutritionally adequate than families on the same budget whose educational level is low. Ignorance of the facts of good nutrition is an important factor in malnutrition, although knowledge alone will not put food on the table when there is no money.

2. There is evidence to suggest that the poor in America suffer from "subtle sub-clinical forms of malnutrition" (Birch, 1964). Certainly congressional hearings on the subject attest to the truth of the statement, and, furthermore, there is a systematic relationship between nutritional adequacy and neurologic maturation and competence in learning (Cravioto et al., 1966). Animal studies in particular have demonstrated a significant interference in brain growth as a result of severe dietary restriction, especially during the first months of life. And, since malnutrition is associated with poverty, it behooves teachers of the poor, we repeat, to take cognizance of a need for relevant health education.

3. Studies of such factors as acute and chronic illness, immunizations, dental care, and the utilization of health services show the same picture: that children reared in poverty "are exposed to massively excessive risks for maldevelopment" (Birch, 1964) in terms of health. There is a dangerous myth among the middle class that the poor have available to them clinics for free health care, and that immunization and dental and medical problems are being adequately cared for. Again, a congressional investigation (in 1971) showed that this was *not* the case, and that health services for the poor were not only inadequate but were worsening.

Why should teachers as teachers, and not simply as humanitarians, be concerned about such problems? We have already pointed out the risks of prematurity in producing children who will have learning problems, and that the status of the learner depends upon his earlier status as a fetus, which depends in turn upon the mother's health care during her childhood. But aside from the special risks associated with prematurity, multiplied when one is also poor, the conditions of submarginal health prevailing among children who were full-term but are being reared in poverty also affect learning ability. The malnourished child is less likely to be responsive to stimulation; he appears apathetic, which provokes apathy on the part of the teacher, resulting in a cumulative pattern of reduced teacher-child interaction (Birch, 1964). It is an effort for teachers to call on the child from whom answers must be dragged, and so they tend to ignore the unresponsive child. And the infrequency of interaction with the very children who need it most continues to contribute to a learning deficit. Finally, in addition to a lack of energy for school learning, there is the very real risk that the conditions of submarginal health may directly affect the developing nervous system and impair the long-term potential of the learner.

The children of the poor are in our schools. As we have said earlier, the classroom teacher as an individual cannot eliminate the effects of poverty from their lives, but we should point out that teacher lobbies might do more in influencing congressional action for medical care, dental care, school meals, and the like than they are presently doing. It comes as a shock to the American visitor to Soviet kindergartens (preschools) to see a dentist's chair in the health office of the school, to meet the school doctor—who is on duty *every* day, *all* day—to see the evidence of remedial care in the way of corrective eyeglasses and the like, to eat the same hearty midday meal as the children, as well as the early morning and late afternoon lighter meals, and to realize that this kind of care for children exists even in poor, backward Soviet republics far removed from the more advanced Republic of Russia. There is clearly something wrong with our priorities.

But the teacher as an individual *does* exert some control over the curriculum; here she can make sure, first, that her students know the facts of good health care as best they are known today, and, second, that children are taught in such a way that they modify their daily living in the light of what they learn.

But before we turn to the health education curriculum, it would be well to point out that dietary and other health problems are not found exclusively in the domain of the poor. The reader may have witnessed the televised congressional hearings on breakfast cereals, at which nutrition experts testified that most of the commercial cereals had little or no nutritional value and at which the manufacturers of these cereals themselves testified that they were counting on the consumer to add milk to the cereal to provide the nutrition! Yet a survey of the eating habits of Americans shortly after the hearings revealed that breakfast habits had not been changed. Certainly with children the power of the Saturday morning television commercials is far greater than the impact of congressional hearings, and these commercials have an impact upon all classes. We do not have data on how many children of the rich, the middle class, and the working class have inadequate diets, but the practices that meet the eye with respect to nutrition are discouraging: the large amounts of sweet and fatty foods, including pastries and French fries, the correspondingly small amounts of fresh fruits and vegetables, the increasing use of chemical substitutes for real foods (imitation milk, orange juice, and so on) and preservatives and other food additives. Particularly appalling was the discovery by one of these writers that some seniors in teacher education at the University of Illinois did not know that vitamin C is a *daily* necessity, since the body does not store it, that they made no effort to see that foods with vitamin C were included in their daily diet, and that, when they wanted to lose weight, they skipped lunch and ate only a candy bar instead!

The pressures of commercial television to be intolerant of any minor aches and pains and to take pills and laxatives also know no class lines.

The problem of exercise, of course, is also one that affects all classes; this we deal with in the physical education section of this chapter.

And, last, there is the frightening problem of drug usage, a relatively new American phenomenon, against which the elementary school child must be armed as best we can arm him.

What we are saying in effect is that, far from being allowed to be slighted, the health curriculum demands more attention from teachers than it is getting now, and that this is true for teachers of all classes of children.

The Health and Safety Education Curriculum

The curriculum for health and safety education embraces the following topics:

Nutrition
Physiology
Dental Care
Communicable Disease Control
Community Health
Safety and First Aid
Drug Abuse

As is true in other subjects, the health and safety curriculum is organized according to a spiral plan. There are generalizations or major themes identified in connection with the various topics listed above, and then these themes are broken down into concepts to be taught at assigned grade levels. Concepts increase in difficulty from grade to grade, but there is a systematic review of the learnings taught at an earlier level, so the net effect is that of a spiral.

Let us take a closer look at the topic Physiology to illustrate curriculum building. Learning is organized around the conventional topics of systems of the body: the skeletal, nervous, digestive, circulatory, and respiratory systems are typically included. Underlying the study of these systems, some broad generalizations that apply to all are identified:

1. There is a basic tendency toward stability or equilibrium in the various systems of the body.

2. When equilibrium is upset by interaction with forces outside or inside the body, regulatory mechanisms go to work to restore equilibrium.

3. There is a relationship between structure and function; the structure of parts of the body determines the function of those parts.

Once major generalizations have been identified, the flow of concepts from grade to grade is roughed out. In connection with study of the skeletal system, for example, children in the primary grades learn:

1. Bones give shape to and support the body, help the body to move, and protect vital organs.

2. The long bones of the body are big and strong; they help to support the body in an upright position.

3. The small bones in the fingers make possible fine work by the hands.

4. Man's backbone is made up of many small bones that make movement easier than would one long bone.

By way of contrast, here are some concepts appropriate for students in intermediate and upper grades:

1. The different parts of the skeleton grow at different rates; in general, development in the upper part of the body precedes development in the lower.

2. There are individual and sex differences in rate of maturation.

3. There is a preadolescent growth spurt that may begin for early developers at ten or eleven years of age; for late developers, it may not begin until fourteen or fifteen years of age.

4. Growth spurts are triggered by hormones in the body whose function is regulated by genes interacting with the environment.

5. Bones in the skeleton are connected by different kinds of joints that permit different kinds of movement.

6. The skeleton of embryos is made up in part of cartilage, permitting easy passage through the birth canal; this elastic tissue is gradually converted into bone whose calcium carbonate composition gives it the hardness essential for upright posture and support.

Included in the study of the skeletal system are relevant concepts about care of the skeletal system. Some of the concepts pertain to exercise, to which we turn in the next section. Some are derived from nutrition. The student learns about the four basic food groups and why it is essential to include foods from each of the four groups in the daily diet. In particular the need for foods from the milk group and the fruit and vegetable group is emphasized.

Evaluation of the effectiveness of health education must be made in terms of what students practice. We are concerned not only that students have the knowledge, but also that they put that knowledge to work to lead more healthful lives. Good teaching practices generally include activities in which children become involved in solving a meaningful problem and putting their knowledge to work. Cooking, for example, is a natural outgrowth of the study of nutrition; children can find out how the four basic food groups are represented in the food of various ethnic groups, and they can prepare that food so as to preserve essential food values. They can investigate the city water supply and find out what an acceptable bacterial count is. They can become astute readers of package labels to evaluate package contents in terms of nutrients and additives. They can analyze TV advertising for the appeals made in the name of good health to sell products that may actually be damaging: the pills to keep one awake, the pills to put one to sleep, the pills to deaden pain or muscle fatigue, the laxatives to keep one young, the "tonics" to pep one up. Involvement in solving meaningful problems is likely to result in effective learning in the health curriculum as well as in other subject-matter areas.

We have mentioned the problem of drugs. A decade ago it would not have been thought necessary to begin education against narcotics and other drugs in the elementary school. Today in both suburban and ghetto schools there *is* a drug problem in the elementary grades. No one knows how great the problem is, but that it *does* exist is attested by the heroin deaths of children under twelve years of age. No one is quite sure, either, how to cope with the problem. But both the federal government and insurance companies publish materials on the effects of drugs, knowledge of which may arm students against ever beginning. Knowledge, too, of the ways of "pushers" and older students who may urge trying a particular drug may help. Certainly teachers should be alert to signs of unusual behavior on the part of students and take appropriate steps to enlist the help of the principal, parents, and a drug clinic in caring for the child.

An important area in the health education curriculum is exercise. There is unanimous agreement on the part of medical experts that exercise is essential to health, and that the alarming increase in heart and circulatory problems stems in large part from the fact that Americans are not physically active enough. Their sedentary habits begin during the school years and are maintained in adult life. Too many children ride in buses or cars to school, sit in the classroom for several hours, stand around on the playground for thirty minutes, and return home for a few hours of TV viewing before and after supper. Yet the status of their arteries in middle age depends upon the development and strengthening of these arteries during the formative years. More and more adults are recognizing the need for regular physical activity and are walking more, riding bicycles, swimming, playing tennis or golf, bowling, or enrolling in exercise classes. Children, too, must recognize the need and start during the elementary school years to build habits of regular exercise.

There are benefits in regular exercise in addition to improved physical well-being. Engaging in sports such as swimming or track promotes release from tension and so contributes to mental as well as physical health. A strenuous period of outdoor play can restore circulation and make the learner more mentally alert for the lessons to follow. And learning to do well in a particular sport can have a positive effect upon one's self-esteem. Erikson (1963) explains the relationship between physical and emotional development by pointing out that mastery of a skill that is valued by the culture contributes to the child's self-concept: becoming "one who can swim" or "one who can ride a two-wheeled bicycle" or "one who can bat a ball" bolsters the child's feelings about himself and has a positive effect upon his emotional well-being.

Today's programs in physical education for elementary schools emphasize exercise, or, more properly, human movement, and physical education teachers attempt to improve human movement through an analysis of the physiology involved and of the reciprocal impact of movement with the environment. For a discussion of this important trend we turn to a statement by Marjorie Souder, Professor of Physical Education for Women at the University of Illinois.

Physical Education in the Elementary School

The question of the relevance of physical education to the elementary school curriculum is at once timeless and timely. Relevance, considered in either the personal or social sense, is dependent upon what the individual knows that enables him to identify and accomplish goals which to him have purpose. What is known about human movement is derived largely from the natural, social, and physical sciences. The subject matter of those sciences provides a framework that is timeless for understanding the movement needs of the human body, the structure of the body for movement, the physical laws that create and govern movement, and the emotional needs that require expression through movement.

The content of the curriculum should embrace the timely as well as the timeless; that is, the personal relevance of human movement will depend largely upon the way in which human movement is utilized as the learning medium. The activities will have personal significance if they allow the child to respond to the world in a meaningful, skilled, productive, active, shared way. If the environment encourages the child to gain a sense of self, to experience limitation and mastery of the self, to sense freedom and fulfillment, then the personal relevance of physical education to the child will be accomplished.

How best to achieve a combination of knowledge and intent or purpose is the contemporary requirement placed on the physical education program. It is the aim of this section to describe a program that combines commitment and goal-directedness in learning with skill in achieving goals of personal significance.

Objectives of Physical Education

Physical education is best defined in terms of the movement-oriented experiences designed to serve major educational goals. The statements prepared by the Physical Education Division of the American Association for Health, Physical Education and Recreation provide insight into the role of physical education in elementary education:

> TO HELP children learn to move more skillfully and effectively not only in exercises, games, sports, and dances but also in all active life situations.

TO DEVELOP understandings of voluntary movement and the ways in which individuals may organize their own movements to accomplish the significant purposes of their lives.

TO ENRICH understanding of socially approved patterns of personal behavior, with particular reference to the interpersonal interactions of games and sport.

TO CONDITION the heart, lungs, muscles, and other organic systems to respond to increased demands by imposing increasingly greater demands upon them.

This, then, is physical education—the modern school subject in which children and young adults study the properties of their own idea—directed movements. (AAHPER, 1965)

Human movement is what physical education instruction should be about. In addition to the formulation of statements regarding the objectives of a program it is also important to clarify the kinds of skills that are important to create, and to identify the kinds of performances that exemplify the attainment of those skills.

In the past, the focus of content in most physical education programs, and consequently the evaluation procedures employed, has been largely directed toward the assessment of specific measurable physical attributes. Such components of physical fitness as cardiorespiratory endurance, strength, flexibility, and speed, as well as measurable skillful performance variables, were the major foci of content development and evaluation in the physical education program. Increasingly, however, attention is being given to the assessment of abilities in spatial orientation, kinesthetic perception, consciously controlled neuromuscular relaxation, and the ability of children to deal with the movement problems of daily living or to predict and adapt to altered situations in the performance of complex games, sports, and dance activities. [Space does not permit the full development of each of these concepts; here we concentrate on movement problems, the area of greatest concern to the classroom teacher. CBL]

The primary focus of the content of physical education for the elementary school child centers around experiences designed to develop a foundation for movement. Following are suggested content areas from which movement problems may be developed. The activities are directed toward increasing the child's awareness of muscle control and factors that influence balance.

Children need to experience:

1. The alternations of body parts around the center of gravity while maintaining balance.
   a. The body parts should be used in a variety of ways in order to identify

the effect of their motion on balance. For example: movements that involve swinging and swaying, rotating (twisting, turning), flexing (bending, curling), stretching.

b. The body weight should be balanced on different parts, and different numbers of parts, of the body.

c. The effect of application of pressure to different body parts and the maintenance of balance. For example: facing a partner and applying pushing and pulling movements to their hands and other body areas. Children should experiment with variations in the distance between their feet.

2. The development of spatial orientation while the body maintains a static position in space.

a. The consistency of a spatial frame of reference while in a variety of positions. For example: balance while on boxes, seesaws, ladders, balance boards, and the like.

3. The influence of muscle tension on body awareness.

a. The creation of tension in all large muscle groups. For example: held balances in various positions by creating tension on each side of the body.

b. The reduction of tension. For example: swinging movements requiring consciously controlled relaxation of muscle groups.

4. The use of sensory modalities in developing postural and balance relationships.

a. The monitoring function of the eyes with movements of body parts in space. For example: activities that require consistent sensory monitoring of eye movement with hand movement.

b. The use of auditory and proprioceptive cues to monitor movements of body parts and the production and reduction of tension. For example: auditory tones of different intensity integrated with varying degrees of tension.

Basic Locomotor Movements

The primary way in which the body moves is by pushing against a resistive force. There are many forms of locomotion, and the primary grades present crucial opportunities to aid in the development of these basic movement patterns.

Walking: The child will have developed relatively purposeful patterns of walking by the first grade. It is particularly important that the walking pattern be assessed in terms of the integration of the antigravity reflex, which maintains postural alignment and orientation to the pull of gravity, and the reflex that enables the child to swing the opposite arm forward as he steps in walking.

1. In phase one of this pattern, the toe of the rear foot leaves the ground and the leg swings forward in a pendular motion. Inertia is

overcome and the surface is met again with the heel first and then the foot, which points straight ahead.

The surface upon which the walking is performed influences the amount of force needed to propel the body forward. According to Newton's law of equal and opposite force the ground is pushing back, causing the body to move forward. The propulsion of the body is therefore greatly affected by the counterpressures and friction of the surface.

Another factor to consider in the execution of this first phase of walking is the movement occurring in the trunk of the body. Newton's law describing the action of the body in motion is relevant to this movement. As the arms swing in natural opposition to the movement of the legs, they counterbalance the tendency of the trunk to continue forward momentum and sideward rotation beyond the base of support. An exaggerated arm swing excessively rotates the trunk, and abrupt inhibition of this movement results in a jerky, uneconomical movement. The arms swing freely and easily in order to counterbalance the smooth swing of the hip and leg.

Speed is increased in this phase of walking by increasing the tempo and length of stride. The push of the toe against the surface initiates this movement and determines the speed and direction of the pushing force. The importance of the amount of force applied to the surface is apparent in movements that appear jerky and uncoordinated. Although the desired speed of travel should determine the amount of pushing force exerted, the rate of movement should always allow for the pendular, forward swing of the legs. The direction of the force applied will be essentially horizontal, although a slight vertical lift is necessary. Excessive amounts of force applied in either direction are uneconomical and unsightly, and should be avoided.

2. During the second phase, both feet are in contact with the surface for a brief period of time. This movement allows for the establishment of a new base of support before the security of the previous base is relinquished. The stability of the body will be directly related to this base of support. The very narrow base that is present when one foot is placed in front of the other gives the appearance of lack of stability. An excessively large base in either a forward-backward or sideward direction will provide too much stability for smooth execution of the next movement, and will tend to make the body sway from side to side.

3. The heel of the foot is placed straight ahead on the surface. The body weight is transferred sequentially forward over the outside border of the foot to the big toe, and the big toe leaves the ground. The transfer of weight should not be accompanied by an excessive relaxation of the muscles of the hip. This relaxation will cause the pelvis to drop laterally and will result in an exaggerated sideward hip sway.

As the foot is placed straight forward, the inner borders should fall along a single straight line. A weaving gait often observed is caused by excessive pelvic rotation. Rotation should be limited to the amount needed to allow the leg to move straight forward.

Good body alignment, in which the head, trunk, and pelvis are balanced, is one of the primary requisites of an esthetic and mechanically efficient walk.

Walking Activities:

1. In good form
2. In place, backward, sideward, turning, and in combinations to make patterns
3. "On tip toes" slowly and lightly
4. With the knees half-flexed
5. On the heels
6. With the knees high
7. Kicking up in front or back
8. With variations in the length of stride and tempo
9. With bending, extending, stretching, twisting, and circling movements of the upper body

Running, Starting, and *Stopping:* Running is a natural part of the development of the modes of locomotion. The skill appears at an early age and undergoes a continuous process of refinement throughout the elementary school years. The combined influences of practice and maturation result in rapid improvement in terms of body movement as well as in the ability to run in variable patterns, to start and stop, and to change direction quickly.

The essentials of the running pattern are evidenced in the actions of the legs in both support and recovery phases of the sequence, in the movement of the arms, and in the position of the trunk throughout the stride pattern.

The force exerted by the pushing leg against the surface is varied in proportion to the demands of the run. Greater force exerted by the driving leg will result in greater speed of the run. Children progressively increase the length of the running stride and amount of force exerted in the movement to increase their running speed. There should also be evidence of a diminution of upward movement of the body with each stride. The direction of the application of force becomes more nearly horizontal in order that all forces may be applied in the direction of the run.

The arm swing should counterbalance the rotation of the body by its natural opposition to the leg swing. The arms should move through a large arc in a vertical plane and at a more vigorous rate of speed. Variability in the amount of arm movement will be demonstrated by children at different age levels, and these variations largely reflect the action of the legs in the running pattern.

Since there is no period in which both feet are in contact with the surface, the stability of the body is diminished when running. This period of nonsupport allows time for the swinging leg to be brought forward quickly. Simultaneous flexion of the lower leg, which brings the heel in close to the buttock, should be observed as the knee of the swinging leg is brought forward. Lengthening this period of nonsupport results in increased length of stride. It is important, however, that the foot that contacts the surface be nearly under the center of gravity of the body. Developmental studies indicate that exaggerated leg and foot movements are diminished progressively in the development toward mature running form.

The trunk is inclined slightly forward during the run, so that the body is in a position that is less stable and more advantageous for motion. This body position also facilitates extension of the support leg at the hip, knee, and ankle which imparts the force required to propel the body forward.

Running, Starting, and Stopping Variations: The nearer to the center of the base the line of gravity falls, the more stable is the body. Conversely, then, the nearer to the edge of the base the line of gravity falls, the more precarious is the balance. Applied to the start of a forward running movement, this principle means that the body should be slightly lowered and inclined forward so that the center of gravity is precariously balanced. The feet should be in a forward-backward stride position; the legs should be flexed; one arm should be brought forward and upward, and the other arm should be extended backward. At the moment of starting, force is applied by the extension of these flexed joints and by the powerful downward swing of the forward arm. The arms continue to assist the forward movement and to counterbalance the leg action. The trunk is inclined slightly forward.

The body in motion now takes on additional characteristics. It possesses an energy of its own. The exact amount of energy is relative to the body weight and to the speed at which the body is moving. This factor has two important implications: it is useful in that it increases the ability of the body to maintain itself in motion, and it may be dangerous if the body energy is not properly controlled. The ability to stop quickly presents two problems: a rapid decrease in the energy of motion and a restoration of balance. These basic movement problems can best be solved by application of the principles already stated: Motion is controlled by increasing the distance over which the energy is lost; and balance is restored by the placement of the limbs to provide an adequate base of support.

Activities to explore running, starting, and stopping variations:

1. Forward Run and Complete Stop
Start: Feet in forward stride position, center of gravity lowered, trunk inclined forward.
Run: Push from both feet (primarily in a horizontal direction). Thrust of forward arm down and back is followed by a forward thrust of the rear arm. Use a forceful thrusting action of the legs will increase the length of stride; the arms are purposefully used for counterbalance.
Stop: On a signal, the last foot pushing from the ground does so in a vertical direction, raising the body slightly into the air. Both feet contact the surface simultaneously in a wide forward-stride position, with the knees flexed and the center of gravity over the rear foot. The momentum of the body is absorbed as it travels over its base of support. The arms are adjusted to assist in the maintenance of balance.
2. Forward Run, Change of Direction
Run forward. On a signal come to a complete stop.
Run to the right (right-angle turn); come to a complete stop on signal.
Repeat the above sequence until the running formation has described a square.
Variation: The same formation is used but the complete stop is eliminated. On hearing the signal, the runner changes direction by executing a right-angle turn, keeping the body in motion.
3. Running while Controlling an Object
    a. Running, dribbling a ball with the feet
    b. Running, balancing an object on the hand
    c. Running, changing an object from one hand to the other
    d. Running, picking up an object from the floor, and continuing to run
    e. Running, rolling a ball to a partner
    f. Running, bouncing a ball around obstacles
    g. Running, bouncing a ball with alternate hands in quick changes from side to side
4. Running Variations
    a. Running-walking combinations
    b. Running with variations in quality and level. For example, slowly, softly, briskly, quickly, high, low

   c. Running, stopping on toes, stopping on one leg, stopping on hands and feet
   d. Running in place, forward, backward, sideward, turning around, and in combinations
   e. Running with rope turning
   f. Running with bending, extending, stretching, twisting, and circling movements of the upper parts of the body

Leaping: The leap is simply an extension of the running pattern and is usually performed to gain horizontal distance or vertical height. As the transfer of weight is made, the pushing force exerted by the leg will be in a vertical or horizontal direction, depending upon the problem to be solved. The body is lifted into the air for a moment of complete suspension with forceful movements of the arms, head, and chest contributing to the total action. As in the walk and run, there is an alternate transfer from one foot to the other.

Activities emphasizing leaping for height, distance, and in combination with other locomotor forms:

1. For distance across to ropes parallel to each other on the floor
2. For height over a rope, or over a balance beam
3. In combination with running, or walking; for example:
   Leap, step, step, step, step
   Run, run, run, leap
   Leap, run, run; leap, run, run
4. With bending, extending, stretching, twisting, and circling movements of the upper body

Jumping and Landing: Jumping is another form of locomotion that serves as a basic skill in movement activities. When applied to sports activities, this skill usually has the components of vertical lift or horizontal reach as the primary goals (for example, center jump and lay-up shot in basketball, spike in volleyball, broad jump, high jump, hop-step-jump in track and field events). Jumping in free locomotor expression, in some gymnastic activities, and in dance forms may have as a primary goal the expression of a percussive quality. A percussive movement is initiated with a sudden, forceful contraction; it spends itself abruptly in a sudden effort and possesses little or no follow-through.

The wide variety of jumping tasks and the range of jumping skill evidenced by children are infinitely varied. Maturational factors such as height, weight, and strength affect performance in jumping. However, improvement in the mechanics involved in jumping may be as important a factor to increased performance as body size.

One of the basic problems of jumping is the attainment of vertical height. In raising the body into the air, the jumper must give careful attention to the various positions of body parts. The functions of balance and vision are controlled by the position of the head. The head should be placed in extension as the eyes focus upon the objective of the arm action. This head position facilitates effective body execution during the jump. By contrast, evidence of an immature form in the vertical jump may be seen in the ineffective head flexion position assumed by many children. The trunk of the body should be inclined slightly forward before the take-off, placing the muscles in a stretched position so that they may exert a more forceful action when joints are extended. The take-off may be executed from one foot or both feet, depending upon the problem to be solved. The take-off is executed by extension of the hips, knees, and ankles, and by flexion of the foot. The arms assist in lifting the body by a forceful forward and upward swing; after the peak of the jump is reached, the nonreaching arm is whipped downward. The downward arm movement serves to tilt the shoulder girdle laterally and raise the hand of the reaching arm higher in reaction.

The gradual absorption of the energy of a moving body protects the joints against injury. When one is landing from a jump, the ankles, knees, and hips should be partially flexed in order to absorb the energy produced by motion. On landing, the direction in which one places the feet (for example, forward-backward, sideward, and so on) will depend upon the problem to be solved in a particular activity.

In order to attain horizontal distance in jumping, the center of gravity is brought forward over the base by an inclination of the trunk and a vigorous swing of the arms in the anteroposterior plane. Prior to take-off the hips, knees, and ankles flex in order to place the muscles on a stretch and overcome the inertia of the body. The sequential extension of these joints and accompanying arm movements provide the force needed to propel the body outward at an angle of approximately 45 degrees. The ability to assume full body extension after the take-off is an important variable in skilled performance. The momentarily held position of extension provides the time needed to flex the lower legs and the thighs and to swing the knees forward. The shortened lever created by sufficient hip flexion enables the legs to be brought forward into position for landing. As the heels touch the ground, the lower leg should be straight in relation to the knee. Upon contact of the heels with the surface there is immediate flexion of the knees to permit an uninterrupted movement of the body weight. The movement of the child's arms both in the preliminary actions and in flight often do not contribute either to the maintenance of balance or to momentum of the body. Characteristically, a child will move his arms sideward while the body is in the air and consequently they will be sideward as his legs come forward for landing. Progressive improvement will be noted in form as the child gives evidence of pulling the arms inward so that they move exclusively in one plane and are in position upon landing to reach forward.

Movement problems described below explore jumping variations, jumping for vertical height and for horizontal distance, and activities designed to practice the landings from jumps. The child should experience

1. Jumping Vertically
   a. Take-off, one foot or both feet
   b. Take-offs, with or without a run
   c. Jumping, pressing head toward an object placed vertically overhead, with or without a run
   d. Jumping, arms swinging forward and backward with rhythmical heel raising, knee flexion, and stretching
   e. Jumping, with arms held at sides, swinging forward and backward or in circles
   f. Jumping, touching an object directly overhead with one hand, with both hands, with and without a run
   g. Jumping over objects, attaining height
   h. Jumping, "scissors" style, or with the legs extended forward and backward
   i. Jumping, upward with partners. Two supports, one child on either side, with handshake grip and support on upper arm, push up on child in middle, while he jumps and pushes at the same time. The arms of the child in the center are kept straight throughout.
2. Jumping Horizontally
   a. Take-off, with one or both feet
   b. Take-off, with or without a run to increase the width of the jump
   c. Standing long jump
   d. Hop-step and jump
   e. Jumping forward, backward, to alternate sides
3. Variations in the Air
   a. Jumping and turning
   b. Jumping, making patterns in the air
   c. Jumping and turning over chalk marks or ropes spaced on the floor
   d. Jumping with hips flexed, knees raised forward
   e. Jumping to catch thrown objects
   f. Jumping from side to side over a rope
   g. Jumping, flexing knees, and kicking feet high in back
   h. Jumping, bending knees up and out to the side
   i. Jumping with legs extended, with arms apart, and sideward
   j. Jumping with back arched in swan-dive position
   k. Jumping, changing directions by adding twists to a vertical direction
   l. Jumping with knees half-flexed, knees fully flexed, knees extended

   m. Jumping, varying slow and fast, heavy and light jumps, big and little jumps

   n. Jumping in threes with runs and leaps (partners on opposite sides of the jumper are close to and slightly in front of him); combine run, run, run, leap, and jump vertically

4. Landings
   a. Controlled landings from a jump
   b. Landings on one or two feet
   c. Landings arriving from a forward, sideward, or backward position from varying heights
   d. Landings and take-offs on balls of feet only
   e. Landing with feet alternately together, sideward, and in a forward-backward stride

Hopping: The hop consists of a transfer of weight from one foot to the same foot. This movement also has the components of vertical height and horizontal distance, depending upon the length of time the force is applied and the distance over which it is exerted.

The following activities explore the locomotor form of hopping in isolated movement and combined with other forms of locomotion. The child should experience:

1. Hopping in good form, emphasizing either height or distance
2. Hopping with free leg flexed high in front, extended forward, sideward, or backward
3. Hopping, changing feet after a definite series
4. Hopping, adding a forward, backward, sideward, or turning direction to the upward direction
5. Hopping slowly and quickly
6. Hopping, combining large and small hops in place
7. Hopping, with rope turning
8. Hopping in combination with walks and runs
9. Hopping, turning in place
10. Hopping with flexing, extending, stretching, twisting, and circling movements of the upper parts of the body

Skipping, Galloping, and *Sliding*: These locomotor forms are combinations of the basic movements already discussed and are performed in uneven rhythmic patterns. The gallop consists of a step with the leading foot and a closing with the opposite foot. The foot that began the step is always leading; the rear foot does not pass the leading foot as it closes.

The slide also consists of a step and close and is usually performed in a sideward direction. The essential difference between the gallop and the slide is in the quality of movement. The slide has a smooth, flowing quality while the gallop is more forceful and staccato.

The skip is a combination of a step and a hop executed on the same foot and has a springy, joyful, rather carefree quality.

The following activities explore skipping, galloping, and sliding movements:

1. Skipping with ropes, in place and moving in different directions
2. Galloping, combined with a slide and a skip
3. Skipping twice, stepping four times, in sequence
4. Sliding four times, skipping once, in sequence
5. Galloping, sliding, and skipping with variation in direction and qualities of movement

Manipulation of Objects

Most sports activities involve the manipulation of either a single object or of one object to control and maneuver a second object. In some sports, balls of various shapes and sizes—basketballs, volleyballs, soccer balls, softballs, and bowling balls—are handled by developing momentum in the object and then releasing it. In other activities, the momentum developed in controlling objects—tennis and badminton rackets, hockey and lacrosse sticks, bats, and clubs—must be transferred by force to the object that is maneuvered.

Manipulative Skills. There are three fundamental types of manipulative skills: those in which the performer maintains contact with an object, such as in lifting, pushing, and pulling activities; those in which momentum is developed in an object and then released, such as in all types of throwing; and those in which momentum of a body part or an implement is transferred to a stationary or moving object, such as in all types of striking. Three patterns of movement performed in overarm, sidearm, and underarm sequences are fundamentally related to the manipulation of objects in elements of throwing and striking.

Overhand Throwing Pattern

An early study by Wild (1938) identified four patterns of throwing and associated their appearance with throwing development according to age schedules. More recent observations by Deach (1950) and Jones (1951) provide information concerning the throwing pattern development as related to age and the difference in throwing ability as related to the sex of the child. Elementary school children will demonstrate improvement in performance at each grade level, with the average performance of boys exceeding the average performance of girls.

The general pattern of movements in the overhand throw is both successive and overlapping. The preparatory movements place the body in a position for the application of effective leverage. The child should assume a forward stride position and begin rotating the body and shifting the weight over the base of support to the rear foot. Simultaneous to this shift of weight is the backward and upward swing of the throwing arm.

The next phase of the sequence involves a step forward in the direction of the throw with the leading foot. At this point, sequential rotation of the pelvis, the spine, and the shoulders takes place. The elbow of the throwing arm is brought forward horizontally, the forearm is extended, and the wrist is flexed just before releasing the ball. It is particularly important at this point that children be assisted in the elimination of the pushing motion, which is persistent in its appearance in both throwing and striking patterns.

The last phase allows for the dissipation of the momentum that has been generated in the production and application of force in the throw. The deceleration of the throwing arm reduces any danger of muscle strain and facilitates a smooth finish of the movement.

Activities that emphasize the production, application, and reception of force in the overhand throwing pattern are given below. The child should

1. Experiment with the production of force in this throwing pattern by
   a. Varying the size and direction of the base of support
   b. Alternating the leading leg between positions of flexion and extension
   c. Alternately releasing an object with and without trunk rotation
   d. Releasing the object using only the momentum of the arm
   e. Releasing the object by increasing the range of motion
   f. Adding a transfer of weight over the base of support
   g. Flexing the knees, rotating the trunk, and swinging the arm right in contact with the ball forcefully, downward
   h. Releasing the object with a pushing motion caused by extending the arm at the elbow
   i. Releasing the object with a whiplike motion (the ball is brought down and back through a long arc to the shoulder level, the elbow is flexed and leads the movement of the hand, the forearm whips forward and the object is released)
2. Experiment with the application of force in this throwing pattern by
   a. Releasing the object at varying points in the arc through which the lever is moving
   b. Releasing the object so that it travels almost directly overhead in a long, high arc; in a straight line; in a line to various spots on the floor
   c. Aiming an object at targets marked on the wall
   d. Aiming an object into circles marked on the floor
   e. Aiming an object through a small hoop held in the air
3. Experiment with receiving the force of an object by

    a. Throwing an object against a wall, turning, and catching it
    b. Jumping into the air to receive a thrown object
    c. Moving toward a ball that is rolled on the floor, receiving it, and executing an overarm throw pattern
    d. Receiving an object that has varying degrees of force
    e. Receiving an object that is rebounding from the floor and redirecting its momentum by executing an overarm throw
4. Experiment with the execution of this overarm striking pattern by
    a. Throwing an object overhead and striking it with the palm
    b. Striking an object that is thrown by a partner
    c. Varying the problems by striking for speed, force, and distance

Sidearm Pattern. The child should

1. Experiment with the production of force in this throwing pattern by
    a. Varying the size and direction of the base of support
    b. Releasing the objects with varying degrees of backswing
    c. Releasing the object with and without trunk rotation
    d. Releasing the ball at varying points along the horizontal arc through which the lever moves
2. Experiment with the application of force in this throwing pattern by
    a. Aiming at targets drawn on the wall
    b. Aiming at circles drawn on the floor
    c. Aiming through a small hoop held in the air
    d. Throwing over ropes stretched at varying heights
    e. Bounce-passing a ball around an object
3. Experiment with receiving the force of an object by
    a. Throwing an object against a wall, turning, and receiving it
    b. Receiving a rolling ball and releasing it in a straight line
    c. Jumping toward a thrown object, turning, and releasing it
4. Experiment with the execution of this sidearm striking pattern by
    a. Dropping a ball to the floor and striking it on the rebound
    b. Holding a ball in one hand and striking it
    c. Striking a thrown ball with both hands clasped together
    d. Varying each problem by experimenting with length of levers

Underarm Pattern. The child should

1. Experiment with the production of force in this throwing pattern by
    a. Varying the size and direction of the base of support
    b. Altering the leading knee between positions of flexion and extension
    c. Varying the length of the backswing
    d. Releasing the object at various points in the arc through which the lever moves
2. Experiment with the application of force in this throwing pattern by
    a. Rolling the ball on the floor

    b. Releasing the ball with a long backswing, flexing the knees, and transferring the weight to the forward foot

    c. Releasing the ball so that it travels in a high arc over varying distances

    d. Aiming at targets drawn on the floor

    e. Aiming at circles drawn on the wall

    f. Throwing through a small hoop held in the air

    g. Throwing over a rope stretched at varying heights

    h. Aiming at objects such as wastebaskets, blocks of wood, boxes, and similar targets

3. Experiment with receiving the force of an object by

    a. Throwing an object against a wall, turning, and catching it

    b. Jumping into an object being thrown

    c. Jumping into an object being thrown, turning, and releasing it

    d. Jumping, turning, and receiving an object being thrown

    e. Running toward an object being rolled on the floor, receiving it, and redirecting it

    f. Receiving objects traveling at various degrees of speeds

    g. Receiving objects traveling at various levels

4. Experiment with the execution of this underarm striking pattern by

    a. Striking an object held in the hand

    b. Striking an object tossed in the air

    c. Dropping a ball to the floor and striking it on the rebound

. . . . . .

The reader will note that what Professor Souder has proposed here constitutes, in effect, a complete curriculum in the area of movement for the elementary school child.

Physical Education and the Classroom Teacher

Classroom teachers usually are responsible for the physical education of their students. Some school systems provide specially trained consultants who will work with teachers in planning appropriate activities, conduct a demonstration lesson, and more or less supervise the program. But it is more common in the elementary school for the teacher to be on her own, and to have to take sole responsibility for an aspect of the curriculum for which she is little prepared.

Fortunately, the contemporary emphasis upon movement as the primary factor in physical education is an emphasis with which the classroom teacher feels more comfortable. With an understanding of basic locomotor movements, teachers can have students engage in the walking, running, leaping, jumping, hopping, skipping, galloping, and sliding activities outlined in the previous section, observe children's movements, and make suggestions to individuals for easier, more grace-ful control of the body. Such activities can be carried out in the school gym or all-purpose room if one is available, the playground, or even the classroom, with furniture pushed back and half the class active at a time.

Instruction in physical education is required by law in most states; so is time for outdoor play or recess. But where the physical education period is an instructional period, recess is typically devoted to free, social play, where children can organize their own games. With some planning with the children before they go outside, the teacher can ensure a more con-structive period for every child. Rope-jumping, baseball, horseshoes, track, jumping contests, volleyball, and running games are activities that take a minimum of organization and equipment.

A steady diet of competitive games that only one child or one group of children can win is unsuited to the young child's stage of develop-ment. Research findings indicate that competition has adverse effects on children's social relations. One study found a significantly greater num-ber of negative behaviors, in the form of hostile remarks and aggressive acts, when second graders painted competitively than when the same group of children painted cooperatively. Furthermore, the hostility in-duced by competitive painting spilled over into the play period that followed. Teachers often note the same effects from playground competi-tion. Relay races in which rival teams work themselves into a frenzy over winning frequently leave the losing teams smarting and all too ready to take out their hurt feelings in insults or accusations directed against the winners. Often these feelings and behaviors are carried back into the school, interfering with the work of the classroom. Running games, tag-ging games, and catching games in which competition is minimized do not, in and of themselves, affect social relations adversely.

Recommended Equipment

The selection of permanent playground equipment is not usually within the province of the classroom teacher. However, it is sometimes possible for teachers to requisition additions to existing equipment that will considerably strengthen the physical education program.

Generally recommended for kindergarten-primary children are the following: climbing apparatus, horizontal bars, horizontal ladders, large wooden boxes, barrels and kegs, walking boards, sawhorses and a ladder, in addition to balls, ropes, and other such expendable supplies. With this equipment, children can climb, hang, and travel hand-over-hand, thus developing agility as well as exercising shoulder, arm, and chest muscles.

The boxes, boards, and sawhorses can be arranged in a variety of ways, to provide seesaws, planks for walking, or higher structures for climbing. Some modern playgrounds are being equipped with very ingenious apparatus that invites dramatic, creative play as well as providing for good physical activity.

Intermediate- and upper-grade children need horizontal bars and ladders scaled to their larger size; climbing ropes, giant strides, and monkey rings are also suitable pieces of equipment. Junior-size basketballs, softballs and bats, and soccer balls are essential to the program.

Whether or not she has a voice in the purchase of equipment, the classroom teacher has the responsibility of giving safety instructions for its proper use. Before introducing new equipment, the teacher plans with the children how it can be used safely. We remind the reader that when children can participate in rule making they are more likely to observe the rules. Planning sessions in which children decide upon the rules, and evaluation sessions to talk over problems in the use of equipment, are helpful. During these sessions, the teacher can help the children to apply appropriate science concepts. Even first graders can learn that sitting on swings is better than standing because broad-based objects are more secure than those with a high center of gravity.

Ideally, equipment and instruction should emphasize not team sports but individual sports, a liking and aptitude for which will carry over into adult life. Fortunately, we are seeing more of this emphasis. There are public schools in ski areas in the Rockies where classes of middle- and upper-elementary school children receive instruction from local ski instructors. Skiing corporations consider it to their advantage to develop zest and aptitude for the sport in young children who will be their customers later on, and so they donate instruction and lift tickets during their less busy times. On a less esoteric basis, public schools arrange with community recreation boards for swimming classes for children to be conducted in public pools. In fact, with the tremendous growth of man-made lakes throughout the country, swimming is more and more available to children, and "every child a swimmer" is becoming a matter of practical necessity.

The physical fitness of adults depends in part upon the amount and kind of physical activity they engaged in during childhood. Many writers have deplored the increasing tendency of young people to ride when they might walk, to sit before a television screen when they might be playing, to spend countless hours chatting or "fooling around" when they might be more active. While a good physical education program in the grades should contribute to physical fitness during childhood, it should also instill in the child a liking for physical activity that will contribute to his health and well-being in later adolescence and maturity.

Summary

Even today there are unmet health needs in this country, extreme among the families of the poor but also existing among the affluent, some of which can be served by more effective health education programs in the schools. Teachers should be concerned about health needs not only because human beings are involved, but also because learning ability is affected by poor health status. This chapter lists topics for inclusion in the health education curriculum and includes some teaching suggestions.

Professor Souder has provided the following summary of her material:

The primary focus of the content of a movement-oriented physical education program for the elementary school child centers around experiences designed to develop a foundation for *movement*. The experiences

Parents, teachers, and children work together. Here, a creative new piece of playground equipment takes shape on a Saturday, as parents, teachers, and children work together on the building. Such cooperative enterprises make for real involvement on the part of all the contributors. The result was playground equipment for young children that provided for many kinds of exercise. Courtesy of M. A. Bonenfant, Lewiston, Maine.

must provide opportunities for the child to develop his capacity for movement and to understand the relationship of that development to himself and the environment in which he lives.

The goals of the program may be attained through problem-solving activities that allow the child to move at his own rate of speed toward discovery of the interrelationships of the sensory and motor responses that are involved in organized, goal-directed sequences of movement. What the child learns is competence in dealing with a nervous system that has a limited capacity for receiving and processing input data. The learning is directed toward the development of strategies for dealing with the stimuli, not toward a set of particular and fragmented performances.

Awareness of the movement potential of the body is basic to the organization of the skilled movements evidenced in sports, dance, gymnastics, and aquatic activities. It involves the differentiation of the coordinates of internal space through the sensing of body parts and their relationship to each other; the effect of the parts on the whole body; and the relationship of the whole body to geometric space and objects in space. The posture, balance, locomotion, and object-manipulation activities presented in this chapter provide specific means by which these competencies may be achieved. The activities should be explored in their infinite variations, both as ends in themselves and as they facilitate the development of specific motor skills.

Various combinations of individuals and environmental components result in the wide range of human movements evidenced in complex movement activities. Movement is initiated by the force created in muscle activity and occurs within space and with rhythm. The environmental restrictions placed upon the individual determinants of motion are manifested in the natural laws that govern movement. The mechanical laws of gravity, balance, motion, leverage, and force are basic to all efficient movement, and knowledge of them and the forces that control them is fundamental to the solution of complex movement problems.

This chapter has introduced a few of the essentials pertaining to the phenomenon of human movement. However, a complete representation of the content of this area and its influences on the individual is not possible in the space available here. In order to understand more clearly the meaning of movement to man, carefully observe a child at play.

READING LIST 13

Allen, J. Movement, Music, Drama, and Art. Chapter II in V. Rogers, (Ed.), *Teaching in the British Primary School*. New York: The Macmillan Company, 1970. This chapter represents what might be called a multimedia approach to physical education. It describes a creative program in a London school where movement is combined with music and drama with happy results.

Birch, H. G. Health and the education of socially disadvantaged children. In C. Lavatelli and F. Stendler (Eds.), *Readings in child behavior and development*, New York: Harcourt Brace Jovanovich, 1972. A pediatrician reviews the research on interrelations among the biology of the child, his environment, and his functional capacities, and points out that the child whose learning abilities are being affected by such factors as malnutrition cannot take full advantage of increased opportunity for learning.

Gilliom, B. *Basic movement education for children: Rationale and teaching units.* Reading, Mass.: Addison-Wesley, 1970. Helpful for the reader who seeks further assistance in the development of movement problems and teaching units.

Physical Education Division, American Association for Health, Physical Education, and Recreation. *This is physical education.* Washington, D.C., 1965. An overview of contemporary concerns and objectives of physical education.

Professional Journals To Become Acquainted With

Journal of Health, Physical Education, and Recreation. American Association for Health, Physical Education, and Recreation, a department of the National Education Association, 1201 Sixteenth St., N.W., Washington, D.C. 20036.

Research Quarterly. American Association for Health, Physical Education and Recreation, 1201 Sixteenth St., N.W., Washington, D.C. 20036.

CHAPTER 14

Evaluation

Elsewhere in this book we have stressed the magnitude of the problems facing the American educational establishment. Viewed at the beginning of the decade of the 1970s, the tasks that lay ahead, while not insurmountable, certainly indicated that a great challenge faced the nation's schools. The 1960s will no doubt be remembered for many of the innovations that characterized that decade—the development of modern curricula, school desegregation, and federal involvement in education. It was during the sixties that great concern was expressed about the question, How much are students learning? This has been a concern for some time, but not for too long a time as one views the educational panorama, past and present.

The fact that elementary education, as one facet of the total educational effort, needs evaluation ought to be self-evident, but how one should go about evaluating remains obscure. The persisting disagreements over the role of the school in a changing society compel the American people to assign a top priority to the evaluating of education. That this is an urgent matter becomes clear when we examine the forecasts freely made in past educational history. It is of interest to reflect on what McGaughy (1937, pp. 383–384) had to say in an early critique. He took the position that intelligence tests could be discarded almost completely as a basis for predicting the probable success of the individual pupil in his school work, but that they would remain as one basis for diagnosis of clinical cases and for use in experiments and in research. Likewise, he predicted that achievement tests would play a minor role in the schools of the future, and that this role would assist in providing a more adequate diagnosis of the observed weaknesses of a few pupils. He asserted that the really important objectives of a good elementary school program could not be measured objectively.

Although things did not turn out quite the way that McGaughy envisioned them, it was observed some thirty years later in the *Carnegie Quarterly* (1966), devoted to a consideration of the need for national assessment, that we cannot describe how close our schools come to accomplishing what they aim to accomplish, identify in any precise way the strengths and weaknesses of the system, or measure progress or the lack of it over time. If this is true, it means that at a time when the national stake in education is very clearly perceived, our educational achievements are not clearly perceived at all. The schools are attacked and defended without solid evidence to support the claims of either attackers or defenders, and public policy is of necessity made largely on the basis of assumption and impressionistic and incomplete evidence.

As we mentioned earlier, in a recent survey Goodlad and his associates viewed the scene through visitations, observations, and interviews in 150 classrooms in 67 schools: 32 kindergartens, 45 first-grade, 26 second-grade, and 18 third-grade classes, and 29 classes at these grade levels classified as "special." *Their purpose was to find out the degree to which frequently discussed ideas for schooling prevail in practice.* Their expectations fell into ten categories, only one of which we will consider in this chapter. This is stated as follows:

> . . . One would expect to find flexible standards of evaluation, with increasing attention to the actual performance of children, rather than comparison with grade, age, or group norms. (Goodlad & Klein, 1970, p. 16)

Goodlad found that two-thirds of his schools used one of three well-known standardized tests—Metropolitan, Iowa, or Otis—in testing the achievement of their pupils, with the Metropolitan accounting for as many schools as the other two tests combined. He observes that he was impressed with the range of tests actually being used in the schools, some twenty-six different ones being employed to appraise achievement, aptitude, reading readiness, and special abilities or psychological factors, although these last were rarely tested in any formal way.

> . . . It is clear that the schools in our sample stayed almost exclusively with measurement of the traditional areas, achievement and intelligence, and measured them with the well-known, long-established instruments. (Goodlad & Klein, 1970, p. 41)

The tests being used in the schools surveyed by Goodlad were almost uniformly of the grade-norm variety and overwhelmingly in the tradition of group achievement and intelligence testing. Criterion-referenced tests —that is, tests designed to get at a child's actual status with respect to some criterion of performance—were virtually nonexistent. Some of the tests used, as in reading, might have been used to diagnose a child's competence in broad areas of performance, but usually they were not employed in this way. Rather, scores were translated into grade equivalents and entered on class record sheets.

> . . . Thus, the visible information available was that a child scored at grade 1.9 in this, 2.2 in something else, 2.9 in that, and 2.6 over all. But

the record sheet did not reveal whether this child had problems with the grapheme-phoneme translation, in composing sentences, or with the cumulative law. So far as tests, records, and interpretations were concerned, individuality was washed away by the universality of grade standards. (Goodlad & Klein, 1970, p. 86)

At another, but certainly pertinent and related level—the high school —the gravity of the situation has also been recognized. In *The College Board Admissions Testing Program: A Technical Report on Research and Development Activities Relating to the Scholastic Aptitude Test and Achievement Tests* (1971), the CEEB supplied answers to the many questions arising about the value, administration, and use of the tests. The aim of the publication was to provide a means for evaluating the technology that supports the testing program: its organization, history and development, demands made on it, and the myriad technical details inherent in the operation and distribution of a testing program of such magnitude.

In *Righting the Balance* (1971), the 21-member Commission on Tests appointed by the CEEB criticized the parent organization for focusing mostly on the interests of colleges and their rather specialized needs, while failing to serve the diverse interests of what should be their prime concern, namely, the students. According to the Commission, the Board Examinations taken by about one and one-half million high school students each year fail to recognize and assess a wide variety of talents, skills, and mental attributes with the result that many students are unfairly penalized. The Commission proposed among other reforms the replacement of the Scholastic Aptitude Test by a flexible assortment of tests that measure not only verbal and mathematical ability, but other dimensions of excellence as well—musical and artistic talents; sensitivity and commitment to social responsibility; political and social leadership; athletic, political, and mechanical skills; styles of analysis and synthesis; ability to express oneself through artistic, oral, nonverbal, or graphic means; ability to organize and manage information; ability to adapt to new situations; characteristics of temperament; and work habits.

Obviously such a program, if instituted, could and probably would correct many existing inadequacies found in evaluation at these higher levels. If the decade ahead is to witness changes that will correct existing faults in evaluation at the elementary level, the high school level, and beyond, it is imperative that there be a deliberate and rational plan of improvement adopted on a scale that is substantial and extensive enough to help the schools accomplish their specific aims and objectives. Much of this improvement could come through innovation, but innovation that is carefully planned.

The Nature of Evaluation

Although the term *evaluation* is relatively new, there persists a rather widespread tendency on the part of educators and others to confuse the various meanings that have become attached to the word. Thus far in this chapter reference has been made to the *testing* aspect or element, and, unfortunately, testing continues to be the primary concern of evaluators. An early work in the field treats evaluation as (1) the application of value to a problem, (2) a label for processes used in gauging teaching competence, (3) a synonym for measurement, (4) the appraisal of curriculum practices and educational resources, and (5) being concerned with the study of the status, or changes, in children's behavior (Shane and McSwain, 1951, pp. 49–52).

Evaluation should not be limited to the application of value to a problem. Nor should it be a synonym for measurement, a means of gauging effective teaching, a way of appraising curriculum practices, or a procedure in studying child behavior. Rather, it is a comprehensive process of which any or all of these variations may be components.

A statement by Hagen and Thorndike on evaluation reveals the direction that began to emerge about a decade ago:

> Evaluation in education signifies describing something, in terms of selected attributes, and judging the degree of acceptability or suitability of that which has been described. The "something" that is to be described and judged may be any aspect of the educational scene, but it is typically (a) a total school program, (b) a curricular procedure, or (c) an individual or group of individuals. The process of evaluating involves three distinct aspects: (a) selecting the attributes that are important for judging the worth of the specimen to be evaluated, (b) developing and applying procedures that will describe these attributes truly and accurately, and (c) synthesizing the evidence yielded by these procedures into a final judgment of worth. (1960, p. 482)

More recently, Stufflebeam (1969) states that evaluation means the provision of information through formal means, such as criteria, measurement, and statistics, to provide rational bases for making the judgments that are inherent in decision situations. For Stufflebeam there are certain functions of decision situations, and he classifies these as *planning, programming, implementing,* and *recycling*. Given these four kinds of educational decisions to be served, he postulates four kinds of evaluation. These he characterizes as *context, input, process,* and *product* evaluation. Decisions served by *context* evaluation would include deciding upon the setting to be served, the goals associated with meeting needs, and the objectives associated with solving problems. Stufflebeam contends that decisions based on *input* evaluation usually result in the specification of procedures, materials, facilities, schedule, staff requirements, and budgets in proposals for funding agencies. Stufflebeam believes the objective of *process* evaluation is to detect or predict, during the implementation stages, defects in the procedural design or its implementation. *Product* evaluation is used to determine the effectiveness of the project after it has run full cycle. Its objective is to relate outcomes to objectives and to content, input, and process, that is, to measure and interpret outcomes. In short, this type of evaluation provides information for deciding to continue, terminate, modify, or refocus a change activity, and for linking the activity to other phases of the change process (Stufflebeam, 1969, pp. 61–68).

Yet another authority, Bloom, deplores the expectations of teachers who bring to the teaching situation a belief that approximately a third of their pupils will adequately learn what they have to teach, while another third will fail, and the remainder will get by, but not well enough to be regarded as "good" students. Bloom argues that if the schools are to provide successful and satisfying learning experiences for at least 90 percent of the students, major changes must take place in the attitudes of students, teachers, and administrators. Changes must also take place in teaching strategies and in the role of evaluation. Therefore, he urges teachers to find the means that will enable students to *master* the subject under consideration. He advances the theory that a learning strategy for mastery may be constructed that takes into account the student's (1) aptitude for particular kinds of learning, (2) quality of instruction, (3) ability to understand instruction, (4) perseverance, and (5) time allowed for learning.

> . . . It is not the sheer amount of time spent in learning (either in school or out of school) that accounts for the level of learning. We believe that each student should be allowed the time he needs to learn a subject. And, the time he needs to learn the subject is likely to be affected by the student's aptitude, his verbal ability, the quality of instruction he receives in class, and the quality of instruction he receives outside of class. The task of a strategy for mastery learning is to find ways of altering the time individuals need for learning as well as to find ways of providing whatever time is needed by each student. Thus, a strategy for mastery learning must find some way of solving problems as well as the school organizational (including instructing time) problems. (Bloom, Hastings, & Madaus, 1971, p. 51)

In quest of such a strategy, Bloom carefully considered some of the *preconditions* necessary, the *operational procedures* required, and the *evaluation of some of the outcomes* of the strategy. Thus, the specification of the objectives and content of instruction is one necessary precondition for informing both teachers and students about expectations.

> . . . The translation of the specifications into evaluation procedures helps to further define what it is that the student should be able to do when he has completed the course. The evaluation procedures used to appraise the outcomes of instruction (summative evaluation) help the teacher and student know when the instruction has been effective. (Bloom et al., 1971, p. 53)

Bloom uses the terms *formative* and *summative* evaluation. What do these labels connote? *Formative* evaluation seeks information for the development of a curriculum or instructional device. Stake (1969, p. 24) feels that findings from *formative* evaluation study are generalized over school setting, teacher and student types, and within the various versions of the particular instructional device, but are not generalized across subject matters and curricula. That writer sees *summative* evaluation as being aimed at giving answers to an educator about the merits and shortcomings of a particular curriculum or a specific set of instructional materials. The findings are expected to be generalizable across large numbers of schools, teachers, and students.

In summarizing this section of the chapter that has dealt with the nature of evaluation, we deem it important to draw attention to the ramifications of the meanings that have been applied to the term *evaluation* over the past few decades. In Chapter 5, "Selection of Content," we mentioned that considerable time and attention were devoted, prior to and during the 1950s, to the development of objectives for elementary education. However, a statement of objectives is not enough; the teacher needs to be able to evaluate the degree to which a given objective has been achieved. Thus the teacher might very well know what the desired pupil behavior is in a given situation, but lack the evaluation instruments needed to provide a picture of the here-and-now situation that she can compare with the previous one, and ultimately make an evaluation.

The Search for Useful Tests

While the teacher might prefer to use her own observations backed up by recorded anecdotes of pupil behavior and specimens of work, in our test-oriented educational culture she will be expected to use standardized tests for evaluation as well. We examine here some standardized tests in the realms of language, literature, and composition as examples of what such tests evaluate.

The *Comprehensive Tests of Basic Skills (Language)*, 1968–1970 (CTBS) are a series of tests with alternate forms (Q and R) for grades 2.5 through 12, divided into four levels that overlap at grades 4, 6, and 8. Test 3, LANGUAGE Mechanics, Test 4, LANGUAGE Expression, and Test 5, LANGUAGE Spelling, are described briefly:

Test 3, LANGUAGE *Mechanics*: Test 3 includes 13 items that measure punctuation and 12 items that measure capitalization. The items measuring ability to punctuate are based on a story and a letter in which the pupil must mark the correct punctuation at places indicated by small black squares. Capitalization is measured in two stories in which each sentence is broken into three parts with a fourth alternative, "N" for "None." The task here is to choose the part of each sentence that contains a mistake; or, should there be no mistake, choose the "None" alternative.

Test 4, LANGUAGE *Expression*: The 30 items of Test 4 measure the correctness and effectiveness of expression. There are 16 correct usage items; 8 of these are based on two stories in which the items are presented in the same format as the capitalization items. Eight more correct usage items are based on sentences for which the pupil selects from four alternatives the word that fits grammatically in the sentence.

Nine items measure the ability to comprehend sentence meaning and to select from four alternatives the word that fits best in the sentence in terms of the author's tone, mood, or form. The final 5 items present four alternative sentences in which the same word is used. The pupil's task is to select the sentence in which the word does *not* fit. It is a process of perceiving inappropriate relationships.

Test 5, LANGUAGE *Spelling*: Test 5 consists of 30 spelling items. In some items the pupil must identify an incorrectly spelled word as the answer from among four words; in others, the pupil recognizes that there are no incorrectly spelled words, in which case he selects "None" as the answer.

Rationale: The Comprehensive Tests of Basic Skills (CTBS) were designed, according to the test makers, to measure the extent to which individual pupils have developed the capabilities and learned the skills that are (1) prerequisite to the study of specific academic disciplines and (2) requisite for functioning in a society based on daily use of language and number. The test makers believe that test items in CTBS measure generally the following abilities: (1) to recognize and/or apply techniques, (2) to translate or convert concepts from one kind of language to another, (3) to comprehend concepts and their interrelationships, and (4) to extend interpretation beyond the stated information.

The intent of the test makers was to develop a complete classification scheme implementing their rationale that would be understood by teachers and could be used for instructional purposes, allowing the teachers to determine major strengths and weaknesses in terms of instructional objectives and content. It is pointed out by the test makers—and this is important—that in the development of the tests, attention was given to long-term trends in curriculum such as those involved in contemporary mathematics programs and in the linguistic approach to the teaching of language arts. Items reflecting these changes were used only when there was a reasonable expectation of achievement by students not oriented to specific teaching approaches. Items were excluded that were unrealistic, that is, which could not be assumed to be based on common experience.

The classification of items consists of two major components: the *process* dimension (skills, objectives) and the *content* dimension (topic, type of material). The broad classifications in the process dimension are (1) recognition and application, (2) translation, (3) interpretation, (4) analysis. Content categories are as broadly representative as possible. LANGUAGE content includes Words, Sentences, Directions, Dialogue, Letters, Articles, Stories, Poems. This classification scheme includes all the typically considered objectives for the language arts curriculum.

As the classroom teacher ponders over the testing materials she recognizes that a major problem that falls upon those charged with the responsibility of selecting standardized language arts tests is that of determining whether the types of test items contained in such instruments are appropriate for contemporary language arts programs. If certain realms or areas thought important by her or by her school are not viewed as being amendable to measurement by the professional test makers, then teachers such as herself are left in the unenviable position of having a program for which they must search for some means of standardized testing. If the measurement of language skills in standard English is felt by the teacher to be significant, then she may find the CTBS LANGUAGE tests of value. In schools where black English is spoken, however, grade equivalent scores on such tests are meaningless.

If the teacher is worried about her literature program, as well she may be, she will find that for many years the profession has been concerned about the quality of literary experiences, if not their quantity, provided children in the elementary school. Huck (1962, p. 307), noted:

> We have no literature program in the elementary school when we compare it with carefully compared developmental programs in reading, spelling, and arithmetic. All our efforts are directed toward teaching children to read—no one seems to be concerned that they do read or what they read.

More recently, Odland (1969, p. 1) stated that beyond the general acceptance of literature in the curriculum of the elementary school, there is evidence of vast differences concerning implementation in terms of content, objectives, methods and approaches, and evaluation procedures. Answers to questions about the teaching of literature might be found, according to that writer, if the focus for research were placed on what children read and on what responses children make to what they read.

One literature test to be considered as the teacher searches for assistance in evaluation of her literature program would be A Look at Literature: The NCTE Cooperative Test of Critical Reading and Appreciation. This is designed for grades 4–6 and appeared in 1969.

A Look at Literature is described in the test manual as a research instrument, designed to measure but a part of literary appreciation, which is viewed as being "the ability to respond critically to specific literary selections." In A Look at Literature "responding" calls for such operations as interpreting, valuing, comparing, inferring, appreciating, restating, attending to, relating, identifying with, and understanding. Selections were chosen to represent as many as possible of the modes of literary expression found in imaginative prose and poetry deemed suitable for children. Thus, under the general heading of prose are found such categories as description, fanciful dialogue, realistic dialogue, fable, myth, fanciful narrative, realistic narrative, and the tall tale. Under poetry are found humorous and lyric subdivisions.

Certain response modes were defined prior to the development of the test and an endeavor made by item writers to compose questions that would fit into one of three categories: translation, extension, and awareness. Translation involves low-level inferences, comprehension of meanings, definition, restatement, and recognition of elements. Extension includes interpretation, prediction, comparison, higher-level inferences, use of the "givens" to go beyond the "givens." Awareness is exhibited by perception of styles and their relationships, recognition of points of view, and of the author's craft and its effects. The categories are not and could not be made mutually exclusive, and thus some questions could be classified in two or even all three of the response modes.

A Look at Literature has two forms, each form containing 50 multiple-choice questions, which are set up in two parts of 25 questions each. The questions are directed at fourteen short literary passages, which include prose and poetry and represent a variety of literary types. Part I of each form of the test is read orally by the teacher while pupils follow reading silently; Part II of each form is read silently by the pupils.

The manual of A Look at Literature quite frankly discusses the limitations of the test. A real limitation on the generalizability of the results of the use of the tests resides in an absence of norms on which to base interpretations of the test scores. The pupils whose test results are reported are a select, not a random, group. By and large, they are middle-class urban and suburban pupils of average and above-average general ability, and they are above-average readers. A Look at Literature possesses potential as an instructional aid in a classroom situation; it is helpful to the teacher in deepening student insight and appreciation of what he reads, but the test needs further development before it will be adequate as a standardized instrument.

When the teacher is desirous of finding a measure of student writing, she really finds that she is in a scarcity situation. Evaluation of self-expression in the schools has been a method subjectively made by the teacher, and in research it has been a method subjectively made by judges. This requires extensive time in both school and research situations. Whether a subjective method of evaluation has been suitable or not for both schools and research programs, educators have not developed any other type of measurement. Some of the problems of essay writing and judging are discussed in detail in the *Handbook for Essay Tests in Educational Testing Service's STEP Series* (1957).

The STEP Essay Tests are free-response tests of writing ability. The student is presented with a brief statement setting forth a topic to write about. He is given thirty-five minutes to read the paragraph and to plan and execute his response. The teacher who is reading the pupil's response to the cue statement is to base the final "grade" on three factors weighted as follows:

Quality of thought	50 percent
Style	30 percent
Conventions	20 percent

"Quality of thought" is defined as the selection and the adequacy of ideas and supplementary details, and the manner of their organization (that is, the way in which their connections are derived from the arrangement of parts). "Style" is defined as clearness, effectiveness, and appropriateness, including matters of structure and diction, emphasis, the means of transition between ideas, and the finer points of simplicity, economy, variety, and exactness of expression. "Conventions" is defined as the proprieties of mechanical form, including grammar and usage, capitalization, punctuation, and the mechanical aspects of the structure of sentences.

Armed with such criteria as these, teachers often have great difficulties in grading student compositions meaningfully. A number of years ago the Illinois English Teachers Association published a bulletin entitled *How Teachers Grade Your Themes* (1966). This stemmed from the discovery that many pupils were unconcerned by the fact that they could see no correlation between the amount of work they put in on a theme and the grade they received. They conceived of the relative success or failure of a paper as a mysterious occurrence over which they had no control; some themes "came off," they felt, while others were "just no good," in spite of their efforts.

The classroom teacher in such areas as language, literature, and composition—beset with doubts as she sought ways of evaluating her program in the language arts through the utilization of commercially prepared tests—felt impelled to try her hand at test making. If she were to succeed in this task, she would have to consider many things that do not ordinarily meet the eye.

The Teacher as Test Maker

The teacher in her role as finder of tests may have had difficulties, but more lies ahead when she shifts her role and performs as a maker of tests. What she is really going to have to concern herself with is summative evaluation.

What was lacking in the *Elementary Evaluative Criteria,* or the *Elementary School Objectives,* was provided by Bloom (1956) in his taxonomies. The *cognitive domain* as seen by Bloom is composed of six subdivisions, of which *knowledge* is the first. Knowledge involves the recall of specifics and universals, the recall of methods and processes, or the recall of a pattern, structure, or setting. The other subdivisions of intellectual abilities and skills consist of *comprehension, application, analysis, synthesis,* and *evaluation.* These five have sometimes been referred to as *understanding.* If the cognitive domain is viewed in this manner, then it is obvious that it can be helpful in analyzing and interpreting educational objectives. Related also are the facets of the *affective domain:* (Krathwohl et al., 1964): *receiving, responding, valuing, organization,* and *characterization by a value or value complex.*

It is quite possible to relate verbal educational objectives to subject matter and to desired behavioral changes on the part of the pupil at a given level. Let us see, for example, how one might do this in a situation encountered in the language arts, *although it should be clear that similar situations are not uncommon and are to be found in any content area.* Certain difficulties are encountered when one endeavors to view the *entire* language arts complex in terms of objectives or purposes. This is not true, however, if one is able to look at what is involved in a specific field within the overall content area. Speech is commonly regarded as falling within the language arts. Huckleberry and Strother (1966, p. 20) state that when we think of speech training for children, we have eight objectives that we try to accomplish: (1) to perceive and understand, (2) to recognize worthwhile ideas, (3) to organize thoughts and feelings, (4) to use appropriate language, (5) to speak with pleasing clarity and loudness, (6) to use appropriate gestures, (7) to adapt to various speech situations, and (8) to listen courteously and critically. The elementary school child has three very significant uses for speech: (1) to aid the process of learning, (2) to assist in developing social competency, and (3) to foster creativity.

It is to be noted that a distinction is made here, in this particular language art, between those *objectives* which are sought by the school and those which may be viewed as pupil *purposes*. A similar distinction should be made in considering objectives and purposes in the other areas of the language arts, such as listening, writing, and reading, as these skills are applied by the pupil as he engages in activities in the realms of language, literature, and composition.

Smith (1967, pp. 59–61) consulted major lists of purposes advanced by authorities in the area of reading from 1924 through 1962 and identified 215 items. From these lists she developed a conceptual framework that is divided into two main sections: the *writers' purposes* and the *readers' purposes*. Thus a writer may have certain general purposes: (1) to entertain, (2) to inform, (3) to influence, or (4) to experiment with literary forms. The elements used by writers in the development of their purposes might include (1) content, (2) grammatical structure, (3) style of writing, (4) vocabulary, (5) literary types (poetry, prose, drama, and so on), (6) literary techniques (climax, rhythm, foreshadowings, flashbacks, setting), (7) point of view, or (8) organization.

Smith (1967, p. 59) believes that there appear to be two major kinds of purposes for reading: first, the broad, general purposes that are sometimes called the life purposes, for which a reader selects and reads particular books or articles. These are called *primary purposes*. Second, the different kinds of comprehension skills have been referred to as making up the *secondary purposes* category.

Examples of *primary purposes*, according to this researcher, are to extend one's range of information, to evaluate possible solutions to social or economic problems, to understand one's self, to achieve esthetic appreciation, and the like. Examples of the *secondary purposes* include understanding the main idea, noting sequential order, making generalizations, and anticipating outcomes.

This same writer points out that reading to understand details and to grasp the main idea is considered basic to all other secondary purposes. Reading to understand ideas in sequential order, to follow directions, to make comparisons, to relate cause and effects of ideas and/or phenomena, and to understand or to reach generalizations and conclusions appears to be dependent upon the reader's skill in reading for details and for main ideas. Interrelated with any or all of the foregoing is reading to anticipate ideas or to predict outcomes, to understand characterization and descriptions, to determine the mood or tone of a selection, to distinguish between fact and opinion and fact and fiction, and to understand sensory imagery. It appears that the reader may be called upon to achieve the foregoing purposes by understanding the literal meanings, the implied meanings, or both the literal and implied meanings.

Smith believes that the primary and secondary purposes appear to be interrelated and dependent upon each other. She states that there is no published research that shows the interdependency among the purposes, but she believes that subjective opinion points to this assumption. Smith feels that many extraneous factors that may be important in reading, but are not readers' purposes per se, are to be noted. These include writers' purposes; style; content of the selections; writers' points of view; the literary type; and techniques used in reading for different purposes such as the selection, analysis, organization, and evaluation of the content and relating the content to one's own personal experiences.

It is difficult to say which comes first, the primary purposes or the secondary purposes. Although it is highly likely that the *teacher* would like to see the primary purposes developed first, it does not follow that this is the way the *child* perceives purpose, nor does the teacher always act as though she considers that the primary purposes ought to come first. This is particularly true when we realize that the secondary purposes are the ones most readily acquired in most school situations. Typically, then, the teacher is likely to stress understanding the main idea; noting sequential order; making generalizations; and the anticipation of outcomes.

The primary purposes, viewed by the teacher as being more difficult to achieve because of their less "tangible" nature, are frequently left to other teachers "up there" (meaning the upper grades and junior high school), because these less tangible purposes are best attained when the child is more "mature." Here the error lies in equating chronological maturity (age in grade in this instance) with mental maturity. It is not necessary to wait until the child is an "old" boy or an "old" girl to advance him toward these more mature habits. This advancement can be furthered and should be furthered from the very outset—from kindergarten on.

As the teacher prepares her specifications and seeks to ascertain levels of accomplishment in the attainment of specific purposes, she must be extremely careful that readability blocks do not intrude. Vocabulary, style, topic, sentence length, pictorial aids, organization of material, and size of type are all factors in readability. Teachers can make their materials more readable by consideration of these factors. That vocabulary is an important factor contributing to difficulty has always been known, but it is by no means easy to express vocabulary ease or difficulty in quantitative terms. Many readability formulas are available today, and in each of them vocabulary is a prominent factor. An objection to many of the formulas is the difficulty of applying them; in short, the degree of statistical knowledge required in some procedures limits the use of the formulas. A second objection, according to Botel (1962, p. 8), is that the formulas do not have a wide range—that is, they do not discriminate between levels of primary materials as well as between levels of inter-mediate or more advanced levels.

It is not necessary to dwell further on the development and use of readability formulas; suffice it to say, the teacher must not place obsta-cles in the path of the pupil by confronting him with difficulties involv-ing comprehension and interpretation if the purpose of the exercise is not directly related to aspects of comprehension and interpretation. It should be obvious, but it is not always so, that if the question posed to the pupil is to get at the ability to find the central thought of a passage, then it is not fair to clutter up the question with concerns that might well lead the pupil away from rather than toward the purpose sought. For the teacher who requires assistance in ascertaining readability level—in short, what words to use in preparing questions and statements toward which ques-tions will be directed, a source such as the *Botel Predicting Readability Levels* (1962) may be consulted. Thus one can learn to discriminate among books at levels ranging from the preprimer through high school, and in a very real sense come to realize that a child can learn to write at these levels.

With this background in mind, let us consider some of the specifics involved. In a given sixth grade, the teacher is wondering about the abilities of her pupils to get at the *central thought* of a passage. Also, she would very much like to ascertain how well pupils are able to respond to *factual* questions. She is concerned, as nearly always, with *vocabulary*. The ability to *follow directions* is important to her goals, and she knows her pupils must continue to grow in their ability to draw *inferences*. Let us ascertain the steps necessary for her to follow if she is to glean the types of information that she feels are important to her in her evaluation of pupil progress.

Let us consider first in detail, the *sixth-grade problem situation*, next a *second-grade situation*, and finally, a *fifth-grade situation*, all involving work in the social studies. *Here we see teachers at work, constructing their own tests!*

How, then, does a teacher develop a passage that will get at these five skills? The passage she might write follows:

Man has always been <u>interested</u> in his own past. Modern explorers have found the beginnings of civilization going back thousands of years. Explorers called archaeologists search for materials from which the story of man can be studied. The materials may be written records, pieces of artwork, or old ruins.

The explorers have developed <u>exact</u> methods of study. The methods <u>center</u> on dating what is found.

The end of World War I marked the beginning of the period of growth in archaeology. In Egypt, an exciting discovery was made. A royal tomb from 1352 years before Christ was found. Finding the 18-year-old king, wrapped in gold and buried with a <u>huge</u> supply of gold objects, <u>awakened</u> the interest of the world.

What kind of question does the teacher pose, then, if her objective is to ascertain if the pupil is able to get at the *central thought* in the above passage?

1. This passage is mostly about
   a. modern explorers.
   b. a royal tomb.
   c. Egypt.
   d. old records.

or

2. Perhaps the best title for this passage would be
   a. *Uncovering Man's Past.*
   b. *The Death of a King.*
   c. *A New Interest in Artworks.*
   d. *Do You Want to Be an Explorer?*

Or, if the teacher is endeavoring to find out what *facts* the pupil is able to glean from his coverage of the passage, she might consider questions such as these:

1. Archaeologists do not search for
   a. new lands.
   b. written records.
   c. artwork.
   d. old ruins.
2. The royal tomb contained
   a. gold objects.
   b. much money.
   c. many old ruins.
   d. written records.
3. According to this passage, an exciting archaeological discovery
   a. was made in Egypt.
   b. is made frequently.
   c. is worth much money.
   d. means much hard work.

If the teacher is interested in finding out how effectively her pupils are able to *draw inferences* from a passage, she would construct questions such as these:

1. From the information presented in this passage, it would seem that the study of archaeology is most nearly like the study of
   a. history.
   b. geography.
   c. law.
   d. engineering.
2. From the information presented in this passage, it is probably true that
   a. archaeology is a rather new study.
   b. gold is a rather new metal.
   c. archaeologists do most of their work in a library. .
   d. man became interested in his history after World War I.

If the teacher is interested in ascertaining to what extent a pupil is able to *follow directions*, the following questions are appropriate:

1. Count the words in the first sentence. Multiply your answer by the number of vowels in the first sentence. The product is
   a. more than 125.
   b. less than 100.
   c. more than 100, but less than 125.
   d. more than 150.
2. Add the number of letters in the first word of this passage to the number of consonants in the fifth word in the first sentence. The answer is equal to the number of letters in the
   a. second word of the second sentence.
   b. first word in the second sentence.
   c. eighth word in the second sentence.
   d. sixth word in the second sentence.

A continuing concern of the sixth-grade teacher is growth in *vocabulary*, and questions such as these would assist her in assessing growth in knowledge in this area:

1. The word exact as underlined and used in this passage means about the same as
   a. precise.
   b. difficult.
   c. incorrect.
   d. exaggerated.
2. The word center as underlined and used in this passage means the opposite of
   a. concentrate.
   b. focus.
   c. converge.
   d. disperse.

In summary, then, in the preceding pages we have demonstrated that a passage can be composed so as to reveal to the teacher that the pupil is at an appropriate level (or is not at such a level) in his ability to get at the central thought of a passage, to respond to factual questions, to follow directions, to draw inferences, and in so doing discloses something of his vocabulary knowledge and growth.

Let us turn now to a consideration of ways in which *the teacher at another grade level proceeds as she writes test items for her second-grade pupils.* Whereas in the sixth grade the concern was with items that sought to get at the *central thought, facts, vocabulary, inference,* and *following directions,* the focus is now on *words in use*—that is, on the *recognition* of words. Following is a group of 10 items that are organized so that the correct response, which the teacher is seeking, is found in the first position in each row:

Words in Use

1. It was time to say _____.	good-bye	girl	with
2. All the children were _____.	reading	thing	yes
3. The boys and girls will _____ something.	give	way	every
4. She will _____ the ball.	catch	over	long.
5. She had _____ hair.	beautiful	neighbor	letter
6. He watched his little _____.	brother	o'clock	stay
7. I bought a _____ at the store.	stamp	move	since
8. It was a very _____ day.	warm	together	joined
9. They rode up on an _____.	elevator	apartment	interest
10. The dress was _____.	wrinkled	rifle	sweep

In contrast to the objective sought by the teacher in the previous set of exercises, the teacher is now concerned with *meaning,* and so she proceeds somewhat differently. Following is a group of 10 words (or phrases) so organized that the correct response, which she is seeking, is found in the first position in each row:

Word Meaning

1. *all of us*	we	I	you	me
2. *something is funny*	laugh	get	home	pushed
3. *little children*	babies	eggs	rain	sun
4. *black*	dark	last	pocket	door
5. *next day*	tomorrow	clothes	right	more
6. *put together*	make	yard	shout	trip

7. *not over*	under	candy	wash	standing
8. *after*	following	forget	listen	weed
9. *near*	close	wonderful	really	excited
10. *suppose*	pretend	finally	danger	shorter

In yet a third situation, the second-grade teacher is concerned with something broader than she had in mind when she was testing her pupils for *words in use* and *word meaning*. She is now seeking what she refers to as *comprehension,* and she feels that in order to get at this skill she must vary her format, for no longer is she satisfied that the recognition of the word as such, or its meaning in isolation, will suffice. Therefore, she composes a "story" and constructs several questions that she feels will reveal the pupils' ability to go beyond the tasks previously executed. All of the correct responses are (a).

Here is her narrative:

> Joseph and Jean went to see grandmother. Mother went with them. Father did not go. He went to the city in the car. Joseph and Jean had a ride on a train. They liked that very much. They had not been on a train before that. Mother had been on a train many times.

1. This story tells about Joseph and Jean
   a. going to see grandmother.
   b. going with grandmother.
   c. riding with father.
   d. going to see mother.
2. Who had been on a train many times?
   a. Mother.
   b. Jean and Joseph.
   c. Jean.
   d. Joseph.
3. Father went
   a. to the city.
   b. to grandmother's house.
   c. with mother.
   d. with Joseph and Jean.

For use with certain members of the class she felt that she might try another type of "story," one that might perhaps be of more interest to some of her second-grade boys. Here is her story, together with questions. All of the correct responses are (a).

> The most important thing about a fireman is that he should know how to put out a fire. But that is not enough. He must also be strong so that he can use the tools needed by firemen. Then, a fireman must be brave when there is danger. To be a good fireman, a man must know what to do and be able to do it.

1. This story tells about
   a. what a good fireman should be like.
   b. how a fire should be put out.
   c. what boys should do if they want to be firemen.
   d. how dangerous fires start.
2. It is most important that the fireman
   a. know what to do.
   b. be strong.
   c. be brave.
   d. be happy.

In a fourth situation, the second-grade teacher found that she had good reason to wonder how her pupils might be faring in "phonics," and so she thought up some questions that she felt would clarify the situation. She knew that she was seeking a quite different kind of reaction, so she devised the following. All of the correct responses are in the first position in each row.

1. They wanted to _____ the box.	lift	gift	sift
2. He was walking in a big _____.	cave	care	cane
3. She put the _____ on the pot.	lid	lip	lit
4. A bee will _____.	sting	sling	swing
5. There was a _____ through the woods.	path	pack	patch
6. The baby made three _____.	messes	messed	messy
7. He lived in an old _____.	shack	shuck	shock
8. The lady _____ to us.	spoke	speak	spike
9. They tried to _____ him.	fool	fowl	foul
10. He cut the _____.	string	strung	strum
11. The man tied it with a _____.	knot	not	cot
12. There was _____ to eat.	lots	lost	slot
13. _____ what did you do?	Then	Ten	When
14. _____ your mother for some.	Ask	Axe	As
15. It was a _____ night.	quiet	quit	quite

In the preceding pages we have presented the concerns of a sixth-grade teacher as she prepares test items for children in an endeavor to assess, in a given situation, what they know about getting at the central thought of a passage, how well they are able to react to factual questions, to follow directions, to draw inferences, and, in general, how their vocabulary is developing. In contrast, we showed how a second-grade teacher—who was concerned with word recognition, word meaning, comprehension, and phonics—found it necessary to develop her testing materials in a somewhat different fashion. In both the sixth-grade and the second-grade situations, the teachers devised "stories" of a narrative character, and in neither case was the intent to link the "story" to a content field or area.

In the fifth-grade class, the teacher is concerned with the develop-
ment of test items within a social studies context. How then, should she
proceed? She is still interested in certain reading skills development, but
how are these advanced in the context of a content field? This is the
passage that she writes:

> Riding through the country may be <u>tiring</u>, <u>especially</u> if you have been
> that way before. However, a look at the signs along the highway may add
> <u>pleasure</u> to the trip.
> You may find that you are passing <u>near</u> Bean Blossom, Indiana, or are
> close to New Diggings, Wisconsin. If you are on <u>Route</u> 41 in Wisconsin,
> you will see such places as Nobob, Nenno, Taycheedah, Oshkosh, and
> Lake Winnebago. The Fox River and the Wolf River are also close by.
> If you are traveling Route 1 in Illinois, you may see Heathsville,
> Russellville, Hardinville, and Friendsville. Grayville and Crossville are
> there, too.
> Next time you take a trip, watch the road signs. You may be able to
> find <u>odd</u> names, too.

The fifth-grade teacher, thinking in terms of social studies content,
wishes to find out if her pupils are able to supply the *central thought* in
the above passage; she constructs this test item:

1. Perhaps the best title for this passage is
   a. Road Sign Fun.
   b. A Trip through the Midwest.
   c. How to Plan a Trip.
   d. Fun on a Trip.

or

2. This passage is mostly about
   a. names of towns.
   b. Wisconsin.
   c. traveling.
   d. highways.

Or, if the fifth-grade teacher is endeavoring to find out what *facts* the
pupil is able to glean from his reading of the passage, she considers items
such as these:

1. Which city is located in the state of Indiana?
   a. Bean Blossom.
   b. New Diggings.
   c. Hardinville.
   d. Nobob.
2. If you are traveling on Route 41, you would
   a. pass near Oshkosh.
   b. pass near Crossville.
   c. be in Indiana.
   d. pass near Bean Blossom.

The fifth-grade teacher is interested in ascertaining how effectively her pupils are able to *draw inferences* from the passage she has prepared, so she constructs questions like these:

1. From the name of the city it is probably true that New Diggings was noted for
   a. mining.
   b. farming.
   c. manufacturing.
   d. flower growing.
2. According to this passage the best fishing would probably be found near
   a. Route 41.
   b. Crossville.
   c. Bean Blossom.
   d. Route 1.

As the fifth-grade teacher is interested in ascertaining to what extent her pupils are able to *follow directions*, she constructs the following test items:

1. In the word Wisconsin, cross out the w, c, and s. The letters you have left spell
   a. is, on, in.
   b. is, con, sin.
   c. we, on, in.
   d. is, on, sin.
2. Write the fifth word in the passage backward. The new word is
   a. yam.
   b. eb.
   c. uoy.
   d. dad.

This teacher is continuously alert to *vocabulary* improvement; she feels that questions such as these would assist her in assessing growth in this area:

1. The word pleasure as underlined and used in this passage means about the same as
   a. enjoyment.
   b. ecstasy.
   c. distress.
   d. contentment.
2. The word odd as underlined and used in this passage means about the same as
   a. unusual.
   b. wonderful.
   c. special.
   d. ordinary.

In summary, then, we have shown that a passage written in a social studies context can be composed in such a manner as to make it possible to extract many questions that will assist the teacher in making determinations respecting the abilities of her pupils to get the main idea of a passage, to respond to factual questions, to follow directions, to draw inferences, and in so doing, to provide some knowledge as to the status of vocabulary development.

Summary

It is too early to ascertain what the results of assessment will be on both national and state levels. Fears have been voiced by Shafer (1971) with respect to assessment in English and by Walker (1971) in the reading field. Results from the first testing in science, citizenship, and writing are beginning to filter in, and the facts reveal that in both rural and urban areas pupils tend to do less well than might be expected.

In the section that has been devoted to discussion of testing procedures, there has been extended treatment of some of the considerations that obtain when one looks to the professional test makers for guidance; and after the criteria developed and used by these professionals has been weighed, the focus is shifted to the teacher as she works in a sixth grade, then a second grade, and finally, in a content area at the fifth-grade level. As the teacher grows in confidence she will find it increasingly more effective and efficient to develop her own testing materials. What has been illustrated rather thoroughly in one language art—reading—can be practiced equally exhaustively in other fields.

There are, of course, some differences to be detected between the standardized test examples provided and the "homemade" tests. We are led to conclude, along with Chauncey and Dobbin (1963, p. 70), that

> . . . For tests that cover short units of instruction, weekly and monthly quizzes, semester examinations, tests in unique courses or experimental classes, and longer units of instruction that involve content or methods different from general practice, most schools depend on testing instruments made by the school staff. For tests that cover longer periods of learning, a year or two, and tests that attempt to measure the more complex learnings, most schools depend on standardized tests. So a school in which testing is done most effectively is certain to employ a combination of homemade and standardized tests in such a way that the two kinds of instruments complement each other when the school uses them to understand and guide the learning processes of students.

READING LIST 14

Bloom, Benjamin S., Hasting, J. Thomas, & Madaus, G. F. *Handbook on forma-tive and summative evaluation of student learning.* New York: McGraw-Hill, 1971. Presents a broad view of evaluation and its place in education and is primarily concerned with its use to improve teaching and learning. Part I deals with procedures in a general way, and Part II provides the teacher of selected subjects and programs with illustrations of those proce-dures and techniques that are likely to have the greatest practical value in each subject field or program.

Hoepfner, Ralph (Ed.) *CSE elementary school test evaluations.* Los Angeles: Center for the Study of Education, UCLA Graduate School of Education, 1970. Presents basically a listing of some of the major goals of elementary education, and against this all published standardized tests are categorized in terms of which objective they most closely meet; a quantifiable test rating was developed, and each test or subtest was evaluated using the MEAN rating system in terms of the appropriateness of the test at grades 1, 3, 5, and 6.

Hedges, W. D. *Evaluation in the elementary school.* New York: Holt, Rinehart and Winston, 1969. Considers the purposes of testing in the elementary school and develops guides for assisting teachers in developing their *own* tests.

Appendix

A capsule view of the history of Federal educational activities is provided in the following list of selected Federal educational legislation*:

Year	Program
1787	Northwest Ordinance—authorized land grants for the establishment of educational institutions.
1862	First Morrill Act—authorized public land grants to the States for the establishment and maintenance of agricultural and mechanical colleges.
1867	Department of Education Act—authorized the establishment of the Office of Education.
1874	Aid to State nautical schools—provides funds for State nautical schools.
1890	Second Morrill Act—provided for money grants for support of instruction in the agricultural and mechanical colleges.
1917	Smith-Hughes Act—provided for grants to States for support of vocational education.
1918	Vocational Rehabilitation Act—authorized funds for rehabilitation of World War I veterans.
1919	Federal surplus property—authorized use of Federal surplus property by educational institutions.
1920	Smith-Bankhead Act—authorized grants to States for vocational rehabilitation programs.
1933	School lunch programs—provided assistance in school lunch programs. The use of surplus farm commodities in school lunch programs began in 1936 and the National School Lunch Act of 1946 continued and expanded this assistance.
1935	Bankhead-Jones Act—made grants to States for agricultural experiment stations.
1937	National Cancer Institute Act—established Public Health Service Fellowship program. Subsequently, fellowships were authorized in legislation concerning other agencies.
1940	School Milk Program—provided funds for cost of milk served to school children.

* From *Digest of Educational Statistics*, USOE 10024–69, 1971, pp. 95–96. Albert R. Munse of the Reference, Estimates, and Projections Branch, National Center for Educational Statistics, had the major responsibility for the development of data for this table.

Year	Program
1941	Amendment to Lanham Act of 1940—authorized Federal aid for construction, maintenance, and operation of schools in federally impacted areas. Such assistance was continued under Public Laws 815 and 874, 81st Congress, in 1950.
1943	Vocational Rehabilitation Act—provided assistance to disabled veterans. School Lunch Indemnity Plan—provided funds for local school lunch food purchases.
1944	Servicemen's Readjustment Act—provided assistance for education of veterans. Surplus Property Act—authorized transfer of surplus property to educational institutions.
1946	George-Barden Act—expanded Federal support of vocational education.
1948	United States Information and Educational Exchange Act—provided for the interchange of persons, knowledge, and skills between the United States and other countries.
1949	Federal Property and Administrative Services Act—provided for donation of surplus property to educational institutions and for other public uses.
1950	Public Laws 815 and 874—provided assistance for construction (P.L. 815) and operation (P.L. 874) of schools in federally affected areas. Housing Act—authorized loans for construction of college housing facilities.
1954	School Milk Program—provided funds for purchase of milk for school lunch programs. Cooperative Research Act—authorized cooperative arrangements with universities, colleges, and State education agencies for educational research. National Advisory Committee on Education Act—established a National Advisory Committee on Education to recommend to the Secretary of the Department needed studies of national concern in the field of education and to propose appropriate action indicated by such studies.
1956	Library Services Act—authorized grants to States for extension and improvement of rural public library services.
1957	Practical Nurse Training Act—provided grants to States for practical nurse training.
1958	National Defense Education Act—provided assistance to State and local school systems for strengthening instruction in science, mathematics, modern foreign languages, and other critical subjects; improvement of State statistical services; guidance, counseling and testing services and training institutes; higher education student loans and fellowships; foreign language institutes and advanced foreign language study and training provided by colleges and universities; experimentation, and dissemination of information on more effective utilization of television, motion picture, and related media for educational purposes; and vocational education for technical occupations necessary to the national defense. Public Law 85–926—Federal assistance for training teachers of the handicapped authorized. Public Law 85–905—authorized a loan service of captioned films for the deaf.

Year	Program

1961   Area Redevelopment Act—included provisions for training or retraining of persons in redevelopment areas.

1962   Manpower Development and Training Act—provided training in new and improved skills for the unemployed and underemployed.

      Public Law 87–477—provided grants for the construction of educational television broadcasting facilities.

      Migration and Refugee Assistance Act of 1962—authorized loans, advances and grants for education and training of refugees.

1963   Health Professions Educational Assistance Act—provided funds to expand teaching facilities and for loans to students in the health professions.

      Vocational Education Act of 1963—increased Federal support of vocational education, including support of residential vocational schools, vocational work-study programs, and research, training, and demonstrations in vocational education.

      Higher Education Facilities Act of 1963—authorized grants and loans for classrooms, libraries, and laboratories in public community colleges and technical institutes as well as undergraduate and graduate facilities in other institutions of higher education.

1964   Civil Rights Act of 1964—authorized the Commissioner to (1) arrange, through grants or contracts with institutions of higher education, for the operation of short-term or regular session institutes for special training to improve ability of elementary and secondary school instructional staff to deal effectively with special education problems occasioned by desegregation; (2) make grants to school boards to pay, in whole or in part, the cost of providing inservice training in dealing with problems incident to desegregation; to provide school boards with technical assistance in desegregation; and required nondiscrimination in federally assisted programs.

      Economic Opportunity Act of 1964—authorized grants for college work-study programs for students of low-income families; established a Job Corps program and authorized support for work-training programs to provide education and vocational training and work experience for unemployed youths; provided training and work experience opportunities in welfare programs; authorized support of Community Action Programs, including Headstart, Follow Through, Upward Bound, education and training activities; authorized the establishment of the Volunteers in Service to America (VISTA).

1965   Elementary and Secondary Education Act—authorized grants for elementary and secondary school programs for children of low-income families; school library resources, textbooks and other instructional materials for school children; supplementary educational centers and services; strengthening State education agencies; and educational research and research training.

      Health Professions Educational Assistance Amendments—authorized scholarships to aid needy students in the health professions and grants to improve the quality of teaching in schools of medicine, dentistry, osteopathy, optometry and podiatry.

Year	*Program*

1965 Higher Education Act of 1965—provided grants for university community
(cont.) service programs, college library assistance and library training and
research; strengthening developing institutions; educational opportunity
grants; insured student loans; teacher-training programs; and under-
graduate instructional equipment. Established a National Teacher Corps
and provided for graduate teacher-training fellowships.

Medical Library Assistance Act—provided assistance for construction and
improvement of health sciences libraries.

National Foundation on the Arts and the Humanities Act—authorized grants
and loans for projects in the creative and performing arts, and for
research, training, and scholarly publications in the humanities.

National Technical Institute for the Deaf Act—provided for the establishment, construction, equipping and operation of a residential school for
postsecondary education and technical training of the deaf.

National Vocational Student Loan Insurance Act—encouraged State and
nonprofit private institutions and organizations to establish adequate
loan insurance programs to assist students to attend post-secondary
business, trade, technical, and other vocational schools.

Disaster Relief Act—provides for assistance to local education agencies to
help meet exceptional cost resulting from a major disaster.

1966 International Education Act—provided grants to institutions of higher education for the establishment, strengthening, and operation of centers for
research and training in international studies and the international aspects
of professional and other fields of study.

National Sea Grant College and Program Act—authorized the establishment
and operation of Sea Grant Colleges and programs by initiating and
supporting programs of education and research in the various fields
relating to the development of marine resources.

Adult Education Act—authorized grants to States for the encouragement
and expansion of educational programs for adults including training of
teachers of adults and demonstrations in adult education (previously
part of the Economic Opportunity Act of 1964).

Model Secondary School for the Deaf Act—authorized the establishment
and operation, by Gallaudet College, of a model secondary school for
the deaf to serve the National Capital region.

Elementary and Secondary Amendment of 1966—in addition to modifying
existing programs, authorized grants to assist States in the initiation,
expansion, and improvement of programs and projects for the education
of handicapped children at the preschool, elementary and secondary
school levels.

1967 Education Professions Development Act—amends the Higher Education
Act of 1955 for the purpose of improving the quality of teaching and to
help meet critical shortages of adequately trained educational personnel
by authorizing support for the development of information on needs for
educational personnel, training and retraining opportunities responsive
to changing manpower needs, attracting a greater number of qualified
persons into the teaching profession, attracting persons who can stimulate creativity in the arts and other skills to undertake short-term or

Year	Program

1967   long-term assignments in education, and helping to make educational
(*cont.*) personnel training programs more responsive to the needs of the schools
and colleges.

Public Broadcasting Act of 1967—establishes a Corporation for Public
Broadcasting to have major responsibility in channeling Federal funds
to noncommercial radio and television stations, program production
groups, and ETV networks directly or through contract; conducts research, demonstration, or training in matters related to noncommercial
broadcasting; and authorizes grants for construction of educational radio
as well as television facilities.

1968   Elementary and Secondary Education Amendments of 1967—in addition
to modifying existing programs, authorized support of regional centers
for education of handicapped children, model centers and services for
deaf-blind children, and recruitment of personnel and dissemination of
information on education of the handicapped; technical assistance in
education to rural areas; support of dropout prevention projects; and
support of bilingual education programs. Also, in order to give adequate
notice of available Federal financial assistance, authorized advance funding for any program for which the Commissioner of Education has responsibility for administration by authorizing appropriations to be included in
the appropriations act for the fiscal year preceding the fiscal year for
which they are available for obligation.

Handicapped Children's Early Education Assistance Act—authorizes preschool and early education programs for handicapped children.

Vocational Education Amendments of 1968—changes the basic formula
for allocating funds; provides for a National Advisory Council on Vocational Education, expansion of vocational education services to meet the
needs of the disadvantaged, the collection and dissemination of information for programs administered by the Commissioner of Education, and
the preparation of a catalog of all Federal education assistance programs.

Higher Education Amendments of 1968—provides new programs to assist
disadvantaged college students through special counseling and summer
tutorial programs and to assist colleges to combine resources for cooperative uses, including closed-circuit television and computer networks.
Also authorizes grants to expand and strengthen student cooperative
programs and to expand programs which provide clinical experiences to
law students.

References

AAHPER. *This is physical education*. Washington, D.C.: American Association for Health, Physical Education, and Recreation, 1965.

Almy, M. Psychological background for the SCIS Elementary Science Program. In W. Jacobson & A. Kondo (Eds.), *SCIS elementary science sourcebook*. Berkeley: University of California, 1968.

Almy, M., et al. *Logical thinking in second grade*. New York: Teachers College Press, 1970.

Almy, M., Chittenden, E., & Miller, P. *Young children's thinking*. New York: Teachers College Press, 1966.

Angelos, J. Nongraded school plan stirs urge to learn among ghetto children. A report on a presentation by Dr. M. C. Hunter. *The Seattle Times,* August 28, 1968, 24.

Archambault, R. D. *John Dewey on education*. New York: Modern Library, 1964.

Arnheim, R. *Toward a psychology of art: Collected essays*. Berkeley: University of California Press, 1966.

Aronoff, F. *Music and young children*. New York: Holt, Rinehart and Winston, 1969.

Ashton-Warner, S. *Teacher*. New York: Simon and Schuster, 1963.

Atkin, J. M. Using behaviorally stated objectives for designing the curriculum: A cautionary note. Paper delivered at the annual meeting of the American Educational Research Association, Chicago, February 1968.

Atkin, J. M., & Karplus, R. Discovery or invention? *The Science Teacher,* September 1962, 29, 45–51.

Ausubel, D. P. Some psychological and educational limitations of learning by discovery. *The Arithmetic Teacher,* 1964, 11, 290–302.

Banks, J. A. Teaching black history with a focus on decision-making. *Social Education,* November 1971, 35, 740–745+.

Barbiana School. *Letter to a teacher by the schoolboys of Barbiana*. Trans. by Nora Rossi & Tom Cole. New York: Random House, 1970.

Barnard, J., Stendler, C., & Spock, B. *Science for tomorrow's world*. Teacher's annotated ed. The Macmillan Science Series. New York: Macmillan, 1966.

Barnes, D. L. What are we teaching in social studies and science? *Education,* October 1960, 81, 121–123.

Baumgartner, L. The public health significance of low birth weight in the U.S.A., with special reference to varying practices in providing special care to infants of low birth weights. *Bulletin World Health Organization*, 1962, **26**, 175.

Becker, W., Madsen, C., Jr., Arnold, C., & Thomas, D. The contingent use of teacher attention and praise in reducing classroom behavior problems. *The Journal of Special Education*, 1967, **21**, 287–307.

Begle, E. (Ed.) *Mathematics education*. The Sixty-ninth Yearbook of the National Society for the Study of Education, Part 1. Chicago: University of Chicago Press, 1970.

Bellack, A. A., et al. *The language of the classroom*. New York: Teachers College Press, 1966.

Bellugi, U. *How the child learns to say no*. Cambridge, Mass.: MIT Press, in press.

Bellugi-Klima, U. *The acquisition of the system of negation in children's speech*. Unpublished doctoral dissertation, Graduate School of Education, Harvard University, 1967.

Bellugi-Klima, U., & Hass, W. Grammatical elements to model for young children. In C. S. Lavatelli (Ed.), *Language training in early childhood education*. Urbana: University of Illinois Press, 1971.

Bereiter, C. Children's problems in coordinating language and reality. Paper presented at a conference on problems of teaching young children, University of Toronto, 1968.

Bereiter, C., & Engelmann, S. *Teaching the disadvantaged child in the preschool*. Englewood Cliffs, N.J.: Prentice-Hall, 1966.

Bernstein, B. Social structure, language, and learning. *Educational Research*, 1961, **3**, 163–176.

Bernstein, B. Social class and linguistic development: A theory of social learning. In A. Halsey, I. Floud, & C. A. Anderson (Eds.), *Education, economy, and society*. New York: Free Press, 1969. Pp. 288–314.

Bernstein, B. A critique of the concept of "compensatory education." In D. Rubinstein & C. Stoneman (Eds.), *Education for democracy*. London: Penguin, 1970.

Bijou, S. W., & Baer, D. M. *Child development*. Vol. 2. *Universal stage of infancy*. New York: Appleton-Century-Crofts, 1965.

Birch, H. G. (Ed.) *Brain damage in children: Biological and social aspects*. Baltimore: Williams & Wilkins, 1964.

Black studies in schools. Education U.S.A. Special Report. Washington, D.C.: National School Public Relations Association, 1970.

Bloom, B. S. *Taxonomy of educational objectives: The classification of educational goals. Handbook I: Cognitive domain*. New York: Longmans, Green, 1956.

Bloom, B. S., Hastings, J. T., & Madaus, G. F. *Handbook on formative and summative evaluation of student learning*. New York: McGraw-Hill, 1971.

Bobbitt, F. *The curriculum*. Boston: Houghton Mifflin, 1918.

Bobbitt, F. *Curriculum-making in Los Angeles. Supplementary Educational Monographs No. 20*. Chicago: University of Chicago Press, 1922.

Botel, Morton. *Predicting readability levels*. Chicago: Follett, 1962.

Brookover, W. B., & Erickson, E. L. *Society, schools, and learning*. Boston: Allyn and Bacon, 1969.

Broudy, H. S. Is there a royal road to musical enjoyment? Speech delivered to the Pennsylvania Music Educators Association, Harrisburg, December 6, 1957.

Broudy, H. S. Can research escape the dogma of behavioral objectives? *The School Review*, 1970, **79**, 44.

Broudy, H. S., Smith, B. O., & Burnett, J. *Democracy and excellence in American secondary education: A study in curriculum theory*. Skokie, Ill.: Rand McNally, 1964.

Brown, M. Vertical groupings. In E. Yeomans (Ed.), *Education for initiative and responsibility*. New York: National Association of Independent Schools, 1967.

Brown, R., Cazden, C. B., & Bellugi-Klima, U. The child's grammar from I to III. In A. Bar-Adon & W. S. Leopold (Eds.), *Child language readings*. Englewood Cliffs, N.J.: Prentice-Hall, 1971.

Bruner, J. S. The course of cognitive growth. *American Psychologist*, 1964, **19**, 1–15.

Bruner, J. S. *Toward a theory of instruction*. Cambridge, Mass.: Harvard University Press, 1966.

Bruner, J. S. Origins of mind in infancy. Address to Division 8 at the 75th Anniversary of the American Psychological Association, Washington, D.C., September 1, 1967.

Bruner, J. S., Olver, R. R., Greenfield, P. M., et al. *Studies in cognitive growth*. New York: Wiley, 1966.

Buck, G. Another phase of the new education. *The Forum*, 1896, **22**, 376–384.

Bundy, McG. The politics of education. Address given at the 18th Anniversary Dinner, Teachers College, Columbia University, May 20, 1968.

Burns, R. F., & Frazier, A. A survey of elementary school social studies programs. *Social Education*, 1957, **51**, 202–204.

Buswell, G. T. The process of reading. *The Reading Teacher*, December 1959, **31**, 108–114.

Campbell, R. F. *Improving education through ESEA: 12 stories*. OE-20122. Washington, D.C.: U.S. Department of Health, Education, and Welfare, 1970.

Campbell, V. N., & Nichols, D. G. National assessment of citizenship education. *Social Education*, 1968, **32**, 280.

Carnegie Quarterly. The gross educational product: How much are students learning? 1966, **14**(2), entire issue.

Carroll, J. B. *Language and thought*. Englewood Cliffs, N.J.: Prentice-Hall, 1964.

Cass, J. Profit and loss in education. *Saturday Review of Literature*, August 15, 1970, 70.

Cazden, C. B. Environmental assistance to the child's acquisition of grammar. Unpublished doctoral dissertation, Graduate School of Education, Harvard University, 1965.

Cazden, C. B. Evaluating language learning in early childhood education. In

B. S. Bloom, T. Hastings, & G. Madaus (Eds.), *Formative and summative evaluation of student learning*. New York: McGraw-Hill, 1970.

Cazden, C. B. Language programs for young children: Notes from England and Wales. In C. S. Lavatelli (Ed.), *Language training in early childhood education*. Urbana: University of Illinois Press, 1971.

Cazden, C. B., Bryant, B., & Tillman, M. Going home and making it: The attitudes of black people toward language education. *Harvard Graduate School of Education Association Bulletin*, 1970, 14(3), 4–9.

Chall, J. *Learning to read: The great debate*. New York: McGraw-Hill, 1967.

Chambers, W., & Murray, J. *I do, and I understand*. Nuffield Mathematics Project. New York: Wiley, 1969.

Champlin, J. R. A spirit in search of substance: Another view of nongradedness. *New York State Education*, May 1969, 56, 18–19.

Chapman, L. Subject matter for the study of art. *Art Education*, 1967, 20(2), 20–22.

Chauncey, H., & Dobbin, J. E. *Testing: Its place in education today*. New York: Harper & Row, 1963.

Chomsky, C. *The acquisition of syntax in children from 5–10*. Cambridge, Mass.: MIT Press, 1969.

Chomsky, C. Language development after six. *Harvard Graduate School of Education Association Bulletin*, Spring 1970, 14(3), 14–16.

Chomsky, C. Write first, read later. *Childhood Education*, 1971, 47, 296–299.

Chomsky, N. A. *Syntactic structures*. The Hague: Mouton, 1957.

Chomsky, N. A., & Halle, M. *The sound pattern of English*. New York: Harper & Row, 1968.

Clegg, A. A., Jr., & Schomberg, C. E. The dilemma of history in the elementary school: Product or process? *Social Education*, 1968, 32, 455.

Clegg, A. B. *The excitement of writing*. London: Chatto & Windus, 1966.

Coleman, J. S., et al. Equality of educational opportunity. Washington, D.C.: GPO, 1966.

The College Board Admissions Testing Program: A technical report on research and development activities relating to the scholastic aptitude test and achievement tests. Princeton: College Entrance Examination Board, 1971.

Cravioto, J., DeLicardie, E. R., & Birch, H. G. Nutrition, growth, and neurointegrative development: An experimental and ecologic study. *Pediatrics*, 1966, 38, 319–326.

CTBS, Comprehensive Tests of Basic Skills: Language. Monterey, Calif.: California Test Bureau, 1969.

Curry, R. L. Subject preferences of fifth grade children. *Peabody Journal of Education*, July 1963, 41, 23–27.

Dady, C. A. Some basic skills expected of incoming first graders. *Curriculum Bulletin No. 131*. Eugene: College of Education, University of Oregon, 1953.

Deach, D. Genetic development of motor skills of children two through six years of age. Unpublished doctoral dissertation, University of Michigan, 1950.

Dean, S. E. Team teaching: A review. In M. Hillson (Ed.), *Change and inno-*

vation in elementary school organization. New York: Holt, Rinehart and Winston, 1965.

Dean, S. E. The future of nongraded schools. In D. W. Beggs, III, & E. G. Buffie (Eds.), *Nongraded schools in action.* Bloomington: Indiana University Press, 1967.

Denny, T., & Weintraub, S. First graders' responses to three questions about reading. *The Elementary School Journal,* 1966, **46,** 441–448.

Deutsch, M., et al. *The disadvantaged child.* New York: Basic Books, 1967.

Dewey, J. The psychological aspect of the school curriculum. *Educational Review,* 1897, **12,** 361.

Dewey, J. *Art as experience.* New York: Minton, Balch, 1934.

Dewey, J. *Experience and education.* New York: Macmillan, 1938.

Dewey, J. *Human nature and conduct.* New York: Modern Library, 1950. (Originally published: New York: Henry Holt, 1922.)

Dick, J. *Rough Rock Demonstration School, Arizona: A Pride of Lions.* Proceedings of the Fourth National Conference sponsored by the U. S. Office of Education Tri-University Project in Elementary Education, Minneapolis, September 19–20, 1968.

Drummond, H. D. Team teaching: An assessment. In M. Hillson (Ed.), *Change and innovation in elementary school organization.* New York: Holt, Rinehart and Winston, 1965.

Educational research and development in the United States. Washington, D.C.: National Center for Educational Research and Development, December 1969 and December 1970.

Educational Researcher: American Educational Research Association Newsletter, October 1970, **21.**

Edwards, D. L. Reading from the child's point of view. *Elementary English,* 1958, **35,** 239–241.

Eisner, E. The challenge to art education. *Art Education,* 1967, **20**(2), 27–29.

Elementary school objectives. (*see* Kearney, N. C.)

Engel, M. The Kenneth Clark design for Washington, D.C., schools. *Audiovisual Instruction,* November 1970, **15,** 5–6+.

Erikson, E. H. *Childhood and society.* (2d ed.) New York: Norton, 1963.

ESSP. *Astronomy.* Books 1–6. Urbana: Elementary School Science Project, University of Illinois, 1966.

Evans, E. D. *Contemporary influences in early childhood education.* New York: Holt, Rinehart and Winston, 1971.

Fallon, B. J. *Fifty states innovate to improve their schools.* Bloomington, Ind.: Phi Delta Kappa, 1967.

Featherstone, J. Schools for children: What's happening in British classrooms. *The New Republic,* August 19, 1967, 157.

Field, D. *Change in art education.* London: Routledge & Kegan Paul, 1970.

Filgamo, M. J. Texarkana battles "Dropout Dilemma!" *Elementary English,* 1970, **47,** 305–308.

Finney, R. L. *A sociological philosophy of education.* New York: Macmillan, 1929.

First grade reading studies. In J. F. Kerfoot (Ed.), *Perspectives in Reading Series No. 5.* Newark, Del.: International Reading Association, 1967.

Flavell, J. *The developmental psychology of Jean Piaget.* Princeton: Van Nostrand, 1963.

Foster, D. E. *A study of first grade children's comprehension of typical first grade social studies content prior to systematic instruction.* Unpublished doctoral dissertation, Colorado State College, 1965.

Fries, C. C. *Linguistics and reading.* New York: Holt, Rinehart and Winston, 1963.

Gage, N. L. Theories of teaching. In Ernest R. Hilgard (Ed.), *Theories of learning and instruction.* The Sixty-third Yearbook of the National Society for the Study of Education. Chicago: University of Chicago Press, 1964.

Gagné, R. M. Elementary science: A new scheme of instruction. *Science*, 1966, **151**, 49–53.

Gahagan, D. M., & Gahagan, G. A. Talk reform: Explorations in language for infant-school children. In *Primary socialization, language, and education, 3.* Sociological Research Unit Monograph Series, B. Bernstein, Director. London: Routledge & Kegan Paul, 1970.

Gardner, D. E. M. *Experiment and tradition in primary schools.* London: Methuen, 1966.

Gartner, A., Kohler, M. C., & Riessman, F. Every child a teacher. *Childhood Education*, 1971, **48**, 12–16.

Goldberg, M. L., Passow, A. H., & Justman, J. *The effects of ability grouping.* New York: Teachers College Press, 1966.

Goodlad, J. I. Classroom organization. In C. W. Harris (Ed.), *Encyclopedia of Educational Research.* New York: Macmillan, 1960.

Goodlad, J. I. The nongraded school. *The National Elementary Principal*, September 1970, **50**, 24–29.

Goodlad, J. I., & Klein, M. F. *Behind the classroom door.* Worthington, Ohio: Charles A. Jones, 1970.

Goodlad, J. I., Von Stoephasius, R., & Klein, M. F. *The changing school curriculum.* New York: Fund for the Advancement of Education, 1966.

Gordon, E. W. (*see IRCD Bulletin* No. 4 and No. 5.)

Gray, W. S. *Education looks ahead.* Chicago: Scott, Foresman, 1960.

Greenbladt, E. L. An analysis of school subject preferences of elementary school children. *The Journal of Educational Research*, 1962, **55**, 554–560.

Hagen, E. P., & Thorndike, R. L. Evaluation. In C. W. Harris (Ed.), *Encyclopedia of Educational Research.* New York: Macmillan, 1960.

Hamilton, W., & Rehwoldt, W. By their differences they learn. In M. Hillson (Ed.), *Change and innovation in elementary school organization.* New York: Holt, Rinehart and Winston, 1965.

Handbook for essay tests in the Educational Testing Service's STEP Series. Princeton: Educational Testing Service, 1957.

Hapgood, M. The open classroom: Protect it from its friends. *Saturday Review*, 1971, **54**(38), 66–69+.

Harding, L. W. Assumptions underlying methods of teaching beginning reading. *Educational Administration and Supervision*, January 1951, **38**, 25–37.

Harris, F. R., Wolf, M. M., & Baer, D. M. Effects of adult social reinforcement on child behavior. *Young Children,* 1964, **20,** 8–17.

Hayweiser, L., et al. *Evaluating behavioral change during a six-week prekindergarten intervention experience.* Syracuse: Syracuse University Research Institute, Final Report, November 1967. ERIC Document 026142.

Heathers, G. Dual progress plan. *Educational Leadership,* November 1960, **18,** 89–91.

Herbart, J. F. *Psychogie als wissenschaft.* Quoted in W. Boyd, *History of western education.* London: A. & C. Black, 1932.

Herman, W. L. How intermediate children rank the subjects. *The Journal of Education Research,* 1963, **56,** 435–436.

Hertzberg, H. W. The new culture: Some implications for teacher training programs. *Social Education,* 1970, **34,** 272.

Hess, R. D., & Bear, R. M. (Eds.) *Early education.* Chicago: Aldine, 1968.

Hillson, M. (Ed.) *Change and innovation in elementary school organization.* New York: Holt, Rinehart and Winston, 1965.

Hillson, M. The nongraded school: A dynamic concept. In D. W. Beggs & E. G. Buffie (Eds.), *Nongraded schools in action.* Bloomington: Indiana University Press, 1967.

Hoetker, J. Limitations and advantages of behavioral objectives in the arts and humanities. In J. Maxwell & A. Lovatt (Eds.), *On writing behavioral objectives for English.* Champaign, Ill.: National Council of Teachers of English, 1970.

How teachers grade your themes. *Illinois English Bulletin,* 1966, **53,** 664 pp. (entire issue).

Huck, C. Planning the literature program for elementary schools. *Elementary English,* 1962, **39,** 307–313.

Huckleberry, A. W., & Strother, E. S. *Speech education for the elementary teacher.* Boston: Allyn and Bacon, 1966.

Hunt, J. McV. *Intelligence and experience.* New York: Ronald Press, 1961.

Hunt, J. McV. Piaget's observations as a source of hypotheses concerning motivation. *Merrill-Palmer Quarterly,* 1963, **9,** 263–275.

Inhelder, B., & Piaget, J. *The growth of logical thinking from childhood to adolescence.* New York: Basic Books, 1958.

IRCD Bulletin No. 4 and No. 5. Gordon, E. W., et al. (Eds.) Decentralization and educational reform. New York: ERIC–IRCD, Teachers College, Columbia University, November 1968–January 1969.

It Works Series: Summaries of selected compensatory education projects. HE 5.237:37069. Washington, D.C.: U.S. Department of Health, Education, and Welfare, 1970.

James, W. *Psychology.* New York: Henry Holt, 1892.

Jenkinson, M. D. Reading: An eternal dynamic. *The Elementary School Journal,* 1970, **71**(1), 1–10.

Jennings, W. Middle school? No! *Minnesota Journal of Education,* January 1967, **47,** 74.

Jensen, A. R. Social class and verbal learning. In M. Deutsch, I. Katz, & A. R.

Jensen (Eds.), *Social class, race, and psychological development*. New York: Holt, Rinehart and Winston, 1968.

Jones, F. A descriptive and mechanical analysis of throwing skills of children. Unpublished masters thesis, University of Wisconsin, 1951.

Joyce, B. R. The primary grades: A review of textbook materials. In C. Cox & B. G. Massialas (Eds.), *Social studies in the United States*. New York: Harcourt Brace Jovanovich, 1967.

Kagan, J., & Moss, H. A. Birth to maturity: A study in psychological development. New York: Wiley, 1962.

Kaltsounis, T. A study concerning third graders' knowledge of social studies content prior to instruction. *The Journal of Educational Research*, 1964, **57**, 345–349.

Karnes, M. B., Teska, J. A., & Hodgins, A. S. *A longitudinal study of disadvantaged children who participated in three different preschool programs*. Urbana: Institute for Research on Exceptional Children, University of Illinois, 1969.

Karplus, R., & Thier, H. *A new look at elementary school science*. Science Curriculum Improvement Study. Skokie, Ill.: Rand McNally, 1967.

Kearney, N. C. *Elementary school objectives*. New York: Russell Sage Foundation, 1953.

Keppel, F. What are the flanking skirmishes? What is the fundamental struggle? *Phi Delta Kappan*, September 1964, **46**, 3.

Kies, K. M. Alternative learning environments: A Philadelphia story. *Childhood Education*, 1971, **47**, 239–243.

Klausmeier, H. J., & Quilling, M. R. Alternative school organization. *Wisconsin Journal of Education*, February 1968, **100**, 9.

Kliebard, H. M. Persistent curriculum issues in historical perspective. In E. C. Short (Ed.), *A search for valid content for curriculum courses. Educational Comment, 1970*, 357. Toledo, Ohio: University of Toledo, College of Education.

Kozol, J. *Death at an early age*. Boston: Houghton Mifflin, 1967.

Krathwohl, D. R., Bloom, B. S., & Masia, B. B. *Taxonomy of educational objectives: The classification of educational goals. Handbook II: Affective domain*. New York: McKay, 1964.

Labov, W., & Cohen, P. Systematic relations of standard and nonstandard rules in the grammars of Negro speakers. *Project Literacy Reports*, July 1967, No. 8, 66–84. Ithaca: Cornell University.

Lavatelli, C. S. *Piaget's theory applied to an early childhood curriculum*. Boston: American Science and Engineering, 1970.

Lavatelli, C. S. A systematized approach to language teaching. In C. S. Lavatelli (Ed.), *Language training in early childhood education*. Urbana: University of Illinois Press, 1971.

Lavatelli, C. S., & Stendler, F. *Readings in child behavior and development*. New York: Harcourt Brace Jovanovich, 1972.

Learning Research Associates. *Teacher support and accountability projects*. New York: Learning Research Associates, 1971.

Le Boeuf, F. Qui docet discit—He who teaches, learns. *The Science Teacher,* 1968, **35**(1), 53–56.

Lee, G. The changing role of the teacher. In J. I. Goodlad (Ed.), *The changing American School.* The Sixty-fifth Yearbook of the National Society for the Study of Education, Part 2. Chicago: University of Chicago Press, 1966.

Levine, M., & Spivack, G. The Rorschach index of ideational repression— Application to quantitative sequence analysis. *Journal of Projective Techniques,* 1963, **27,** 73–78.

Linguistics in school programs. A. H. Marckwardt (Ed.). The Sixty-ninth Yearbook of the National Society for the Study of Education, Part 2. Chicago: University of Chicago Press, 1970.

Lovell, K. *The growth of understanding in mathematics: Kindergarten through grade three.* New York: Holt, Rinehart and Winston, 1971.

Lowenfeld, V. *Creative and mental growth.* (3d ed.) New York: Macmillan, 1957.

Maccoby, E. M., & Zellner, M. *Experiments in primary education: Aspects of Project Follow-Through.* New York: Harcourt Brace Jovanovich, 1970.

McGarry, D. D. The crisis in education: Will Christian schools survive? In W. B. Kolesnik & E. J. Power (Eds.), *Catholic education: A book of readings.* New York: McGraw-Hill, 1965.

McGaughy, J. R. *An evaluation of the elementary school.* New York: Bobbs-Merrill, 1937.

McLoughlin, W. P. The phantom nongraded school. *Phi Delta Kappan,* 1968, **49,** 248.

McLure, W. P., & Pence, A. M. *Early childhood and basic elementary and secondary education: Needs, programs, demands.* National Finance Project, Special Study No. 1. Urbana: Bureau of Educational Research, University of Illinois, 1971.

Marland, S. P., Jr. The education park concept in Pittsburgh. *Phi Delta Kappan,* 1967, **48,** 329.

Mayhew, K. C., & Edwards, A. C. *The Dewey school.* New York: Atheling Books, 1965.

Miller, N., & Dollard, J. *Social learning and imitation.* New Haven: Yale University Press, 1941.

Moore, D. A critical review of methods of teaching language skills to lower class preschool children. In C. S. Lavatelli (Ed.), *Language training in early childhood education.* Urbana: University of Illinois Press, 1971.

Moore, W. J. Children view reading. College of Education, University of Illinois, 1970, mimeo.

Morsell, J. A. Racial desegregation and integration in public education. *The Journal of Negro Education,* 1969, **38,** 276–284.

National Education Association. *Report of the committee of ten on secondary school studies.* New York: American Book, 1894.

National Education Association. *Schools for the 60's.* New York: McGraw-Hill, 1963.

The New York Times. Semple, R. B., Jr. Head Start pupils found no better off than others. April 13, 1969, 1.

The New York Times. Stevens, W. K. Tests indicate T.V. program improves children's skills. January 28, 1970, 19.

The New York Times. Malcolm, A. H. Sesame Street rated excellent: 2-year study finds it helped children of poor learn. November 5, 1970, 32.

Newmann, F. M. Evaluation of programmed instruction in the social studies. *Social Education,* 1965, **29,** 295.

Nichols, R. G. Speaking and listening. In A. Schiller et al. (Eds.), *Language and how to use it.* Bk. 4, teacher's ed. Glenview, Ill.: Scott, Foresman, 1969.

Nickerson, N. C., Jr. Regroup for another try. *Minnesota Journal of Education,* November 1966, **47,** 16.

Odland, N. *Teaching literature in the elementary school.* Champaign, Ill.: National Council of Teachers of English, 1969.

Ogle, R. *The impact of three preschool programs upon certain personality variables.* Unpublished doctoral dissertation, The Graduate School, University of Illinois, 1971.

Original papers in relation to a cause of liberal education. *The American Journal of Arts and Science,* 1829, **15,** 308–309.

Orr, D. B., & Graham, F. Retention by educable mentally retarded children of material presented by simultaneous reading and listening. Pittsburgh, American Institutes for Research in Behavioral Sciences, May 4, 1967.

Palmer, J. R. Selection and use of textbooks and audio-visual materials. In B. G. Massialas & F. B. Smith (Eds.), *New Challenges in the social studies.* Belmont, Calif.: Wadsworth, 1965.

Paxton, T. What did you learn in school today? A record by Cherry Lane Music, 142 E. 34th St., New York, 1962.

Piaget, J. *The child's conception of number.* London: Routledge & Kegan Paul, 1952.

Piaget, J. How children form mathematical concepts. *Scientific American,* 1953, **89,** 74–79.

Piaget, J. *The origins of intelligence in children.* New York: Norton, 1963.

Piaget, J. Development and learning. In R. E. Ripple & V. N. Rockcastle (Eds.), *Piaget rediscovered.* Ithaca: Cornell University School of Education, 1964.

Piaget, J., & Inhelder, B. *The child's concept of space.* London: Routledge & Kegan Paul, 1956.

Popper, S. H. Why don't elementary school principals raise some hell? *The National Elementary Principal,* 1970, **49,** 59–62.

Preston, R. C. The reading status of children classified by teachers as retarded readers. *Elementary English,* 1953, **30,** 225–227.

Raths, L. E., Harmin, M., & Simon, S. B. *Values and teaching.* Columbus, Ohio: Merrill, 1966.

Righting the balance. Report of the Commission on Tests. Princeton: College Entrance Examination Board, 1971.

Robinson, A., Foster, C. C., & Ogilvie, D. H. (Eds.) *Black studies in the university.* New York: Bantam Books, 1969.

Rogers, V. R. *Teaching in the British primary school*. New York: Macmillan, 1970.

Rosenthal, R., & Jacobson, L. *Pygmalion in the classroom*. New York: Holt, Rinehart and Winston, 1968.

Rudman, H. C. The informational needs and reading interests of children in grades 4 through 8. *Elementary School Journal*, 1955, **55**, 502–512.

The Schools Council. *Mathematics in primary schools*. London: Her Majesty's Stationery Office, 1966.

Schrag, P. *Voices in the classroom: Public schools and public attitudes*. Boston: Beacon, 1965.

Sealey, L. G. W. Looking back on Leicestershire, *ESI Quarterly Report*, Spring–Summer 1966, 40.

Seeley, L. Culture epochs. In C. A. McMurry (Ed.), *Second yearbook of the National Herbart Society*. Bloomington, Ill.: The Society, 1896.

Senesh, L. Organizing a curriculum around social science concepts. In J. S. Gibson (Ed.), *New frontiers in the social studies: Action and analysis*. New York: Citation Press, 1967.

Shafer, R. E. A national assessment in English: A double-edged sword. *Elementary English*, April 1971, **48**, 188–195.

Shane, H., & McSwain, E. T. *Evaluation and the elementary curriculum*. New York: Holt, Rinehart and Winston, 1951.

Shaplin, J. T. Team teaching. In P. Woodring & J. Scanlon (Eds.), *American education today*. New York: McGraw-Hill, 1963.

Sigel, I. E., & Mermelstein, E. Effects of nonschooling on Piagetian tasks of conservation. Paper presented at the meeting of the American Psychological Association, Chicago, September 1965.

Silberman, C. *Crisis in the classroom*. New York: Random House, 1970.

Skinner, B. F. The science of learning and the art of teaching. *Harvard Educational Review*, 1954, **24**, 86–97.

Slobin, D., & Welch, C. Elicited imitation as a research tool in developmental psycholinguistics. In C. S. Lavatelli (Ed.), *Language training in early childhood education*. Urbana: University of Illinois Press, 1971.

Smith, B. O., et al. *A study of the logic of teaching*. Urbana: Bureau of Educational Research, University of Illinois, 1962, mimeo.

Smith, H. K. The responses of good and poor readers when asked to read for different purposes. *Reading Research Quarterly*, Fall 1967, **3**, 53–83.

Smith, R. O., & Cardinell, C. F. Challenging the expanding environment theory. *Social Education*, 1964, **28**, 141–142.

Snedden, D. Case group methods of determining flexibility of general curricula in high schools. *School and Society*, March 17, 1923, **17**, 314–320.

Sowards, G. W. A working seminar on the improvement of the social studies curriculum. Cooperative Research Report No. F-013, U.S. Office of Education. Stanford: Stanford University, 1963, mimeo.

Stake, R. E. Language, rationality, and assessment. *Improving educational assessment and an inventory of measures of affective behavior*. Washington, D.C.: Association for Supervision and Curriculum Development, National Education Association, 1969.

Stauffer, R. G. The verdict: Speculative controversy. *The Reading Teacher*, 1966, **19,** 564. (a)

Stauffer, R. G. Some tidy generalizations. *The Reading Teacher*, 1966, **20,** 4. (b)

Stendler, C. B. *The developmental approach of Piaget and its implications for science in the elementary schools*. Booklet to accompany The Macmillan Science Series. New York: Macmillan, 1966.

Stendler, C. B. The transition from concrete operational thinking to formal thought. Paper read at the National Science Teachers Association National Conference, New York City, February 1967.

Stephens, J. M. *The process of schooling*. New York: Holt, Rinehart and Winston, 1967.

Stone, I. F. Some comments on a visit to the Ocean Hill–Brownsville schools. *I. F. Stone's Weekly*, November 4, 1968.

Stone, S., & Quinn, F. How to be a super space saver. *Nature and Science*, March 2, 1970, **7,** 6–7.

Strickland, R. *The language arts in the elementary school*. (3d ed.) Lexington, Mass.: Heath, 1969.

Stufflebeam, D. L. Evaluation as enlightenment for decision making. *Improving educational assessment and an inventory of measures of affective behavior*. Washington, D.C.: Association for Supervision and Curriculum Development, National Education Association, 1969.

Taba, H. Implementing thinking as an objective in social studies. In J. Fair & F. Shaftel (Eds.), *Effective thinking in the social studies*. The Thirty-seventh Yearbook of the National Council for the Social Studies. Washington, D.C.: The National Council for the Social Studies, 1967. (a)

Taba, H. *Teacher's handbook for elementary social studies*. Reading, Mass.: Addison-Wesley, 1967. (b)

Thelen, H. A. *Classroom grouping for teachability*. New York: Wiley, 1967.

Thorndike, E. L. Mental discipline in high school studies. *The Journal of Educational Psychology*, 1924, **15,** 236–245.

Tumin, M. Procedures for effecting educational change. *Art Education*, 1967, **20**(2), 7–14.

Turner, T. Individualization through inquiry. *Social Education*, 1970, **34,** 72.

Tyler, R. *Basic principles of curriculum and instruction*. Chicago: University of Chicago Press, 1950.

Venezky, R. L. Linguistics and spelling. In A. H. Marckwardt (Ed.), *Linguistics in school programs*. The Sixty-ninth Yearbook of the National Society for the Study of Education, Part 2. Chicago: University of Chicago Press, 1970.

Walker, J. L. Obstetrical complications, congenital malformations, and social strata. In *Mechanisms of congenital malformations*. New York: Association for the Aid of Crippled Children, 1954.

Walker, J. L. National assessment of reading. *The Reading Teacher*, 1971, **24,** 711–714+.

Weber, G. A. Do teachers understand learning theory? *Phi Delta Kappan*, 1965, **46,** 433–435.

Weber, L. *The English infant school and informal education*. Englewood Cliffs, N.J.: Prentice-Hall, 1971.

West, E., & Gardner, W. The role of the social studies in developing values. Background Paper No. 11. *Preparation and evaluation of social studies curriculum.* University of Minnesota, Minneapolis, n.d., mimeo.

Wetzel, R. *Behavior modification techniques and the training of teacher's aides.* Tucson: Early Childhood Education Center, University of Arizona, August 1969. ERIC Document 040150.

White, R. W. Motivation reconsidered: The concept of competence. *Psychological Review,* 1959, **66,** 297–333.

Whittemore, R. By inquiry alone? *Social Education,* 1970, **34,** 283.

Wild, M. The behavior pattern of throwing and some observations concerning its course of development in children. *Research Quarterly,* 1938, **9**(3), 20–24.

Wohlwill, J., & Lowe, R. C. Experimental analysis of the development of the conservation of number. *Child Development,* 1962, **33,** 153–167.

Wolf, M., Giles, D., & Hall, A. Experiments with token reinforcement in a remedial classroom. *Behavior Research and Therapy,* 1968, **6,** 51–64.

Yates, A. (Ed.) *Grouping in education.* New York: Wiley, 1967.

Zigler, E. Motivational determinants in the performance of retarded children. *American Journal of Orthopsychiatry,* 1966, **36,** 848–856.

Zigler, E., & Butterfield, E. C. Motivational aspects of changes in IQ test performance of culturally deprived nursery school children. *Child Development,* 1968, **39,** 1–14.

Name Index

Allen, J., 320
Allen, J. E., Jr., 196
Almy, M., 224, 230–231, 245
Angelos, J., 132
Archambault, R. D., 93
Arnheim, R., 274–275
Aronoff, F., 291
Ashton-Warner, S., 206
Atkin, J. M., 14, 79–82, 110, 228
Ausubel, D. P., 78, 82

Baer, D. M., 69, 70
Banks, J. A., 164
Baratz, J. C., 220
Barnard, J. A., 232–233, 235, 248
Barnes, D. L., 137
Baumgartner, L., 295
Bear, R. M., 70
Beberman, M., 250
Becker, W., 71, 72, 176
Beggs, D. W., 111, 134
Begle, E., 254, 264–265, 269
Bellack, A., 85
Bellugi, U., 171
Bellugi-Klima, U., 170, 178
Bereiter, C., 114, 118, 175, 176, 213, 214
Berelson, B., 158, 159
Bernstein, B., 172, 174, 192
Betts, E., 280
Bijou, S. W., 69, 70
Birch, H. G., 295, 296, 321
Bloom, B. S., 108, 109, 118, 326–327, 333, 344
Bobbitt, F., 88, 89, 94, 96, 109
Botel, M., 335
Brookover, W. B., 122
Broudy, H. S., 33, 34, 98, 284

Brown, M., 126
Brown, R., 170
Brueckener, L. J., 270
Bruner, J. S., 40–41, 48, 49, 58–60, 78, 79, 82, 83, 142, 234
Bryant, B., 173
Buck, G., 92
Buffie, E. G., 134
Bundy, McG., 5
Burnett, J., 33, 34
Burns, R. F., 136
Burrows, A., 195
Buswell, G. T., 197
Butterfield, E. C., 66

Campbell, V. N., 104, 157
Cardinell, C. F., 139
Carroll, J. B., 182
Cass, J., 212
Cazden, C. B., 170, 173, 177, 180, 184, 195
Chall, J., 219
Chambers, W., 266–267
Champlin, J. R., 124
Chapman, L., 270
Charters, W. W., 97
Chauncey, H., 343
Chomsky, C., 168, 188, 206
Chomsky, N., 170, 187
Clark, K., 16
Clegg, A. A., 140, 186
Clune, W., III, 29
Cohen, P., 172
Coleman, J. S., 9, 12–14, 29
Coons, J., 29
Cravioto, J., 295
Cuisenaire, G., 257, 269
Czek, F., 280

Subject Index

Page numbers in italics indicate illustrations.

Ability grouping, 121–123, 133
American Association for the Advancement of Science (AAAS) Project, 225–228
  changes resulting from, 231–235
  evaluation of, 230–231
American Educational Research Association, 211
Apperception, 91
Art, curriculum, 271–282
  content of, 279–281
  deficiencies of, 271–275
  discovery methods in, *80*
  functions of, 275–278
  and developmental stages, 274
  as expression of innate perceptions (Arnheim), 274–275
  films, 280
  place in American values, 271
  and self-expression, 274–275
  and social studies, *149*
  visual- versus haptic-mindedness, 274–275
Astronomy, 228–230
Audiovisual aids, 3, 143, 154, 160, 280
Auto-instructional devices, 15, 68, 73–76
  See also Programmed learning; Teaching machines

Bank Street curriculum model, 115
Barbiana, children of, 29
  School, 173
Basal reading programs, 206–209

Behavior shaping (*see* Behavioral modification)
Behavioral modification, 63–66, 69–73, 76–77, 115
Behavioral objectives, and curriculum theory, 97–99
  federal government and, 14–15
  movement, 109–110
Behaviorism, 62–82
Bereiter-Engelmann program, 214–215
Bestorites, the, (Arthur), 22, 196
Biological Sciences Study Committee (BSSC), 222
Black English, 172–173
Black music, 288, 290–291
Black studies, 116, 163–164
Botel Predicting Readability Levels, 335
British Infant and Primary Schools, 14, 18–21, 28, 65, 121, 213
  and evaluation, 269
  and "family grouping," 126–127
  and the "integrated day," 126–127
  Nuffield Mathematics Project, 268
  and the open curriculum, 99–100, 114–115
  and science, 242–243
  and spelling, 188
  and writing approach to reading, 205–206
Busing, 7, 9, 131–132, 214

Capitalization, 186–187
Carnegie Foundation, 4, 18, 21, 216
Center for Applied Linguistics, 173